RECORDS

OF THE

COURT OF ASSISTANTS

OF THE

COLONY

OF THE

MASSACHUSETTS BAY

1630–1692

PRINTED UNDER THE SUPERVISION OF

JOHN NOBLE

CLERK OF THE SUPREME JUDICIAL COURT

Vol. II.

Southern Historical Press, Inc.
Greenville, South Carolina

This volume was reproduced
from a personal copy located in
the Publishers private library

All rights reserved. No part of this publication may be reproduced,
stored in a retrieval system, transmitted in any form, posted
on the web in any form or by any means without the
prior written permission of the publisher.

Please direct all correspondence and book orders to:
SOUTHERN HISTORICAL PRESS, Inc.
1071 Park West Blvd.
Greenville, SC 29611

Published 1904 by:
 The County of Suffolk, MA
ISBN #978-1-63914-655-0
Printed in the United States of America

PREFACE.

VOLUME I. of the Records of the Court of Assistants, covering the period from 1673 to 1692, was issued in 1901.

Volume II., now issued, takes in the period from the settlement of the Colony to 5 March, 1643-4.

This volume, though containing the records of a period earlier than that in the former volume, has been numbered Volume II. for the reasons given in the preface to the first volume.

Part I. is taken from the first volume of the Records of the Colony of the Massachusetts Bay in the State Archives, and has been printed, like the earlier volume, with an exact adherence to the originals, and is a reproduction of them in every particular, so far as the difference between print and manuscript will allow.

It has also been compared with a contemporaneous copy of the same (made by Thomas Lechford to 28 January, 1641), referred to below.

Part II. comprises a copy of a portion of the records of the Court of Assistants, extending from 28 October, 1641, to 5 March, 1643-4, recently discovered in the so-called Barlow Manuscript Copy, or duplicate, of the records of the Colony of the Massachusetts Bay, which was bought for the Boston Public Library in 1890. This was published by order of the City Council of Boston, by William H. Whitmore, Record Commissioner, in his Bibliographical Sketch of the Laws of the Massachusetts Colony.

In the record of the Court for 5 March, 1643-4, there are at the end three subsequent entries, the latest being 30 May, 1644.

The same exact adherence to the original has been kept as in Part I.

As stated in the preface to Volume I., these earliest records, thus preserved, are not, as has been often assumed, the complete record of the proceedings of the Court through those periods, as they contain substantially only criminal matters or matters of public concern. Civil suits do not appear therein, although it is evident that such suits were tried before this Court from the very first. This appears among other proofs from the entry under date of 4 March, 1633-4, on page 40 of this Volume II., mentioning a judgment against Joseph Twitchell. It also appears, from the numerous references to such causes, as early as 1639, in Lechford's Journal. See also the Order of the General Court, in 1634, as to the entry of Actions. (Mass. Col. Rec., Vol. I., p. 129.)

See, also, an Order of the General Court, carrying out a suggestion of Lechford in 1639, which was made at the September Session of the same year:

"Whereas many iudgments have been given in o^r Courts, whereof no records are kept of the evidence and reasons whereupon the verdict and iudgment did passe, the records whereof being duely entered and kept would bee of good use for president to posterity, and a releife to such as shall have just cause to have their causes reheard and reveiwed, it is therefore by this Court ordered and decreed that henceforward every iudgment, wth all the evidence, bee recorded in a booke, to bee kept to posterity."

(Massachusetts Colony Records, i, 275.)

When Volume I. was issued it was proposed that the present volume should contain three parts, and expected that it would complete the records of this Court, so far as they were extant or could in any way be reproduced at the present day. It has been found, however, that Part III., described in the former preface, must contain such an amount of matter as would make, if included herein, an unwieldly volume, and delay the issue of this.

Part III., as heretofore designated, will accordingly be issued separately as Volume III., and at as early a date as possible.

It attempts, so far as material anywhere accessible allows, to fill the gap in the records between March 4, 1643, and March 4, 1673, a period where no continuous or consecutive record is to be found, and to reproduce, as far as may be possible, the doings of the Court of Assistants in these years.

It will consist of restored fragments of records taken from certified copies of judgments, verdicts, executions, etc., found among the Court Files of Suffolk, and among the files in the offices of the several counties; in the State Archives; among ancient manuscripts in the possession of the Massachusetts Historical Society, and in various other places, giving authoritative information as to the action of the Court of Assistants during that period. In some cases additional information obtained from contemporaneous sources, not easily accessible, will be added in notes to explain or amplify the record. These fragments of records relate largely to civil causes. Their value as historical material will be evident, and also in carrying out the purpose expressed in the preface to Volume I., of gathering matter for the study of the origin, development, and methods of procedure of this Colonial Court of ultimate resort and supreme jurisdiction, and as contributing to a study of the history of the Commonwealth and of its jurisprudence.

JOHN NOBLE.

SUPREME JUDICIAL COURT,
OFFICE OF THE CLERK,
JANUARY 1, 1904.

COURT OF ASSISTANTS.

RECORDS, SO FAR AS RECOVERED OR REPRODUCED,
FROM 1630 TO 1644.

[IN TWO PARTS.]

EXPLANATION OF MARKS AND CHARACTERS.

MARKS.

A mark over a letter indicates an omission of one or more letters.

A caret ᴀ indicates one or more words omitted in the original.

Brackets [   ] indicate words or letters in the original which are illegible or doubtful or apparently erroneous.

Parallels ‖   ‖ enclose words interlined in the original.

CHARACTERS.

ff	signifies	ff or F.
ñ	"	ner, nor, or no.
p̃	"	par or per.
℘	"	por or pro.
ⱶ	"	Per.
ṽ	"	ver.
ℯꝛ	"	&c. (etc.)

PART I.

COURT OF ASSISTANTS.

RECORD 1630–1641.

FROM THE FIRST VOLUME OF THE COLONY RECORDS
IN THE MASSACHUSETTS STATE ARCHIVES.

PART I.
1630—1641.

COURT OF ASSISTANTS RECORDS.

[Taken from the first volume of the Records of the Colony of the Massachusetts Bay, in the State Archives, and compared with a copy thereof in the Boston Public Library (made by Thomas Lechford to January 28, 1641) which will, for convenience here, be referred to as the L. copy. Differences, other than unimportant literal ones, will be indicated by foot-notes. The original record is in the handwriting of Secretary Simon Bradstreet till May, 1636, and thereafter in the handwriting of Secretary Increase Nowell.]

[55]   The first Court of Assistants holden att Charlton August 23th Año D̃m 1630.

Present

M^r. Jo: Winthrop Gou̅n^r
M^r. Tho: Dudley Deput Gou̅n^r
S^r. Rich: Saltonstall k^t
M^r. Robte:* Ludlowe
M^r. Edward Rossiter

M^r. Increase Nowell
M^r. Tho: Sharpe
M^r. Will: Pinchion
M^r. Sim:† Bradstreete

1.‡   Imp^r, it was ꝓpounded howe the ministers should be mayntayned, M^r. Wilson & M^r. Phillips onely ꝓpounded.

It was ordered that houses should be built for them with convenient speede, att the publique charge. S^r. Rich: Saltonstall vndertooke to

---

* Roger is written in the margin in a modern hand.   † "Simon" in L. copy.

‡ The marginal numbers and titles seem to have been entered in connection with some index or codification of laws and orders. Many of them are in the handwriting of Edward Rawson, the Secretary from 1650 to 1686. The marginal entries in the Library copy are different.

see it done att his plantacon for Mr. Phillips and Mr. Goūnr att the other plantacon for Mr. Wilson./

2.   It was ꝓpounded what should be their prsent mainetenance.

Ordered that Mr. Phillips should haue allowed him 3 hogsheads of meale, 1 hogshd of malte, 4 bushells of Indean corne, 1 bushell of oatemeale, halfe an hundred of salte fishe, for apparell and other ꝓvisions xxˡ, or els to haue xlˡ giuen him in money ꝑ anñ to make his owne ꝓuisions if hee chuse it the rather, the yeare to begin the first of September nexte.

It. that Mr. Wilson should haue after xxˡ ꝑ anñ till his wife come ouer, his yeare to begin the 10th of July ~~nexte~~ last all this to be att the comon charge those of Mattapan ‖ & Salem ‖ onely exempted./

3.   It was ꝓpounded what should be Mr. Gagers maintenance.

Ordered that hee should haue a house builded him against the nexte springe, is to haue a cowe giuen him & xxˡ in money for this yeare to begin the 20th of June ‖ (1630) ‖ & after xxxˡ ꝑ anñ. all this to be att the comon charge.

4.   It was ordered that James Peñ should haue 20 nobles ꝑ anñ & a dayes worke of a man att springe from eūy able famyly to helpe build his howse, his yeare to begin the 1th of September nexte. his imployemt to be as a Beadle to attend vpon the Goūnr, and alwaies to be ready to execute his coṁands in publique businesses.

5.   It was ordered that there should be a Court of Assistants helde att the Goūnrs howse on the 7th day of Septembr nexte being tuesday to begin att 8 of the clocke.

courts.

referred till the nexte Court./   It was ꝓpounded whither there should not be a Court helde eūy first tuesday in eūy moneth, & a Geñall Court the last wednesday in eūy tearme./

6.   It was ordered that, in all ciuill accõns the first ꝓcesse or suṁons by the Beadle or his deputy shalbe directed by the Goūnr or Deputy Goūnr or some other of the Assistants being a Justice of the peace, the next ꝓcesse to be a capias or distringas att the discrecõn of the Court./

proces.

[56]

7. It was ordered that Morton of Mount Woolison should presently be sent for by pcesse.

rates.
8. It was ordered that carpenters joyners brickelayers sawers* and thatchers shall not take aboue 2^s a day, nor any man shall giue more vnder paine of x^s to taker & giuer/. and that sawers shall not take aboue 4^s — 6^d ye hundred for boards, att 6 scoore to the hundred, if they haue their wood felled & squared for them, & not aboue 5^s — 6^d if they fell & square their wood themselues./

iustices.
9. It was ordered that the Gouern^r & Deputy Goū^r for the tyme being shall alwaies be Justices of ye peace. and that S^r. Rich: Saltonstall M^r. Johnson M^r. Endicott & M^r. Ludlowe shalbe Justices of the peace for the p^{r}sent tyme, in all things to haue like power that Justices of peace hath† in England for reformačon of abuses and punishing of offend^{rs}. and that any Justice of the peace may imprison an‡ offend^r, but not inflict any corporall punishm^t wthout the p^{r}sence & consent of some one of the Assistants.

·[10] 6.
[2]
boates.
It was ordered that noe pson shall vse or take away any boate or Cannoe without leaue from the owner thereof in paine of ffyne & imprisonm^t, att the discrečon of the Court./

Memorand. to estimate the nexte Court day the charges y^t M^r. Goū^r hath beene att in entertaineing seūall publique psons since his landing in Newe England./

[57] A Court of Assistants holden att Charlton the 7th of September 1630.

Present

The Gouern^r	M^r. Nowell
Deputy Goūnor	M^r. Coddington
S^r. Rich: Saltonstall, k^t	M^r. Ludlowe
M^r. Johnson	M^r. Rossiter
M^r. Endicott	M^r. Pinchon
M^r. Sharpe	M^r. Bradstreete

Capt. Endicott beinge formerly chosen an Assistant did nowe take the oath of an Assistant in the presence of the Court.

---

* "Sawyers" in L. copy.   † "Have" in L. copy.   ‡ "Any" in L. copy.

Courts.

It was ordered that eũy third tuesday there should be a Court of Assistants helde att the Goũnoʳs howse (for the tyme being) to begin ‖ att ‖ 8 of the clocke in the morneing, eũy Assistant not being present att that tyme to be fyned att the discreõon of the Court.

James Peñ did now take the oath of Beadle.

Mʳ. Ludlowe Mʳ. Rossiter & Mʳ. Pinchon by the geñall consent of the Court is* fyned a noble a peece for their absence from the Court after the tyme appoyncted.

Thomas Morton punished.†

It is ordered by this present Court, that Thomas Morton of Mount Wolliston ‡ shall presently be sett into the bilbowes, & after sent prisoner into England by the Shipp called the Gifte, nowe returneing thith[er] that all his goods shalbe seazed vpon to defray the charge of his transportaõon, paymᵗ of his debts, & to giue satisfacõon to the Indians for a Cannoe hee vniustly tooke away from them & that his howse, after the goods are taken out, shalbe burnt downe to the ground in the sight of the Indians for their satisfacõon, for many wrongs hee hath done them from tyme to tyme./

It is ordered that Mʳ. Clearke shall pay vnto John Baker the soñe of xxxviijˢ in recompence, for the damage hee receaued by a bargaine of cloath, wherein Mʳ. Clearke dealte fraudylently with the said John Baker as hath beene ꝑued vpon oath.

[58] It is ordered that Mʳ. Patricke & Mʳ. Vnderhill shall haue allowed them for halfe a yeares ꝓvision, 2 hogsheads of meale, 4 bushells of malte, 10ˡ of powder, & leade to make shott, also howseᵣoome ꝓuided for them & 15ˡ 12ˢ in money to make other prouisions. all this to be done att the publique charge their yeare to begin from the tyme they begin to keep howse.

Boston, Dorchester, & Water Toune.

It is ordered that Trimountaine shall be called Boston, Mattapan Dorchester, & the Towne vpon Charles Ryver Waterton. /

3- (2) Plantations.

It is ordered that noe ꝑson shall plant in any place within the lymitts of this Pattent, without leaue from the Goũnʳ and Assistants, or the maior ꝑte of them.

Also that a warrant shall presently be sent to Aggawam, to coñand those that are planted there forthwith to come away.

---

* "Are" in L. copy.   † In modern hand.   ‡ "Wollaston" in L. copy.

A Court of Assistants holden att Charlton 28th of Septembr 1630.

Present

The Goũnr   Mr. Nowell
Deputy Goũnr   Mr. Coddington
Capt. Endicott   Mr. Bradstreete
Mr. Ludlowe   Mr. Rossiter
                    Mr. Pinchon.

1.   It is ordered that those of Dorchester whoe bought certayne cattell of the merchts of Dorchester, shall pay vnto Nich: Stower 9 bushells of meale or of Indian corne or 9l of beaur for the keepeing of the said cattell according to an agreemt. made wth him.

4— 2.
Indian.   It is ordered that noe pson whatsoeur. shall either directly or indirectly, imploy or cause to be imployed or to their power pmitt any Indian to vse any peece vpon any occaõon or pretence whatsoeuer, vnder payne of xl ffyne for the first offence & for the 2* offence to be ffyned & imprisoned att the discreõon of the Court./

5— (3)
Servants.   It is further ordered that noe servt. eithr. man or maide shall either giue sell or trucke any comodytie whatsoeur, without lycence from their maister dureing the tyme of their service vnder paine of ffyne & corporall punishmt. att the discreõon of the Court.

[59]   John Woodbury is chosen Constable of Salem & Thom[as] Stoughton constable of Dorchester, to contynue in that office for a yeare & after till newe be chosen.

John Woodbury did nowe take the oath of a Constable.

Strong waters seized on.   It is ordered that all Rich: Cloughes stronge water shall presently be seazed vpon, for his selling greate quantytie thereof to seũall mens servts which was the occaõon of much disorder drunckenes & misdemeanr.

6.
Rates for Workmn.   It is ordered that noe maister carpenter mason joyner or brickelayer shall take aboue 16d a day for their worke, if they haue meate and drinke, & the second sort not aboue 12d a day vnder payne of xs both to giuer & receauer./

It is ordered that Mr. Patricke & Mr. Vndrhill shall haue allowed

---

* "Second" in L. copy.

them 6ˡ 8ˢ in money to buy them howseholde stuffe, & for helpe to washe brewe & bake [xx]*

Gray sent.

Thomas Gray is inioyned vnder the penalty of xˡ to attend on the Court in pson this day 3 weekes to answer to dyvers things obiected against him & to remoue himselfe out of the lymetts of this patt[ent] before the end of March nexte.

Sʳ. Rich: Saltonstall is ffyned 4 bushells of malte for his absence from the Court.

Corne. 6.

It is ordered that noe pson inhabitting within the lymitts of this Pattent shall either directly or indirectly giue sell trucke or send away any Indian corn to any Englishe without the lymitts of this Pattent or to any Indian whatsoeuer without licence from the Goũnʳ. & Assistants.

Gouldsworth, Pickrin, censr.

It is ordered that John Goulworth shalbe whipped and afterwards sett in the stocks for fellony comitted by him whereof hee is convicted by his owne confession also that Henry Lyñ shalbe whipped for the like offence, & John Boggust & John Pickryn to sitt in the stocks 4 howers togeathʳ. att Salem for being access[ary] therevnto.

For Capᵗ Patrick & Capᵗ Undʳhill 50ˡⁱ.

It is ordered that there shalbe collected & levied by distresse out of the seũall plantaĉons for the maintenance of Mʳ. Patricke & Mʳ. Vnderhill the soɱe of 50ˡ, vz: out of Charlton 7ˡ Boston 11ˡ Dorchestʳ 7ˡ Rocsbury 5ˡ Waterton 11ˡ Meadford 3ˡ Salem 3ˡ Wessaguscus 2ˡ Natascett 1ˡ.

Rates.

It is ordered that Labourers shall not take aboue 12ᵈ a day for their worke, & not aboue 6ᵈ & [meate &] drinke vnder paine of xˢ.

[60]   Septembʳ 28ᵗʰ 1630.

A Jury impanneld to inquire concerning the Death of Austen Bratcher.

Rich: Browne	Nich: Vpsall
Willɱ Aspynwall	John Johnson
Abraham Palmʳ.	Edward Converse
Nich: Stower	Ralfe Sprage
Peter Palfry	Giles Sexton
Roger Williams	Abraham Pratt
Willɱ Bunell† —	Francis Smyth
	George Dyar —

---

* "xxⁱⁱ" in L. copy.   † "Bunnell" in L. copy.

Austen Bratcher dyeing lately att M{r} Cradocks plantaçon was vewed before his buryall by dyv{rs} psons vz —

Tho: Graues	Thomas Reade	
James Crugott	Rich: Lynton	⎫
Thomas Ward	John Jarvis	⎬ absent.
Thomas Paynt{r}.	Arthur Ellis.	⎭
Will͞m Barsham		

The Jureys Verdict

Wee finde that the strookes* giuen by Walter Palmer were occationally the meanes of the death of Austen Bratcher & soe to be manslaught{r}./

Walter Palmer hath bound himselfe in 40{l}. & Ralfe Sprage & John Sticklett hath† bound themselues in 20{l} a peece for Walter Palmers psonall appearance att the nexte Courte to be holden att Boston the 19{th} of Octob{r} nexte to answer for the death of Austen Bratcher./

[61]   September 18{th}. 1630.

Vpon vew of the dead body of Will͞m Bateman

An Inquisiçon taken att Charlton the 18{th} day of Sept{br} Año D͞n͞i 1630 before John Winthrop, Esq{r}. & Gou͞n{r}. & Isaack Johnson Esq{r}. one of the Assistants & Justice of ⌃Peace

Vpon the oathes of

Walt{r} Norton Esq{r}.	Richard Browne
Nich: Stowre	Robte Hardinge
Ralfe Sprage	Richard Garrett
Will: Cheesebrough	Thomas Willms
John Stickland	Daniell
Rich: Norman	John Baker
	Will͞m Bateman

whoe say, vpon their oathes that the afores{d} Will͞m Bateman was sett on shore vpon the necke of land neere Pullen poynte in the bay of Mattachusetts by a shallop of one M{r}. Wright (which brought him from Plimouthe) vpon wednesday last being very sicke & weake & beinge lefte there with one M{r} Ralfe Glouer & others, whoe hadd a shallop in that place, but being forced to leaue her there because the

---

* " Stroakes " in L. copy.   † " Have " in L. copy.

winde was contrarie, they returneing home lefte him such p̄visions as they hadd, & a   & fire, but when they returned to their boate vpon Friday last they found the said Will͞m Bateman dead about the highwater marke neere their boate aboute a stones cast from the place where they lefte him — Soe the Jury p̄sents that hee dyed by gods visitac͠on.

Evidences, M͞r. Ralfe ~~Sprage~~ Glouer Elias Ma͞wacke Giles Sexton & James Browne. er.

[On page 62 and 63 is a record of a General Court 19 Oct., 1630, and a list of those desiring to be made freemen. Page 64 is blank.]

[65] A Court of Assistants holden att Boston Nouemb͞r 9th. 1630.

Present
The Go͞un͞r
Deputy Go͞un͞r.
S͞r. Rich Saltonstall
M͞r. Ludlowe
Cap͞t. Endicott
M͞r. Coddington
M͞r. Pinchon
M͞r. Bradstreete

It is ordered that whereas the vsuall rate of beau͞r hath beene after 6ˢ. the pound, it shalbe hereafter lefte free for eu͞y man to make the best p̄ffit & im̄puem͞t of it that hee can.

Repealed.   It is ordered, that eu͞y Englishe man that killeth a wolfe in any p͞rte within the Lymitts of this pattent shall haue allowed him 1ᵈ. for eu͞y beast & horse & oᵇ.* for eu͞y weaned swyne & goate in eu͞y plantac͠on to be leuied by the Constables of the sᵈ plantac͠ons.

3
Ferry encouragᵈ.

It is further ordered that whosoeuer shall first giue in his name to M͞r. Go͞un͞r that hee will vndertake to sett vpp a fferry betwixte Boston and Charlton & shall begin the same att such tyme as M͞r. Go͞un͞r shall appoynct, shall haue 1ᵈ. for eu͞y pson & 1ᵈ. for eu͞y 100 waight of goods hee shall soe transport.

M͞r. Clearke is p̄hibited cohabitac͠on & frequent keepeing company with M͞rˢ. Freeman, vnder paine of such ~~company~~ punishm͞t as the Court shall thinke meete to inflict.

M͞r. Clearke & M͞r. Freeman hath bound themselues in xxˡ apeece that M͞r Clearke shall make his psonall appearance att the nexte Court to be holden in March nexte, & in the meane tyme to carry himselfe in good behav͞r towards all people & espetially towards M͞rˢ. Freeman, concerneing whome there is stronge suspic͠on of incontinency.

It is ordered, that Rich Diffy, servᵗ to Sʳ. Richard Saltonstall shalbe whipped for his misdemean͞r towards his maister.

---

* Obolus or half penny.

A Jury impannel[ ] for the Tryall of Walter Palmer concerneing the Death of Austin Bratcher.

Mr Edmond Lockwood	Rich: Morris
Will͠m Rockewell	Will͠m Balston
Christopher Conant	Will͠m Cheesbrough
Will͠m Phelpes	John Page
Will͠m Gallard*	John Balshe
John Hoskins	Laurence Leach

The jury findes Walter Palmer not guilty of manslaughter whereof hee stoode indicted & soe the Court acquitts him.

[66] A Court of Assistants holden att Boston Nouemb^r 30th 1630.

Present

The Go͠vn^r	M^r. Nowell
The Deputy Go͠vn^r	M^r. Pinchon
S^r. Rich: Saltonstall	M^r. Coddington
M^r. Ludlowe	M^r. Bradstreete.

S^r Ri: Sa: find 5. S^r. Rich. Saltonstall is fyned v^l for whipping 2 se͠vall psons without the presence of another Assistant contrary to an act of Court form͠ly made.

Ord^r about Wm Knop. It is ordered that whoesoeuer imployeth Willm Knopp or his sonne in any worke shall pay the one halfe of their wages to S^r. Rich. Siltonstall, & whoeuer buyeth boards of them shall pay one halfe of the price to S^r. Richard, till the money hee hath disbursed for them be satisfyed.

Barth Hill cens. ~~John H~~ Bartholmewe Hill is adiudged to be whipt for stealeing a loafe of breade from John Hoskins which himselfe confesseth.

Rate for ye ministers. It is ordered that there shalbe 60^l collected out of the se͠vall plantac͠ons folloveing for the mainetenance of M^r. Wilson & M^r. Phillips, vz: out of Boston 20^l. Waterton 20^l. Charlton 10^l. Rockesbury 6^l. Meadford 3^l. Winnett-semett 1^l.

J^{no} Bakers cens. It is ordered, that John Baker shalbe whipped for shooteing att fowle on the Sabboth day ℈r.

---

* " Gaylard " in L. copy.

It is further ordered that Thomas Moulton shall pay vnto Mʳ.
Ralfe Glouer xlˢ before the 8ᵗʰ day of Decembʳ nexte
or els to be whipped for the wronge hee did Mʳ.
Glouer in comeing from Plymoth being maister of his boate, & leaue-
ing him without a pylott.

Tho Moulton sent.

[67]   A Court of Assistants holden att Boston 1ᵗʰ of March 1630–31.*

Present

The Gouernʳ	Mʳ. Pinchon
Deputie Goũnʳ.	Mʳ. Nowell
Sʳ. Rich: Saltonstall	Mʳ. Sharpe
Mʳ. Ludlowe	Mʳ. Coddington
Capt. Endicott	Mʳ. Bradstreete.

It is ordered that Mʳ. Aleworth Mʳ. Weauʳ Mʳ. Plastow Mʳ.
Shutʳ Cobbett† & Wormewood shalbe sent into England by the shipp
Lyon, or soe many of them as the ship can carry the
rest to be sent thither by the 1ᵗʰ of May nexte if
there be optunitie of shipping, if not by the nexte
shipp that returnes for England as psons vnmeete to inhabit here,
& that Sʳ. Christopher Gardnʳ. & Mʳ. Wright shalbe sent as prisoners
into England by the shipp Lyon nowe returneing thither.

Seuʳll persons sent prisoners home.

Further, it is ordered, that the busines concerneing Mʳ. George
Ludlowe expressed in a certaine petition sent out of England to the
Goũnʳ. er shalbe referred to t[he] Goũnʳ & Deputy
Goũnʳ. & the rest of the Assistants resident att
Boston (or some 3 of them the Goũnʳ [&] Deputie
being 2 thereof) to receaue his answer, and determyne the busines.

Ordr about Mr Ludlow.

Mʳ. Tho: Stoughton, Constable of Dorchester is
ffyned vˡ for takeing vpon him to marry Clemᵗ Briggs
& Joane Allen, & to be imprisoned till hee hath p̃d
his ffyne.

Mr Tho: Staughton fined.

It is ordered that if any pson within the Lymitts of this Pattent, doe trade trucke or sell any
money eithʳ siluer or golde, to any Indian, or any man
that knoweth of any that shall soe doe & conceale the
same shall forfe[it] twenty for one —

7   (4)
Indian not to be traded wth in mony.

---

* See Winthrop I. 38, 39, for meetings in December, 1630.
† " Mʳ. Cobbett " in L. copy.

<small>Indian not to be entrteynd as serv^{ts}</small>
Further it is ordered that whateuer pson hath receau[ed] any Indian into their ffamylie as a serv^t shall discharge themselues of them by the 1th of May nexte, & that noe pson shall hereafter intertaine any Indian for a serv^t without licence from the Court.

<small>Nich: Knop find for deceite.</small>
Nich: Knopp is fyned v^l for takeing vpon him to cure the scurvey by a water of noe worth nor value, which hee solde att a very deare rate, to be imprisoned till hee pay his ffine or giue securitye for it, or els to be whipped & shalbe lyable to any mans accōn of whome hee hath receaued money for the s^d water.

[68]

<small>Wellust sallery.</small>
Jost Weillust is chosen survey^r of the ordinanc & cannouneere for which hee is to haue allowed him 10^l p ann.

<small>Elfords & suretys bond.</small>
John Ellford hath bound himselfe in C m̃ks, & Roger Connant & John Woodbury hath bound themselues in 40^l a peece for John Ellfords psonall appearance att the first Court to be holden in Novemb^r nexte to answere for the death of Thomas Puckett.

M^r. Willm Pelham & M^r. Edmond Lockewood hath ꝓmised to pay to the Court the some of v^l. for Nich: Knopp before the last Court of May nexte.

Att a Court att Waterton March 8th 1630–31.

P^rsent

The Goūn^r　　　　　M^r. Nowell
Deputie Goūn^r　　　M^r. Pinchon
S^r. Rich: Saltonstall　M^r. Coddington
M^r. Ludlowe　　　　 M^r. Bradstreete.

<small>Indians recompence for 2 wiggwams, burnt by S^r Ri: Sal[:man]:</small>
Vpon a complaynte made by Saggamore John & Pet^r. for haueing 2 wigwams burnt which vpon examinacōn appeared to be occacōned by James Woodward serv^t to S^r. Rich: Saltonstall it was therefore ordered that S^r. Richard should satisfie the Indians for the wronge done to them (which accordingly hee did by giueing them 7 yards of cloath) & that his said serv^t. should pay vnto him for it att the end of his tyme the some of l^s.

Tho: Fox sent.	It was ordered that Tho: Foxe serv^t to M^r. Cradocke shalbe whipped for vttering mallitious & scandilous speeches, whereby hee sought to traduce the Court as if they hadd taken some bribe in the busines concerneing Walter Palmer./
Courts legality. 9	Further (in regard the number of Assistants are but fewe & some of them goeing for England) it was therefore ordered that whensoeuer the number of Assistants resident within the Lymitts of this Jurisdicc͠on shalbe fewer then 9, it shalbe lawfull for the maior p^{r}te of them to keepe a Court and whatsoeu͠ orders or acts they ~~shall~~ make shalbe as legall & authenticall as if there were the full number of 7 or more.

[69] Att a Court of Assistants holden att Boston March 22th 1630–31.

Present

The Gouern^r	S^r. Rich: Soltonstall
The Deputie Gou͠n^r	M^r. Pinchon
M^r. Ludlowe	M^r. Sharpe
M^r. Coddington	M^r. Bradstreete.
M^r. Nowell	

Workmens wages at liberty. Rates.	It is ordered (that whereas the wages of Carpent^{rs} Joyners & other artificers & workemen were by order of court restrayned to pticul^r som͠es) shall nowe be lefte free & att libertie as men shall ‖ reasonably ‖ agree.
Armes for all inhabitants to be provided. 10	Further it is ordered that eu͠y Towne within this Pattent shall before the 5th of Aprill nexte, take espetiall care that eu͠y pson within their Towne (except magistrates & ministers) as well serv^{ts} as others, be furnished with good & sufficient armes allowable by the Capt. or other officers, those that want & are of abilitie to buy them themselues, others tha[t] are vnable to haue them pvided by the Towne for the present, & after to receiue satisfacc͠on for that they disburse when they shalbe able.
Cardes & dice 11 (5) to be made away wth.	It is likewise ordered that all psons whatsoeuer that haue cards dice or tables in their howses shall make away with them before the nexte Court vnder paine of punishm^t./

Johnson acknowledgt of 13ˡⁱ debt to Srː Rich.

Richː Johnson confesseth to owe vnto Srː Richard Saltonstall (all accompts cleared) the some of 13ˡ. wᶜʰ hee promiseth to pay after 2ˢ p̄ weeke, therefore it is ordered that those that setts Johnson on worke shall pay vnto Sʳ. Richard out of his wages the sᵈ 2ˢ p̄ week.

Crib, Cable, & Trowent sent. to be whipt.

It is ordered that Beniamyn Cribb John Cable & Morris Trowent shalbe whipped for stealeing 3 piggs of Mʳ. Ralfe Glouers.

Richː Louge confesseth to owe vnto Mʳ. Ludlowe the some of 3ˡ — 18ˢ — 4ᵈ. which hee p̄misseth to pay him after 2ˢ. p̄ weeke till it be all satisfied.

It appeares by Sʳ. Richː Saltonstalls note of disbursm̄ᵗˢ that Willm̄ Knopp owes him the some of 19ˡ vˢ, as was evidenced to the Court by Richard Browne & Ephraim Childe being men indifferently chosen betwixte them to iudge thereof.

[70]   A Court of Assistants holden att Boston Aprill 12ᵗʰ 1631.*

Pʳsent,

The Goū̄nʳ   Mʳ. Nowell
Deputie Goū̄nʳ   Mʳ. Pinchon
Mʳ. Ludlowe   Mʳ. Bradstreete.

Watches, when to begin.

It is ordered that there shalbe a watch of 4 kept eū̄y night att Dorchester & another of 4 att Waterton the watches to begin att Sunsett.

Disturbance of yᵐ 12 (6)

Further it is ordered that if any p̄son shall shoote of any peece after the watch is sett, hee shall forfeict 40ˢ. or if the Court shall iudge him vnable then to be whipped, the second fault to be punished by the Court as an offence of an higher nature.

13

Ammunition, eū̄y man to provide.

It is likewise ordered, that eū̄y man that findes a muskett shall before the 18th day of this moneth (& soe alwaies after) haue ready 1ˡ of powder 20 bulletts & 2 fathome of match vnder penaltie of xˢ for eū̄y fault. — moderated 470 : †

Traineinge once a week.

It is ordered that eū̄y Captaine shall traine his companie on Saterday in euerie weeke.

---

* See Winthrop I. 52.
† This number, which is not in the Lechford copy, is a reference to an order of the General Court passed in June, 1641, and numbered 470 in the margin of the record. See Mass. Col. Records, Vol. I., p. 307.

Travellers not to go vnarmed.   Further it is ordered that noe pson shall travell single betwixte theis plantacons & Plymouthe nor without some armes though 2 or 3 togeath^r.

A Court of Assistants holden att Boston May 3 1631.

Present

The Goūn^r
Deputie Goūn^r
M^r. Ludlowe
Capt. Endicott

M^r. Nowell
M^r. Pinchon
M^r. Bradstreete

It is ordered that Thomas Chubb shall be freed from the service of M^r. Sam^ll Maūacke & shall become serv^t to Willm̄ Gayllerd of Dorchester.

It is ordered that John Legge serv^t to M^r. Humfry shalbe seuerely whipped this day att Boston, and afterwards soe soone as conveniently may be att Salem for strikeing Richard Wright when hee came to giue him correccōn for idleness in his maist^rs worke.

[71]   Tho: Walford of Charlton is ffyned xl^s. & is inioyned hee and his wife to depte out of the lymits of this Pattent before the 20th day of October nexte vnder paine of confiscacōn of his goods for his contempt of authoritie & confrontinge officers &c.

Walford to dep^t ye patent.

It is ordered that for this yeare if the cowes horses or goates of any mans in any plantacōn ~~shall~~ (Salem excepted) shall trespasse & doe hurte in the corne of another, that the owner of the cattell shall make full satisfaccōn for the damage done by them, & that all swine that are found in any mans corne shalbe forfeict to the publique, out of wch the p^rtie damnyfied shalbe satisfied, if ye swine soe forfeicted be of that value, if not the owner is to make full recompence in other goods.

Trespasses in corne, own^rs of cattle to pay.

Swyne forfeited &c.

It is ordered that Thomas Bartlett serv^t to M^r. Pelham shalbe whipped for his vniust selling of his maisters tooles, & that Sam^ll Hosier & John Page shall returne either the tooles they bought of him or the prices thereof to M^r. Pelham.

Tho: Bartlets sent.

John Norman sen^r. is ffyned x^s for his not appearing att the Court being sum̄oned.

A Jury impanneld to inquire concerneing an acc̃on of Battry complayned of by Thomas Dextor against Capt. Endicott

Rich: Browne	Henry Wolcott
Willm̃ Clearke	Sam¹¹ Hosier
Alex: Wignall	John Stickland
John Dillingham	Isaac Sternes
John Gosse	Daniell Fince
John Johnson	Edw: Converse.

The Jury findes for the plantiffe and cesses for damages xlˢ.

[On page 72 and the beginning of page 73 is the record of a General Court 18 May, 1631. The rest of page 73 and pages 74 and 79 contain lists of freemen admitted from 1631 to 1634. Between pages 74 and 79 there were at the time the pages of the book were numbered two leaves paged 75, 76, 77, and 78. These are now in the first part of the original volume and are paged, beside the old paging, (1), (2), (9), and (10). The order in which Lechford made his copy, about the year 1640, indicates that these two leaves with other miscellaneous matter were then at the end of the original volume, and that the first pagination took place at a later date after these two leaves had been inserted between pages 74 and 79. In fact, the first numbering of the pages of the original seems to have been done by Rawson, the Secretary after Nowell. The leaf paged 75 and 76 contains the oaths for the governor and for the council. That paged 77 and 78 contains the "Answer" of John Pratt and the action of the court thereon. This has no date, but it appears from a mention of it by Winthrop, in his History of New England, page 173, to have been at a meeting of the Court of Assistants Nov. 3, 1635. It will be found below at the end of Part I.]

[80]   A Court holden att Boston June 14ᵗʰ 1631.

Present
The Goũnʳ   16
Deputy Goũnʳ   (8)
Mr. Ludlowe   [svᵗ]
Capt. Endicott
Mr. Nowell   Licence.
Mr. Pinchon
Simon Bradstreete. 17

It is ordered that noe man within the limitts of this Jurisdicc̃on shall hire any p̃son for a servᵗ for lesse time then a yeare, vnles hee be a setled housekeep also that noe p̃son wˢoeuer shall trauell out of this pattent eithʳ by sea or land without leaue from the Governʳ Deputy Goũnʳ or some other assistant, vnder such penalty as the Court shall thinke meete to inflict.

It is ordered that the Constables of the seũall plantac̃ons shall giue notice to the creditʳˢ of Capt. Levett John Boggust & Henry Lauson to be att the nexte Court to make p̃fe of their debts that they may receiue satisfacc̃on for the same, soe farr as their goods will afford.

Vpon the reading of certaine Artickles concerneing a geñall trade of beavʳ agreed vpon by Capt. Endicott & dyvʳˢ others. It was ordered that the p̃sons interest‸ therein shall giue a meeteing before the nexte

Court att such tyme & place as Capt. Endicott shall appoynct, to discide such differences as are betwixte them, & for such as they cannot end to bring them to the nexte Court there to be determined.

John Maisters's.*
M^r. John Maisters hath vndertaken to make a passage from Charles Ryver to the newe Towne [12]† foote broad & [7] foote deepe for which the Court ꝑmiseth him satisfacc̄on according as the charges thereof shall amount vnto.

It is ordered that Phillip Swaddon shalbe whipped for runing away from his maister Robte Seely, intending to goe to Virginia.

It is ordered that Phillip Ratliffe shalbe whipped haue his eares cutt of fyned 40^l & banished out of ye lymitts of this Jurisdicc̄on, for vttering mallitious & scandalous speeches against the gou̅m^t & the church of Salem &c., as appeareth by a ꝑticul^r. thereof, ꝙued vpon oath.‡

Licence.
18
It is ordered that noe ꝑson w^tsoeuer shall buy corne or any other ꝑvision or merch^table com̄odity of any shipp or barke that comes into this bay without leaue from the Gou̅n^r or some oth^r of the Assistants.

Chickatabut.
Chickataubott is fyned a skyn of beau^r for shooteinge a swine of S^r. Rich: Saltonstalls.§

Ja: Browne ꝑmiseth payem^t.
Will̄m Almy is ffyned ij^s vi^d for takeing away Mr Glouers cannoe without leaue.

19
[Edwd Converse undertakes] to keep Charlestown Ferry.
Edw: Converse hath vndertaken to sett vpp a fferry betwixte Charlton & Boston for which hee is to haue ij^d for eu̅y single ꝑson & 1^d a peece if there be 2 or more.

It is ordered that M^r. Pelham shall pay vnto Tho: Goilthayt the som̄e of v^l (whereof 5 nobles is already p̄d) wch the Court hath awarded him to pay to make good a covenant betwixte them.

[81]   A Court of Assistants holden att Boston July 5th 1631.

Pr̃sent,
The Gou̅n^r
Deputy Gou̅n^r
M^r. Ludlowe
M^r. Nowell
M^r. Pinchon
S: Bradstreete.

It is ordered there shalbe levyed out of the seu̅all plantac̄ons the som̄e of thirty pounds for the makeing of the creeke att the Newe Towne, vz.: Winettsem^t 15^s Wessaguscus 40^s Saugus 20^s Natascett 10^s Waterton v^l Boston v^l Dorchester 4^l 10^s Rocksbury 3^l Salem 3^l 15^s Charlton 4^l 10^s.

20
Ilands
Further it is ordered that all the Ilelands within the Lymitts of this pattent vz. Conants Ileland

---

* In modern hand.
† "20" in L. copy.
‡ See Winthrop I. 56.
§ See Winthrop I. 56.

Noddles Ileland Tompsons Ileland togeath' with all other Ilelands within the lymitts of our pattent shalbe apppriated to publique benefit & vses, & to remaine in the power of the Gou̅n' & Assistants (for the time being,) to be lett & disposed of ‖ by ‖ them to helpe towards publique charges, & that noe pson w'soeu' shall make any vse or benefitt of any of the said Ilelands, by putting on Cattell, felling wood raiseing slate &c. without leaue from the Gou̅n' & Assistants for the time being. This order to take place imediately after the first of Octob' nexte.

Asistants to make sumons.
21 (9)
Court.

It is further ordered that eu̅y Assistant shall haue power to graunt war'ts. sumons & attatchm'ts, as occaco̅n shall require, & that the acts of the Court shalbe authenticall if they passe onely vnder the Secretaryes hand for y'e tyme being.

‖The Saggamore of Aggawam is banished from comeing into any Englishe mans howse for the space of a yeare, vnd' the penalty of 10 skins of beav'.‖

Att a Court holden att Boston July 26th. 1631.

P'sent,
The Gou̅n'
Deputy Gou̅n'
M'. Ludlowe
Capt. Endicott
M'. Nowell
M'. Pinchon
S: Bradstreete

[22] (10)
Fyres.

For the p'servaco̅n of howses hay boards timb' &c it was ordered that noe pson whatsoeuer within the Lymitts of o' Pattent shall burne any ground any yeare till the first of March, vnder such penalty as the Court shall thinke meete to inflict; & if any pson be desirous to burne any of his owne ~~corne~~ ground for corne before that time, hee shall make full satisfacco̅n for the damage it doeth in case any be occaco̅n'd thereby. Altred &c 442.*

Lucy Smith.

Lucy Smyth is bound as an apprentice with M'. Roger Ludlowe for 7 yeares ~~for wch~~ dureing w'ch tyme hee is to finde her meate drinke & cloathes, & att the end of her yeares to giue her the some of v'l.

Watch.
3.

It is ordered that there shalbe a watch of sixe & an offi[cer] kept eu̅y night att Boston, 2 whereof are to be of Boston 2 of Charlton and 2 of Rocksbury.

---

* This refers to an order of the Gen'l. Court passed Nov., 1639, and numbered 442 in the margin of the record.

<small>4.</small>
Traineing.

It is further ordered that eūy first thursday in eūy m[oneth] there shalbe a geñall traineing of Capt. Vnd'hills com[pany] att Boston & Rocksbury, & eūy first Friday in eūy moneth there shalbe a geñal traineing of the remaind[r] of them [that] inhabitt att Charlton Misticke & the newe Towne att [some] convenient place aboute the Indian wigwams, the traine[ing to] begin att one of the clocke in the afternoone.

[82.] It is ordered that Frauncis Perry shalbe whipped for his ill speeches & misbehav[r] towards his maister.

M[r]. Frauncis Aleworth is chosen Leifeten[t] vnto Capt. Southcoate, & Capt. Southcoate hath liberty graunted him to goe for England ꝑmiseing to returne againe wth all convenient speede.

A Court of Assistants holden att Boston August 16th, 1631.

Present,
The Goūn[r]
Deputy Goūn[r]
M[r]. Ludlowe
M[r]. Nowell
M[r]. Pinchon
S: Bradstreete

Debts.
28 [11]

It is ordered that any bill assigned to another shalbe good debt to the ꝑty to whome it is assigned, also that such debts due vpon bill shalbe p̄d before any other & that the ꝑty that giueth such bills shall renewe them vpon demaund & deliūy in of the olde bill.

Shep. Cole Gibbings fined 5 m'ks a peece.

It is ordered that M[r]. Shepheard and Robte Coles shalbe ffyned 5 m̄ks a peece & Edward Gibbons xx[s] for abuseing themselues disorderly with drinkeing to much stronge drinke aboard the Frendshipp, & att M[r]. Maūacke his howse at Winettsem[t]. discharged, 409.*

Wignall.

M[r]. Alex: Wignall is ffined 5 m̄ks for the like offence att the same time.

Garrets executors.

It is further ordered that the execut[rs] of Rich: Garrett shall pay vnto Henry Harwood the some of 20 nobles, according to the ꝓporc̄on that the goods of the said Rich: Garrett shall amount vnto.†

Swadden freedom.

It is ordered, that Phillip Swaddon shalbe sett free from his maister Robte Seely vpon the payem[t] of x[s] to his maister.

M[r]. Gennison, Ensi.

M[r]. Will[m] Gennison is chosen anchient to Capt. Pattricke.

---

* This refers to an order of the Gen[l]. Court passed Sept., 1638.
† See Winthrop I. 39.

OF THE MASSACHUSETTS BAY.

A Court of Assistants holden att Boston Septembr 6th 1631.

Prsent,
The Govnr
Deputy Govnr
Mr. Ludlowe
Mr. Nowell
Mr. Pinchon
S: Bradstreete.

Govr Winthrop 600 [acres at] Misticke.

It is ordered that Henry Lyn shalbe whipped and banished the plantacon before the 6th day of Octobr nexte for writeing into England falsely & mallitiously against the govmt & execucon of Justice here.*

There is graunted to Mr. Govnr 600 ac of land to be sett forth by mks & bounds neere his howse att Misticke to enioy to him & his heires for euer.

It is ordered John Dawe shalbe seuerely whipped for intiseing an Indian woman to lye wth him. Vpon this occacon it is ꝑpounded withr adultery eithr wth English or Indian shall not be punished wth death./ Referred to the nexte Courte to be considered of.†

[83] Mr. Alex: Wignall is ffined 40s. bound to his good behavr & enioyned to remove his dwelling to some setled plantacon before the last of May nexte, for drunkenes & much misdemeanr by him comitted att the plantacon where nowe hee dwelleth.

A Court of Assistants holden att Boston Septembr 27th 1631.

Present,
The Govnr
Deputy Govnr
Mr. Ludlowe
Mr. Nowell
Mr. Pinchon
S: Bradstreete.

25
Rates.

It is ordered that Sawers shall not take aboue 12d a scoore for boards if they have their wood felled & squared for them, & not aboue 7s the hundred after 5 scoore to the hundred if they fell & square their wood themselues.

Willm Phelpes is chosen constable of Dorchester.

It is ordered that Josias Plastowe shall (for stealeing 4 basketts of corne from the Indians) returne them 8 basketts againe be ffined vl & hereafter to be called by the name of Josias & not Mr. as formly hee vsed to be, & that Willm Buckland & Tho: Andrewe shalbe whipped for being accessary to the same offence.‡

A Court of Assistants holden att Boston Octobr 18th 1631.

Prsent,
The Govnr
Deputy Govnr
Mr. Ludlowe [26]
Capt. Endicott 12
Mr. Nowell
Mr. Pinchon
S: Bradstreete.

[13]

It is ordered that if any man shall have carnall copulacon with another mans wife be she Englishe or Indian they ‖both‖ shalbe punished by death. [This was confirmed the first month 1637 or 1638.§]

---

* See Winthrop I. 61.   † See Winthrop I. 60, 61.   ‡ See Winthrop I. 61.
§ This, which appears to have been written by Increase Nowell, is not in the L. copy.

The constable of Rocksbury returnes the receipt of M^r. Shepheards ffine of 5 m̄ks & soe it remaines in his hands to be accomptable for it. M^r. Goūn^r is to haue 40^s of it wch hee p̄d for ferryeing the watch from Charlton to Boston.

₂₇
Tho: Grays censure. quare.*

It is ordered that Thomas Grayes howse att Marble Harb^r shalbe puld downe, & that noe Englishe man shall hereafter giue howseroome to him or intertaine him vnder such penalty as the Court shall thinke meete to inflicte.

₂₈

It is ordered that there shalbe taken out of the estate of M^r. Crispe & his company the som̄e of xij^l j^s v^d & deliūed to John Kirman as his ꝑp goods, & after the whole estate to be Inventoryed, whereof the s^d John Kirman is to haue an 8th p^rte, this to be done with all convenient speede by theis 5 com̄ission^rs or any 3 of them vizt : M^r. John Masters M^r. Robte Feakes† M^r. Edward Gibbons Epharim Childe Dan^ll Fynch ℈c.

₄₁
Corn in payment.

It is further ordered that corne shall passe for payem^t of all debts at the vsuall rate it is solde for except money or beav^r be expressley named.

[84] Att a Meeteing of Assistants att Boston February the 3 1631.

P^rsent,
The Goūn^r
Deputy Goūn^r
M^r. Ludlowe
Capt. Endicott
M^r. Nowell
M^r. Pinchon
S: Bradstreete

Rate.

It was ordered, there should be three scoore pounds levyed out of the seūall plantac̄ons within the Lymitts of this Pattent towards the ~~pallasading~~ makeing of a pallysadoe aboute the newe Towne vizt. : Waterton ‡ viij^l the newe Towne iij^l Charlton vij^l Meadford iij^l Saugus & Marble Harb^r vj^l Salem iiij^l x^s Boston viij^l Rocksbury vij^l Dorchester vij^l Wessaguscus v^l Winettsem^t xxx^s.

Knowers bond.

Thomas Knower hath bound himselfe in x^l to make his ꝑsonall appearance att the nexte Court to be holden att Boston the first Tuesday in March nexte to answer to such things as shalbe obiected against him./

---

* This marginal note is in the handwriting of Edward Rawson.
† "Feke" in L. copy.   ‡ See Winthrop I. 70.

A Court of Assistants, holden att Boston March 6th 1632.*

29

Present,
The Goũnr
Deputy Goũnr
Mr. Ludlowe
Capt. Endicott
Mr. Nowell
Mr. Pinchon
S: Bradstreete

30
Armour to be
prvided for by
service, &c.

It is ordered that noe planter within the Lymitts of this Jurisdicõon returneing for England shall carry either money or beavr with him wthout leave from the Gounr (for the time being,) vnder paine of forfectinge the money or beaver soe intended to be transported.

As an addiõon to an order made the 22th of March 1630 it is ordered that if any single pson be not ꝓvided of sufficient armes, allowable by the Capt. or Leifetents before the 10th of Aprill nexte, ₍shalbe compelled to serue by the yeare with any maister that will retaine him for such wages as the Court shall thinke meete to appoynte.

It is ordered that Courts hereafter shalbe helde eũy first Tuesday in eũy moneth.†

Robert Coles.‡

It is further ordered that Robte Coles of Rocksbury shalbe fined xxs for being drunke att Charlton in Octobr last, & is inioyned to confesse his fault to the Court, (nowe comitted in extenuateing his offence) the nexte Court & after att the Geñall Court.

Tho: Knower hath bound himselfe in xl to make his psonall ||appearance|| att the nexte Court to answer to such things as shall be obiected against him.

[85]   A Court of Assistants holden att Boston Aprill 3 1632.§

Present,
The Goũnr
Deputy Goũnr
Mr. Ludlowe
Capt. Endicott
Mr. Nowell
Mr. Pinchon
S: Bradstreete

Catching foule.

Tho: Knower was sett in the bilbowes for threateing the Court that if hee should be punist, hee would haue it tryed in England whither hee was lawfully punished or not.

It was ordered, that noe pson wtsoeuer shall att any shoote att fowle vpon Pullen Poynte or Noddles Ileland but that the sd places shalbe reserved for John Perkins to take fowle wth netts.

Vpon Robte Coles confession of his faulte comitted the last Court in extenuateing of his offence of drunkenes the Court remitted his ffyne & further confession enioyned him the last Court.

---

* See Winthrop I. 70, 71, for Meetings Feb. 17 and March 5.
† See Winthrop I. 71.   ‡ In modern hand.   § See Winthrop I. 72.

31

Sarah Morley is putt as an apprentice to M{r}. Nathanaell Turner of Saugus for the space of nyne yeares from this Court for w{ch} tearme hee is to finde her meate drinke & cloathing.

32
Connants
Iland, or Gou{rs}
Garden, gr{r}ted to
John Winthrop,
Esq{r}, Gou{r}.

The Ileland called Conant's Ileland, with all the lib{r}ties & previlidges of fishing & fowleing, was demised to John Winthrop Esq{r} the p{r}sent Go⃞n{r} for the tearme of his life for the ffine of fforty shillings & att the yearely rent of xij{d} to be paid to the Treasurer vpon the 25{th} day of March & it was further agreed, & the said John Winthrop did covenant & ꝑmise to plant a vineyard and an orchyard in the same, in consideracõn whereof the Court did graunt that att the end of the said tearme the lease hereof should be renewed to the heires or assignes of the said John Winthrop for one & twenty yeares, payeinge yearely to the Go⃞n{r}, for the time being, the fifth p̱{r}te of all such fruicts & ꝓffitts as shalbe yearely raysed out of the same, & soe the same lease to be renewed from time to time vnto the heires & assignes of the said John Winthrop with the said reservacõn of the said fifth p̱{r}te to the Go⃞n{r} for the time being, & the name of the said Ileland was * changed, & is to be called the Go⃞n{rs} Garden. ꝓvided that if the heires or assignes of the said John Winthrop shall att any time suffer the said Ileland to lye wast, & not imꝑue the same, then this p{r}sent demise to be voide.

[86]

March 6{th} 1632.†

33
Charles Toune
& New Toune
bounds.

It is agreed vpon by the p̱{r}tyes whose names are here vnderwritten By vertue of an order of Court ffor the appoincted‡ & setting out the bounds of CharlesTowne & Newe Towne,

First it is agreed that all the land impaled by Newe Towne men with the necke therevnto adioyneing whereon M{r}. Graues dwelleth shall belonge to the said Newe Towne & that the bounds of Charles Towne shall end att a Tree marked by the said pale, & to passe alonge from that tree, by a straight lyne vnto the mydway betweene the westermost p̱{r}te of the greate lott of land of John Winthrop Esq{r}. nowe Go⃞n{r} of the Englishe Colony in the Massachusetts, & the

---

* "Is" in L. copy.
† A similar entry will be found following the record of 7 Nov. 1632.
‡ "Appointing" in L. copy.

neerest p̱rte thereto of the bounds of Waterton. In witnes whereof weȝ have herevnto sett oʳ hands the day & yeare aforesaid.

> Tho: Mayhewe,
> Nath: Turner,
> George Alcocke.

[Page 87 is blank. Page 88 contains the record of the General Court May 9, 1632.]

[89]   A Court of Assistants holden att Boston June 5ᵗʰ 1632.*

Pʳsent
The Goūnʳ
Deputy Goūnʳ
Mʳ. Nowell
Mʳ. Pinchon
Mʳ. Ludlowe
Mʳ. Winthrop, Juʳ
S: Bradstreete.

Day of Thanks- giving.

The Court takeing into consideraĉon the greate m̄cy of god vouchsafed to the Churches of god in Germany and the Pallattinate ꝯ hath appoyncted the 13ᵗʰ day of this pʳsent moneth to be kept as a day of publique thanksgiueing throughout the seūall plantaĉons.†

Compā goods securd.

It is ordered that the goods of the company of husbandm̄ shalbe Inventoryed by the Beadle, & pʳserued here for the vse and benefitt of the said company.

36
200 acres of land grᵗ to Tho: Dudley, Esqʳ.

It was further ordered that there shalbe 200 aĉ of land sett out by m̄ks & bounds on the west side of Charles Ryver ouer against the Newe Towne to enioy to Thomas Dudley Esqʳ. Deputy Goūnʳ to him & his heires for euer.

bever.
37

It was likewise ordered that eūy planter inhabiting wᵗʰin this Pattent shall pay to the Court towards the defrayeing of publique charges xijᵈ for eūy pound of beavʳ that hee shall trade for with any Indian within this Pattent or that hee brings into the Pattent haveing traded the same with any forraine Indean. Rep. 207.‡

Trucking houses.

Also it is agreed that there shalbe a trucking howse appoyncted in eūy plantaĉon whither the Indians may resorte to trade to avoide there comeing to seūall howses.

Josias Plaistow estat to be inquʳd after.

There is a Com̄ission graunted to Mʳ. Pinchon & Mʳ. Maūicke Senʳ. to make inquiry & to take depositĉons of the creditors of Josias Plastowe & th[ere] witnesses, that it may appeare what debts are oweing by him, & soe his estate to be pʳserued here till the nexte Court.

---

* See Winthrop I. 73, for meeting May 1.   † See Winthrop I. 79.
‡ This refers to an order of the Genˡ. Court, March, 1635, repealing the first order.

[90]   A Court holden att Boston July 3 1632.

Prsent
The Govnr
Deputy Govnr
Mr. Ludlowe
Capt. Endicott
Mr. Pinchon
Mr. Winthrop
S: Bradstreete
Mr. Nowell.

Capt. Endicott being chosen an Assistant att the geñall Court did nowe take an oath to his place belonging, in the prsence of the Court.

It is ordered that Joist Weillust shall haue allowed him v^l towards his transportačon into his owne Country whith^r. according to his desire hee hath free leaue to goe.

It is ordered that Thomas Dextor shalbe bound to his good behav^r till the nexte geñall Court, & ffined v^l for his misdemean^r & insolent carriage & speeches to S: Bradstreete, att his owne howse also att the geñall Court is bound to confesse his fault.

38
Jo: Endicotts land.*

There is a necke of land lyeing aboute 3 myles from Salem cont. aboute 300 ac of land graunted to Capt. Jo: Endicott to enioy to him & his heires for euer called in the Indean tonge Wahquamesehcok in English Birchwood, bounded on the south side with a Ryver called in the Indean

Mr. Endicotts farme.

tounge Soewamapenessett, comonly called the Cowe Howse Ryver. bounded on the North side with a Ryver called in the Indean tongue Conamabsqnooncant, comonly called the Ducke Ryver. bounded on the East wth a Ryver leadeing vpp to the 2 form ryvers, wch is called in the Indean tongue Orkhussunt, otherwise knowen by the name of Wooleston Ryv^r. bounded on the west with the maine land.

39
Sam: Skelton.

There is another necke of land, lyeing aboute 3 myles frō Salem cont. aboute 200 ac graunted to M^r. Sam^{ll} Skelton to enioy to him & his heires for euer called by the Indeans Wahquack bounded on the south vpon a little Ryv^r called by the Indeans Conamabsqnooncant vpon the North abutting on another Ryver called by the Indeans Ponomeneuhcant & on the East on the same ryv^r also there is graunted to M^r. Skelton one ac of land, on wch his howse standeth. & 10 ac more in a necke of land abutting on the South ryver, vpon the harb^r Ryv^r on the north, vpon Willm Allens ground on the East & vpon M^{rs}. Higgensons ground on the west. likewise there is graunted to M^r. Skelton 2 ac more of ground lyeing in Salem, abutting on the South ryv^r on the East vpon the Maine vpon the west, on Capt. Endicotts ground on the south & on John Sweetes ground on the North.

---

* In modern hand.

Bateman.* Willm Parks doeth p̃mise if S^rieant Bateman comes noe more to satisfie M^r. Pinchon w^t shalbe thought meete by 2 indifferent men for 3 leaden waights by him lost, & 12 p̃re of stockins wch the said Bateman solde to M^r. Pinchon for good ones but p̃ued badd & moath-eaten./

[91] John Smithe is bound as an apprentice with M^r. John Wilson for fyve yeares from this Court dureing wch tearme M^r. Wilson is to finde the said John Smyth meate drinke & appell, & att the end of the said time is to giue vnto him the sõme of fforty shillings.

J^no Smith bound to M^r. Wilson.

It is likewise ordered that those goods wch were sent ouer with the said John Smythe shall remaine in the hands of M^r. Wilson for wch hee is to be accountable to those y^t sent them ouer.

Bond for Appearance. Bryan Bincks & Peter Johnson hath bound themselues ioynctly & seũally in x^l a peece that they shall not dep̃t out of the Pattent w^thout leave from the Goũn^r & shalbe ready to attend vpon the Court, when they shalbe called to giue an account of their company goods.

John Smyth hath likewise bound himselfe in x^l to be acomptable for his companyes goods nowe Inventoryed & remaineing in his hands.

Drunkenes punisht. M^r. James Parker is ffined xl^s & bound to his good behav^r till the nexte Court for his misdemean^r and drunkenes comitted aboard the Virginia shipp.

M^r. Sam^ll Dudley is ffined xl^s for the like offence att the same time.

40
Military officers care. It is ordered that the Capt. & Officers shall take especiall care to search all peeces that are brought into the ffeild for being charged & that noe p̃son w^tsoeuer shall att any time charge any peece of service wth bulletts or shott other then for defence of their howses or att co[m̃au]nd from the capt. vpon such penallty as the Court shall thinke meete to inflict.†

[92] A Court holden att Boston August 7th 1632.‡
P^rsent,
The Goũn^r
Deputy Goũn^r
M^r. Ludlowe
M^r. Nowell
M^r. Pinchon
M^r. Winthrop
S: Bradstreete

Vpon further consideraçon of Justice to be done vpon the murder of Walter Bagnall & vpon readeing a l̃re from those of Plymouthe being written in answer of a l̃re sent to them aboute it It is ordered that a boate shall be sent forth sufficiently manned with

---

* In modern hand. † See Winthrop I. 80.
‡ See Winthrop I. 82 for meeting Aug. 8. See also I. 86.

comission to deale with the Plantaçon to the Eastward, & to ioyne with such of them as shalbe willing thereto, for examinaçon of the murder of the said Walter Bagnall & for app^rhending of such as shalbe found guilty thereof, & to bring the prison^rs into the Bay it is referred to the Goũn^r to take order herein.

It is ordered that the remaind^r of M^r. Allens stronge water, being estimated aboute 2 gallands shalbe deliũed into the hands of the deacons of Dorchest^r. for the benefitt of the poore there, for his selling of it to dyv^rs psons tymes to such as were drunke wth it, hee knowing thereof.

It is ordered that James Woodward shalbe sett in the bill-bowes for being drunke att the Newe Towne.

There is iij^l of Knops fine of v^l remitted.

4.
It is ordered that the Capt. shalbe mainetained by their seũall companies.

41
M^r. Willm̃ Pinchon is chosen Treasurer for this yeare nexte ensueing, & till a newe be chosen./

A Court holden att Boston Sept. 4th 1632.

Present,
The Goũn^r
Deputy Goũn^r
M^r. Ludlowe
Capt. Endicott
M^r. Tresu^r
M^r. Nowell
M^r. Jo: Winthrop
S: Bradstreete.

It is ordered that Robte Shawe shalbe seuerely whipt for wicked curseing sweareing iustifyeing the same & gloryeing in it as hath been ꝓved by oath.

John Stickland is ffined iij^l for his refuseing to watch att the Capt. co[mãu]nds.

Saggamore John ꝯ ꝓmised against the nexte yeare ‖ & soe * euer after‖ to fence their corne against all kinde of cattell.

Josuah Barnes is bound as an apprentice to M^r. Paine for 5 yeares from his landing for 4^l p añ wages and v^l att the end of his tearme to be paid to him by his said maister.

It is ordered † Willm Hamon shalbe sett in the bilbowes for being drunke.

M^r. Turner is chosen Constable of Saugus for this yeare & till a newe be chosen, & did nowe take an oath to his place belonging.

There is order giuen to M^r. Tres^r to pay 40^s to Richard Waterman for killing a woulfe aboute 2 monthes since in Salem plantaçon.

---

* "For" in L. copy.   † "Ordered that" in L. copy.

[93]
Capt[s]. salle[r]y[s].

There is likewise order graunted to M[r]. Tresurer to pay Capt. Vnderhill & Capt. Pattricke a quart[r]s exhibic͠on.

M[r]. Feaks Leift.

M[r]. Rob[t]e Feakes* is chosen into the place of leifeten[t] to Capt. Pattricke.

Hopkins sent.

It is ordered that Richard Hopkins shalbe seuerely whipt & branded with a hott iron on one of his cheekes for selling peeces & powder & shott to the Indeans. Hereupon it was ꝑpounded if this offence should not be punished hereafter by death   referred to the nexte Court to be determined.†

A Court holden att Boston ~~Nov.~~ Octob[r] 3 1632.

P[r]sent,
The Go͠vn[r]
Deputy Go͠vn[r]
M[r]. Ludlowe
Capt. Endicott
M[r]. Tresu[r]
M[r]. Nowell
M[r]. Winthrop
S: Bradstreete.

M[r]. Batchil[r] silenst.

Bever trade.

[42?]

House for beadle, e[c].

M[r]. Tresurer hath ꝑmised to giue xxv[l] for this yeare for his beav[r] trade for w[ch] his 12[d] in the pound is remitted.

It is ordered that there shalbe a howse of correcc͠on & a house for the Beadle built att Boston wth w[t] speede conveniently may be.

M[r]. Batchel[r] is required to forbeare exerciseing his guifts as a past[r] or teacher publiquely in o[r] Pattent vnlesse it be to those hee brought with him, for his contempt of Aucthority & till some scandles be removed.

It is agreed that the Beadle shall have viij[l] exhibic͠on for this yeare.

It is ordered that James Woodward shalbe whipt for runing from his maist[r] M[r]. Gibbons, & absenting himselfe from his service, in recompence whereof hee shall doe him 6 weekes worke when his time comes out.

E: Burton find.‡

Edward Burton is ffined v[l] for his contempt of aucthority in refuseing to come to the Court being sum͠ond by the Go͠vn[r] and 40[s] for drunkenes

43
Saugus to build wear.‡

It is ordered that Saugus plantac͠on shall haue liberty to build a ware vpon Saugus Ryver, also they haue ꝑmised to make & continually to keepe a good foote-bridge vpon the most convenient place there.

It is ordered that Alex: Miller & John Wipple shall giue iij[s] iiij[d] apeece to their maister Israell Stoughton for their wastfull expence of powd[r] & shott.

---

* "Feke" in L. copy.   † See Winthrop I. 88.   ‡ In modern hand.

Leifeten{^t} Aleworth hath liberty graunted him to returne to England by the shipp Lyon.

44
Simon Bradstreet.
60 acres.

There is 60 ac̃ of meadowe ground graunted to Simon Bradstreete in the marshe ~~ground~~ against the Oyster banke where hee shall chuse to inioy to him & his heires for euer.

[94]
45
Nich: Frost cens.

It is ordered that Nicholas Frost, for thefte by him comitted att Damerills Cove vpon the Indeans for drunkenes and fornicac̃on of all w{^ch} hee is convicted, shalbe fined v{^l} to the Court & xl{^l} to Henry Way & John Holman, shalbe seuerely whipt & branded in the hand with a hott iron, & after banished out of this Pattent, with penalty that if euer hee be found within the lymitts of the said Pattent, hee shalbe putt to death : also it is agreed that hee shalbe kept in boults by Henry Way & John Holman till his ffines be paid, dureing w{^ch} time hee is to beare his owne charges.

Boston y{^e} fittest place for meetings.

It is thought by geñall consent that Boston is the fittest place for publique meeteings of any place in the Bay.

It is ordered that from the 1{^th} of March nexte eũy p̃son shall satisfie for the damages his swine shall doe in the corne of another.

Tobacco p̃hibited.

It is further ordered that noe p̃son shall take any tobacco publiquely vnder paine of punishm{^t} also that eũy one shall pay j{^d} for euery time hee is convicted for takeing tobacco in any place, & that any assistant shall haue power to receave evidence & giue order for the levyeing of it as also to giue order for the levyeing of the officers charge this order to begin the 10{^th} of Novemb{^r} nexte.

Geo: Dyar constable.*

George Dyar is chosen Constable of Dorchest{^r} for this yeare nexte ensueing & till a newe be chosen & did nowe take an oath to his place belonging.

A Court holden att Boston Novemb{_r} 7{^th} 1632.

P̃sent,
The Goũn{^r}
Deputy Goũn{^r}
M{^r}. Ludlowe
M{^r}. Tres{^r} *46*
M{^r}. Nowell
M{^r}. Winthrop
S: Bradstreete.

For preservac̃on of good timb{^r} for more necessary vses It is ordered that noe man shall fell any wood for paleing but such as shalbe vewed & allowed by the nexte Assistant, or some whome they shall depute to doe the same, this order not to extend to ground that is or shall be assigned to p̃ticul{^r} p̃sons.

---

* In modern hand.

<small>Differ betw Ch. & New. referd.</small>
<small>47</small>
<small>Charlestown & Newton.*</small>

It is ordered that the difference betwixte Charles-Towne & Newe-Towne ||for ground|| shalbe referred to Mr. Mawicke Junr. Mr. Alcocke Mr. Turner & John Johnson to vewe the ground wood & meadowe, & soe to sett downe the bounds betwixte them.

<small>48</small>

It is ordered that the necke of land betwixte powder horne hill & pullen poynte shall belonge to Boston to be enioyed by the Inhabitants thereof for euer.

<small>49</small>

It is likewise ordered that the Inhabitants of Boston shall haue liberty to fetch wood from Dorchester necke of land for 20 yeares the ꝓpriety of the Land to remaine to Dorchester.

[95]
<small>50</small>
<small>Committe abt Dor & Rox bounds.</small>

Capt. Traske Mr. Conant Willm Cheesebrough & John Perkins are appoincted by the Court to sett downe the bounds betwixte Dorchester and Rocksbury. Ralfe Sprage is chosen Vmpire.

<small>51</small>
<small>100 acrs to Mr. Ludlow.</small>

There is 100 ac̄ of land graunted to Mr. Roger Ludlowe to inioy to him & his heires for euer lyeing betwixte Musquantum chappell & the mouthe of Naponsett.

<small>Jno Finch find.</small>

John Finch is ffined xs for wanting armes for his man & for being absent himselfe from traineing.

<small>Hen Lin find.</small>

Henry Lynn is ffined xs for absenting himselfe from traineing.

Mr. Mathewe Cradocke is ffined iiij¹ for his men being absent from traineing dyvers times.

<small>52</small>
<small>Capt. to traine but once a mo.</small>

It is ordered that the Capt. shall traine their companyes but once a monethe.

<small>Sr Ri: Salt amerst.</small>

It is ffurther agreed that Sr. Richard Saltonstall shall giue Saggamore John a hogshead of corne for the hurt his cattell did him in his corne.

[53?]
<small>No reward for killing wooluos.</small>

It is ordered that neithr Englishe nor Indeans shall haue any more rewards giuen them for killing woolfes.

<small>54</small>
<small>50 acres mea to Jno Winthrop, Esqr.</small>

There is aboute 50 ac̄ of mead ground graunted to John Winthrop Esqr prsent Govr lyeing betwixte Cobbetts howse & Wanottymies Ryver.

---

* In modern hand.

<small>55</small>
Land to Jn⁰ Humphry, Esqʳ.

It is referred to Mʳ. Turner Peter Palfry & Roger Conant to sett out a pporc̃on of land in Saugus for John Humfry Esqʳ.

<small>56</small>
Mʳ. Phillips 30 lot.

Mʳ. Phillips hath 30 ac̃ of land graunted him vpp Charles Ryver on the south side begininge att a Creeke a lyttle higher then the first Pynes, & soe vpwards towards the ware.

Robt Huit sent.

It is ordered that Robte Huitt & Mary Ridge shalbe whipt for comitting fornicac̃on togeather of wᶜʰ they are convicted.

There is iiijˡ of Tho: Dexters ffine of vˡ forgiuen him./

6ᵗʰ Mʳch 1632.

Charlestown & Newtown bounds.

It was agreed by the parties appointed by the Court ℓ That all the ground impaled by Newe towne men, wᵗʰ the neck whereon Mʳ. Grave[s] his house standeth shall belong to Newe towne, & that the bounds of Charlestowne shall end at a tree mʳked by the pale, & to passe along from thence by a straight line vnto the midway betwixt the westermost part of the Governoʳˢ greate lot, & the nearest part thereto of the bounds of Watertowne.*/

[96]   A Court holden att Boston March 4ᵗʰ 1632.†

Pʳsent,
The Goũnʳ
Deputy Goũnʳ
Mʳ. Ludlowe
Capt. Endicott
Mʳ. Tresʳ.
Mʳ. Nowell
Mʳ. Winthrop, Jun
S: Bradstreete

There is administrac̃on graunted to Roger Ludlowe Esq of the goods and chattells of John Knight whoe disceased in Novembʳ last.

Mʳ. Batchiler at libʳty.

The Court hath reversed the last act against Mʳ. Batchelʳ wᶜʰ restrained him from further gathering a Church wᵗʰⁱⁿ this Pattent.

Mʳ. Dexters sent. for reproaching yᵉ Court.

It is ordered that Thomas Dexter shalbe sett in the bilbowes disfranchized & ffined xlˡ for speakeing repᵖchfull & seditious words against the Goũmᵗ here established & findeing fault to dyvʳˢ wᵗʰ the acts of the Court sayeing

---

* This entry is in the handwriting of Increase Nowell. See also above before the record for June 5, 1632.

† See Winthrop I. 96, 97, for Meeting of Council Nov. 23, and Meeting of Assistants Dec. 4, 1632.

this captious goḕmᵗ will bring all to naught adding that the best of them was but an Atturney &c.

Boston & Rox. bounds. It is agreed that the bounds form̃ly sett out betwixte Boston & Rocksbury shall continue, onely Rocksbury to enioy the conveniency of the creeke neere therevnto.

Rate for capᵗ. salery. Boston is cessed vˡ Charlton iiijˡ Rocksbury vjˡ Waterton vjˡ Newe-Towne vjˡ Meadford iiijˡ for the maintenance of Capt. Vnderhill & Capt. Pattricke for halfe a yeare.

Sᵗ. Morris, ensign to Capᵗ. Vnderhill. Sʳieant Morris is chosen Ancient to Capt. Vnderhill.

Thomas Wincall is ffined xxˢ for drunkennes.

A Court holden att Boston Aprill 1ᵗʰ 1633.

Present,
The Goḕnʳ
Deputy Goḕnʳ
Mʳ. Ludlowe
Capt. Endicott
Mʳ. Tresurer
Mʳ. Nowell
S: Bradstreete

Edw Convʳs allow for ferryin officers. There is xjˢ vᵈ allowed to Edward Converse for ferryeing Officers ouer the Water.

2. Agawam planta. It is ordered that noe pson wᵗsoeuer shall goe to plant or inhabitt att Aggawam without leave from the Court except those that are already gone vz. : Mʳ. John Winthrop Junʳ Mʳ. Clerke Rob̃te Coles Thomas Howlett John Biggs John Gage, Thomas Hardy Willm̃ Perkins Mʳ. Thornedicke, Willm̃ Sʳieant.

3. The price of corne form̃ly restrained to 6ˢ the bushell is nowe sett at liberty to be solde as men can agree.

Nodles Island gʳted to Mʳ. Mauericke on rent. Noddles Ileland is graunted to Mʳ. Samˡˡ Maw̃acke to enioy to him & his heires for euer, yeilding & payeing yearely att the gen̄all Court to the Goḕnʳ for the time being eithʳ a fatt weather a fatt hogg or xlˢ in money, & shall giue leave to Boston & Charles-Towne to fetch wood contynually as their neede requires from the Southerne pte of the sᵈ Ileland.

[97]

50 acʳs to Mʳ. Blackston. It is agreed that Mʳ. ||William|| Blackestone shall haue 50 ãc of ground sett out for him neere to his howse in Boston to inioy for euer.

Ezekiell Richardson is chosen constable of Charlton for this yeare nexte ensueing & till a newe be chosen.

It is ordered that if any swine shall in fishing time come within a quarter of a myle of the stage att Marble Harb{r} that they shalbe forfected to the owners of the s{d} stadge & soe for all other stadges within theis Lymitts.

Damage by swine.

It is ordered that Joyce Bradwicke shall giue vnto Alex: Becke the some of xx{s}, for ꝑmiseing him marriage w{th}out her ffrends consent & nowe refuseing to pforme the same.

Joyc Bradwick fined 20.

John Sayle being convicted of fellonyously takeing away corne & fishe from dyvers psons the last yeare & this, as also clapboards &c is censured by the Court after this mann: That all his estate shalbe forfected out of w{ch} double restitucon shalbe made to those whome hee hath wronged shalbe whipt & bound as a serv{t} with any that will retaine him for 3 yeares & after to be disposed of by the Court, as they shall thinke meete.

61
J{no} Sayles sent.

John Sayle is bound with M{r}. Coxeshall for 3 yeares for w{ch} hee is to giue him 4{l} p ann: his daughter is also bound w{th} him for 14 yeares. M{r}. Coxeshall* is to haue a sowe w{th} her, & att the end of her time hee is to giue vnto her a cowe calfe.

61

[Page 98 is blank. Page 99 has the record of a General Court May 29, 1633.]

[100]   A Court holden att Boston June 11{th} 1633.

Present,
The Go{u}{r}
Deputy Go{u}{nr}
M{r}. Ludlowe
M{r}. Tres{r}
M{r}. Nowell
M{r}. Coddington
M{r}. Winthrop
S: Bradstreete.

Dixon in bilboes.

It is ordered that Willm Dixon shalbe sett in the bilbowes for disordering himselfe with drinke.

J{no} Pemb{r}ton sent.

It is likewise ordered that John Pemerton shalbe whipt bound to his good behav{r}, & enioyned to make his appearance att the nexte Court for comitting fornicacon with Eliz: Marson.

John Webb is sett at liberty from his maister Willm Parks.

There is leave graunted to Tho: Sellen to plant att Aggawam.

Thanksgiving.†

The 19{th} day of this moneth is appoyncted to be kept as a day of publique thanksgiueing throughout the seu{er}all plantacons, &c.‡

9· ꝗ ꝫ ſ— 9ᷣ /·, ꝛ / §

---

* "Coggeshall" in L. copy.   † In modern hand.   ‡ See Winthrop I. 104.

§ These shorthand words, which are in the margin of the original record, may be conjecturally rendered as follows :—

     Gi[ve] out call soon.   G[ive] on[e] to [   ].

[101]

Present,
The Govr
Deputy Govnr
Mr. Ludlowe
Mr. Endicott
Mr. Tresr
Mr. Nowell
Mr. Coddington
Mr. Winthrop
S: Bradstreete.

[Rat: 150li.]
Govr. salary.*

Robt Allen find.

James White fined.

Jno Bennet find.

65
Non to sell wine,
&c. wtht licenc.

66
(13)
Fen: to pay damage in case.

Alexr Wignalls goods to be inventoried.

67
Charle Towne liberty.

A Court holden att Boston, July 2 1633.

Mr. Endicott being chosen an Assistant att the Genall Court did nowe take an oath to his place belonging.

64   Mr. Ludlowe Mr. Tresr & Mr. Nowell are chosen as comittees to take an accompt of the debts due to the Govnr & to certifie the same att the nexte Court that they may be discharged.

It is ordered that there shallbe Cll ||150li|| giuen to the Govnr for † this present yeare towards his publique charges & extraordinary expences.‡

Robte Allen is ffined vs for absenting himselfe from Court being sumoned to be there as a witnes &c.

James White is ffined xxxs for drunkenes by him comitted att Marblehead on the Sabboth day.

John Bennett is ffined xs for being drunke att Marblehead.

It is ordered that noe pson shall sell either wine or stronge water without leave from the Govnr or Deputy Govnr. this order to take place a fortnight hence & after the Constable of the same plantacon hath published the same, & that noe man shall sell, or (being in a course of tradeing) giue any stronge water to any Indean.

It is ordered that if any corne fence shalbe by the inhabitants of the Towne iudged insufficient, & the owner thereof forbeare mending of it more then 2 dayes after warneing giuen, the Inhabitants shall mend the said fence, & the corne of the owner of the said fence shalbe liable to pay the charges of the mending thereof.

Mr. Woolridge & Mr. Gibbons are appoyncted to Joyne wth Mr. Graues & Mr. Geneson§ to Inventory the goods & chattells of Alex: Wignall.

It is ordered that the ground lyeing betwixte the North Ryvr & the creeke on the north side of Mr. Mawacks & soe vpp into the Country shall belonge to the inhabitants of Charlton.

---

* In modern hand.   † " For " omitted in L. copy.
‡ See Winthrop I. 105.   § " Gennison " in L. copy.

34 RECORDS OF THE COURT OF ASSISTANTS

Left Mason recompd.

Order is giuen to the Tres{r} to deliu to Leifetent Mason x{l} for his voyage to the Eastward, when hee went about the takeing of Bull.

68 Tho: Lambs liberty.

There is demised to Tho: Lambe of slate in slate Ileand 10 poole towards the water side & 5 poole into the land for 3 yeares payeing the yearely rent of ij{s} vj{d}

69 Ralf Glous good admtrd on.

Administracon is graunted to M{r}. Mayhewe of the goods & chattells of M{r}. Ralfe Glover disceased &c.

Swyne may be killed.

It is ordered that it shalbe lawfull for any man to kill any swine that comes into his corne, the p{r}ty that owes the swine is to haue them being kild, & allowe recompence for the damage they doe &c.

[102]   A Court holden att Boston August 6{th} 1633.

Present,
The Go{u}n{r}
Deputy Go{u}n{r}
M{r}. Ludlowe
M{r}. Tres{r}.
M{r}. Nowell
M{r}. Coddington
M{r}. Winthrop
S: Bradstreete.

Woolrd find.

M{r}. John Woolridge is ffined 1{s} for distemping himselfe w{th} drinke aboard M{r}. Graues his shipp.

70 Cartbridg.

It is agreed that there shalbe a sufficient cartbridge made in some convenient place ouer muddy riuer & another ouer Stony ryver, to be done att the charge of Boston & Rocksbury. M{r}. Coddington M{r}. Colbran & M{r}. Samford are chosen to see it done for Boston, M. Tres{r} Jehu Burr & John Johnson for Rocksbury.

71 Ram goats restreined

It is further ordered that if any ram goate be found amongst Ewe goates betwixte the first of July & 10{th} of Novemb{r} it shalbe lawfull for any man to sease on him before witnesses, & to convey him to some safe place till the said 10{th} of Novemb{r} & then halfe of him is to goe to the publique & the other halfe to the p{r}ty that seases on him this order to take place on thursday nexte.

A Court holden att Boston Sep{t} 3 1633.

Present,
The Go{u}n{r}
Deputy Go{u}n{r}
M{r}. Ludlowe
M{r}. Tres{r}
M{r}. Nowell
M{r}. Coddington
M{r}. Winthrop
S: Bradstreete.

Shatswell find.

John Shotswell is ffined xl{s} for distemping himselfe with drinke att Aggawam.

*Rob{t} Coles find for drunkenes. See p. 107.**

Robte Coles is ffined x{l}: & enioyned to stand w{th} a white sheete of pap|| on his back|| wherein a drunkard shalbe written in greate lres, & to stand therew{th} soe longe

*108?

as the Court thinks meete, for abuseing himselfe shamefully wth drinke intiseing John Shotswell wife to incontinency & oth^r misdemean^r.

Walfords goods sequestrd, to pay his debts.
It is ordered that the goods of Thomas Walford shalbe sequestred & remaine in the hands of ~~The~~ Anchient Gennison to satisfie the debts hee owes in the Bay to seuall psons.

72
Russells estat adm^sted.
There is administracon graunted to Willm Gallard & Willm Rockwell of the goods and chattels of John Russell of ~~Rocksbury~~ Dorchester whoe disceased August 26th 1633.

Desbres estat adm^red.
Administracon graunted to M^r. John Moody of the goods & chattels of Thomas Desbre disceased, & soe to remaine in his hands to be accomptable for them.

Differenc. bet. Dilling: & Dexter referd.
By consent of John Dillingham Richard Wright & Thomas Dexter the differences betwixte them are referd to M^r. Endicott & M^r. Nowell, & power is graunted them by the Court to depose witnesses heare & determine the said differences.

Sept 3, 1633

[103]

Capt. Jno Stones sent
Capt. John Stone for his outrage comitted in confronting aucthority abuseing M^r. Ludlowe both in words and behaviour ‖assalting him &‖ calling him a iust as * ‖e^r‖ is ffined C^l & phibited comeing ~~into~~ within this Pattent w^thout leaue from the Goum^t vnder the penalty of death.†

73
All hands to Boston Fort except, e^r.
It is ordered (according to a former order att the genall Court) that eu^y hand (except magistrates & ministers) shall aford there helpe to the finishing of the ffort att Boston till it be ended.

Mr. Palmer.‡
M^r. Palmer is ffined x^s for absenting himselfe being warnd to serue of a jury.

Alex^dr Wignall find 10^li for dru. quarr. & contempt.
Alex: Wignall is ffined x^l for drunkenes quarrelling breach of an order of Court & contempt of aucthority.

Rich: Arnold estat admstd on.
Administracon graunted to Willm Stitson of the goods & chattells of Richard Arnoll of Wenetsem^t disceased.

Mr. Jno Winthrop, Jur, liberty, e^r.
There is liberty graunted to M^r. John Winthrop Junr. & to his assignes to sett vpp a trucking howse, vpp merrymak ryver.

---

* " A just asse " in L. copy.   † See Winthrop I. 111.   ‡ In modern hand.

<small>M^r. J^{no} Barkroft^s ackno.</small>

M^r. John Barcrofte doeth acknowledge to owe vnto o^r Sou͠aigne [the] the King the some of xl^{li} & M^r. Sam^{ll} Mau͠acke the some of xx^l ℘. The condicon of this recognizance is that Jane Barcrofte wife of the said John shall be of good behav^r. towards all ⱕpsons.

A Court holden att Boston Octob^r. 1th 1633.

<small>The Gou͠n^r
Deputy Gou͠n^r
M^r. Ludlowe
M^r. Tres^r
M^r. Nowell
M^r. Coddington
S: Bradstreete.</small>

<small>M^r. Perkins & Tho: Dexter fined.</small>

It is ordered that S^rieant Perkins shall carry 40 turf[es] to the ffort as a punishm^t for drunkenes by him comitted.

also it is ordered that Thomas Dexter shalbe ffined xx^s for the like offence.

<small>74
Absent from trayng.</small>

It is ordered that if any trained sold[ier] shalbe absent from traineing, vpon their traineing dayes haueing lawfull warneing ₐ shall forfect v^s & that it shalbe lawfull for one of the S^rieants appoyncted by the Capt. of the company to levy: vnles wthin 2 dayes after it be demaunded || ~~vnles~~ || the p^rty offending bring a certificate from the nexte Assistant that hee had a necessary occaɔon to be absent.

<small>Octob^r 3, 1633.</small>

<small>Workmen wages limitted</small>

It is ordered that maister Carpenters, Sawers, masons clapboard-ryvers bricklayers, tylars, joyners wheelewrigh[ts] mowers ℘ shall not take aboue 2^s a day findeing themselues dyett, & not aboue 14^d a day if they haue dyett found them, vnder the penalty of v^s both to giuer & receau͠ for eu͠y day that there is more giuen & receaved also that all other inferior workemen of the said occupaɔons shall haue such wages as the Constable of the said place & 2 other inhabitants that hee shall chuse shall appoynct.

[104] also it is agreed that the best sorte of labourers shall not take aboue 18^d a day if they ~~have~~ dyett ~~found~~ themselues & not aboue 8^d a day if they haue dyett found them vnder the aforesaid penalty both to giuer & receauer.

<small>October 1th, 1633.</small>

likewise that the wages of inferior labou^{rs} shalbe referd to the Constable & 2 other as aforesaid.

m^r. Taylours shall not take aboue 12^d a day & the inferior sorte not aboue 8^d if they be dyeted vnder the aforesaid penalty & for all oth^r worke they doe att home ⱕp̃ɔonably & soe for other worke that shalbe done by the greate by any other artificer.

75

further it is ordered that all workemen shall worke the whole day alloweing convenient tyme for foode & rest this order to take place the 12th of this p'sent moneth.*

76

(14)
Idlenes to be punisht.

It is further ordered that noe pson howse houlder or oth', shall spend his time idely or vnpffitably vnder paine of such punishm'ent as the Court shall thinke meete to inflicte & for this end it is ordered that the Constable of eũy place shall vse spetiall care & deligence to take knowledge of offenders in this kinde, espetially of comon coasters vnpfittable fowlers & tobacco takers & to p'sent the same to the 2 nexte assistants, whoe shall haue power to heare & determine the cause, or if the matter be of importance to transferr it to the Court.

day of Thanksgiving.

77

plantacõns.†

In regard of the many & extraordinary mercyes wch the Lord hath beene pleased to vouchsafe of late to this Plantacõn vz. a plentifull harvest, Ships safely arriued wth psons of spetiall vse & quallity ⟨&⟩ it is ordered that wednesday the 16th day of this present moneth shalbe kept as a day of publique thanksgiueing through the seũall plantacõns.† And whereas it is found by comon experience that the keepeing of Lectures att the ordinary howres nowe obserued in the fore-noone to be dyvers wayes p'iudiciall to the comon good, both in the losse of a whole day & bringing oth' charges & troubles to the place where the Lecture is kept.

78
Times for lectures.

It is therefore ordered that hereafter ~~all~~ ‖noe‖ Lecture shall begin before one a clocke in the afternoone.

It is ordered that there shalbe 400¹‡ collected out of the seũall plantacõns to defray publique charges vz. —

Boston . . .	48¹	00ˢ	00ᵈ	Saugus . . .	36¹	00ˢ	00ᵈ
Rocksbury . .	48	00	00	Salem . . .	28	00	00
Newe-Towne .	48	00	00	Wenetsem' . .	08	00	00
Waterton . .	48	00	00	Meadford . .	12	00	00
Charlton . . .	48	00	00	Aggawam . .	08	00	00
Dorchester . .	80	00	00				

Sũm tot 412¹ 00 00.

---

* See Winthrop I. 116.   † "Plantations &c." in L. copy.   ‡ So in the original.

[105] A Court holden att Boston Novemb^r 5th 1633

Present
The Goūn^r
M^r. Ludlowe
M^r. Nowell
M^r. Tresu^r
M^r. Coddington
S: Bradstreete.

80
Secret to name & sumō^n juryes 14 days, e_r

Price of corne 6^s p bush.

Ord^r ab^t swyne.

1. It is ordered that when all the plantacōns in the bay hath done 2 dayes worke a peece att the ffort, there shall order goe forth to Salem Aggawam & Saugus to send in their money for 3 dayes worke towards it for eūy man except magistrates & minister.

2. It is ordered that ꝑces shall be directed by the Secretary to the Beadle, for the warneing of 24 Jurors 14 dayes before the Court to be named by the Secritary.

It is likewise ordered that corne of the Country shall passe att 6^s the bushell till the nexte Court.

Further it is agreed that noe man shall giue his swine any corne, but such as being vewed by 2 or 3 neighbors shalbe iudged vnfitt for mans meate.

also that eūy plantacōn shall agree howe many swine eūy ꝑson may keepe winter & sumēr aboute the plantacōn this order to take place 10 dayes hence.

81
M^r. Rich: Browne allowed to keep a ferry.

Ensigne Morris discharged.

82

M^r. Rich: Browne is allowed by the Court to keepe a fferry ouer Charles Ryver against his howse, & is to haue 2^d for eūy single ꝑson hee soe transports & j^d a peece if there be 2 or more.

Ensigne Morris is discharged of his place of Ensigne & M^r. Thomas Mooteham chosen in his roome.

S^rieant ~~Morris~~ ‖Stoughton‖ is chosen Ensigne to Capt Mason.

It is ordered that James Peñ the Beadle shall haue allowed him by the Tresurer the somē of 30^l to builde a howse, wch is to be for his vse while hee remaines in the place of Beadle, & after to be disposed of as the Court shall thinke meete.

[106] ~~Att a Meeteing of Assistants & some of the com[ilty] att Boston January 17th 1633~~

~~Present~~
~~The Goūn^r.~~
~~Deputy Goūn^r.~~
~~M^r. Ludlowe~~
~~M^r. Tresurer~~
~~M^r. Nowell~~
~~M^r. Winthrop~~

Novemb^r. 8th 1633.

<small>83
Comodities to be sold, not exceeding 4^d per shilling p^{r}fit.</small>

Whereas by order of Court holden in Octob^r last the Wages of workemen were reduced to a certainety in regard of the greate extorcon vsed by dyvers psons of little conscience & the greate disorder wch grewe herevpon, by vaine and idle wast of much precious tyme, & expence of those imoderate gaynes in Wyne stronge water & other supfluities, nowe least the honest & conscionable workemen should be wronged or discouraged by excessiue prizes of those comodityes, wch are necessary for their Life & comfort: Wee have thought it very iust & equall, to sett order also therein. Wee doe therefore hereby order, that after publique notice hereof, noe psons shall sell to any of the Inhabitants within this Jurisdiccon, any pvision, cloathinge, Tooles, or other Comodities above the rate of ffoure pence in a shilling, more then the same cost or might be bought for ready money in England Vpon paine of forfecting the valewe of the thinge solde (Except Cheese wch in regard of the much hazard in bringing, & Wyne, Oyle, Vineger, & stronge Waters wch in regard of leakeing may be solde att such rates (pvided the same be moderate) as the buyer & seller can agree.)

And for Lynnen & other Comodities wch in regard of their close stowage, & small hazard, may be afforded att a Cheap rate, wee doe advise all men to be a rule to themselues, in keepeing a good Conscience assureing them that if any man shall exceede the bounds of moderacon wee shall punish them seuerely.*

[107]   A Court holden att Boston March 4th ~~1634~~ 1633.

<small>Psent,
The Goun^r.
Deputy Goun^r.
M^r. Ludlowe
Capt. Endicott
M^r. Tresurer
M^r. Nowell
M^r. Coddington
S: Bradstreete.</small>

<small>84
Swamps free.</small>

It is ordered that all the Swamps conteyneing aboue 100 a^c either belonging to any Towne or not shall lye in comon for any free inhabitant to fetch wood att seasonable tymes wthout pjudice to the inhabitants where the same is, (that swampe onely excepted lyeing within the Newe-Towne pale towards the Bay.)

<small>M^r. Dumer rat.</small>

It is ordered that M^r. Dumer shalbe rated viij^l to the publique stocke vizt v^l x for his estate in Rocksbury & l^s in Saugus the Tresury is to lose the rest that hee was rated in Saugus.

---

* See Winthrop I. 116.

Mr. Downings cattle to be rated.	The Court hath ordered that Mr. Dillingham shalbe rated for the cattell hee is possessed of, of Mr. Downeings.
Boston mrket.	It is ordered that there shalbe a markett kept att Boston vpon eũy thursday the fifth day of the weeke.*
Mr. Turnr, capt.	Mr. Nath: Turner is chosen capt. of the millitary company att Saugus.
Sayles cens.	It is ordered that John Sayles † shalbe seuerely whipt for runing from his maister Mr. Coxeall.‡
Twitchells releas.	It is ordered that yl of the iudgemt against Joseph Twitchwell shalbe abated it appeareing to the Court that Joseph Mannering hadd not paid the same as was formly conceaued.§
Mr. Morris, left.	Mr. Rich: Morris is chosen Leifetent to Capt. Vnderhill.
85 Land not to be bought of Ind. wthout leaue.	It is ordered that noe ꝑson whatsoeuer shall buy any land of any Indean without leaue from the Court.
Tarlings cens.	Christopher Tarling is to be whipt for stealeing victualls from his mr. & for runing away.
Mr. Wm Dennison, cõstable.	Mr. Willm Dennison is chosen Constable of Rocksbury.

John Chapman is ffined xxs for selling boards att 8s ꝑ 10[0] contrary to an order of Court & is [remitted vpon ꝑmise of 300 of 4 inch planke towards the sea ffort.]‖

~~It is ordered that euy Assistant shall move all newe comers (wch haue not adventured in the comon stocke) that they thinke fi[t] to contribute towards the Sea fort, & if they find any averse to desire the helpe of the nexte Assistant, & yet if neede require to acquaint the Court therewth.~~

Ri: Wms find.	Rich Williams is ffined xls for drunkenes comitted att Bowmans howse.
Wm Cooley find.	Willm Cooley is ffined 40s for the like offence.
Tmo Haukins & Jno Vauhan fined.	Tymothy Hawkins & John Vauhan ffined xxs a peece for mispending their tyme in company keepeing ~~strong~~ drinkeing stronge water, & selling other contrary to an order of Court.

---

* See Winthrop I. 125.   † "Sayle" in L. copy.   ‡ "Coggeshall" in L. copy.
§ This entry is evidence that there was a record of the Court of Assistants in civil actions distinct from the record in criminal cases and in matters of an administrative nature.
‖ The words in brackets are written in the original in the margin.

Allowed to the witnes bound ouer to the Court to giue evidence against them vs.

[108]
March 4th 1638
Edwd How find.

Edward Howe is ffined xxs for selling stronge water contrary to an order of Court.

Robt Coles disfranchisd for drunkenes, & to weare lettr D.

It is ordered that Robte Coles for drunkenes by him comitted att Rocksbury shalbe disfranchized, weare about his necke & soe to hange vpon his outward garmt a D: made of redd cloath & sett vpon white, to contynue this for a yeare & not to leave it of att any tyme when hee comes amongst company, vnder the penalty of xls for the first offence & vl the second, & after to be punished by the Court, as they thinke meete, also hee is to weare the D outwards, & is enioyned to appeare att the nexte geñall Court & to contynue there till the Court be ended.*

Josiah† Harris put aprentice to Frā Weston.

Josuah Harris is bound as an apprentice with Frauncis Weston for 5 yeares from this day his said maister findeing him meate drinke & cloathes.

Bounds between Boston & Roxbury.‡

Ensigne Stoughton Tho: Ford & Willm Felpes & Willm Galard are appoyncted to sett out the bounds betwixte Boston & Rocksbury wch is nowe in difference betwixte them.

86
Mistick Wajre to Mr. Winthrop & Mr. Craddock.

The Ware att Misticke is graunted to John Winthrop Esqr pr̃sent Goũnr & to Mr. Mathewe Cradocke of London mercht to enioy to them & their heires for euer

87

Vpon consideracõn of the vsefullness of a moveing ffort to be builte 40 ffoote ~~wide~~ longe & 21 ffoote wide, for defence of this Colony & vpon the ffree offer of some gentlem̃ lately come ouer to vs of some large som̃es of money to be imployed that way, it is thought fitt that this matter shalbe moued to such men of ability as haue not borne their prte in the greate charges of the ffoundacõn of this Colony & for this end it is desired that eũy Assistant shall vndertake the busines for treateing with such as are within the Townes where they dwell & if they see fitt they may desire some other of the Assistants to ioyne wth them.

There is xl p̃mised Mr. Steuens for his care & expedicõn in this worke to be p̃d when the worke is finished.

---

* See Winthrop I. 125.   † So in the original.   ‡ In modern hand.

[109]   Gyven & pmised towards the Sea Fort

March 4 1633.
Mr. Haynes	. . . .	l¹
Capt. Turner	. . . . . .	xⁱ
Mr. Coxeall	. . . .	vˡ
Rich: Wright 4 inch plancke	.	400
John Chapm̄ 4 inch planke	.	300
Mr. Aspinwall	. . . . . .	lˢ
John Johnson	. . . . . .	xxˢ
Mr. Nowell	. . . .	iijˡ
Frauncis Johnson	. . . .	xlˢ
Josuah Hewes	. . . . . .	xxˢ
James Peñ	. . . .	xxˢ
Mr. Willm Dennison	. . . .	xlˢ

Aprill 1ᵗʰ 1634.
Mr. Harding	. . . . . .	iijˡ
Mr. George Alcocke	. . . .	xlˢ
Mr. Israell Stoughton to be pd within 9 or 10 monthes	.	xxˡ
Mr. John Coggin *	. . . .	vˡ
Tho: Reade	. . . . . .	xxˢ
Mr. Parker of Rocksbury	. .	lˢ
Mr. Dumer	. . . .	xxxˡ
Phillip Tabor, 4 inch plancke	.	200
Garrett Church, 4 inch plancke,		200
Mr. John Wilson	. . . . .	iijˡ

144ˡ & 1100 4 inch pl.

[Page 110 is blank.]

[111]   A Court holden att Boston Aprill 1ᵗʰ [1634.]

[Present]
The Goūnr
Deputy Goūnr
Mr. Ludlowe
Mr. Endicott
Mr. Tresurer
Mr. Nowell
Mr. Coddington
Mr. Winthrop
S: Bradstreete.

88
Sam: Dud.
Dan: Den.

There is a thousand acres of land & greate p[ond] † graunted to John Haynes Esqr ffyve hundred ac graunted to Thomas Dudley Esqr Deputy Goūnr [three] hundred to Mr. Samˡˡ Dudley & two hundred acres [Mr.] Daniell Dennison all lyeing & being aboue the ffalls [on the] Easterly side of Charles Ryver to enioy to them & [their] heires for euer.

---

* "Cogan" in L. copy.
† These places on pages 111 and 112, which are worn off and illegible in the original record, are filled out from the Lechford copy.

OF THE MASSACHUSETTS BAY.   43

89
200 acrs to Mr. Nowell.

There is Two hundred acres of land graunted to Mr. I[ncrease] Nowell lyeing & being on the westside of the North Ryv otherwise called the three myle brooke.

90
Mr. Oldams graunt.

There is ffyve hundred acres of land graunted to Mr. Jo[hn] Oldham, lyeing neare mount ffeakes on the north-wes[t side] of Charles Ryver.

91
Imprvement of farmes.

It is ordered that if any man that hath any greate quan[tity] of land graunted him & doeth not builde vpon it or imp[ve] within Three yeares it shalbe ffree for the Court to disp[ose] of it to whom they please.

92
Mr. John Wilsons grant of his farme of 200 acres.

There is Two hundred acres of land graunted to Mr. Jo[hn] Wilson pastor of the church of Boston lyeing nexte [the] land graunted to Mr. Nowell on the south & nexte Meadf[ord] on the north.

Jno Lee cens.

It is ordered that John Lee shalbe ~~ffined~~ whipt & ffined for calling Mr. Ludlowe false-hearted knave & hard-hearted knave heavy ffriend &r.

Tho: Fox sent.

Thomas Foxe is ffined xs for want of appearance being sum̄ to giue evidence against John Lee.

Ro: Moulton const: Charls.

Robte Moulton is chosen Constable of Charlton & sworne.

93
Mr. Stoughtons liberty to build a weare.

Mr. Israell Stoughton hath liberty graunted him to builde a Myll a Ware & a Bridge ouer Naponsett Ryver & is to sell the Alewyves hee takes there att 5s the thousand.

94   (15)
Runaways to be sent home.

It is ordered that if any boy (that hath bene whipt for runing frō his maister) be taken in any other plantačon, not haueing a note from his maister to testifie his business there, it sh[albe] lawfull for the Constable of the said plantačon to whip him a[nd] send him home.

Mr. Jno Tilley estat admstred on.

There is power graunted to Mr. Ludlowe & Mr. Coggin* to inventory & take into safe keeping the goods & chattells of Mr. John Tilley to satisfie such debts as hee ownes † in ye B[ay]

The price of corne is lefte at liberty to be solde as men can a[gree]

Mr. Chester bound our.

Mr. Chester hath bound himselfe in xl to appeare at the nexte [Court] to be holden in June to answer to such things as shalbe obiected against him.

---

* "Cogan" in L. copy.   † "Owes" in L. copy.

Garrett Church & Phillip Tabor hath bound themselues [in] xl^s a peece to appeare then to giue testimony agst M^r. Ch[ester] for selling comodities contrary to order.

<small>95
Ilands grnted
t[o Boston.]</small>

Long Iland, Deere Iland & Hogg Iland graunted to Boston for [21 years] for the yearely rent of ij^l * to be paid [to the Treasurer upon the] first day of the second [moneth commonly called April]

[112]

[ib] 1634

[96?]
(16)
[Resi]dents oath.

It was further ordered that eūy man of or above the age of Twenty yeares whoe hath bene or shall hereafter be resident within this Jurisdicc̄on by the space of Sixe monethes as an householder or ~~Soldier~~ ‖soiorner‖ and not infranchised shall take the Oath herevnder written before the Goūn^r or Deputy Goūn^r or some Two of the nexte Assistants, whoe shall haue power to convent him for that purpose, and vpon his refuseall, to binde him ouer to the nexte Court of Assistants: ~~where~~ ‖And‖ vpon his refuseall the second tyme hee shalbe banished, except the Court shall see cause to giue him further respite†

The Oath.

I doe heare sweare and call god to witnes that being nowe an inhabitant within the Lymitts of this Jurisdicc̄on of the Massachusetts, I doe acknowledge myselfe lawfully subiect to the Aucthoritie and gouerm^t there established, And doe accordingly submitt my pson family and estate to be ꝑtected ordered, & gouerned by the Lawes & constituc̄ons thereof. And doe faithfully ꝑmise to be from time to time obedient and conformeable therevnto and to the Aucthoritie of the Goūn^r, & all other the magistrates there, and their success^{r}s, and to all such lawes orders sentences & decrees as nowe are or hereafter shalbe lawfully made decreed & published by them or their success^{r}s. And I will alwayes indeav^r (as in duty I am bound) to advance the peace & wellfaire of this body pollitique, and I will (to my best power & meanes) seeke to devert & prevent whatsoeuer may tende to the ruine or damage thereof or of ye Goūn^r Deputy Goūn^r or Assistants or any of them or their success^rs, And will giue speedy notice to them or some of them of any sedic̄on, violence treacherie or oth^r hurte or euill wch I shall knowe heare or vehemently suspect to be plotted or intended

---

* "Three pounds" in L. copy.   † See Winthrop I. 128.

against them or any of them, or against the said Comon-wealth or goūmᵗ established. Soe helpe mee God.

[113]

97

(17)
Assurance of lands.

> It was further ordered that the Constable & [foure] more of the cheife inhabitants of eūy Towne (to be chosen by all the ffree men there, att some meeteing there) with the advise of some one or more of the nexte Assistants shall make a surveyinge of the howses backeside corne feildes moweing ground, & other lands impoved or inclosed or graunted by speciall order of yᵉ Court of euery ffree inhabitant there, & shall enter the same in a booke (fairely written in words att lenght & not in ffigures) with the seūall bounds & quantities by the neerest estimačon, & shall deliuer a transcript thereof into the Court within sixe monethes nowe nexte ensueing, & the same soe entered and recorded shalbe a sufficient assurance to eūy such ffree inhabitant his & theire heires and Assignes of such estate of inheritance or as they shall haue in any such Howses Lands or Franketenem's.

The like course shalbe taken for assurance of all Howses & Towne-Lotts of all such as shalbe hereaftʳ Enfranchised, & eūy sale or graunt, of such Howses or Lotts as shalbe from time to time entered into yᵉ said booke by the said Constable & foure Inhabitants or their successʳˢ, (whoe shal be still supplyed vpon death or removeall,) for which entry the purchaser shall pay sixe pence, & the like sume for a Coppy thereof, Vnder the hands of the said surveyers or Three of them. See [sᵗ] 190.*

[The next two pages are marked 112ᵃ and 113ᵃ and contain lists of freemen 1634-5. Pages 114 to 118 contain the General Court record of May 14, 1634.]

[119] A Court holden at Newe Towne June 3 1634.

Pʳsent
The Goūnʳ
Deputy Goūnʳ
Mʳ. Winthrop, Senʳ
Mʳ. Haynes
Mʳ. Tresurer
Mʳ. Pinchon
Mʳ. Nowell
Mʳ. Winthropeᵀ
S: Bradstreete.

Ordeʳ as to
Jnᵒ Burslyˢ
lāmes

Eltweed Pumery sworne constable of Dorchester.
Whereas Thomas Lane late servᵗ to John Burslyn, by the pvidence of god is fallen lame & impotent, & hath since remayned att Dorchestʳ, where hee hath bene chargeable to that plantačon, & like soe to contynue, it is therefore ordered that the Inhabitants of Wessa-

---

* This is a reference to the order of March 4, 1634-5, on page 139 of the original record, which is marked in the margin 190.   † "Junʳ" in L. copy.

guscus shall send to Dorchester for the said Thomas Lane, & shall pay for all the charges they haue beene att in keepeing him dureing his aboade att Dorchest^r.

M^r. John Winthrop Junr being chosen an Assistant att the last genall Court did nowe take an oath to his said place belonging in presence of the Court.

Robt ffibbins releas

By consent of Willm Gallerd † admistrat^r to John Russell & Robte ffibbin it is ordered that in consideracon of some service pformed att Sea by the said Robte Fibbin & 3 monthes servis in Newe England, that the said Robte Fibbin shalbe sett free, & haue 1^l 13^s 5^d forgiuen him wch hee ought to his said maist^r John Russell./

Damag donne by ye swyne of Charls Toune

M^r. Thomas Mayhewe is intreated by the Court to examine what hurt the swyne of Charlton hath done amongst the Indean barnes of Corne on the north side of misticke, & accordingly the inhabitants of Charlton pmiseth to giue them satisfaccon.

Ord^r ab^t Ralph Glouers estate

M^r. Thomas Mayhewe being admistrat^r of M^r. Ralfe Glouer, hath nowe exhibited an Inventory of the said estate into the Court, there is therefore day giuen till the first tuesday in August nexte for the Creditors of the said Ralfe Glouer to make their demaunds of such debts as are due to them, or els the said estate shalbe devided betwixte those that then comes in the other to be excluded.

[120] A Court of Assistants holden att Newe Towne July 1th 1634.

Present
The Go$\bar{u}$n^r
Deputy Go$\bar{u}$n^r
M^r. Winthrop
M^r. Haynes
M^r. Endicot
M^r. Tresurer
M^r. Pinchon
M^r. Nowell
S: Bradstreete

Robt Way to continue wth Ensign Gennison, &^{r}.

It was ordered that Robte Way shall remaine with Ensigne Gennison till hee make it appeare to the Court that hee hath lawfully assigned him to some other, hee confessing hee was assigned to him by his maist^r Way.

W^m. Almy fined.

Willm Almy is fyned x^s for not appeareing att the last Court being sumond & is inioyned to bring to the nexte Court an Inventory of the goods hee receaved of Edw: Johnson, duely prized by indifferent men.

Dorchester to pay 3^{li} for Tho: Lane.

It is ordered that the Tresurer shall pay vnto the Deputy Go$\bar{u}$n^r & some other the Inhabitants of Dorchester the some of Three pounds, being charges they haue bene att with Thomas Lane an impotent pson.

---

* "Gaylard" in L. copy.

Isack Allirton fined.

It is ordered that M^r. Isaack Allerton shall pay the some of xl^s to M^r. Willm Dennison for charges ~~of~~ ‖ in ‖ suyte aboute a debte of an hundreth pound.

New Townes addition of accommodation by meadows.

It is further ordered that the Inhabitants of Newe Towne shall inioy the meadowe on the north side of ye pond (Except that wch John Chapm̄ hath already mowen) & after to be decided by the gen̄all Court to whome it shall belonge.

Differences betwene Jno Tilley, M^r. Marriner, & Jno Coggan referd to a com̄itt.

By consent of M^r. Marryner his company & John Tylley the difference betwixte them is referred to John Winthrop Senr. Esqr. M^r. Willm Peirce M^r. Thomas Beecher & M^r. Stagg, also the difference betwixte M^r. John Coggin* & John Tylley for money payde by M^r. Coggin* to the shipps company, by their consent is referd to the p^rtyes before menc̄oned as likewise the difference betwixte John Tylley & Henry Cogan is referd to the p^rtyes aforesaid ═ in this reference there is a bill of 33^l of Jo. Tylley ~~agst~~. excepted.

[121]   A Court holden att Newe Towne August 5th 1634.

Present,
The Goūn^r
Deputy Goūn^r
M^r. Winthrop, Senr.
M^r. Haynes
M^r. Humfry
M^r. Endicot
M^r. Tresurer
~~M^r. Coddington~~
M^r. Pinchon
M^r. Nowell
S: Bradstreete.

Day Thanks.

It was ordered that Wednesday the 20th of this moneth shalbe kept as a day of publique thanksgiueing throughout the sev̄all plantac̄ons for the safe arriueall of shipps and passengers this sum̄er &c.†

Ipswich.

It is ordered that Aggawam shalbe called Ipswitch.†

50^s

It was witnessed vpon oath that James Rawlens tooke xviij^d aday & meate and drinke for 10 dayes worke, for one of his serv^ts for weedeing corne, contrary to an order of Court & therefore is to pay 5^s for ev̄y day hee hath soe transgressed.

Jno Humphry, Esqr sworne.

John Humfry Esqr being chosen an Assistant att the last gen̄all Court did nowe take an oath to his place belonging in presence of the Court.

Richd Cornish.

Rich Cornishe hath bound himselfe in x^l for his wyves psonall appearance att the Court ‡ in Octob^r [next] to answer to such things as shalbe obiected against her.

---

* " Cogan " in L. copy.   † See Winthrop I. 137.   ‡ " To be holden " in L. copy.

Frā Godson find.

Frauncis Godson hath bound himselfe in x¹ for his psonall appearance att the Court to be holden in Octobr nexte to answer for breach of an order of Court ~~for~~ in takeing to greate wages &c.

Sam: Hosier, constā.

Samˡˡ Hosier chosen & sworne Constable of Waterton.

Kathe: Gray to be whipᵗ, &c.

It was ordered that Katherine Gray shalbe whipt for her filthy & vnchast behavr wᵗʰ Thomas Elkyn.

Rī: Hitchcock bound ouer to yᵉ Court.

Rich Hitchcocke hath bound himselfe in xx¹ to make his psonall appearance att the Court to be holden the first tuesday in Octobr nexte to answer to such things as shalbe obiected against him.

Widdō Bozworthˢ prouission.

It was ordered that such moneyes as shalbe layde out for the mainetenance of Widd: Bosworth & her famyly shalbe payde againe by the Treasurer.

Robᵗ Way to abide wᵗʰ Edwᵈ Burton.

Whereas it was made knowen to the Court that Robte Way was lawfully assigned by Ensigne Gennison to Edward Burton it was therefore ordered that the said Burton shall keepe the said Way according to covenant.

Mr. Aspinwalls oath to be taken, &c.

John Humfry Esqr. & Mr. Increase Nowell was desyred by the Court to take deposicōns of the witnesses of Mr. Aspinwall in a case betwixte Sr Willm̄ Brewerton* Ba[rᵗ] & the said Mr. Aspinwall.

[Pages 122 to 131 contain the General Court record for Sept., 1634. Page 132 is blank.]

[133]   Att a Court, holden at Newe Towne, Octobr 6ᵗʰ, 1634.

Præsent
The Goūnr
Deputy Goūnr
Mr. Winthrop
Mr. Haynes
Mr. Endicott
Mr. Pinchon
Mr. Nowell
Mr. Winthrop Jur
Mr. Bradstreete.

Ensigne Jennison.

It is ordered that Ensigne Jennison shalbe ffyned the some of xx¹ for vpbraydeing the Court with Iniustice, vttering theis words I pray god deliuer mee from this Court professing hee had wayted from Court to Court & could not haue iustice done him — &c.

Mr. Crafords goods invento.

It is ordered that Leiuetenᵗ Feakes,† Mr. Rich: Browne Mr. Pendleton & Epharim Childe shall take an Inventory of the goods & chattells of Mr. Craford lately disceased & returne the same into the nexte Court.

---

* "Brereton" in L. copy.   † "Feke" in L. copy.

OF THE MASSACHUSETTS BAY.   49

Damage in Thos Richards corne.

It is ordered that Mr. Hull, Willm Gallerd * Eltweed Pumery Mr. Willm Hill & Mr. Willm Haythorne shall haue power to heare & determine the seūall trespasses that hath bene done, by the swine of seūall psons, in the corne of Thomas Richards, as also for the charge hee hath bene att in keepeing his corne & for other charges incident therevnto.

Clement Briggs find for entge Indean.

Clemt Briggs is ffined xs for intertaineing an Indean without leaue & is enioyned forthwith to discharge himselfe of him.

Kir[k]mans damg.

John Kirman tooke oath hee was sumond by Rich: Kent to appeare this day att the Court to answer him in an accōn of trespasse & nowe psecutes not, soe the Court hath giuen him xs damage.

Jno Lees cens. for reproaching ye Gournor.

It is ordered that John Lee shalbe whipt & ffyned xlli† for speakeing repchfully of the Goūnr sayeing hee was but a Lawer's clerke, & what vnderstanding hadd hee more then himselfe, also taxeing the Court for makeing lawes to picke mens purses, as also for abuseing a mayde of the Goūn's pretending love in the way of marriage, when himselfe professes hee intended none, as also for intiseing her to goe with him into the cornefeild ℯr.

Sam: Hall find for drunk.

Samll Hall is ffined vs for drunkenes by him comitted a shipboard himselfe freely confessing his offence.

Ri: Lamberts bond forfeited.

Rich: Lambert hath forfected his bond of xl wch bound him to appeare att this Court. And it is ordered that Beniamin Gilham & Robte Walker shall haue vs apeece allowed them, being witnesses sumoned to appeare./

John Humfry, Esqr. is deputed by the Court to take deposicōns of the witnesses to the will of Willm Payne lately disceased.

[134]

Agawams damag. by Charls Towne swyn.

Vpon a Complaynt of ye Saggamore of Aggawam for hurte done in his corne by the Swine of Charlton, it is ordered that Mr. Nowell shall heare his witnesses, & appoynct what satisfaccōn hee shall haue, & whoe shall giue it, & to binde ouer to the Court those that refuse payemt.

---

* " Gaylard " in L. copy.   † xx changed to xlli.

Att a Court holden att Newe Towne Novembʳ 7ᵗʰ 1634.

Present
The Goũnʳ
Deputy Goũnʳ
Mʳ. Winthrop
Mʳ. Haynes
Mʳ. Tresurer
Mʳ. Pinchon
Mʳ. Nowell
Mʳ. Bradstreete.

Olliuʳ goods sequestred.

It is ordered that the goods and chattells of Christopher Ollyver nowe in the custody of Roger Williams & Thomas Okam, or the proceede thereof, shalbe sequestred & remaine in the hands of Mʳ. Israell Stoughton, till the said Christopher Olyver shall satisfie such debts as are due from him to Mʳ. Israell Stoughton & John Hoskins, Senʳ./

Hen: Brights censure for swearing.

It is ordered that Henry Bright shalbe set in yᵉ Bilbowes for swearing.

Ens: Rich: Dauenport sent for, for defacīng his coulors.

It is ordered that Ensigne Damford shalbe sent for by warᵗ with comaund to bring his colʳs with him to the nexte Court as also any other that hath defaced the said colʳs.*

Wᵐ Knop bound ouer.

Willm Knopp is bound in xˡ to appeare att the nexte Court & to abide the sensure of the Court for sweareing./

Seuᵉrall, for age, dismisᵗ from trayⁿg.

Mʳ. John Beniamin, Willm Pan[t]ry & Henry Goldston are (by reason of their age & infirmities) dismissed from traineing onely they are to haue in readines att all tymes sufficient Armes for themselues besides for their servᵗs.

Xopʳ: Grant find for drunkenes 20.

Christ: Graunt is ffined xxˢ for drunknes by him comitted./

Pᵗ of Jnᵒ Lees fine remitted him.

There is 30ˡ of John Lee his ffines of xlˡ remitted him./

[135]   Att a Court holden att Newe Towne March 3 1634.†

Present,
The Goũnʳ
Deputy Goũnʳ
Mʳ. Winthrop
Mʳ. Haynes
Mʳ. Endicott
Mʳ. Tresuʳ
Mʳ. Pinchon
Mʳ. Nowell
S: Bradstreete.

Consᵗb. find.

The constable of Dorchestʳ is ffined xxˢ for not retorneing his warᵗ for the last Levy into the Court.

The constable of Boston is ffined the somē of xxˢ for yᵉ like.

Lockwoods writings.

It is ordered that Ruth Lockwood widd shall bring all the writeings that her husband lefte in her hands, to John Haynes

---

*See Winthrop I. 146.

†See Winthrop I. 150, for Meeting of Assistants Nov. 27, 1634. See also I. 154, for Meeting of Ministers Jan. 19, 1634-5.

Esqr. & Simon Bradstreete on the third day of the nexte weeke, whoe shall detaine the same in their hands till the nexte Court, when they shalbe disposed of to those to whom they belonge.

<small>Ed[w:] Hubbard, cons^tble.</small>

Edmond Hubbert Senr. chosen constable of Charlton for this year nexte ensueing & till a newe be chosen.

<small>M^{rs}. Ann Loomans goods to be inventō.</small>

It is ordered that the goods & chattells of M^{rs}. Ann Looman shalbe Inventoryed by 3 or 4 of the ffreemen of Rocksbury & retourned into the Court in Aprill nexte. M. Pinchon is desired to appoynct the men that shall doe it.

<small>J^{no} Stanley estat diuided & setled.</small>

Whereas John Stanley dyed intestate in the Way to Newe England, & lefte three children vndisposed of, the yongest whereof is since disceased haveing also lefte an estate of cxvj^l in goods & chattells &c. It is therefore ordered with the consent of Thomas Stanley brother to the said John disceased, that hee shall haue ||forthwith|| the some of lviij^l of the s^d estate putt into his hands, in consideracon whereof the said Thomas Stanley shall educate & bring vpp John Stanley sonne of John Stanley disceased, findeing him meate drinke & appell, till hee shall accomplishe the age of xxi yeares & att the end of the said tearme shall giue vnto the said John Stanley the some of ffifty pounds./

Also it is further ordered with the consent of Tymothy Stanley another brother of the afores^d John Stanley disceased that the other lviij^l of the aforesaid estate shalbe putt into the hands of the said Tymothy Stanley in consideracon whereof the said Tymothy shall educate & bring vpp Rueth Stanley daughter of the afores^d John Stanley disceased findeing her meate drinke & appell, till shee shall attaine the age of one & twenty yeares, & att the end of the said tearme or att the day of her marriage with Tymothy Stanleyes consent, shall giue vnto the s^d Ruth Stanley the some of thirty pounds, provided if eyther of the said children shall dye before the expiracon of the said tearmes, then the p^rty whoe kept the said Childe shall stand to the order of the Court for payeing soe much to the survyveing childe as the Court shall appoynct.

[136]

<small>March 3. 1634.

Ri: Coka^{rs} sent. to be whipt.</small>

It is ordered that Rich: Cokar shalbe whipt here this day, & on the fifth day of the nexte weeke att Boston, for intiseing seūall psons, that were servants, to run away to the Dutch Plantacon & to steale dyv^{rs} things to carry with them./

Sam: Johnsons sent.   Also it is ordered that Sam^ll Johnson shalbe whipt for the like offence.

It is referd to John Humfry & John Endicott Esqr. to heare & determine all matters of difference concerneing the estate of Willust disceased, wch is betwixte any that layes claime to any p^rte thereof./

[On pages 137 to 145 is the record of the General Court 4 March, 1634–5.]

[146]   Att a Court holden att Newe Towne Aprill 7th 1635.

Present
The Gou͠n^r.
Deputy Gou͠n^r.
M^r. Winthrop
M^r. Haynes
M^r. Tresu^r.
M^r. Pinchon
M^r. Nowell
S: Bradstreete.

It is referd to John Haynes Esqr. & M^r. Robte Feakes* to audit the accompts betwixte Edward Howe & Willm̄ Knopp, to sweare witnesses, & examine them what they can say in the case, & to make returne thereof into the nexte Court.

Ens. Genisons fine remit.   Ensigne Jennisons ffine of xx^l is remitted him vpon his submission & acknowledgem^t of his offence.

Nahaton find 2 skins bevar.   It is ordered that Nahanton shall giue two skins of beav^r to M^r. Blackestone, for damage done him in his swine by setting of trapps &c.

Ab^t Plow Pattent.   Further it is ordered that Capt. Traske shall pay to John Kirman, out of the estate of the Company of husbandm̄ the some of ffoure & twenty pounds, eleven shillings & fyve pence being the remainder of the eight pte of the said estate, wch was by order of Court gyven the said John Kirman Provided if hereafter it shall appeare, that there is not soe much due to ye said John out of the said 8th pte, that then hee shalbe accomptable for the same.

Lockwood estate.   It is refered to † the church of Waterton with the consent of Robte Lockwood execut^r of Edmond Lockwood disceased, to ‡ dispose of the children & estate of the said Edmond Lockwood (gyven to them) to such psons as they thinke meete, ~~as also to take an accompt~~ wch if they pforme not within foureteene dayes, it shalbe lawfull for the Gou͠n^r. John Haynes Esqr. & Simon Bradstreete to dispose of the said children & estate as in their discreco͠n, they shall thinke meete, as also to take an accompt of the said Robte Lockwood, & giue him a full discharge.

---

* ffeke in L. copy.   † Ordered that in L. copy.   ‡ May in L. copy.

Mountagues censū: It is ordered that Griffin Mountague shalbe sett in the bilbowes, for stealeing boards & clapboards from M^r. Wilbore & is enioyned to remove his habitacon from Muddy Ryver before the nexte genall Court vnder the penalty of v^l.

Willm̄ Swifte promiseth to gyve x̄x^s towards the cure of his late servant being infirme & lame.

It is referd * to M^r. Tresurer & M^r. Pinchon to examine & prepare the business betwixte M^r. Coxeall [&] Sayles his daughter & John Levens & to returne the same into the nexte Court.

Hewards sent.   Ordered that John Heward † shalbe whipt for sweareing & stealeing.

226
The line betwixt Roxbury & New Towne.

The lyne betwixte Rocksbury & Newe Towne ‡ is layde out to run south west from Muddy Ryver, neere that place wch is called M^r. Nowells bridge, a tree being marked on foure sydes & from the mouthe of the ryver to that place, the southe syde is for Rocksbury & the north syde for Newe Towne ‡ by mee   p̄ Willm̄ Jennison.

[147]   Willm̄ Colbran John Johnson & Abraham Palmer being appoynoted by the genall Court to lay out the bounds betwixte Waterton & Newe Towne ‡ did make this returne into the Court.—

227

Bounds betwixt Water Towne & New Towne.

It is agreed by vs whose names are here vnderwritten, that the bounds betweene Waterton & Newe Towne shall stand as they are already from Charles Ryver to the greate freshe pond & from the tree marked by Waterton & Newe Towne on the south east syde of the po[n]nd§ ouer the pond to a white poplar tree [on the norwest syde of the pond, & from that tree] ¶ vpp into the Country norewest & by west, vpon a straight lyne by a merydian compasse, and ffurther that Waterton shall have one hundreth rodds in lenght above the Weire, & one hundreth rodd beneath the weire in lenght, & threescoore rodd in breadth from the Ryver on the southe syde thereof, & all the rest of the ground on that syde the River to lye to Newe Towne.

Willm Colbran
John Johnson
Abraham Palmer.

---

* It is ordered & referred in L. copy.   † Heyward in L. copy.   ‡ Newton in L. copy.
§ Pond in L. copy.   ¶ These eleven words omitted in the L. copy.

[On pages 148 to 152 is the record of the General Court for May, June and July, 1635. Page 153 contains lists of freemen 1635 and 1636.]

[154]   Att the Court holden in June 2 1635.

P'sent,
The Goūnr
Deputy Goūnr
Mr. Winthrop
Mr. Dudley
Mr. Pinchon
Mr. Nowell
Mr. Hough
Mr. Dumer
Mr. Bradstreete.
Forfect.

Perkins bill.

It was ordered that war^t shalbe sent to Norton to bring into the nexte Court a bill of v^l made by Goodm̄ Perkins to Thomas Wade, y^t it may be safely kept till it appeare, to whome it is due, the money being gyven, (as the Court is informed) to Jonathan Wade his brother./

Mr Humfry is ffined x^s for his absence from ye Court.

Richd Kings goods ad m̄st^d on by Rich: Bishop.

There is administracōn graunted to Richard Bishopp (in the behalf of his wife) of the goods & chattells of Richard King disceased./

In the cause of the children & widdowe of Edward* Lockwood (the elders & other of the church of Waterton being p'sent) & vpon consideracōn of the order of court in Aprill last, made in the case,† wch was found not to have bene observed, because the estate was not computed & apportioned, It is nowe ordered with consent of all pties, vizt the Church of Waterton the widd̄: of the said Edmond lyveing, & the execut^r, haveing consented to the former order, that the present Goūn^r & the Secretary shall have power to call pties, & witnesses, for findeing out the true estate, & haveing consideracōn of the vncertainety of the will, & the debts, & other circumstances, to apporcōn the remainder of the estate to the wife, & children, according to their best discrecōn, & then the Church of Waterton is to dispose of the elder children, & their pcōns, as shalbe best for their Christian educacōn, & the preservacōn of their estate.

Com̄ittee ab^t ship Thund^r.

It is ordered with the consent of John Cogan John Tylley Willm̄ Hill Henry Wulcott, & Humfry Pynney that the arbitrators chosen by them, vz. M^r. Willm̄ Haythorne, ‡ Will: Halford, Roger Williams, & Rich Collicott, shall have full power to make a ffinall end of all differences, & accompts betwixte the said pties, concerneing the shipp Thunder, wch the Court enioynes them to pforme before this day fortnight & to returne into the nexte pticular Court, what they have done herein, & in the meane tyme all execucōns concerneing the shipp Thunder to be re-

---

* So in the original.   † Cause in L. copy.   ‡ Hathorne in L. copy.

speted. Also it is ordered that the arbitrators shall have power to examine witnesses vpon oathe./

[155] Att the Court holden att Newe Towne July the 7th 1635.

Present,
The Govnr
Deputy Govnr
Mr. Winthrop
Mr. Dudley
Mr. Tresurer
Mr. Pinchon
Mr. Hough
Mr. Nowell
Mr. Bradstreete
Mr. Dumer.

Steven Terry was sworne Constable of Dorchestr for a yeare & till a newe be chosen./

Lands sold by Chickatabut to Mr. Pinchon.

It is ordered that Ensigne Jennison & Mr. Woolridge shall require the Indians that were present with Chickataubut when hee solde certaine Land aboute Massachusetts to Mr. Pinchon, or knewe what it was, to sett out the sevall bounds thereof, & to returne the same to the Govnr before the last day of this weeke Mr. Smyth & Goodman Wright are allowed to goe alonge with them./

Order to remburse Mr. Henry Sewall as to ye Bos[worths]

In consideracon of money disbursed by Mr. Henry Seawall for the transportacon of Edward Bosworth & his ffamyly, It is ordered that Jonathan Bosworth shall pay to Mr. Seawall the some of vl vpon the 29th of Septembr. nexte, Willm Buckland vl on the said 29th of Septr Nathanaell ‖Bosworth‖ vl ls att the said day & ls more that day twelue moneth, & Beniamyn Bosworth xxxs on the said 29th of Septr. & iijl xs att midsumer nexte, all theis somes to be paide to the said Mr. Seawall.

Also it is agreed that the forenamed pties shalbe bound one for another for the payment of the said somes att the sevall dayes of payemt.

Francis Toby

Ordered that Frauncis Toby (for misdemeanr by him comitted) shalbe bound to his good behavr, & shall putt in suretyes for the same, or els to remaine in holde./

John Love is ffined xs for drunkenes.

[156] Att the Court holden att Newe Towne August 4th 1635.

Present,
The Govnr.
Deputy Govnr.
Mr. Winthrop
Mr. Dudley
Mr. Tresurer
Mr. Pinchon
Mr. Nowell
Mr. Hough
Mr. Dumer
Mr. Bradstreete.

Willm Gallerd* & Willm Rockwell executors of John Russell hath exhibited into Court an Inventory of the goods & chattells of the said John Russell disceased.

Wannertons sent.

John Holland being att the Eastward affirmeth that Mr. Thomas Wonnarton threatned to sinke his boate if hee would not pay him a debt that Henry Way ought † him, &

---

* Gaylard in L. copy.   † Owed in L. copy.

called him roage & knave, & said they were all soe in the Bay, & that hee hoped to see all their throates cutt, & that hee could finde in his heart to begin with him, & therevpon strucke him vpon the head, and when the said Holland tould him, if Way ought him any money hee might recouer it by lawe, to wᶜʰ Woñarton answered that they had noe lawe for them but to sterue * them. the like Bray Wilkinson & Roḇte Ellwell witnesseth against Woñorton Wherevpon it was ordered, that the said Woñarton should putt in sufficient suryties for his good behavʳ & in the meane tyme to remaine in durance./

His cens.

There is admistraĉon graunted Willm̄ Stitson of the goods & chattells of Roḇte White disceased, & it is ordered that all his creditʳˢ shall repaire to the Deputy & Tresurer, before the nexte Court, whoe shall haue power to examine witnesses &c. & such debts as they shall finde due they shall giue warᵗ to the said admistratʳ to pay, & those that are doubtfull shalbe transferd to the Court./

Admistraton to Wᵐ Stitson of Robᵗ. Whites estate.

Mʳ. Hutchingson witnessed vpon oath that Arthur Holbidge tooke 2ˢ 6ᵈ a day of him for 30 dayes worke, Richard Bulgar 6 dayes Thomas Munt 9 dayes, & James Hawkens 36 dayes, all att 2ˢ 6ᵈ a day & soe haue all forfected vˢ aday according to the order of Court./

Seuʳall fforfectˢ abᵗ wages.

Mʳ. Cogan witnessed vpon oath that James Hawkins tooke 2ˢ 6ᵈ a day of him for 14 dayes.

There is xˢ graunted to John Pyke, for his charges being brought from Ipswᶜʰ as a witnes against John Mustlewhite.

Jnº Pikeˢ allow. as a witnes.

The Court hath enioyned Willm̄ Wills to pay to Gyles Gibbs the som̄e of xvjˢ for ffellony by him comitted./

Wᵐ Willis cens.

With the consent of Mʳ. Humfry Mʳ. Hough & Richard Wright, the difference aboute two heifers that Richard Wright kept is referd to Mʳ. Winthrop Mʳ. Dudley & Mʳ. Nowell, whoe hath power gyven them to examine witnesses vpon an oath & soe putt an end to the difference.

It was ordered that Arthur Holbidge shall putt in surytye for his good behavʳ for contempt by him comitted, & in the meane tyme to be imprisoned./

Arthur Holbidg sent.

Ordered that James Hawkins fforfects shall forthwᵗʰ be levyed, &

---

* Starve in L. copy.

in case hee hath noe goods, his body shalbe taken & imprisoned till it be payde.*

[157]
Jn⁰ Russells nuncupative will.

John Russell merchant disceased att Dorchest ͬ August 26ᵗʰ 1633 & before his death being of a disposeing vnderstanding, did make his last will, in the presence of Mʳ. John Warham Past ͬ of the church of Dorchest ͬ Tho: Moore, John Moore, & Tho: Deway in the words followeing or to the same effect.

Halfe of my estate I giue to the church of Dorchest ͬ & halfe to my brothers Henry Russell & Thomas Hyatt, except my mans tyme, wᶜʰ I giue to my man, & hee desired that in the disposeing of his goods to Dorchest ͬ, there should be espetiall respect hadd to olde Dorchest ͬ people nameing Goodm̄ Caping.

John Warham

This was testifyed vpon the oathes of the said witnesses taken in Court Septʳ 3 1633

The mʳke of   I   Thomas Moore
The m̄ke of Tho: Deawy O
John Moore.

Att the Court holden att Newe Towne Septembʳ 1ᵗʰ 1635.†

Present
The Goūnʳ.
Deputy Goūnʳ.
Mʳ. Winthrop
Mʳ. Dudley
Mʳ. Tresurer
Mʳ. Hough
Mʳ. Nowell
Mʳ. Bradstreete
Mʳ. Dum̄er.

Stor[ey] sent.

Scarlet sent.

Forfeits.
Dixons bond forfeit.

It was ordered that Andrewe Storyn shalbe whipt for runing from his maistʳ.

Ordered that Robte Scarlett shalbe whipt for runing from his maister.

Willm̄ Dixon hath forfected his recognizance of xxˡ; Edward Converse & James Browne xˡ a peece being bound for Dixons appearance att the Court.

It was ordered that the goods and chattells of Willm̄ Dixon shalbe attatched & kept safely to satisfie the Court for the fforfect of his recognizance.

how dischargd.

Ordered that Richard Bulgar Thomas Munt James Hawkins & Arthur Holbidge shall pay iijˢ a peece weekely to the marshall towards the discharge of their fforfects.

It is ordered that Mary   servᵗ to Mʳ. Bartholmewe shalbe whipt for runing from her maistʳ & shall serve him 6 weekes after her terme is ended.

---

* The last four words not in L. copy.
† See Winthrop I. 166, under date Sept. 1, 1635; "At this general court was the first grand jury."

Mr. Thatcher admstd on Mr. Jos͞e Aueryˢ estate.

There is admͪstrac͞on graunted to Mʳ. Anthony Thacher of the goods & chattells of Mʳ. Joseph Avery disceased, wᶜʰ hee is to Inventory & returne the same into the nexte Court, & the said goods are to remaine in his hands till further order be taken the[rein.]

[158] An Inventory of the Goods and Chattells of Joseph Avery, disceased.

Due to him from John Emery Carpenter	07ˡ	00ˢ	00ᵈ
It: from Robte Andrewes of Ipswich wᶜʰ he confesseth to be due & to be pᵈ forthwᵗʰ	02	00	00
It: from Mʳ. Willm Hilton or a sowe & piggs to that valewe testis Rich: Kent.	02	16	00

From Rich: Kent of Ipswᶜʰ ten bushells of Indean corne which hee acknowledgeth.

John Emery denyes his debt but Richard Knight Nicholas Holte & John Knight all three of Newberry can & will testifie & proue it to be due, onely hee was by condic͞on to pay the said 7ˡ in his worke, wᶜʰ hee was to doe so [soone] as Mʳ. Auery did call vpon him for it, out of wᶜʰ said 7ˡ there is something paide in labʳ already as hee can make to appeare.

₽ me Antho[ny] Thatcher.

Att the Court Novembʳ 3 1635.*

Present
The Goṽnʳ.
Deputy Goṽnʳ.
Mʳ. Winthrop, Senʳ.
Mʳ. Dudley
Mʳ. Humfry
Mʳ. Tresurer
Mʳ. Pinchon
Mʳ. Hough
Mʳ. Dumer
S: Bradstreete
Mʳ. Nowell.

It was ordered that the Deputy Goṽnʳ & Mʳ. Winthrop Senʳ. shall have power to examine all witnesses vpon oath concerneing an acc͞on of the case brought by Mʳ. Hough against Mʳ. Mav͞acke.

Order abᵗ Tho: Coleman.

Whereas Thomas Coleman hath contracted with Sʳ. Richard Saltonstall & dyvers other gentlem͞ in England, & here for the keepeing of certaine horses bulls & sheepe in a gen͞all stocke for the space of three yeares, & nowe since his comeing hither hath bene exceedeing necligent in dischargeing the trust com͞itted to him, absenting himselfe

---

* See Winthrop I. 173, John Pratt "questioned" at this Court. For his answer and the action of the Court thereupon see below at the end of Part I. — For a court Oct. 6, 1635, see below.

for a longe tyme from the said cattell, as also neclecting to provide howseing for them by reason whereof many of the said cattell are dead already & more damage like dayly to accrue to the said gentlem̄. It is therefore ordered that it shalbe lawfull for the said gentlem̄ to devide the oates & hay provided for the said cattell amongst themselues, & soe euery one to take care of their owne cattell for this winter.

John Pease to be whipt.

Ordered that John Pease shalbe whipt & bound to his good behav^r for strikeing his mother M^{rs}. Weston, & derydeing of her & for dyvers other misdemean^{rs} & other evill carriages.

Robt Coles allow.

There is x^s damages graunted Rob̄te Coles, to be paid by M^r. ffawne, whoe sum̄oned him to app̱e att this Court & ꝑsecutes not against him.

Jno Cole to be whipt for stealing.

Ordered that John Cole shalbe whipt for stealeing a sheete and a p̱re of shoes.

Nich^o ffrost.

Ordered that Nich: ffrost shalbe imprisoned till the nexte Court when a tryeall is to passe vpon him for comeing into this Jurisdicc̄ being form̄ly banished.

Isabell Sucket, adm̄st.

There is adm̄stracon graunted to Isabell Sackett of the goods & chattells of her husband lately disceased./

Forfects.

[It] was lefte in trust wth him [by a] friend, to sell for him.*

Sam^{ll} Cole hath forfected xx^s for selling 2 quarts of beare at ij^d a quart.

M^r. Nowell is ffined iij^s iiij^d for selling wyne./

[On pages 159 to 164 is the record of the General Court for September, 1635, and also a record as to the bounds of certain towns.]

[165]   Att the Court holden att Newe Towne Octob^r 6th 1635.

Present
The Goūn^r.
Deputy Goūn^r.
M^r. Winthrop
M^r. Dudley
M^r. Treasurer
M^r. Pinchon
M^r. Hough
M^r. Nowell
S: Bradstreete.

Servants ruñg away.

It was ordered that Clem^t Cole Peter [P]yford Simon Bird, Willm̄ Barker,† Willm̄ Downes, & George Wilby shalbe whipt for runing from their maisters, & for stealeing a boate & dyv^{rs} others things with them, as also shall giue satisfaccon to the Country for their charges in sending to fetch them home, & likewise shall serue their said maisters twice soe longe att the end of their

---

* This marginal entry was written by John Winthrop Senr. and refers probably to Mr. Nowell's "wine." See marginal note in shorthand under the date March 1, 1635 (page 61).

† Baker in L. copy.

tyme, as they have bene absent from their masters service, by reason of their runing away & for Cole & Byford* the Court will consider of some further punishm⁺ for them./

Ordered that Dan¹¹ White shalbe seuerely whipt & ffyned v¹ for stealeing a golde ring & a hankerchiue, out of wᶜʰ ffine satisfacčon shalbe made to those that have bene att charges in keepeing him after hee was apprehended./

R.

A theife punisht.

Whereas Beniamyn Felton hath brought into this Country one Robte Scarlett a knowen theife, whoe since his comeing hither hath comitted dyvers fellonyes &c as appeareth by his examinačon,

It is therefore ordered that the said Scarlett shalbe seuerely whipt & branded in the forehead with a T & after sent to his said maister whome the Court enioynes to send the said Scarlett out of this Jurisdiččon, & in the meane tyme to be lyeable to satisfie for such damages, as his said serv⁺ shall doe to any p͟son, & also shall pay xˢ to Mʳ. Stileman the Constable for his charges in keepeing him & bringing of him to the Court./

Forfect.

It was ordered that Richard Longe† shalbe ffined v¹ for contempt of aucthoritie, & for ryveing dyvʳˢ good trees into clapboards, and selling of them from Waymothe Towne, the wᶜʰ trees hee was appoyncted to fell for shingles for the ffort att Castle Ileland & that the said money shalbe gyven to the Towne of Waymothe towards the makeing of a bridge there./

Mʳ. Seawall injoyned to p͟vide for Mʳˢ. Sewalls prouision.

With the consent & att the desire of Henry Seawall & Ellen his wife the Court hath ordered that his saide wife shalbe att her owne disposeall, for the place of her habitačon & that her saide husband shall allowe her, her weareing appell & xx¹ p ann͠ to be paide quarterly, as also a bedd with furniture to it.

Joshua Hues.

Josuah Huyes‡ hath fforfect vˢ for knyves & iiijˢ vjᵈ for a sythe wᶜʰ hee solde for above iiijᵈ in the shilling p͟ffitt.

Forfects.

Edward Gyles was ffined xlˢ for knoweing his wife carnally before marriage.

John Galley was ffined xxˢ for the like offence.

---

* Pyford in L. copy. † Or Louge. Long in L. copy. ‡ Hughes in L. copy.

[166]   Att the Court holden att Newe Towne March 1th 1635.*

Present
The Goūnr.
Deputy Goūnr.
Mr. Winthrop
Mr. Dudley
Mr. Tresur
Mr. Pinchon
Mr. Nowell
Mr. Hough
Mr. Dumer
S: Bradstreete.

Robt Way servant to Wm Hosier, & to pay er

It was ordered that all the bills & writeings aboute one Robte Way shalbe delivēd into the Court, & that Ensigne Jennison Edward Burton & Samll Hosier shall pay xxs apeece to Willm Almy, as also that the said Robte Way shalbe taken from Mr. Stoughton where nowe hee is, & putt to the said Willm Almy, & him shall serve till hee hath satisfyed the some of iijl wch if hee doe, hee shall pay xxs thereof backe againe to Samll Hosier.

Wm. Almys satisfačon from James Luddam.

Whereas in a suite betwixte David Johnson & Willm Almy concerneing one James Ludam sometimes servt to either of them there was a iudgemt of vl graunted to Willm Almy against David Johnson, but upon some consideračon execučon was respited, & nowe by consent of all ptyes, it was agreed that the said vl shalbe borne equally betwixte them, that is to say that the widd Johnson shall pay fyve nobles & James Ludam the some of fyve nobles to the said Willm Almy & hee to loose the rest.

Fine.
Rich: Phelp find 40s for drunkenes.

Richard Phelpes was ffyned xls for drunkenes.

Anthō Cops bond forfeited.

Anthony Coop fforfected his recognizance of xll for nonappance.

Differenc between Mr. Dumer & Mr. Burr refed.

The difference betwixte Mr. Dumer & Jehu Burr aboute Mr. Dumers swine spoyleing his corne, is by their consent referd to the ffinal determinačon of Willm Parke goodm Potter & goodm Porter.

Seur bonds forfeited, as H: Jocely, Jno Pick[ring], & Nick. Frost.

Henry Joslyn gent. John Pickrin & Nicholas Frost all of Paskataq have forfected their recognizance of Cl for not apping att this Court.

Griffin Mountagu forfited his bond, 20.

Griffin Montague fforfected his recognizance of xxl for nonappance.

James Luddam find 40s for being drunk.

James Ludam was ffined [xls] for drunkenes & it is ordered that Knight the witnes, shalbe pd out of it./

†

[Pages 167 to 174 contain the record of a General Court 3 March 1635-6. Page 174 has also the following record.]

* See Winthrop I. 175-7, for meetings of the Magistrates Jan., 1635-6.

† Shorthand conjecturally rendered:— "Tell the Court about Mr. [Now]ell." See marginal note under the date Nov. 3, 1635 (page 59).

Att the Court holden att Newe Towne Aprill 5th 1636.

Present,
The Goūnr.
Deputie Goūnr.
Mr. Winthrop, Senr.
Mr. Dudley
Mr. Tresur.
Mr. Pinchon
Mr. Nowell
Mr. Houghe
M Dumer
Mr. Bradstreete.

Vpon the appearance of Nicholas ffrost att this Court, & his sheweing iust cause whie hee was detained from the last Court the sd Nich ffrost, Henry Joslyn gent. & John Pickrin are discharged of their recognizance of C¹ & the said Nich: ffrost hath bound himselfe in xxˡ to appeare att any Court hereafter, vpon sumons to answer to such things as shalbe obiected against him./

Wm. Shepheard sent. for Theft.

Ordered that Willm Shepheard servt to Willm Sumer shalbe whipt for stealeing victualls from his mr. & beanes from the Indians.

Wm. Perkins sent. for being drunk, D.

Ordered that Willm Perkins shall (for drunkenes & other misdemeanrs by him comitted) stand att the nexte geñall Court one houre in publique vewe, with a white sheete of pap on his brest, haveing a greate D made vpon it, & shall attend the pleasure of the Court till hee be dismissed.

Georg Ropps sent to be whipt for strikeing his mr, Mr. Garford, &c.

Ordered that George Ropps shalbe seuerely whipt here this p'sent Court, & againe after some convenient tyme att Salem, att some publique meeteing there, for strickeing his maistr Mr. Garford, throweing him downe & spurneing him with his feete being downe, & the Court hath intreated John Endicott Esqr to see his correccõn gyven./

Wm. Barker sent. for theft.

Ordered that Willm Barker * shalbe whipt for stealeing Bacon cheese &c from Ralfe Tompkins./

[Pages 175 to 177 contain records of the General Court from March 3, 1635-6, to May 25, 1636. From here the original record is in the handwriting of Increase Nowell.]

[178]   the 7th of the 4th mo @ 1636

A quarter Court held at Boston the 7th of the 4th Mo @ 1636: †

present
the Governor
the Deputy Govr.
Mr Tho: Dudley Seni
Mr Rich'd Bellingham

John Jobson shipmaster vndertooke & bound himselfe in a sum set‡ of 10ˡ to answear for ffrancis Tobey any damage not exceeding 10ˡ./

Ed: Bendall.

Edwd Bendall was fined 40s to the Compⁿ, & [10s] to the sentry & to returne

---

* Baker in L. copy.

† See Winthrop II. 344, case between Richd Beggarly and wife for divorce heard by the "Governour and Council and assistants" June 2, 1636.

‡ In Assumpsit in L. copy.

Mʳ John Haynes
Mʳ Williā Codding-
ton
Mʳ Roger Herlack-
ingden
Mʳ Richʳd Dummer
Increase Nowell
Mʳ John Humfrey
Mʳ John Endecot.

Phillip consᵗ.

to prison till hee acknowledg the iustice of the Court, & pay his fine. Hee after acknowledged his sinn, paid his fine, & was discharged./

Whetle, Bairstow, Wales, cens.

John Whitele, Willi: Bayrstow, & Tymothy Wales were censured to be whiped 6 stroaks a peece for drunkennes./

John Philips was chosen Cunstable of Dorchester, & tooke his oathe to that place belonging.

Mʳ Moses Maverick paid the Govʳnoʳ 40ˢ rent for Nodles Iland.

Tho: Miller comītt.

Thomas Miller pylote, & mate to Mʳ ffearnes in the Hectoʳ was comīted for certeine seditious & opprobrious speaches, saying wee are all rebells, & traytors, & hee would iustify it to the Governoʳˢ face, & that hee had bene twice at yᵉ Counsell table, & would go againe, & doubted not but to bring some to scourge vs.*

The 6ᵗʰ Day of the 7ᵗʰ Mᵒ @ 1636:
A quarter Court kept att Boston.

pʳsent
The Governoʳ
Deputie Governoʳ
Mʳ John Haynes
Mʳ Richʳd Bellingā
Mʳ Willī: Codding-
ton
Mʳ Willi: Pinchon
Mʳ John Winthrope
Iuniʳ
Mʳ Roger Herlak-
enden
Mʳ Tho: Dudley
Mʳ John Humfrey
Mʳ Richʳd Dummer
Mʳ Symon Brad-
streete
Increase Nowell.

It was ordered that John Olyver & Robᵗ Marten should veiwe the land beyond monotoquid ryver, & bring a plot of the same.

[Jam]es Clarke & Joane Clarke were ~~accused~~ ‖suspected‖ of fornication but no cleare pufe.

Shorthose sent.

Robert Shorthose for swearing by the bloud of god was sentenced to have his tongue put into a cleft stick, & to stand so by the space of haulfe an houre.

Comitt.

It was ordered that Mʳ Dudley Mʳ Endecot, & Mʳ Bradstreete or any two of them should examine the accounts betweene Mʳ Richʳd Saltonstall & Edwᵈ. Dillingam, & report to the Court how they find the estate of John Dillingam, & his wife deceased.

Mʳ Oldams estate.

It was ordered that Mʳ Haynes, Mʳ Harlakenden, & Increase Nowell or any two of them should examine ₐ busines concᵉrning Mʳ Ouldams estate, & debts: & Mʳ Hutchinson & Mʳ Mayhewe to gather vp the debts & estate, & bee accountable to the Courte.

---

* See Winthrop I. 187, and II. 344.

Jnº. Whites bond.   John White being bound vpon recognizance forfeted ten pounds.

Petr Bussackrs sent.   Peter Bussaker was censured for drunkennes to bee whiped, & to have twenty stripes sharply inflicted, & fined 5ˡ, for sleiteing the magistrates, or what they could do, saying they could but fine him.

Edw: Woodley sent.   Edward Woodley for attempting a rape, swearing, & breaking into a house was censured to be severely whiped 30 stripes, a yeares imprisonment, & kept to hard labor wᵗʰ course dyot, & to weare a Coller of yron.

Eliz: Aplegaᵗ sent.   Elisabeth the wife of Thomas Aplegate was censured to stand wᵗʰ her tongue in a Cleft stick for swearing, raileing & revileing./

[Pages 179 to 183 contain the General Court record from Sept. 8th to Oct. 28th, 1636. Page 183 has also the following record.]

A quarter Courte houlden at Boston the 6ᵗʰ Day of the 10ᵗʰ Mº @ 1636:

pʳsent
The Govʳnoʳ
the Deputy Govʳnoʳ
Mʳ Thom: Dudley
Mʳ John Haynes
Mʳ Richᵈ Bellingham
Mʳ John Humfry
Mʳ John Endecot
Mʳ Will: Coddington
Mʳ Richard Dumer
Mʳ Jnº Winthrope Iunʳ
Mʳ Symon Bradstreet
& Increase Nowell, se:

The same order was renewed, wᶜʰ was formerly agreed vpon betweene Mʳ Richʳd Saltonstall, Mʳ Apleton & Mʳ Edwᵈ Dillingam & the same gentlemen to whom the cause* was referd to have power to determine or to report to the Courte.

Will: Clarke being convicted of severall thefts was censured to bee severely whiped, & Comited to prison till the ship returne, & then to bee sent home./

Anthony Robinson being convicted of fornication comited by him 3 times by his owne Confession was censured to bee whiped, & to have 20 stripes sharply layd on. Hee was also enio[y]ned to appeare at the next quarter Courte after the expiration of his time, & the meane while to bee of good behavioʳ./

[On pages 184 to 190 is the General Court record from Dec. 7, 1636, to April 18, 1637.]

---

* The words "did belong" are inserted here in L. copy.

[191] A Quarter Courte houlden at Boston the 7ᵗʰ Day of the First Mº @ 1636 :*

p^rsent
The Gov^rno^r
the Deputy Govr.
Mr Dudley
Mr Haynes
Mr Bellingham
Mr Coddington
Mr Herlakenden
Mr Humfry
Increase Nowell.

Woodly, release.   In regard the imprisonment of Edward Woodley doth prove p^riuditiall to his m^r, the Courte (if the mayde shall professe her freedome from feare before Mr Haynes) doth release the said Woodley to his master./

Louells sent.   Weybro Lovell wife of Capt. Lovell being p^rsented by the grand jury for light & whoarish behavio^r, was seriously admonished to repent, & walke humbly, chastly, & holily./

Em^rsons bond.   John Emerson being accused by Edith Pitts forfeted 100ˡ.

George Kendrick & Will: Hatche forfetted 50ˡ a peece for want of John Emerson's appearance. These were discharged the 4ᵗʰ mº. 1638.

Jā Heyden freed.   James Hayden was admited to be free because of his m^r. his former ꝑmise before the act of the Courte made against it./

Moultons rate to be repajd him.   It is thought equall by the Court that the towne of Salem should repay goodman Robert Moulton the money taken of him for the last 1200ˡ rate./

W^m. James cens.   Will: James being p^rsented for incontinency knowing his wife before marriage, was sentenced to bee set in the bilboes† at Boston the 5ᵗʰ in the afternoone, & in the stocks at Salem vpon the next Courte day, & bound in 20ˡ./

The power formerly granted to Mr Dudley, Mr Endecot, & Mr Bradstreete, is granted to Increase Nowell & Thom: Mayhewe, to examine the acccounts betweene Mr Rich^rd Saltonstall, Mr Apleton, & Edward Dillingam./

Louell admonisht.   Capt. Lovell was admonished to take heede of light carriage.

Tim^o Tomljns.   Tymothy Tomlins was contented to take onely x^s of John Stretton.

A Capias was graunted to John Stretton to bring Kibbe & Elwell before the Governo^r.

Tho: Petet cens.   Thom: Pettet for suspition of slaunder, idlenes, & stubbornenes is censured to bee severely whiped, & to bee kept in hould.

---

* 1636-7?   † The L. copy has also here " upon the next court day."

Attachment was ~~sent~~ ‖ordered‖ for Will: Powell to appear the 28ᵗʰ pʳsent for contempt, & to answear to the accusation of Tho: Pettet./

<small>Jnᵒ Trumble find 20ᵘ.</small> John Trumble was fined 20ˡ to the Comon Wealth resting till the next quarter Court, & bound in 40ˡ to appeare the first tewsday in the 4th month @ 1637./

Mary Bowler was adiudged to make double restitution for the things stoalen by her from others./

[On pages 192 to 196 is the record of the General Court 17 May, 1637, and also the list of freemen from May, 1636, to March, 1638-9. The following record is on page 195.]

The First of the 4ᵗʰ Mᵒ @ 1637 :

Mʳ Richʳᵈ Saltonstall being chosen an Assistant by the Generall Court this day tooke the oath to that place belonging./

[197] A Quarter Court houlden at Boston the 6ᵗʰ Day of the 4ᵗʰ Mᵒ @ 1637 :

<small>pʳsent
the Governoʳ
the Deputy Govʳnoʳ
Colo: Jnᵒ Endecot
Mʳ Richʳd Bellinghā
Mʳ Jnᵒ Winthrope Iunior
Mʳ Roger Herlakenden
Mʳ Rich: Saltonstall
Mʳ Israell Staughton
Increase Nowell.</small>

<small>Sweet find.</small> John Sweete being pʳsented by the grandiury for shooting a woolfe dog of Colonell Endecots, in Colonell Endecots owne yard was fined 5ˡ & to bee imprisoned dureing the pleasure of the Courte./

<small>Andʳson find.</small> Robert Anderson for his contempt was fined 50ˡ, & sent to prison till hee shall give satisfaction./

<small>Jnᵒ Hathaway, for adultery.</small> John Hathaway being accused of adultery wᵗʰ Margaret Seale wife of Edward Seale, James Peñ & Samuell Coles testified that hee confessed it to them : so the grandiury found the byll of inditement to bee true though ʌ

<small>Robᵗ Allen & Margᵗ Seale, for adultery.</small> Robᵗ Allen & Margaret Seale being accused of adultery confessed the fact ; so the grandiury found the byll of inditemᵗ to bee true.

<small>Mathue Bridg bound ouer.</small> Mathewe Bridg being accused to bee guilty of the vntimely death of John Abbot the said Mathewe, & John Bridge his father were bound in 40ˡ for his appearance at the next quarter Courte to bee held the first tewsday in the 7ᵗʰ mᵒ at Boston.

In regard Phebe Seales was by order of Court put

Order abt Phebe Seales free frō Jnᵒ Cogshall.

app'tice to John Coggesall of Boston m̃chant, who at the instant request of the Courte accepted the same, & for that the said girle hath ᵱved over burthensome to him, the Court (as formerly) so nowe have thought it iust to ease him of it, & whereas the said girle was put by the said John Coggeshall to one John Levins of Roxberry to bee kept at a certeine ₍ₐ₎ ; It is now ordered that Mʳ Deputie calling to him Mʳ Brenton, & Will: Parks chosen by the said 2 ᵱties shall have power to end the difference betweene the said parties, & to set downe such order for the ease & discharge of the said John Coggesall & disposeing of the said Phebe as they shall thinke equall.

Jnᵒ Palmer costs gʳ to him.

John Palmer was graunted 10sˢ costs against Georg Woodwar[d] for not ᵱsecuting his suite haveing sum̃oned the said John to appeare this quarter Courte.

15ˡⁱ of Jnᵒ Trumbles 20 fine remitted him.

John Trumble being formerly fined 20ˡ fifteen pound of the said 20ˡ is remited, & the other 5ˡ hee hath a yeares time granted him to satisfie the same.

Rich: Osbornes injunction.

Richᵈ Osborne was enioyned to give an account to the Cunstable weekely * how hee doth imᵱve his time, & if hee neglect, further order to bee taken, by puting him to the Castle.

Isack Davies to be sent home to his wife in Eng.

Isaack Davies was ordered to bee sent whom to his wife to England, & the care thereof is com̃ited to Salem./

Binfeildˢ children, how disposed.

Wheareas John Binfeild† dyed leaving 2 child'n vndisposed of, the charge of the one was ordered to bee defrayed by Mʳ Cradock, hee haveing the goods of the deceased, the other child being disposed of by the Country./

Edwᵈ Seales sent. to be whip. for drunkeness.

Edward Seale for his beastly drunkennes was censured to bee set in the bilboes till the end of the Court, & then to bee severely whiped.

Geo: Munings find for selling beer.

George Munnings was fined 20sˢ for seling beare & keeping a house of intertainement without license./

Sam: Cole find.

Samuell Cole was fined 10sˢ for selling a quart of beare a[t] 2ᵈ, & was licensed to sell such claret & white wine as is sent f[or.]

---

* Wm Kelly in L. copy.
† Benefeild in L. copy.

Rob't Long find.

Rob't Longe was fined 10ˢ * for seling a qʳt of beare at 2ᵈ, and was licensed to sell such claret & white wine as is sent for.

[198]
Wiͫ Balston find.

William Baulston was fined 10sˢ for selling a qʳt of beare at 2ᵈ.

James Brownes cens.

James Browne was censured for drunkennes to bee set two houres in the bilboes vpon the market day at Boston publikely

& the said James Browne was fined 40sˢ for selling strong water to the Indians wᵗʰout license.

Benja: Hubburd admonishᵗ.

Beniamin Hubberd was also solemly admonished of his failing for being in Company wᵗʰ James Browne & the rest, & often drinking of the strong water bottle† wᵗʰ them, & not reꝓving them.

Gorg Woodwards costs.

George Woodward was ordered to give Rich'd Chadwell 6ˢ 8ᵈ because hee called him for a witnes from Saugust ‡ by warrant.

John Knight, of Newbury, licenst.

John Knight of Neweberry was licensed to keepe an [ordinary, & give]§ intertainement to such as neede.

Nicho: Vpshall, of Dorch. licenct.

Nicholas Vpsall of Dorchester was licensed to keepe an ordinary, & give intertainement to such as neede./

Wᵐ Knopˢ cense.

Willi: Knop was enioyned vpon paine of 100ˡ & imprisonment to bring in sureties wᵗʰin 8 dayes for his appearance at the next quarter Court to answear what shalbee obiected about his speaches of Mʳ Vaine oʳ late governoʳ./

Mʳ. Sam: Maůrick injunction.

Mʳ Samuell Maverick was enioyned to keepe in his hands of the goods of Robert Anderson to the valew of 50ˡ starling for his fine, for his contempt offered, & to deliver him the rest of his goods./

A day of thanksgiving.

The 5ᵗʰ day of the next weeke, being the 15ᵗʰ of this month was appointed to bee kept a day of thanksgiveing in the severall Churches./

Wᵐ. Baulston liͫ.

Willi: Baulston is licensed to keepe a house of intertainement, & is licensed to sell such claret & white wine as is sent for./

---

    * 20ˢ in L. copy.
    † The word bottle not in L. copy.
    ‡ Lynne in L. copy.
    § These three words omitted and the words " house of" substituted in L. copy.

OF THE MASSACHUSETTS BAY. 69

Schooler sent for, & old Jno Bayly.
Order was appointed to bee given to the Cunstable of Neweberry to app^rhend Schooler, Bayly * & dwelling beyond merrimack† to appear at the Court at Ipswich or before the magistrates there, who have power to take further order as they shall see cause.

Hen: Kingman, of Weymouth, licenct.
Henry Kingman of Waymoth is licensed to keepe a house of intertainement./

[On page 199 and the first part of page 200 is the General Court record of Aug. 1, 1637. The rest of page 200 contains the following record.]

The 5th Day of this 7th Month 1637.

prsent
the Gov^rnor
the Deputy Govr
Mr Rich: Bellinghā
Mr John Winthrope iu:
Mr Rich: Saltonstal
Mr Israel Staughtō
Increase Nowell

The quarter Court was adiourned till the 19th of this 7th month because of the Synode kept at Newetowne for the setling of things in difference amongst vs.

The 7th Day of the 7th Month @ 1637.

The Generall Courte by the Generall Consent of all present was adiourned to the 26th of this 7th month, & the pticuler Courts in the severall places to bee kept the last Tewsday of the 8th month./

Freemen, 2.
Mr George Moxham & Mr Tymothy Dalton were made free this 7th day.

The 19th of the 7th M°, @ 1637.

A quarter Courte held at Boston, & Newetowne because of the Conference.

the Gov^rnor
the Deputy Govr.
Col: John Endecot
Mr John Humfrey
Mr Rich: Bellingham
Mr Israell Staughton
Mr Rog^r Herlakenden
Mr Rich: Saltonstall
Increase Nowell.

J^{no} W^{ms}, murd^r.

Wm Schooler for murd^r.

John Williams being indited about the death of John Hobbe‡ confessed that hee killed the said Hobbe, so the Jury found him guilty of murther.§

William Schooler being indited for the death of Mary Scholee¶ the Jury found him guilty of murthering the said Schoolee.§

---

* Not in L. copy.   † Merrimack river in L. copy.
‡ Hobbey in L. copy.   § See Winthrop I. 241, 321.
¶ Schooley in L. copy.

Mary Osborn acq^d. Mary Osborne the wife of ____ Osborne being indited about the death of her daughter, found* the byll Ignoramus.

J^no Hathaway, adulty. John Hathaway being indited for adultery was found guilty.

Robt Allen, adult. Rob^rt Allen confessed Adultery, & was found guilty.

Marga^rt Seale, adult. Margaret Seale the wife of ____ Seale confessed adultery & was found guilty.

The grandiury men.

John Holgrave
Daniell Raye
Will: Parke†
Isaack Morrell
Jonathan Wade
Will: Bartholmew
Rich^rd Joanes
Rob^rt Harding
Samu: Wilbore‡
Henry Kingman
Rich^rd Adams
Edmond Hubberd seni:
Thom: Hamond
Abrah: Palmer
Brian Pendleton
Thom: Cakebread.

The Jury of Life & Death.

Ralph Hudson
Samuell ffinch
Willi: Curtis
Willi: Barsham
John Smyth
John Holman
John Holland
Nicholas Vpsall
John Geepin
Ezechi:§ Richardson
Thomas Squire
Rich^rd Betscombe.

[201]

Bromfeilds sent. William Brumfeild being examined about theft confesed that hee had stoalen above 5^l from his m^r, & about an elle of cloth, & for his stealeing, ploting to run from his m^r. lying, drunkennes, & idlenes was censured to make double restitution to bee branded, & bee severely whiped.

Georg Spencers sent. George Spencer who received 6s^s of the said Brumfeild was censured to make double restitution, & bee whiped.

Georg Barlow sent. George Barlow for his idlenes was censured to bee whiped.

---

* "The Grand Jury found" in L. copy.   † Parkes in L. copy.
‡ Gibones in L. copy.   § Elizabeth in L. copy.

OF THE MASSACHUSETTS BAY. 71

<small>Jnº Hogges sent.</small>

John Hogges being accused of drunkennes confessed it, & was fined 3ˡ.

<small>Jacob Smith dischard.</small>

Jacob Smyth was discharged for want of evidence vpon his imprisonment.

<small>Mathew Bridg acquᵗ.</small>

Mathew Bridge appearing, & no evidence comeing in against him, hee was quit by ꝓclamation.

<small>Mʳ. Jnº Green find & banisht.</small>

Mʳ John Greene of new ꝓvidence was fined 20ˡ, & comīted vntill the fine of 20ˡ bee payd, & enioyned not to come into this iurisdiction vpon paine of fine, or imprisonment at the pleasure of the Courte for speaking contemptuously of the magistrates.

<small>Mʳ. Jnº Stretton find, xˡⁱ.</small>

Mʳ John Stretton was fined xˡ for lending a gun to an Indian four dayes.

<small>338
Gurlings land to be sold.</small>

It was ordered that Mʳ Joseph Weld & Mʳ John Beniamin (being authorished) should make sale of Mʳ Gurlings land for satisfaction of the creditoʳs in ꝓportion if it come to short, & if an overplus bee, that to remaine in the hands of Mʳ Beniamin.

<small>Mʳ. Rob: Saltonstalls deed for his creditors.</small>

The 23ᵗʰ * of this 7ᵗʰ m° 1637 Mʳ Hugh Peters delivʳed into the court a deed of Mʳ Robert Saltonstall makeing over all the estate that hee hath, or shall have to satisfy his Creditoʳs.

[The rest of page 201 and pages 202 to 213 contain the General Court record from Sept. 26 to Nov. 20, 1637.]

[214] At a quarter Court held at Newetowne the 5th Day of the 10ᵗʰ M° @ 1637.

<small>pʳsent,
the Governoʳ
Deputy Govʳnoʳ
Mʳ Bellingham
Mʳ Herlakenden
Mʳ Staughton
Increase Nowell</small>

<small>Mʳ Rich:
Brownes
satisfaction
for 5ˡⁱ 10
from Curtiss
Jesop, &c.</small>

Whereas there came into this Courte Richʳd Browne of Watertowne on the behalfe of John Woolcot, & William Curtis of Roxberry, & by mediation of the Court the said Willi: Curtis was willing & did agree to pay vnto the said Richʳd Browne 5. 10ˢ wᶜʰ hee was indebted to one John Jesop, now out of this iurisdiction, in satisfaction of 5. 10ˢ dewe by the said Jesop to the said John Woolcot † this Court doth order that vpon payment of the said 5ˡ 10ˢ by the said Curtis, the said John Woolcot,‡ & the said Richʳd Browne, & their executoʳs shalbee alwayes lyable to save harmlesse the

---

    * 13th in L. copy.   † Wolridge in L. copy.   ‡ Wollcott in L. copy.

said Willi: Curtis against the said Jesop for the said 5ˡ 10sˢ till a sufficient discharge bee oth{r}wise had from him.

Luke Henbury{s} sent., for theft, to be whipt, e{r}.

Luke Henberry being convicted of theft was censured to bee severely whiped, & for runing away./

Hen: Harwood{s} invento.

The inventory of Henry Harwood of Charlstowne was p{r}sented to this Court being 46ˡ 17ˢ 8ᵈ * & the debts 4ˡ. Edw{d} Conv{r}se, Rob{r}t Long, & Rob{r}t Hale were the apraissers.

368

Joane Drakɜ will & invent.

The Inventory of Joane Drake w{th} a Coppey of her will was presented to the Court being 28ˡ 1ˢ 5ᵈ. Willi: Cheesbro James Penniman, & Willi: Huet were the appraisers. She gave ¼ of her goods at Boston in N. E. to John N[o]tt,† to her sister Duglas 2ˡ, to her nephew to whom shee was a witnes 20ˢ to buy him a bible, the rest of her goods heare in Newe England to Samuell Bellingham, & all [her] goods in ould England shee gave them equally between her two sisters there.

the disposeing of these shee leaveth to her m{r} as executor.

Georg Woodwards costs.

There is 5sˢ damages graunted George Woodward to bee paid by Willi: Dinely, who sumoned him to appear at this Court, and causing him to attend, did not ꝓsecute ag{a} him.

Sam: Freemans costs.

There is 13ˢ 4ᵈ damages granted Sam: Freeman to bee paid by John Gay, who sumoned him to appear at this Court, and causeing him to attend w{th} 2 witnesses ꝓsecuted not against him.

[215] At a quarter Court held at Newetowne the 6{th} of the First Month @ $\frac{1637}{1638}$: ‡

p{r}sent,
The Governo{r}
the Deputy Gov{r}no{r}
M{r} Bellingham
M{r} Humfrey
M{r} Herlakenden
M{r} Staughton
Increase Nowell.

Jose Faber.

Joseph ffaber being complained of for selling of wine w{th}out order was find 10ˢ for sel̶l̶g a gallon.

Hollard.

Angell Hollard being p{r}sented for a libell acknowledged his fault of himselfe volentarily, & was fined 20sˢ./

Brigg bond for his wife.

Clement Briggs is bound in xˡ for his wifes appearance at the next quarter Court

Arthu{r} Warren, for accompā Briggs wif.

the p{r}sentment of Arthur Warren for keeping Company w{th} Clement Briggs wife was found to bee true.

---

* 8ᵈ omitted in L. copy. † Natt in L. copy. ‡ 1637 in L. copy.

Laur: Waters bound for his wife.	Lawrence Waters is bound in x^l for his wife's appearance at the next quarter Court.*
Lef^t How^s bond App.	Leift Howe is bound in 20^l to appear at the next quarter Court.
368 Gurlings land sold.	The sale of Mr Gurlings land by Mr Beniamin & Mr Joseph Weld to Mr Andrews is confirmed, & appointed to bee layd out by Mr Damfort, Mr Colebran, and Goodm̄ Bridge./†
Jno Woolridg admonisht for his drunkenes.	John Woolrige appearing vpon the inditement of the grandiury confessed his fraude & drunkennes in ould England for wch hee was sharply reproved & seriously admonished./
Xtopher Grant find 5 for excess. drinking.	Christopher Graunt appearing vpon p^{r}sentment for being in company, & drinking more then was convenient was fined 5^s./
Hen: Bright dismis^t.	Henry Bright appearing was dismissed
	Mullinder appearing was dismissed
Nicholas Busby, an attach. issue out ag^t him.	Nicholas Busbey not appearing an attachment was granted against him to appeare at Boston the 22th p^{r}sent at Boston.
Tho: Smith‡ attach^t ag^t him.	John Smyth not appearing attachment was granted against him to appear at Newetowne the 27th§ p^{r}sent.
Tho: Starr find 20 for speaking ag^t the law.	Thomas Starr being accused for speaking against the order of Court about swine, & the same ⱷved that hee said the law was against gods law, and hee would not obey it: so hee was com̄ited, & enioyned to acknowledg his fault the 14th at the gen^{r}all Court, & was fined 20^l, & to give security for his fine, or pay the same before his releasement./
Attachm^t gted ag^t seū person, as Edw: Lambe, &c.	attachment was graunted ag^a Nic^o¶ Theale to appear the 4th [m^o.]
	attachment was granted ag^a Edward Lambe to appear the 4th m^o.

attachm^t was graunted ag^a John Bennet.
attachm^t was granted ag^a Philip Deare.

Tho: Evar, cons^t of Charls Tō.	Tho: Ewar was chosen Cunstable of Charlestowne, & tooke his oath to discharge the said office god helping the 24th, first [m^o.]

---

* This paragraph not in L. copy.   † John Bridge in L. copy.   ‡ So in the original.
§ 22 in L. copy.   ¶ Richard in L. copy.

[Pages 216 to 224 contain the General Court record for March and May, 1638.]

[225]

Qu^{rt} Court, 5: 4: 38.

p^rsent.
The Governo^r
The Deputy Gov^rno^r
Mr Endecott
Mr Bellingham
Mr Saltonstall
Mr Stoughton
Mr Bradstreete
Mr Herlakenden
Incr: Nowell.

Ric: Colli.

Gurlins land.

Difference betweene M^r. Whit. & M^r. Woolcot referr'd.

Edith Pitts abused.

M^r. Hen: Sewalls beating his wife referd to Ipsw.

Robt Bartlet sent. for swearing, his toung in a cleft stick.

Jno Smith sent.

Kath: Cornish admonish^t.

At A Courte of Assistants held at Cambridge the 5th Day of the 4th M^o @ 1638: being a q^rter Courte.

M^r. Skeltons estat. set.

It was ordered wth the Consent of Mrs Baggerly that the increase of Mr Skeltons Cattle should bee divided according to Mr Skeltons will, & that the goods & household stuffe wch belongs to the 3 eldest child'n should be divided by some of the Church of Salem, & comitted to the Church of Salem./

Richrd Collicot & John Buslin were fined 6^s 8^d a peece for absence when the Court sat in the afternoone being Jurymen.

Mr Willard & Mr Spencer are ioyned wth oth^{rs} formerly appointed about M^r. Gurlins land./

Mr Richrd Bellingham, Increase Nowell, & Mr Mayhewe are appointed they or any two of them to examine witnesses vpon oathe & to heare & examine all things concerning Mr White & Mrs Woolcote,* & to do it wthin 14 dayes, & Mrs Woolcot is to bring in a pfect inventory, & distinguish the goods inventoried between his & the Childrens leaving to the Court to give order about them.

Samuell Jackson & Edith Pits did appear, & give in their evidence ag^t John Emerson of Scituate about his abusing the said Edith./

Henry Seawall being p^rsented by the grandiury for beating his wife is referd to the Court of Ipswich to examine, & hee to appear wthout any new summons./

Rob^rt Bartlet being p^rsented for Cursing & swearing was Censured to have his tongue put in a Cleft sticke.

John Smyth of Meadford for swearing being penitent was set in the bilboes.†

Katherine vxor Rich: Cornish was found suspitious of incontinency, & was seriously admonished to take heede.

---

* Wolcott in L. copy.
† This paragraph not in L. copy.

Clem^t Brig wife enjoy. not to accompā Arth: Warren.	Clement Brigs his wife is enioyned not to come into the Company of Arthur Warren.

Willi: Busbey being p^rsented for drunkennes it was found the falling sicknes.

Laurenc͡e Waters wife & others admonish^t.	Laurence Waters Wife was enjoyned to give John ffinch 18^d & Nico: Theale to give Jno ffinch 18^d & Edw^a Lambe to give him 2^s & lambe was fined 15^s 6^d for his contempt, & all of them were admonished to avoyde dancing.

John Bennet & Philip Deare were referd to Salem for their drunken[es.]

Newbery find 6.8.	The towne of Newberry was fined 6^s 8^d, & enioyned to repaire y^{ir} defects before the Court in Septemb^r.
Ips. find 6.8.	The towne of Ipswich is fined 6. 8^d, & hath lib^rty till the 7th m° to repair their defects.
Lin find 20^s.	The towne of Linn is fined 20^s, & enioyned to mend their wayes before the next Court./
Charl Tō find 6.8.	The towne of Charlestowne is fined 6^s 8^d & hath lib^rty till the 7th month.
Tho: Ewar find 40 for leauing his pitt open.	Thomas Ewar is fined 40^s for the leaving his pit, or well open in wch a child was drowned./
Camb. find 5.	The towne of Cambridge was fined 5s^s & to p^rpare before the next Court.
Boston traū y^eir p^rsent.	The towne of Boston trav^rse their p^rsentment./
Edmund Hubbard find 40.	Edmond Hubberd Senior was fined 40^s for leaving a pit open in wch a child was drowned./
Franc͡ Westons wife set in the bilboes 2 howers.	Francis Westons wife was censured to bee set 2 houres in the bilboes hear & 2 houres at Salem vpon a lecture day.
Dor^{ch} find 6.8.	The towne of Dorchester was fined 6. 8^d & hath liberty till Septemb^r next.
Rox. find 6.8.	The towne of Roxberry was fined 6. 8^d & hath lib^rty till the 7th month.
Weymouth find 6. 8.	The towne of Waymoth was fined 6^s 8^d & hath lib^rty till the 7th month next.
Hingh. find 6.8.	The towne of Hingham was fined 6. 8^d & hath a months lib^rty.

John Holgrave is referd to Salem./

76   RECORDS OF THE COURT OF ASSISTANTS

<small>Tho: Gray to be seuly whip^t & banish^t.</small>   Thomas Gray was censured to bee severely whiped, & the former execution of banishment to bee inflicted.

<small>Jno Leg & Wm Edmonds bonds for y^{eir} wives.</small>   John Leg bound in 40^l & Willi: Edmonds bound in 40^l to ~~bring~~ ‖carry‖ their wifes to Salem Court & Rob^rt Keyes bound in 20^l to appear.

<small>Robt Cole.</small>   Rob^rt Cole was enioyned to pay the witnesses 10^s & so was discharged.

<small>Jno Emersons bond.</small>   John Emerson is bound to the good behavio^r for twelue months & bound in 40^l to appeare at the quarter Court in this iurisdiction the 4th m^o. 1639./

George Pye a more * was to remaine wth Mr Cradock vntill advise from England, & advise to bee sent to Rye./

Rob^rt Morgan, Edw^a Hall, & Rich: Lambert are referd to Salem./

[226]   A Courte of Assistants held at Boston the 4th of the 7th Month @ 1638: †

<small>p^rsent,
the Governo^r
the Deputie Gov^rno^r
Mr Endecott
Mr Bellingham
Mr Herlakendon
Mr Bradstreete
Mr Stoughton
Mr John Winthrop iuni:
& Increase Nowell.</small>

The Cunstables of Cambridg & the Cunstables of Boston are fined 10s^s a peece for not returning their warrants in time wth the names of the Jury men./

<small>Hen: Collens find.</small>   Henry Collens is fined 5^s for not appearing when hee was called to serve vpon the grand iury./

<small>Katherin, wife of Sam: finch, whipt for speaking ag^t magist^s & church^s.</small>   Katherine the wife of Samuell ffinch being accused for speaking against the magistrates, agā the Churches, & against the Elders was censured to bee whiped, & comited till the gene^rall Court./

Holloway is bound in 20^l to appear at the next Courte.

John Crosse being warned to appear about his servant Clement Manning who miscarried the said Crosse was discharged.

<small>Geor: Horn find for being distempred by drink.</small>   George Horne is fined 10^s for distemper wth drinke wch his m^r. Willi: Denne vndertooke to see satisfied./

John Smyth bound in 20^l to appear at the next Courte./

<small>Wm South whipt & banish^t.</small>   William South is censured to bee severely whiped, & kept to the Generall Courte./ by whom hee was banished to returne no more vpon paine of death./

---

* So in the original. Moor?
† See Winthrop I. 274, mention of an action against one Gillow at this Court.

M^r. Jno Winthrō took his oath. Mr John Winthrope iunior tooke the oath of Assistants.

The busines of Capt Lovells is referd to Mr Roger Herlak[e]nden & Increase Nowell to examine all things about it both estate & debts./

Edwd Wilson will & estate. The Inventory of Edward Wilson, amounting to 48^l 2^s 00^d, was delivered into the Court this 4th day of the 7th m^o./ by Thom: Wilson, executor of the aforenamed Edward, & was received de bene esse./

Jane Drakes legacy to Jno not. It was ordered wth the consent of Mr Rich^{r}d Bellingham that the said Mr Bellingham should deliver Willi: Cheesbro for John Nott 6^l in satisfaction for his ¼ p^{r}te of all the goods & chattels given him by his aunt Joane Drake this to bee dd p^{r}sently & the said Mr Bellingham to bee dischar[g]ed thereof vpon delivery of the same.

Agreem^t betw. Jno & W^m ffiske. The agreement betweene Mr John ffiske & his brother William made by Mr John Endecot, Willi: Hathorne John Woodberry & Jeffrey* Massey was approved in Court wth the consent of p^{r}ties that the said Jno shall returne 200^l of the estate in his hands to his brother Willi: & Willi: shalbee bound to give vnto his said Brother John, if hee dies vnmarried before hee comes to the age of 24 yeares the sume of 100^l, & the said Willi: did release to the said John in Court all his Interest in the land./

391-
Ad m̄straĉon to Robt bills estate. John Knowles (haveing married the widow of Ephraim Davies who was sister to Rob^{r}t Bills) was granted administration of the estate of Rob^{r}t Bills.

Siluest^r Bauldwins estate. The will of Silvester Bauldwin was p^{r}sented into the court & his wife Sarah & sonne Rich^{r}d were alowed executors according to the will.

[On pages 227 to 234 and part of page 235 is the General Court record for September, 1638. The following Quarter Court record begins on page 235.]

A quarter Courte houlden at Boston the 4th day of the 10th month @ 1638:

p^{r}sent,
the Governo^r
the Deputie Go:
Mr John Endecot
Mr Rich^{r}d Saltonstall
Mr Symon Bradstreete

George Walton was fined 10s^s for swearing, & paid it in Court.

John Kinge, Willi: Reeves, & John Davies appearing were discharged till further information bee given about the murtherer they tooke from the iland.

---
* Geoffrey in L. copy.

Mr John Winthrop, iuni
Mr Israell Stoughton
Increase Nowell.

Robᵗ Shorthose was comitted for saying if the magistrate had any thing to say to him hee might come to him, hee was released binding himselfe in 20ˡ to appear at the next Court, & to bee of good behavioʳ the meane time.

James Luxfoard & Beniamin Hubberd are bound in 10ˡ a peece for the appearance & good behavioʳ of Robᵗ Shorthose.

The Indian   wᶜʰ had bene kept in prison was released being required to send or Bring satisfaction for the Cowe, or else satisfaction should bee taken frō Na[v]igan *

Thomas Hollaway appearing was discharged.

John Holgrave being pʳsented by the grandiury for drawing wine against an order of Court was declared to have forfeted xˡ & for causing his daughter to deliver a paper to a Jury man out of Court hee was fined xˢ hee was also by the Jewrye found gilty of contempt, & to have broken the rule of hospitality & the peace wᶜʰ were remitted him./

Thomas Wilson for takeing above double tole was fined xˡ & being pʳsented for standing above sixe months excomunica[te] hee was enioyned to appeare at the next Courte.

Samuell Basse for his contempt was fined 5ˡ./

Richʳd Turner for being notoriously drunke was fined 2ˡ.

Canooes.
William Blanton appearing was enioy[n]ed to appeare at the next court † wᵗʰ all the men that were in the Canooe wᵗʰ him, &   Aplegate, wᶜʰ owned the Canooe out of wᶜʰ the 3 psons were drowned./ & it was ordered that no Canooe should bee vsed at any fferry vpon paine of 5ˡ nor no Canooe to bee made in oʳ iurisdiction before the next generall Court vpon paine of 10ˡ.

Also order was appointed to bee given to Richʳd Right ‡ to stave that Canooe, out of wᶜʰ these psons were drowned.

Dorothy the wife of John Talbie being by her owne confession guilty of the vnnaturall & vntimely death of her daughter Difficult Talbye was by the Jury found guilty, & so was condemned to bee hanged./§

William Androws haveing made assault vpon his mʳ. Henry Coggan struck him diverse blowes, & wickedly conspired against the life of his said mʳ., & not onely so: but did conspire also against the peace,

---

* Naviganset in L. copy.   † These last six words not in L. copy.
‡ Wright in L. copy.   § See Winthrop I. 279.

& welfare of this whole Comon welth was censured to bee severely whiped, & delivered vp as a slave to whom the Court shall appoint.

[236]   John Haslewood being found guilty of severall thefts, & breaking into severall houses was censured to bee severely whiped, & delivered vp a slave to whom the Court shall appoint.

Gyles Player being found guilty of severall thefts, & breaking into houses was censured to bee severely whiped, & delivered vp for a slave to whom the Court shall appoint.

John Bickerstaffe was censured to bee severely whiped for comitting fornication wth Ales Burwoode.

Ales Burwoode was censured to bee whiped for yelding to Bickerstaffe w^thout crying out, & concealing it 9 or 10 dayes.

Katherine Cornish is respited vntill the Court the first m°.

Attachm^t to bee sent out for Ibrooke, & Ralph Smythe.

Rob^rt Abell for want of sufficient witnes was discharged.

Clement Brigs was not found gilty of extortion & so was discharged.

The towne of Waymoth was fined 10s^s for defect in their high wayes, & day was given them till the next Courte.

The towne of Dorchester for a defective high way was fined 5s^s, & had day given them vntill the next Courte.

The towne of Boston were fined 10s^s for their defective high ways ||& want of a watch house || & day was given till the next Courte.

Attachment was to bee sent out for Edward ffuller.

Henry Webb was discharged for want of sufficient witnes.

The Towne of Concord was fined 5s^s for want of a paire of stocks & a watch house.

The towne of Watertowne for want of a paire of stocks was fined xs^s & had day till the next Courte.

Isaack Sternes & John Page were fined 5s^s for turning the way about, & day was given till the next Courte.

Thomas Cornehill * appearing, & being licensed was discharged.

The wife of Josua Verin was referd to Salem.

An Attachment to bee sent out for George Richards.

Willi: Ballard huiring no other but such as had lots was discharged.

John Coggan † was in like sort discharged because those wch hee huired were other mens servants./

---

* Cornall in L. copy.
† Cogan in L. copy.

The towne of Cambridge was fined 10s⁵ for want of a watch house, pound, & stocks, & time was given them till the next Courte.

John Bets appeared, & was discharged there being not evidence sufficient to ᵱve his overselling./

The towne of Charles towne was fined 5s⁵ for want of a watch house, & time was given till the next Courte.

John Poole for abuseing his servant was fined 5ˡ.*

John Cooper iunior was comitted to his father for correction.

ffrancis ffelmingham & Willi: Pester appearing for want of witnes were discharged./

Mʳ Willi: Goose is respited vntill his returne.

Mary the wife of Thomas Oliver for disturbing the Church of Salem was comitted to prison vntill shee should find sureties for her good behaviour & appearance at the ∧ †

[237] Richard Geaves & Peter Bussaker for quarrelling and fighting are referd to the Court at Salem.

Richʳᵈ Hollingsworth for prophaning the saboth in travelling was censured to bee set in the stocks vpon a lecture day at Salem./

The towne of Ipswich was fined 10s⁵ for defective high wayes, & time was given them till the next Court to repair them./

Anthony Emery was fined 20s⁵ for a pound breach, & enioyned to give Thomas Coleman 13ˢ 4ᵈ for his charges.

Thomas Savory for his grosse lying was referd to the Court at Ipswich.

The towne of Neweberry was fined 5s⁵ for want of a paire of stocks, & time was given them till the next Courte to make them.

Thomas Terry was enioyned to appear at the next Courte to answear further.

An Attachment was granted for Jarvice Mudge to appeare at the next Courte.

John Haward being chosen Cunstable for the towne of Dedham did take his oath the 5ᵗʰ 10ᵗʰ mᵒ 1638.

Thom: Brooke being chosen Cunstable for the towne of Concord did take his oath the 8ᵗʰ 10ᵗʰ mᵒ 1638.

409 ∧ ‡ Ewar was alowed executrix of her husband Thom Ewar, deceased.

An Attachment was granted for John Harrison, genᵗ.

---

* See Lechford's Note Book, p. 25.
† See Winthrop I. 281.
‡ The widow Ewar in L. copy.

[238]   A Quarter Court held at Boston the 5th day of the first month
@ 1638 or 1639

present,
The Governor
the Deputy Gover
Mr Endicott
Mr John Winthrope,
in:
Mr Richrd Saltonstall
Mr Israell Stoughton
& Increase Nowell

John Davies for grosse offences in attempting lewdnes wth divers woomen was censured to bee severely whiped both heare & at Ipswich, & to weare the letter V vpon his breast vpon his vppermost garment vntill the Court do discharge him.

John Greene dying in the house of Daniell Brewar, administration was granted to the said Brewar./

Willi: Blanton, Willi: Potter, Robrt Thorpe, Henry Neale, John ffitch, & Thomas Aplegate appearing were discharged wth an admonition not to adventure too many into any boate.

Thomas Boyse haveing attempted a rape wth Sara Jusall was censured to give the mayde 5l, & to bee whiped & imprisoned a time.

Willi: Judson appearing was discharged.

Isaack Deesbury was comitted & fined 5l for stealing at Pecoit out of wch the 3 witnesses are to have 5s a peece, & the psecutor 10ss.

Ralph Smyth appearing was discharged.

Richrd Ibrooke for tempting 2 or more maydes to vncleannes was fined 5l to the country, & 20ss a peece to the 2 maydes Rebecca Phippen & Mary Marsh.

Thomas Aplegate was appointed to have 29ss for his Canooe, when the armes wch hee borrowed are returned back as good as they were when he borrowed them.

James Meadecalfe not being returned from Pascataque Mr Samu: Maverick had granted him liberty till the next Court to bring him in./

Edward Saunders being sick at Pascataque Nicolas Davyson had liberty till the next Court to bring him in./

John Hogges,* for swearing Gods foote, & cursing his servant, wishing a poxe of g[o]d take you was find 5l./

John Harrison not appearing a new attachment was granted.

Chaulkley the wife of Robert Chalkley not appearing attachment was granted for her to appear at the next courte.

Ricrd Silvester was fined 12s for selling strong water, wch hee paid into the Court.

Robert Shorthose was set in the bilboes for sleiting the magistrate in his speaches.

---
* Hoggs in L. copy.

James Ludden had granted his 10s⁸ against Cutshamache, who warned him to appear, & did not come to ꝑsecute./

Edmond Audley is granted administration of the goods of ffrancis Dent deceased vpon the testimony of John Winge, & Sargent Davies,* vpon oath./

An Attachment was granted for John Harrison.

An Attachment for   Chaulkley, the wife of Rob't Chaulkley.

[From page 239 to page 253 is the General Court record for March, May and June, 1639. Page 254 contains lists of freemen for May and June, 1639, and also the first part of the following Quarter Court record.]

The 4th day of the 4th month @ 1639   A Quarter Court held at Boston

pʳsent,
the Governoʳ
the Deputy Govʳ
Mʳ Endecott
Mʳ Bellingham
Mʳ Rich: Saltonstall
Mʳ Stoughton
Mʳ Bradstreete
Increase Nowell

Yᵉ following 3 pages omitted a[s] qʳᵗᵉʳ Courts †

Rich'd Silvester for speaking against the law about hogs & against a perticuler magistrate was fined ten pounds, whereof the three witnesses to have 6ˢ 8ᵈ a peece./

Henry Laurence was for the pʳsent discharged about Capt. Bonito his servant./ ‡

Mʳ Samuell Maverick being bound in ten pounds for the appearing of James Meadcalfe forfetted his recognisance.

Mʳ Nicho: Davison being bound in ten pounds for the appearing of Edward Saunders forfetted his recognisance./

John Stretton vpon evidence of his repentance was freed from his bond to the good behavioʳ wᵗʰ an admonition./

John Emerson appearing was discharged of his recognisance.

Thomas Bushrode haveing warned David Phippen, Joseph Androws, & Henry Coggan to appear at this Court, & himselfe not appearing to ꝑsecute the Court gave iudgment for 10ˢ a peece to bee alowed them, & if payment bee not made, execution to bee granted them.

Samuell Norman was Comitted for want of security, & was censured to be whipped, for saying if ministers wᶜʰ come will but raile against England some would receive them./

[255] Katherine the wife of Samu: ffinch ꝑmised to go to the ordinances, & to carry herselfe dutifully to her husband./

---

* First written Damport.
† This marginal entry is in Rawson's hand.
‡ See Lechford's Note Book, p. 51.

Mʳ John Harrison appearing was fined 10sˢ for his former not appearing, & admonished not to vse gameing./

John Palflin* for   was fined 20sˢ & vpon his submission hee was remitted 10ˢ, & paid in the other 10ˢ. I. N.†

John Gibons for   was fined 10ˢ by the Governoʳ Deputy, & Treasurer & paid it (to the Treasurer [oxi])‡

William Bartlet for distemperedness in drinking & lying was fined 20ˢ by the Governoʳ Treasurer, & Secretary./

Ellen Peirce was fined 40shˢ for Cursing & wicked imprecations, & to pay the 2 witnesses 2ˢ a peece./

Elisabeth Chaulkley ‖of Charlestowne‖ was enjoyned to give double restitution for the eggs & things wᶜʰ shee stoale./

All townes had respit to bring in the transcripts of their lands vntill the nexte Courte./

Mʳ Goouch of Newberry for selling strong water wᵗʰout leave was fined 10sˢ.

John Bayly was fined 5ˡ for buying land of the Indians wᵗʰout leave wᵗʰ condition if hee yeld vp the land to be remitted./

Edmond Greenliffe was referd to Ipswich Courte.

Thomas Hale § was also referd to the Court at Ipswich./

The p'sentment of Ipswich for defective high wayes was avoyded for want of witnes, & for vncerteinty.

Goodman ffoster & Henry Archer are referd to Ipswich Court.

Daniell Clarke is referd to Ipswich Courte also./

ffrancis Perry is referd to the Court at Salem.

John Elford & Willi: James had respite till the next Courte.

The wife of Hugh Burt was fined 40ˢ for cursing & swearing./

Adam Haukes is referd to the Court at Salem./

Edmond Audeley is referd also to Salem./

John Haule ¶ about correcting his boy was discharged./

Linn was fined 10ˢ for their bad wayes, & to mend them by the next Court, & to lay the ferry in a convenient place.

Robᵗ Longe was discharged for want of ꝓufe./

Mʳ John Woolrich & William Bachiler had respite till the next coʳt.

Charlestowne was discharged about Richʳd Lowdens lot./

---

* Paulflin in L. copy.
† These initials of Increase Nowell are not in the L. copy.
‡ These four words not in L. copy.
§ Hall in L. copy.
¶ Haul in L. copy.

Thomas Cornehill* was fined 30ˡ for severall offences selling wine wᵗʰout licence, & beare at 2ᵈ a quart. hee had warning the 10ᵗʰ 4ᵗʰ mº.†

Robert Turner was discharged for want of proofe./

Boston was fined 20sˢ for defective high wayes, & enioyned to repair them vpon the penalty of 5ˡ the stocks were ready compleate.

The widow Hudson was discharged, her husband being dead./

Roxberry was fined 10ˢ for daming vp the nearest way from Boston to Dorchester & had liberty till the next Court to make the way so as a loaden horse carrying a sack of Corne may passe./

Roxberry was fined 2ˢ 6ᵈ for the defectivenes of the bridge at Muddy Ryver & had liberty to amend it till the next Courte.

The pʳsentment of the bridge at Dorchester brooke is discharged for want of proofe./

Willi: Dennison & Thomas Wilson had liberty till the next Courte./

[256] Dorchester had liberty to vse Sergent Collicots house for a watch house./

The pʳsentments of Dorchester high wayes & bridges were discharged for want of proofe./

Nicho: Ellen was fined 40sˢ for idlenes & disorderly liveing & had liberty till the next court to settle himselfe./

Captaine Staughton was fined 40ˢ for releasing his man before the expiration of his time./

Waymoth was fined 10sˢ for their bad way at the steping stones & were enioyned to amend it by the next Court vpon paine of 5ˡ.

Thom: White had 10sˢ granted him being a witnes./

Mʳ Waltham & Mʳ Richʳds were fined 5ˢ for want of scales & weights in their mill, & to ꝑvide them by the next Courte.

Mʳ Waltham was fined 3ˡ for takeing too much tole in some aboue double what was dew, whearof 20ˢ to bee given the witnesses.

Ralfe Allen was fined 10ˢ for releasing a servant before the expiration of his time./

Hingham had liberty to vse their meeting house for a watch house.

Hingham was acquited from the pʳsentment about Thom: Turners lot it being but reserved for him./

Dedham was fined 2ˢ 6ᵈ for want of a paire of stocks./

fferdinando Adams was discharged the pʳsentmᵗ not beeing found oppʳssion./

---

* Cornell in L. copy.
† See Lechford's Note Book, p. 55.

Willi: ffuller, wch kept the mill at Concord was fined 3^l for grosse abuse in overtoaling./

The towne of Concord was discharged the lot* to Robert Edwards being but reserved for him.

Rob^rt ffletcher was discharged being not found faulty./

Concord was fined 5^s for want of a watch house.

Watertowne was fined 5s^s for want of a paire of stocks, & enioyned to prepare them by the next court, vpon paine of 40s^d./

John Gosse for comon railing was disfranchised, fined 20^l & comitted to prison./

Willi: Hamon not appearing attachment was granted for him.

Watertowne was discharged of the p^rsentm^t for the high way to the mill for want of proofe./

Watertowne is fined 10^s for the bad way at John Pages, & enioyned to make good the way vpon paine of 5^l./

Daniell Abbot is departed to new p^rvidence./

Cambridg is fined 5s^s for want of a pound./

Cambridg is discharged from the p^rsentment about stoping fish it being p^rsently reformed./

John Masters having licence was discharged./

Cambridg was fined 10^s for defective high wayes, & enioyned to repair them by the next Court vpon paine of 40s^s./

Cambrige was enioyned to repair their wayes at long swampe & vine brooke leading to Concord vpon paine of 5^l./

The p^rsentment of John Chairyes† wife was mistaken

The will of Joseph Harvy wth his inventory was delivered into the Court amounting to forty eight pounds 2^s & 9½^d.‡

The will of Mr Abraham Mallows was delivered in

M^r ‖John‖ Beniamin gave in the Account of Richd Gurling whereby onely 4^s appeareth remaining dew to widow Gurling.

[257] A Quarter Court held at Boston the 3th day of the 7th month @ 1639:

p^rsent
The Governo^r
The Deputy Govr
Mr Endecott
Mr Humfrey
Mr Bellingham

John Stacy iunior for being distempered with drinke was set in the stocks.

Ralfe Warriner was fined 10^s for being at excessive drinking at Thom: Grayes at Marble Heade./

---

* Of the lot in L. copy. † Cayries in L. copy. ‡ 9^d o^ḃ in L. copy.

Mr Saltonstall
Mr Winthrope, iuni
Mr Bradstreete
Mr Stoughton
Incr: Nowell.

Nicholas Merry was fined 40s^s for seling strong water.

John Neale for runing away and stealing was censured to bee severely whiped, & comitted to his master to bee kept chained./

Mr. Wades servant, Rich: Wilson, [s^c.]

Rich'd Wilson for stealing 8^l of money & diverse small things from his m^r Samuel Wade was censured to bee put fourth to servise for 3 or 4 yeares except hee can procure 10^l, also hee is to have a T set vpon his vpmost garment, the servise is to bee wth his m^r, if his m^r will have him, or else to bee put out by the Countrey./

Rich^{r}d Turner for being drunke was fined 20s^s./

Willi: Davies for sondry drinkings at his house was fined 3^l./

Robert Penyer is bound in 10^l to appear at the next Court. Thom: Turner & John White are bound in 5^l a peece for Peniars appearance.

Thom: Bushrode being accused of defaming the government was Comited & fined 6.13^s 4^d, wch paying to bee discharged./

Hugh Burt had 20^s of his fine remitted him, & pd in 20s^s & is discharged.

Marmaduke Peirce being accused of suspition of murther, & the matter not appearing cleare it was refered vntil the next quarter Court, & the Jewry was enioyned then to appeare.*

Daniell Clarke being found by the Jewry to be an imoderate drinker was fined 2^l whereof 3s^s was paid the Jewry, & the other 37^s pd I. N.

John Simpson was enioyned to pay Capt Jeanison 8^s, & Mr Browne 5s^s, haveing warned them to appear, & not psecuting./

John Wedgwood for being in the Company of drunkards was to bee set in the stocks at Ipswich./

Rich^{r}d Cooke is granted 20s^s against Thomas Robinson for vniust molestation./

Jarvise Mudge appearing ⋀

John Pemberton being warned by John Baker to appear at the Court at Boston, & Baker not appearing to psecute, the Court granted John Pemberton 50s^s damage./

John Kempe for filthy vncleane attemp[t]s wth 3 yong girles was censured to bee whiped both heare, at Roxberry & at Salem very severely & was Comitted for a slave to Leif^t Davenport/

---

* See Lechford's Note Book, p. 139. Also Winthrop I. 318.

Willi: Androws, who was formerly Comitted to slavery for his ill & insolent Carriage, is released (upon his good Carriage) from his slavery, & put to Mr Endecott hee ꝑmising to pay Henry Coggan 8^l, & so Androws is to serve Mr Endecot the rest of his time.

Mathewe Edwards for puting his hand vnder a girles Coates was censured to bee whipped.

Thom: Knore for selling a potfull of strong water wthout license was fined 5s^s.

·Nicholas Davison for swearing an oath was ordered to pay 20s^s, wch hee consented vnto.

John Hogg for his drunkennes was fined 10s^s.

John Kitchen for shewing books wch hee was comanded to bring to the Governo^r, & forbidden to shew them to any other, & yet shewed them to other was fined 10s^s.

[258] John Joanes for defileing his wife before marriage was fined 20s^s.

John Davies vpon his good Carriage was discharged from wearing the V wch was formerly enjoyned him./

Rich^r Silvester had 6^l of his fine respited vpon his good behaviour, & hee paid in the other 6^l./

Thom: Gray, for being drunke, prophaning of the name of god, keeping a tipling house, & drawing his knife in the Courte, was censured to bee severely whiped & fined 5^l.

Richrd Redman & Thom: Warner, for quarelling were fined 5^s a peece, & paid it in./

John Lee is discharged of his fine haveing paid 5^l formerly

Richrd Perry iunior was granted 5^l damages for the long wanting of the 27^l wch should have bene formerly p^d & was deferred vntill this weeke past, & the trouble about it.

Mr Thomas Lechford for going to the Jewry & pleading wth them out of Court is debarred from pleading any mans cause hereafter vnless his owne, & admonished not to p^{r}sume to meddle beyond what hee shalbee called to by the Courte.* [ordered]

William Gutrige † was enioned to take Care of Ales Burwood vntill hee may bee lawfully discharged of her.

Thomas Millard, Ephraim Pope, ffrancis Gold ‖& Thom: Burkbee‖ being watchmen drinking severall times strong water were imprisoned, & Burkbee &   were set in the stocks for being drunke.

---

* See Lechford's Note Book, p. 117.
† Gurtridge in L. copy.

Edward ffuller & Edward Convers were bound in 20¹ a peece for the appearing of Edward ffuller at the next Courte./

[On pages 259 to 269 is the General Court record for Sept. and Nov., 1639.]

[270]   the 31ᵗʰ of the 8ᵗʰ m°, 1639:

A Court held at Boston for small Causes not exceeding 20ˡⁱ except for strangers

prsent,
The Governor
The Deputy Govr
Mr Bellingham
Mr Stoughton
& Incr: Nowell.

John Woolrige for his drunkennes was fined ten pounds whereof 8¹ was paid mee In: Nowell, & 2¹ is in the hands of Mr Coddington.

Rich'd Joanes for his Cheating, was censured to bee whiped, & put to the assigne of the party wronged to make satisfaction for the money wᶜʰ hee did receive, & hath spent.

Edward Convers brought in Edward ffuller, & stands bound againe for him to appear at the next Court./

John Johnson is by order of Court freed from training paying ten shillings p annum to the company./

Thomas Marriner (servant formerly to Robert Smyth) is for the prsent discharged vnlesse his master hereafter can shew sufficient Cause to the Contrary./

Willi: Powell for resisting the surveyar is fined 40sˢ./

John Clois is admonished to vse his servant Peter Tylls well, or else the said Peter to bee discharged, & to take course, that hee may bee taught his trade of a seaman by himself or others

Mr Israell Stoughton being formerly fined 40sˢ is discharged of the same it being remitted because hee could not hould his servant haveing no Covenant./

Robert Penyar appearing his surety was discharged: but an attachment was granted against Penyar for going away vndischarged.

Edward ffuller & Thomas Sheppe for being distempered wᵗʰ wine were enioyned to appear at the next Court./

Richard Penne not Appearing forfected his recognizance of ten pounds./

the 8ᵗʰ Day of the 9ᵗʰ month @ 1639

Thomas Symonds was enioyned to appear at the quarter Court about Mr Eatons house, & the Colledge.

Robᵗ Driver was enioyned to appear at the quarter Court./

Abraham Morell was enioyned to appear at the quarter Court./

Tacye for swearing was fined 10sˢ wᶜʰ Mr Trerice vndertooke.

[271] A Court of Assistants or Quarter Court held at Boston the 3th of the 10th m°, 1639:

present,
the Governo^r
the Deputy Govr
Mr Endecott
Mr Bellingham
Mr Humfrey
Mr Saltonstall
Mr Winthrope, iu:
Mr Stoughton
& Incr: Nowell.

Mr John Hogges* was remitted three pounds of his fine of five pounds.

An Attachment was granted against the wife of Sam: ffinch for her appearance at the next Court./

Rich^rd Pepper for his extortion was fined 5^l./

The towne of Roxberry for neglect of their order about swine was fined ten pounds: but they are to bee exempted, wch did endeavo^r to execute the order.

James Luxford being p^rsented for haveing two wifes, his last marriage was declared voyde, or a nullity thereof, & to bee divorced not to come to the sight of her whom hee last tooke, & hee to bee sent away for England by the first opportunity, all that hee hath is appointed to her whom hee last married, for her, & her children, hee is also fined 100^l, & to bee set in the stocks an houre vpon a market day after the lecture, the next lecture day if the weather ꝑmit, or else the next lecture day after.

Mr Samu: Maverick paid in 5^l of his recognisance of 10^l the other was respited, till it appear whether it may bee recovered from James Meadecalfe.

the Iury which went vpon Peirce
Nicho: Willis
Robert Scot
John Button
Griffin Bowen
Willi: Dade
Steven ffosditch
James Garret
Rob^rt Cutler
Willi: French
Thom: Brigham
Rob^rt Saund^rs
Rog^r Shawe

a.

Marmaduke Peirce being indited vpon suspition of murther was found not guilty; but was bound to the good behavio^r, & to appeare at the next Court, & to pay the witnesses, & Nico: Davies was bound in 20^l for his appearance./†

Elnor Peirce her husband was bound in 10^l for her good behavio^r, & to bring her to stand in the market place the next market day wth a paper for her light behavio^r.

Quick was appointed to stand in the market place wth a paper for her light behavio^r the next 5th day.

a.

Lewes Hewlet for his extortion was fined 20s^s, & was bound over in 10^l to the ~~next~~ Court ‖the first month‖ for his contemptuous speaches./

Jane Robinson for disorder in her house, drunkennes, & light behavio^r was censured to bee severely whiped./

---

* Hoggs in L. copy.
† See Lechford's Note Book, p. 139. Also see Winthrop I. 318.

Margaret Hindersam* was censured to stand in the market place wth a paper the next market day, for her ill behavio^r, & her husband was bound in 5^l for her good behavio^r, & to bring her to the market place at the time appointed for her to stand there./

Thomas Dickerson was censured to bee severely whiped, & condemned to slavery./

Robert Penyar for his vnclean attempt, & his flying when hee should have appeared was censured to bee whiped./

John Vaughan is to appear at the next Court./

a.
Isaac Deesbro is bound in 10^l to appear at the next Court at Salem, & at the next quarter Court at Boston.

a.
John ffarrington is bound wth Deesbro in 10^l for his appearance./

[272]   Mr Thomas Allen appearing was discharged the painting being before his time, & disliked of him./

Sa.
The towne of Salem, for not keeping Constant watch ‖this sumer‖ was fined 10s^s./

An Attachment was granted against Ipswich because none appeared to answer for their defective wayes, & 10s^s costs./

Concord for not giveing in a transcript of their lands was fined 5s^s, & for neglecting their watch 10s^s./

Dedham for want of weights & measures was fined 5s^s.

Cambridge for defect of the way at Vine brooke & long swampe are referd to the former fine of 5^l.

And for want of stocks are fined 5s^s.

And for neglect of a constant watch are fined 10s^s.

442
Charlestowne meeting house is alowed for a watchhouse.

Linn for not keeping constant watch is fined 10s^s.

And for want of sealed weights is fined 5s^s.

And for not giveing in a transcript of their lands 5^s.

Boston for defect of their wayes between Powder Horne Hill & the written tree is fined 20s^s & enioyned to mend them.

Dorchester for not bringing in a transcript of their lands are fined 5s^s.

Waymoth for want of a sufficient watch house is fined 5^s.

And for neglect of keeping constant watch is fined 10^s.

And for not delivering in a transcript of their lands is fined 5s^s.

---

* Hindersham in L. copy.

And ‖Waymoth‖ for not looking to the execution of their order about swine Waymoth is fined 3ˡ.

Hingham for not making sufficient fences is fined 5sˢ & hath time to mend their fences till the 4ᵗʰ month./

And for defect in their high wayes are fined 10sˢ.

And for not keeping Constant watch Hingam is fined 10sˢ.

Leifᵗ Duncan is appointed to take an Inventory of the goods of Sarah Lishe — to pay the legacies, & to keepe the rest till further order./

The Governoʳ had leave to keepe a Naviganset* Indian, & his wife./

[273] A Courte held at Boston the 30ᵗʰ of the 11ᵗʰ mᵒ 1639:

present,
the Governoʳ
the Deputy Govʳ
Mʳ Bellingham
Mʳ Humfrey
& Increase Nowell.

William Waltham for being drunke aboard the ship called the Bristowe Marchant, wᶜʰ hee confessed was fined twenty shillings it being the first time that hee was knowen to bee drunke, & so was seriously admonished, & dismissed. ‖This 20ˢ was paid in‖

John Vaughan haveing defiled & refused to marry her was Comitted to prison till hee should give sufficient security to ꝑvide both for the mother & the Child, or marry her whom hee hath defiled./†

A Court of Assistants held at Boston for a Quarter Court the 3ᵗʰ day of the first month 1639–1640:

present,
the Governoʳ
the Deputy govʳ
Mʳ Bellingham
Mʳ Humfrey
Mʳ Winthrope iuni:
Mʳ Saltonstall
Mʳ Bradstreete
Mʳ Stoughton
& Incr: Nowell.

Richᵈ Pepper his fine of 5 pounds is remitted to 6ˢ 8ᵈ wᶜʰ hee paid

Thom: Davenport for huiring John Parish to cast baules of paste wᵗʰ Copperas in them, & cast it into a mans yard was admonished seriously to take heed of doing the like.

There is ten pounds delivered the Governoʳ by one that had failed by taking too great prizes for his Comodities ‖hee‖ havᵍ. satisfied the parties whom hee sould the Comodities vnto./

Thom: Blumfeild is appointed administratoʳ to his father John Blumfeild deceased & to have the house & ground, & the lame daughter to have the overplus of the goods not disposed of./

the will & inventory to bee recorded./

---

* Narhiganset in L. copy.
† These last seven words not in the L. copy.

Samu: Basse his fine of 5ˡ vpon his petition was remitted him

Micha: Iver being called, & not appearing forfected his recognisance.

This Courte gave way to the Governoʳ to free his servant Thom: Philips so far as they have power.

Hester Ketcham is freed from her servise wᵗʰ her mʳ John Woolrige, & the said mʳ enioyned to give   Ketcham 20sˢ charges & the said mʳ, John Woolrige, is bound to his good behavioʳ, & enioyned to appear at the Court the 7ᵗʰ mº next, & to put in sufficient caution for the good behavioʳ & appearance.

Mʳ John Coggan had authority given him to receive of Mʳ Willi: Tyng 9. 8sˢ for wᶜʰ Mʳ Coggan is to free Mʳ Ting as the Court shall direct, & bee responsall for the same./

John Knight is bound in 5ˡ to appear at the Court at Boston the 2ᵈ month.

John Dunvard bound his land, & 20ˡ more to appear at the next Court.

Lewes Hewlet, not appearing forfected his recognisance of 10ˡ.

Isaack Deesbro & John Farrington forfected their recognisance.

Marmaduke Peirce appearing was discharged being enioyned to pay the witnesses as hee should bee able.

Mʳ Henry Seawall for his Contemptuous speach & carriage to Mʳ Saltonstall was enioyned to acknowledg his fault publikely at Ipswich Court, & to bee of good hehavioʳ, & was enioyned to appear at the next quarter Court vnles the Court of Ipswich do release him from the good behavioʳ & from his appearance at the quarter Court. hee bound him selfe in 66ˡ 13ˢ 4ᵈ for his appearance & good behavioʳ./

[274]   The 30ᵗʰ of the 2ᵈ month @ 1640

A perticuler Court held at Boston for small Causes.

present,
The Governor
The Deputy Govʳ
the Treasu: Mʳ Bel: *
Mʳ Stoughton
& Increase Nowell.

Thomas Buckmaster being in distres is granted thirty bushells of corne, & money to make it vp ten pounds, wᶜʰ was appointed to be paid him by the treasurer.

John Clare is fined 20sˢ for being drunke, wᶜʰ Christofer Grant vndertooke to satisfy.

John Pope for his unchast attempt upon a girle, & dalliance wᵗʰ maydes, & rebellios or stubborne carriage against his master was censured to bee severely whiped.

---

* Mʳ Bel: not in L. copy.

John Danvard being accused of uncleannes was bound in 20¹ to appear at the Court the 4th month vnles hee avoyde out of Waymoth before that, & to pay the Cunstable 20ˢ for witnesses.

George Palmer having comitted folly wth Margery Rugs through her allurement, because hee confessed volentarily, hee was onely set in the stocks, & so dismissed.

Margery Rugs for intiseing & allureing George Palmer was censured to bee severely whiped.

Charles towne haveing chosen Robᵗ Longe to sell wine this Court doth alow him till the quarter Court.

Boston haveing chosen William Hudson to keepe an ordinary this Court doth alow him till the quarter Courte.

Nathaniell Travell appearing was admonished to acknowledg his offence in his scandolos & slaunderos speaches of severall psons, wᶜʰ hee ꝑmised to do, & to take advise, & so the Court discharged him upon triall./

[Pages 275 to 280 contain the record of the General Court 13 May, 1640. Page 281 contains lists of freemen for May and September, 1640.]

[282] At a quarter Court houlden at Boston the 2th day of the 4th mo @ 1640:

pʳsent,
Mʳ Deputy Bel:,
Mʳ Winthrope, seni
Mʳ Endecott
Mʳ Humfrey
Mʳ Winthrope iuni
Mʳ Saltonstall
Mʳ Stoughton
Incr: Nowell.

Leonard Bowtle * for neglecting to obey a warrant served by the Cunstable was fined 10sˢ./

Mʳ Browning for seling strong water was fined 5ˢ witn: to ha: 2ˢ of it

Mʳ Tynge & Mʳ. Davison are desired to examine the accounts between Mʳ Joanes & Mʳ. Mayhewe./

Muddy River bridge.† The Charge of Muddy ryver bridge being 15ˡ 3ˢ 6ᵈ was ordered to bee alowed as followeth By Boston, 6ˡ: by Roxberry 5ˡ: Dorchester 1ˡ 7ˢ 8ᵈ Watertowne 1. 7. 11ᵈ Cambridge 1ˡ 7ˢ 11ᵈ./

George Hurne is Comited to bee layd in yrons & to bee whiped to morrow for his insolent & contemptuous carriage.

John Hogge not appearing ₍ₐ₎

James Davies for his unquietnes wth his wife was enioyned to appear at the next Court of Assistants.

---

* Buttolph in L. copy.
† In modern hand.

Henry Chapman for not obeying a presse was fined 5s^s.

Mr John Woodbridg is discharged of his p^{r}sentment for releasing a servant paying 2^s 6^d.

Robert Tucker for upbraiding James Brittain calling him lyar, & saying hee could que him so being a witnes, was fined 20^s, & enioyned to acknowledg the wrong hee had done Brittaine.

Mr Peter Bulkeley is granted the Corne of Alexander Thwayte & to bee responsall for it if hee come to answere the suite./

Willi: Powell for his sinn in geting his wife wth child before marriage was fined 40s^s. Deniing it often, & [a]* confessing.

Thom: Gray was censured to bee severely whiped for his drunkennes & other misdemeano^{rs} at Marbleheade, wch Mr Endecot tooke the Care of by undertaking it.†

gooddy ffinch was censured to bee severely whiped to morrow, & so kept in prison./

Thom: Savory for breaking a house in the time of exercise was censured to bee severely whiped, & for his theft to bee sould for a slave vntil hee have made double restitution.

Henry Allein & Clement Weaver for drunkennes were fined 10s^s a peece.

Mr Barnard for giveing a gallon of strong water amongst certein persons at worke at his house wherof Allen & Wever were two was fined 3^l.

Robt Abels busines is refered to Mr Stoughton to inquire.

Elisabeth Lovel was admonished for her imodest exp^{r}ssions, enioyned to pay the witnesses, & so was dismissed./ ‡

John Downham for geting his wife wth child before marriage was fined 20s^s./

Hingham being p^{r}sented for defective wayes & bridge, & the Court being certified by hen: Smyth that they are mended they were fined 2^s 6^d, & discharged./

Edward Converse was fined 10^s because the ferry had bene neglected./

Thomas Bell being setled since the p^{r}sentment is respited.

the way of Dorchester being p^{r}sented is deferd to veiwe.

Mr Rich^{r}d Dumer for want of weights & scales [w^{ch}] were supplied 5^s.

---

* After in L. copy.
† See Lechford's Note Book, p. 149.
‡ These last nine words not in L. copy.

Neweberry for want of towne weights & measures fined 6. 8ᵈ.
Salem for neglecting their watch was fined 10sˢ:

[283]   The 30ᵗʰ of the 5ᵗʰ m° 1640

pʳsent,
the Governoʳ
the Deputy go:
Mʳ Winthrop, se:
Mʳ Stoughton
Incr: Nowell.

John Tower for his disturbance of the peace & his offence thereby against the Comōn welth is fined five pounds:

Two indian weomen were adiudged to bee whiped for their insolent carryage, and abusing Mʳˢ Weld./

Elisa: Bennet was censured to bee whiped for her unchast miscarriage

Mʳ John Hogges for his drunkennes is fined five pounds

John White is bound in 10ˡ for to bee of good behavioʳ, & not to come into the Compª of Bulls wife alone, & to appear at the quarter Court the first 3ᵗʰ day of the 10ᵗʰ m° next

John Wily & George Orrice bound themselues in 5ˡ a peece for the forenamed John White

Hope the Indian was censured for her runing away, & other misdemeanoʳ to bee whiped hear & at Marble heade.

Isaack Hart bound himselfe in 20ˡ to bee of good behavioʳ & Mʳ Roḃt Saltonstall bound himselfe in 10ˡ for the said Isa: Hart his good behavioʳ till hee deṗt out of the plantation, or bring a note frō that hee is free from fear.

Joell Jenkin is bound over to the next genʳall Court for geting his mʳ. his daughter wᵗʰ child:

The 20ᵗʰ of the 3ᵗʰ m° @ 1640

pʳsent,
the Deputy go:
Mʳ Winthrop, se:
Increase Nowell.

Henry Illery being drunke the night before, & calling Walter Merry knave, & saying further to him a member a dog hee was fined 10ˢ, & to go to prison till hee have paid it./

John Barnes likewise : for being distemped with wine was fined 10sˢ:

Daniell Hutchins bound himselfe in 10ˡ to appear at the Court to answer for neglect of the 2 children in the ship, wᶜʰ were comīted to him./

Willi: Kilcup & Rich: Haines bound themselues in 5ˡ a peece for the appearance of Dani: Huchins.

6ᵗʰ m° 27 Henry Bright tooke his oath for to discharge the place of survayar of the armes in Watertowne this year, & till a new bee chosen.

[284] A quarter Court held at Boston the first of the 7ᵗʰ mº 1640:
A Record of a former business.

present,
the Governoʳ
the Deputy goː
Mʳ Winthrope, seː
Mʳ Endecott
Mʳ Humfrey
Mʳ Stoughton
Mʳ Bradstreete
Mʳ Winthrope, juː
Increase Nowell
Mʳ. Saltonstall.

In the matter between Andrewe Coleman & Williː Swift, it is ordered by the Court, that whereas the said Andrewe Coleman by his letter of attorney dated the   day of   anno Dñi 1636 made unto John Haynes Esqʳ gave him the said John Haynes powʳ & authority to sue & compound wᵗʰ the said Williː Swift for & upon one bond of Cˡ bearing date the   day of   in the yeare ∧ wherein the said Williː Swift as a surety was bound wᵗʰ Roger Spring principall debtoʳ, & Josua Smyth another suerty for the paymᵗ of fifty two pounds unto the said Andrew Coleman upon a certeine day past, & thereupon the said John Haynes agreed, & compounded wᵗʰ the said Williː Swift, And the said Williː Swift morgaged his house, & lands at Watertowne aforesaid unto the said John Haynes in behalfe of the said Andrew Coleman by one deed, or writing dated in or about the month of   in the year 1636 aforesaid. And wheras the said Williː Swift alleageth that the said Andrew Coleman hath already recovered for part of the said debt the sume of eighteen pounds & five shillings from John Smitheman, & Williː Stacy iunior of Bocking Clothiers, wᶜʰ they owed to the said Williː Swift, & that since the said morgage made, the said Andrew Coleman hath contrary to the said agreemᵗ arrested, & troubled the said Williː Swift in England for the said debt, & recovered from him seaven pounds & ten shillings more, wᶜʰ in all being twenty five pounds, & fifteen shillings cometh to halfe the said debt, wanting but five shillings, & that halfe thereof is as much in equity as hee being a surety wᵗʰ another ought to pay, & the other surety the said Joseph * Smith being a man of sufficient estate ought to pay the other halfe, This Court hath ordered, that the possession of the said house, & lands shall remaine in the hands of the said John Haynes till midsomer next, to the end the said Williː Swift may make what proofe hee can of the pʳmises in the mean time, and then this Court will set downe a finall order in the pʳmises, as shalbee agreeable to equity.†

If the Court bee pleased to record this order I consent to it.

Joː Haynes.‡

---

* Josua in L. copy. In Lechford's Note Book it is Josiah.
† See Lechford's Note Book, p. 174.
‡ This signature as well as the record is in the hand of the Secretary.

John Woolrige appearing was discharged frō his band haveing carried himselfe orderly for ought wee heare

John Porter & Henry Tuttle being chosen cunstables of Hingham did take the oathe to them belonging.

Thomas Tylestone, & Edward Winshot were fined 6^s 8^d a peece for not attending the iury when they were called

It was referd to Mr Willi: Tynge & Mr Willi: Peirce to examine the books about the goods wch came in the Charles was* are wanting of persons absent./

Thomas Baguley for seeking to get a mayde wthout her freinds consent is bound to his good behavio^r, & if hee trouble her by p^{r}fering any newe suite, or make any disturbance, it is to bee accounted a breach of the good behavio^r./

Rich^{r}d Cluffe for saying shall I pay 12^d for the fragments wch the grandiury roages have left hee was bound to his good behavio^r & fined three pounds, sixe shillings, & eight pence, wch was discounted by Mr Rob^{r}t Saltonstall upon account.

Edmond Mathewe was admonished to take heede of pilfering.

Mr Samu: Maverick bound himselfe in 120^l for the Comp^a of the Charles to answer such actions as are or shalbee brought.

[285] Thomas Dickinson is discharged from his slavery & comīted to Ensigne Rich^{r}d Walker./

John Turner & William Rich^{r}ds are referd to Mr Ginner & Thomas White to settle things betweene them.

Evan Thomas haveing a wife, & four children is alowed twenty bushells of corne at harvest, & what necessary charge goodm̄ Button is at to bee alowed him.

Jonathan Hatch was censured to bee severely whiped, & for the p^{r}sent is comīted for a slave to Leift Davenport.

Rec^d òf Ipswich for their attachment 10^s they haveing set out newe highwayes nearer then the former, as they informed./

Walter Merries two servants were censured to bee whiped for runing away, & delivered to their maister./

450— Mr Atherton Hoffe,† Mr Thom: Leveret, & Mr Thom: Colebron, have authority, & order to sell the house & ground, wch was Mr Mellows to bee disposed of by them for the good of the sixe children till they come to age, or marry, & the eldest sonne to have a double portion.

---

* So in the original. It is *what* in L. copy.   † Haugh in L. copy.

Mr Samu: Winslew* is sworne surveyar of the armes at Colechester.

John Gosse had ten pounds of his fine of 20ˡ remitted.

John Burrows for going into other mens houses in the night & upon the lords day in the time of exercise was censured to bee whiped./

the 8ᵗʰ Day of the 8ᵗʰ mᵒ 1640

John Knight for his drunkennes swearing, & other disorder was censured to bee severely whiped./

Daniell Houchens † haveing given satisfaction to the father of the children wᶜʰ were neglected is freed from his attendance at the Courte any further./

15. John Davies, & Henry Messenger are bound in 20ˡ a peece, & each for other to appear at the next generall Courte.

John Crabtree Willi: Hudson & John Hill ‡ bound themselues in 20ˡ a peece that what shalbee adiudged by the Courte to bee overpaid shal bee returned to Mr Hibbens./

[On pages 286 to 292 is the record of the General Court for October, 1640.]

[293] A perticuler Court held at Boston the 29ᵗʰ 8ᵗʰ mᵒ 1640:

pʳsent,
the Governoʳ
the Deputy Govʳ
Mr Winthrope, seni:
Mr Isra: Stoughton
& Incr: Nowell.

Henry Edwards, & Willi: Hudson are discharged from their recognisance./

Beniamin Pauly for his distemper wᵗʰ wine was ordered to pay 10ˢ, & paid in the same./

Nicho: Davison byll of 200ˡ being delivered into the Court by　　Sill was ordered to bee kept by the secretary.

Joseph Shawe & Nicho: Byram are granted administration of the goods of Abraham Shawe deceased./

Willi: Hamond deposed that Edmond Greenliffe served him wᵗʰ warrants to appear at two Courts, & causing him to appear did not ꝓsecute. Hamond was granted against the said Greenliffe 20sˢ.

John Porter, John Ottis, Thom: Minard, & Natha: Baker being called to bee witnesses were granted 6ˢ a peece &　　　Graves § 1ˢ all to bee paid by the Country./

John Dutton for swearing, stealing, & drunkennes was censured to bee severely whiped./

John Parker was granted 20ˢ against Thom: Clay for not ꝓsecuting, causing him to attend 3 dayes wᵗʰ witnesses./

---

* The final w seems to have been cancelled. It is Winsley in L. copy.
† Hutchins in L. copy.　　‡ John Hill not in L. copy.　　§ Or Geaves.

Attachment was granted to Thomas ffowle against Thomas Owen to attach such goods as are in his possession for performance of his bargaine of corne./

It is ordered Mr Stoughton should heare busines betweene Rich'd Lange, & the towne of Waymoth, & Mr Stoughton hath power to call for the towne booke, & make report to the co^rt if the cause do require it./

[294] A quarter Court held at Boston the first day of the 10th m^o 1640

p^rsent,
Mr Governo^r
Mr Deputy
Mr Winthrope, seni:
Mr Humfrey
Mr Saltonstall
Mr Winthrope, iuni:
Mr Stoughton
& Increase Nowell.

The towne of Cambridge upon ꝑufe that the way at vine brooke & long smap* was repaired before the declaration of the defect was discharged of the fine of 5^l.

Watertowne ffreemen promising to yeld to ev^ry townsman his ꝑportion alike according to rule, w^thout respect to freedome or not freedome were dismised

George Richardson is bound to the good behavio^r in 20^l, & to appear at the quarter,† the 10th m^o 1641. Henry Curtis & Willi: Knope are bound for George Richardson [in 10^l.]

Giles Player haveing taken from the deputy governo^r a boate & other things of 15^l valewe, & from Leift Davenport the worth of 5^l hee is comitted to them till they bee satisfied./

Joell Jenkin upon his repentance was discharged./

Rob^rt Rendall is deferd till the next quarter court./

The towne of Braintree were enioyned to make their pound, stocks, & watchouse by the quarter court in the first month.

Dorchester, & Roxberry the bridge, & way being repaired were discharged./

Boston the wayes being newe layde out had time to repair them between powder horne hill & the written tree till the ^

Mr Thomas Lechford acknowledging hee had overshot himselfe, & is sorry for it, ꝑmising to attend his calling, & not to meddle wth controversies was dismised.‡

Willi: Bartlet the pilfering not being ꝑued was discharged newe sumons was to bee sent for Robert Bartlet./

Charlstowne meeting house was formerly alowed for theire watch house./

---

* So in the original. *Swamp* in L. copy.
† Co^rt in L. copy. ‡ See Lechford's Note Book, pp. 117, 176.

Samuell Dunkin there being a mistake in the presentment as appeared by the witnes was discharged./

Concord & Sudberry in regard of the snow were deferd till the quarter Court in the first month./

Willi: Wake was councelled to go whom* to his wife, & upon his p̄mise so to do, his repentance, & testimony of his good behavio^r hee was discharged./

Salem.†   Salem meeting house is alowed for their watch-house.

Robert Crosse is remited to Ipswich Court./

James Hubberd is discharged the hurt being little, & done unwiting the other pressing in upon him./

Linn was enioyned upon paine of 10^l to repair their wayes by the quarter court in the 4th m° next./

Lin.†   Linn meeting house is alowed for their watch-house.

Rowley p^rsentments are deferd till the quarter court in the next first month.

Colechester p^rsentm^{ts} are deferd till the quarter court the first month.

Hampton p^rsentm^{ts} are deferd till the quarter c^rt p° m°.‡

Hingam.†   Hingham meeting house for the p^rsent is alowed for their watch house.

Christopher Batte for selling his servant his time is referd to the Court at Ipswich.

It was ordered that John Twogood should bee sent to his dame the wife of Thomas Marshfeild at Conecticot by Rob^{rt} ffeñ, the father of the said Twogood haveing put him a servant to Tho: Marshfeild.

[295]   the com̄ission about Mr Edmond White & Mrs Woolcote § is renued for Mr Deputy Bellingham, Incr: Nowell, & Mr Thomas Mayhewe to examine the accounts.

Mr Collens, Mr Sparhauke, & goo: Bridge¶ are desired to heare businesses betwen John Smyth, & his father Jeremy Norcros, & examine accounts, & settle things if they can, if not to make report to the Courte, if there bee cause./

Henry Stevens for fiering the barn of his m^r, Mr John Humfrey hee was ordered to bee servant to M^r. Humfrey for 21 years from this day toward recompencing the losse./

---

* Home in L. copy.   † In modern hand.   ‡ Quarter Court the first moneth in L. copy.
§ Wolcott in L. copy.   ¶ John Bridge in L. copy.

Samu: Hefford* haveing bene much misused by his m{^{r}}. Jonathan Wade hee is freed from the said M{^{r}} Wade, & is put to John Johnson for three yeares, & to have 6{^{l}} wages p @, & for the other 1½ years it is referd to the court./

Rich{^{r}}d Nicoles case is referd to the Court at Ipswich

Daniell Bacon is granted 10{^{s}} costs against Rich: Neve because hee served him w{th} a warrant, & p{^{r}}secuted not./

George Rich{^{r}}dson is granted 10{^{s}} costs against James Smyth hee haveing served him w{th} a warrant p{^{r}}secuted not.

Jonathan Wade is bound in 40{^{l}} to bee of good behavio{^{r}}:

M{^{r}} Rich{^{r}}d Parker for seling ½ lb or ¾ lb of gunpowder‖ to an Indian‖ being ignorant of the law against it is respited til the gen{^{r}}all co{^{r}}t.

M{^{r}} Henry Webbe his man Roger T[o]le for seling 2 lb of gunpowder to an indian not knowing the law is respited till the gen{^{r}}all co{^{r}}t

John Stowe for seling shot ‖ to an indian ‖ not knowing the law is respited

M{^{r}} Thom: Clarke his man seling 8 lb of shot to an indian is respited

Rich{^{r}}d Collecot forgeting the‖ law‖ against mending indians guns haveing got 2 of their locks to bee mended is respited for his fine till the next gen{^{r}}all co{^{r}}t

Micha: Willis is discharged being ignorant whose the locks were./

M{^{r}} Henry Waltham his sonne being lately dead, & hee discovering his sonne had given 3{^{l}} to the publike though no other knew of it was discharged./

goo: Button is alowed 10{^{l}} 8{^{s}} 9{^{d}} for the charge w{th} Tho; Evans.

Bewet, for heresy, banisht.

the Jury found Hugh Buets† to bee gilty of heresy, & that his person & errors are dangeros for infection of others.‡

It was ordered that the said Hugh Buet should bee gone out of o{^{r}} iurisdiction by the 24{th} p{^{r}}sent upon paine of death, & not to returne upon paine of being hanged./

the Court granted the iury 12{^{s}} for their servise

Jury y{$_t$} tryed Buets.

the names of the Jury that tryed Buets

Edward Rainsford	John Rugells
James Browne	Griffin Crofte
John Martin	Isaack Johnson
John Haule	Jonathan Negus
Thom: Goble	Rich{^{r}}d Trusdell
Daniell Brewar	Christo: Gibson

---

* Hofford in L. copy. † Buett in L. copy. ‡ See Winthrop II. 19.

It was ordered that Alexander Beck should have 24 bushels of corne for Mary Joanes for the time past, & for the time to come a bushell of corne a weeke, & to have two blankets & a rug to keepe her warme./

[296]   A Court at Boston the 28th 11th mo 1640.

p'sent,
the Governor
the Deputy govr
Mr John Winthrope
se:
Mr John Humfrey
Mr John Winthrope,
iu:
& Increase Nowell.

The will of Ann Bunting was given in, & the witnesses depo: *

John Holland Edward Brecke, & John Sherman being returned for Iury men, & not appearing when they were called they were fined 5s a peece.

The will of † George Alcock was given in & the witnesses deposed, & also the praisers of the inventory were deposed.

Thomas Hawkins for his scurrillous speaches was enioyned attendance, but upon the petition of the gentlemen hee was remitted./

Samuell Haukes for swearing, cursing, lying, theft, & unclean speach, was censured to bee set an houre in the stocks to morrowe & have a clefte stick on his tongue while the Court thinks meete, & was comitted the meane while./

William Carpenter being chosen cunstable of Waymoth for the year ensuing tooke his oath to that place belonging./

John Hogg for his drunkennes, wastfulnes, & idlenes was censured to bee comitted to Leift Davenport till the next Court./

Walter Knight forfected his recognisance of 5l by not appearing

Thomas Dexter forfected his recognisance of 5l being bound for the appearance of Walter Knight, who appeared not

Mr. James Parker is alowed to marry Thomas Clifton & Mary Butterworth w(th)in a month:

Ordered by consent of Henry Waltham marchant, & Welthia ‡ the wife of Thomas Richards of Waymoth that all matters in difference hearafter mentioned shalbee referred to Mr Neweman, Mr Parker, & Edward Bates, of the same towne, who by this Court have power, or any two of them to appoint a miller to keepe the mill for both parties: to set downe an equall valewe for the rent of Mr Walthams part of the house, wch shee is to enioy till her husband returne (if hee returne this sumer) & to heare & determine all accounts, & reckenings betweene them, for wch end they, or any two of them have heareby authority to

---

* Deposed in L. copy.   † Mr. in L. copy.   ‡ Welthian in L. copy.

examine witnesses upon oathe, this to bee in force till the next Court of Assistants.*

[That part of the Library copy which is of records of a later date than the above, 28 Jan., 1641, appears to have been made, in part at least, by Samuel Symonds. See Transactions Colonial Society of Massachusetts, Jan., 1898 (page 144).]

[297] A quarter court held at Boston the 2th day of the first m^o 1640–1641 †

p^{r}sent,
the Gov^{r}no^r
the deputy go:
Mr Winthrope se:
Mr Endecott
Mr Humfrey
Mr Saltonstall
Mr Winthrop iu
Mr Stoughton
Mr Bradstreet
Incre: Nowell

Christopher Graunt for his cruell usage of his servant Nicholas Gilberd was fined ten pounds, & bound to his good behavio^r

Garret Church & John Stebben bound themselues in 20^l a peece for Grants good behavio^r till the next quarter court

Robert Stedman a iury man not appearing was fined 6^s. 8^d.

John Hogg upon the security of Samu: Grames, & Thomas Munte they haveing the goods in their possession for their security wch hee was let have to keepe till hee went for England, & then to deliver them to his use./

Walter Edmonds being chosen cunstable of Concord did take his oathe

Susan Starr is granted administration of the estate of her husband Thoma: Star, & the inventory of 49. 6. 9^d was shewed in co^{r}t

Rich^{r}d Hollingworth upon occation of the death of Rob^{r}t Baker was fined 10^l: to bee paid to the wife, & children of the said Rob^{r}t Baker his negligence being the occation of his death.

Rob^{r}t Bartlet appearing, & there appearing a mistake in the p^{r}sentment hee was discharged

Robert Rendall being tryed by the grand iury was not found gilty

Henry Palmer bound himselfe in 40^l for his wifes good behavio^r & appearance at the next quarter co^{r}t when free from being wth child, & fit to come abroad./

Mr John Morecroft is fined 20^l for his unfit carrige, & bound to his good behavio^r.

also the forenamed John Morecroft is to pay 20^l of the 40^l wch hee forfected for want of Will: Bell his appearance ‡

---

* See Lechford's Note Book, p. 195.   ‡ See Mass. Hist. Soc. Coll., 4th Series, Vol. 7, p. 308.
† See Winthrop II. 43, mentions presentment of Governor Bellingham.

Walter Knight appearing was fined 10¹ for his rude speaches and contemptuous ∧ For security hee made over a bill of 11¹

Rich^rd Ponton is put to John Reade for 8 yeares from the first of the 11th m° last past with his owne consent.

John George is put to Mr John Winthrope seni: for 8 yeares with his owne consent./

An attachment was granted against Nicholas Bacons cattle for the payment of his rent to Mr John Coggan./

sumōns & attachment was granted ag^t the estate of J^no Sampson.

the difference between Mr William Tynge & Mr Robert Tompson is referd to the arbiterment of M^r ffoule & Capt. Gibons.

Mr Rich^rd Dumēr had his fine of 5^s remitted the p^rsentm^t being upon a mistake as was testified:

Thomas Carter Senio^r, & Edward Joanes being chosen Cunstables for Charles towne did take the oath appointed for that place

John Johnson of Roxberry is freed from training in regard of other publike servise w^thout any pay to the Company./

[Blank space.]

Thomas Foxe was enioyned to pay 5^s or appear at the next court./

[298]   A Courte at Boston the 29th 2^d m° 1641:

p^rsent,
the Gov^rnor
the Deputy gov:
Mr Winthrop sen:
Mr Humfrey
Increase Nowell.

Rich^rd Wilson for his grosse abuse of his m^r. Thom: Cheesholme in base revileing speaches, & refusing to obey his lawfull commaunds was censured to bee severely whiped

Edward Page it being testified that his m^r. confessed hee was not to bee turned over, nor serve his wife if hee dyed the said Edw^a was freed by the Courte./

Mr Joseph Kinge for uncomely & obscean speaches was sharply reprehended, & for distemper in drinking wine hee was fined fourty shillings to bee paid w^thin ten dayes to the treasurer

Mr Henry Pitts for his uncomely speaches & obscean was sharply reprehended, & for distemper in drinking wine hee was fined fourty shillings to bee paid to the treasurer w^thin ten dayes.

William Browne for his obscean, & filthy speaches was sharply reprehended, & admonished not to use such base speaches./

Samu: Sherman was enioyned, & ꝑmised to appear at the next Court./

Thomas Turner, Thom: Collier, & John Sutton bound themselues in 40ˡ a peece to appear at the next court, to answer for the things taken up of John Hardies rack.*

Thomas Baguley, for seling his servant his time contrary to order of court was fined ten shillings./

Mighill Bacon senʳ upon the certificate of Richʳd Beres, Hugh Mason, Willi: Williams, & Thomas Hastings, that full satisfaction hath bene given was discharged, it being declared to bee a mistake of ignorance./

[Blank space.]

John Barnes for some distemp in drinking wine, was required to give 10ˢ, wᶜʰ hee consented vnto.

A quarter Court held at Boston the first of the 4ᵗʰ m° 1641:

pʳsent,
the governoʳ
the Deputy govʳ
Mʳ Winthrope
Mʳ Dudley˙
Mʳ Saltonstall
Mʳ Humfrey
Mʳ Bradstreet
Mʳ Winthrop iu
Mʳ Stoughton
Increase Nowell.

Edward Johnson of Charlstowne being warned to serve upon the iury (& not appearing) was fined 6ˢ 8ᵈ:

James Dane for makeing an indian drunk was fined 20sˢ.

Mʳ John Longe for his distemper in drinking & giving wine to others is fined 3ˡ.

A warrant was ordered to to examine all that tooke up any thing of the rack,* & send a perfect inventory, & in any thing doubtfull they are to take the advise of Mʳ Peck minister & Mʳ Newmã

John Whitney was chosen Cunstable of Watertowne & tooke oath

There was granted to Goodm̃ Nutt, Marten Vnderwood, John Whitney, Henry Kemball, & John Witheredge alowance for 83½ yʳd of cloth valewed at 12ᵈ ₚ yʳd

Joane Abell being pʳsented for being drunke it being found to bee a mistake shee was discharged./

Mʳ Edward Tomlins retracting his opinions against singing in the churches was discharged

Thomas Patience for want of proofe was referred to Mʳ. Endecot

Edward Adams was enioyned to returne to his wife./ & being questioned for other things was discharged for want of ꝓoffe.

the towne of Roxberry is enioyned to make a sufficient way between the buriing place & the gate upon paine of 20sˢ forf:

---

* Wrack in L. copy.

Roxberry is also enioyned to repair the other way over the swamp toward Dorchester mill upon paine of 20ˢ forfett.

Ipswich was enioyned to repair their wayes by the next qʳtʳ Court upon paine of forfeture of 10ˡ for the way to Salem. for theyr way toward Rowley they have 6 months to repair it./

[299] Cambridg was certified to have repaired the way towʳd Concʳd.

Cambridg for the way between Watertowne & Roxberry is inioyned to repair it wᵗʰin 6 mᵒ upon paine of 3. 6. 8ᵈ.

Waymoth defective way is certified to bee mended./

Salem is enioyned to amend the short swampe wᵗʰin a month & the other wayes wᵗʰin 6 months upon paine of 5ˡ.

Boston in inioyned to mend their wayes upon paine of 20ˢ.

Watertowne is discharged. & Liñ is discharged./

Salsberry was enioyned to amend their way upon paine of 20ˢ.

Salsberry for want of weights & measures is fined 2. 6ᵈ.

Rowley was enioyned to mend their way vpon paine of 20ˢ wᵗʰin a month./

Dorchester way to bee mended vpon paine to forfet 20ˢ.

Hampton for want of weights & measures is fined 2. 6ᵈ.

Concord to pay 10ˢ for neglecting watch & not appearance.

the wife of Robʳt Lewes * for her dishonoring the name of god was censured to bee whiped./

Enoch Hunt for his oppʳssing practice & extorsion was enioyned to make restitution, pay the witnesses, & was fined 3ˡ.

Waymoth is remited the 3ˡ fine about neglecting their hogs.

Roxberry is remited the 10ˡ fine for neglecting their hogs.

Robʳt Lewes & John Madox were discharged the pʳsentmᵗ being mistaken, their answer being iudged reasonable.

Jonathan Thing for ravishing Mary Gree[n]feild was censured to bee severely whiped heare & at Ipswich [& fined 20ˡ to bee paid in three yeares to Sam: Greenfeild.] †

Cambridge was enioned to give Squa Sachim so much corne as to make up 35 bushels, & 4 coates for the last year, & this.

Christopher Grant appearing was discharged frō further appance

John White appearing was discharged

John Skidmer is fined 10ˢ for seling strong water to Indians

Abraham Morrell is fined 5ˡ for seling his servant his time

Samu: Sherman is fined 20ˢ for selˢ his servant his time

---

* Lews in L. copy.

† This part within brackets not in L. copy.

the wife of Rich'd Carter appearing shee was admonished, & enioyned to bring her husband to bee bound for her good behavio'

Willi: Pilsberry & Dorothy Crosbey were bound to the good behavio', & to appear at the next Court bound in ten pounds

& hee was enioyned to ‖ worke wth ‖ goo: Wiswell 2 dayes in the weeke & goo: Cheny one day in the weeke for five yeares:

M' Bu'slin was referd to the Court at Salem

Davy * Hickbourne for his grosse misdemeano', & foule miscarriage was censured to bee severely whiped, to weare an iron coller till the co't please, & serve his m' 3 weekes longer for lost time, & trouble of his m'.

M' John Longe bound himselfe in 20¹ to bee of good behavio', & to appear at the next quarter court./

John & Elnor Peirce were admonished to see better order bee kept

Willi: Knop for selling bear 2 years unlicensed was fined 5¹.

Alexand' Becke was granted 8 bushells of corne more then a bushell a weeke for his trouble wth Mary Joanes.

Henry Webbe & George † Stoader cunsta: of Boston had granted them power to gather in the estate of Paul Yonge, & to pay the debts, & to give account:

John Barnes was enioyned to pay 10^s, or appear at the co't to answer for a second distemp in drinking too much, wch hee not appearing is to pay.

[Pages 300 to 312 contain the record of the General Court for June, 1641.]

[313]   the 29th 5th m° @ 1641

p^rsent
the Gov'no'
the Deputy
M' Winthrope
M' Dudley
M' Humfrey
M' Stoughton
Incr: Nowell.

At a co't at Boston George Bowen being absent when hee was called to serve upon the iury, was fined 5s^s.

James Laurence for goeing out of his m'. his house in the night unseasonablely ag^t his exp'sse order was censured to bee sharply whiped & also for keeping company wth a leaude woman./

William Pilsberry for defileing his m'. his house was censured to bee whiped./

Dorothy Pilsberry was censured to bee whiped for her uncleannes, & defileing her m'. his house./

---

* David in L. copy.   † George, changed to Anthony, in L. copy.

Mary Osborne for her grosse miscarriage in giveing her husband quick silver, & other abuses was censured to bee severely whiped./

Mary ffelton the wife of Beniamin ffelton for her severall thefts frō Mʳ Webbe, Mʳ Parker, Mʳ Stoader, & Mʳ Eldreds man to the valewe of 8. 15. 11ᵈ the things were restored, & her husband undertooke, & bound himselfe to restore the valewe of the goods taken away to each of them./

[Blank space.]

[314] A Quarter Coʳt at Boston the 07ᵗʰ 7ᵗʰ m° 1641

pʳsent,
the Governoʳ
the Deputy go:
Mʳ Winthrope, se:
Mʳ Dudley
Mʳ Humfrey
Mʳ Saltonstall
Mʳ Stoughton
Mʳ Bradstreete
Incr: Nowell

Thomas Carter senioʳ Cunstable of Charlstowne is fined 6. 8ᵈ for warning the iury men too late & for a rong day, wᶜʰ was two dayes too late.

Edward Larkin being warned to serve upon the iury, & not appearing is fined 5ˢ : ‖ This fine is remitted, the Cunstable mistaking, & warning for a wrong day.‖

The rates of wharfige & litrige are referd to the genʳall Court, to bee brought in by the towne of Boston:

Willi: Wells is enioyned in 10ˡ to answere for oppʳssion

Mʳ Nicholas Trerice for his miscarriage in Court, is fined fourtye shillings

Thomas Owen for his adulteros practises was censured to bee sent to the gallos wᵗʰ a roape about his neck & to sit upon the lather an houre the roapes end throwen over the gallos & so to returne to prison

Sara Hales the wife of Willi: Hales was censured for her miscarriage to bee carried to the gallos, wᵗʰ a roape about her neck, & to sit an houre upon the lather the roaps end flung over the gallos, & after to bee banished.

Willi: Lampson hath liberty to fell 300 trees, on the other side of Chebacco, so it bee not in the limits of any towne

Anthony Stoader confessing his fault in his unfiting speach to the governoʳ in affronting of him is fined 13⅓ˡ.*

Captaine John Vnderhill being indited upon ꝑclamation no witnesses comeing in hee was acquited.†

John Kilmaster, John Knop, & John Knight for their distemper were admonished, & dismissed./

Mʳ Samuell Maverick being found gilty of a confederacy wᵗʰ Thom:

---

* See Winthrop II. 38.   † See Winthrop II. 13, 41.

Owen to breake prison, consealing of it, & letting bee upon his iland was fined one hundred [1]:

Mr Chidley for confederating & consealing was fined 13⅓^l.

Mr Ducket for confederacy & consealing was fined 26⅔^l.

Mr Wollaston for consealing being privy was fined 13⅓^l.

Mr Oateley for consealing was fined 13⅓^l.

Thorne for consealing hideing & suppliing was fined 6⅔^l.

Willi: Cope for consealing was fined 6⅔^l.

Mary Wilbee for consealing & consenting was fined 6⅔^l.

Thomas Owen for ^escaping out of breaking prison was fined 20^l to bee paid w^thin a weeke, or to bee severely whiped.

Sara Hales for escaping to pay 13⅓^l or be whiped & banished

Mr Dutchfeild, Mr Williams, & Mr Hale were admonished to take heede of the like consealment.

Mr William Collens being found to bee a seducer, & his practices ꝓved such, hee is fined one hundred pounds, & to bee kept close prisoner till his fine bee paid, & then hee is * banished upon paine of death.†

Francis Hutchinson for calling the Church of Boston a whoare, a strumpet, & other corrupt tenents,‡ hee is fined 50^l, & to bee kept close prisoner till it bee paid, & then hee is § banished upon paine of death.†

Margery Mathew¶ widow of Thom: Mathew¶ is alowed to sell her husbands house, land, & goods toward paym^t of her husbands debts, reserving her necessary cloaths & beding, wch were hers before marriage being ꝑply her owne./

[The next record of the Court of Assistants in the L. copy is of the date 28 Oct. 1641. The record of the Court of Assistants as found in the first volume of the Colony Record ends here. The following is the answer of John Pratt and the action of the Court thereon referred to above under the date of November 3, 1635. (See the note on page 58.) This John Pratt record was paged at one time 77 and 78. It is now paged 9 and 10 in the original volume. (See above page 15.) The whole, including the signatures at the end, was written by the Secretary, Simon Bradstreet.]

[77]   The Answer of mee John Pratt, to such things as I he[are &] ꝑceave obiected against mee, as offensive in my lre.

ffirst geñally w^tsoeuer I writt of the imꝓbabilitie or impossibility of subsistance for o^rselues or o^r posterity without tempting god o^r with-

---

* Is to bee in L. copy.   † See Winthrop II., 38.   ‡ Tennets in L. copy.
§ Then to bee in L. copy.   ¶ Mathews in L. copy.

out extraordinarie meanes, it was with theis two regards first I did not meane that wch I said in respect of the whole Country, or o^r whole Pattent in geñall: but onely of that compasse of ground wherein theis townes are soe thicke sett togeather & secondly I supposed that they intended soe to remaine, because (vpon conferrence with divers) I found that men did thinke it vnreasonable that they or any should remove or disperse into other pts of the Countrie. And vpon this ground I thought I could not subsist myselfe, nor the Plantaĉon nor posteritie. But I doe acknowledge, that since my lre there have bene ~~foure~~ sundry places newly found out as Neweberry Concord & others (and that within this Pattent,) wch will afford good meanes of subsistance, for men & beasts, In w^ch & other such like newe plantaĉons, if the Townes shalbe fewer & the bounds larger then theis are, I conceave they may lyve comfortably. the like I thinke of Conecticott, with the plantaĉons there nowe in hand, & w^t I conceave soe sufficient for my selfe, I conceave soe sufficient also for my posteritie & concerneing theis Townes heare soe thicke planted, I conceave they may subsist, in case that besides the conveniences wch they have already neere hand, they doe impue ffermes somew^t further of, & doe also apply themselues to, & doe impue the trade of fishing, & other trades. As concerneing y^t intimaĉon of the Comonwealth builded vpon rocks sands & salte marshes, I wishe I hadd not made it, because it is construed contrarie to my meaneing, wch I have before expressed And whereas my lres doe seeme to extenuate the iudgem^t of such as came before, as haveing more honestie, then skill they being scollers, cittyzens tradsmen &c my meaneing was not soe geñall as the words doe import, for I had an eye onely to those, that hadd made larger reports into England of the Country then I found to be true in the sence aforesaid. And whereas I may seeme to imply, that I had altered the myndes or iudgem^ts of the body of the people, magistrates & others, I did not meane this in respect of the goodnes o^r badnes of the Land, in the whole plantaĉon, but onely in poynte of removeall, & spredding further into oth^r pts they afterwards conceaveing it necessarie, that some should remove into other places here & there of more inlargem^t. and whereas I seeme to speake of all the magistrates & people, I did indeed meane onely all those with whome I hadd any private speech aboute those things & as for the barrenes of the sandy grounds &c. I spake of the[m] as then I conceaved, but nowe by experience of myne owne, I finde that such ground, as before I accounted barren, [78] yet being manured & husbanded doeth bring forthe more fruict then I did expect. As for the not p̱sping of the Englishe graine vpon this ground, I doe since that time see that rye & oates haue p̱sped better than I expected, but as for the other kindes of graine, I doe still question whither they will come to such p̱fecc̃on as in o{^{r}} natiue countrie from whence they come. And whereas I am thought geñally to charge all that haue written into England, by way of comendac̃on of this land as if what they hadd written were geñally false, I meant it onely of such excessiue comendac̃ons, as I see did exceede, & a[re] contrary to that w{^{ch}} I haue here expressed.

And as concerneing that w{^{ch}} I said, that the gospell would be as deare here as in England I did it to this end, to putt some w{^{ch}} intended to come hither onely for outward comoditie, to looke for better grounds, ere they looke this way.

As for some grounds of my returneing, w{^{ch}} I concealed from my ffriends for feare of doeing hurt, I meant onely some p̱ticul{^{r}} occac̃ons & apprehencons of myne owne, not intending to lay any secrett blemishe vpon the state, and whereas I did expresse the danger of decayeing here in o{^{r}} first loue &c I did it onely in regard of the many folde occac̃ons & businesses, w{^{ch}} here att first wee meete withall, by w{^{ch}} I finde in my owne experience, (and soe I think doe others also) howe hard it is to keepe o{^{r}} hearts in that holy frame w{^{ch}} some tymes they were in, where wee hadd lesse to doe in outward things: but not at all intending to impute it as necessary to o{^{r}} condic̃on, much lesse as a fruicte of o{^{r}} precious liberties, w{^{ch}} wee enioy, w{^{ch}} rather tend to the quickening of vs, wee improueing the same as wee ought. This my answer (according with the inward consent & meaneing of my heart) I doe humbly com̃end to the fav{^{r}}able considerac̃on & acceptance of the Court desireing in this as in all things, to approue myselfe, in a conscience voyde of offence towards god & man.

John Pratt.

Of this answer of John Pratt before written, voluntarily by him made, as wee are witnesses, soe doe wee also ioyne w{th} him in humble desire vnto the Court that it may be fav{^{r}}ably accepted & what euer fayleings are in the łre in regard of the manner of expressions (w{^{ch}} may seeme hardly to suite w{th} theis his interpretac̃ons,) wee doe desire the indulgence of the Court to passe ouer without ffurther question/.

Peter Bulkeley ⎫
John Wilson ⎬
Thomas Hooker ⎭

Whereas John Prat of Newe Towne being called before vs att this pʳsent Court, & questioned for a lre wᶜʰ hee wrote into England, dated wherein hee raysed an ill report of this Countrie, did desire respite till the nexte day to consider of his answer, hee hath nowe deliūed in this before written, wᶜʰ vpon his free submission & acknowledgemᵗ of his error the Court hath accepted for satisfacc̄on & therevpon p̄doned his sᵈ offence, & gyven ordʳ. yᵗ it shalbe recorded & such as desire coppyes thereof may have the same/.

        John Haynes Goū̄nʳ.
        Rich Bellingham
        John Winthrop
        Tho. Dudley
        John Humfry
        Willm̄ Coddington
        Willm̄ Pinchon
        Atterton Houghe
        Increase Nowell
        Simon Bradstreete

PART II.

COURT OF ASSISTANTS.

RECORD 1641–1644.

FROM A CONTEMPORANEOUS COPY NOW IN THE
BOSTON PUBLIC LIBRARY.

PART II.
1641–1644.

COURT OF ASSISTANTS RECORDS.

[Taken from the copy of the Massachusetts Colony Records now in the Boston Public Library and known as the Barlow Copy. This portion of that copy has been printed in W. H. Whitmore's Bibliographical Sketch of the Laws of the Massachusetts Colony. The first part of the copy in the Public Library, extending to Jan. 28, 1641, is in the handwriting of Thomas Lechford. (See above, page 1, headnote to Part I.) The rest of that copy, or part of it, as stated above in the note on page 103, appears to have been made by Samuel Symonds. (See Transactions Colonial Society of Massachusetts, Vol. V., p. 144, January, 1898.) Through the whole copy the paragraphs are numbered successively in the margin from 1 at the beginning to 3450 at the end. As these marginal numbers are not in the original record now extant in the State Archives from which the first part of the copy was made, it is evident that the lost record from which the part of that copy now printed was made did not have them, and they are therefore omitted here.]

[277]   At a Co^{r}t the 28th. 8th. Moth. 1641.

Present.   The Governo^r. M^r. Winthrop.
                M^r. Dudley. Increase Nowell.

Luxford.   James Luxford was Ordered to bee delivered to his three Credito^{rs}.

Voysey fined.   M^r. Symon Voysey for striking M^r. Constable was comitted, & fined to give M^r. Constable, 10^{lb}.

Waltham. Brittaine bound for Wilson.   M^r. Henry Waltham, & James Brittaine, were bound for Gawen Wilson his appearance at ye next Co^{r}t.

Knight comitted.   John Knight is comitted vntill hee find sureties.

At a Quarter Co^{r}t at Boston the 7th. of the 10th. Mth. 1641.

Eliot. Tee.   Jacob Eliot deposed to the will, & Inventory of John Tee.

Smith. Prichard.	John Smith is graunted five shillings against William Prichard.
Richardson discharged.	John Richardson appearing, & testimony given of his good carriage, hee, & his sureties were discharged.
Wilson, & sureties discharged.	Gawen Wilson appearing, hee, & his sureties were discharged.
Voca[s] fined or whipt.	John Vocar was censured to pay ten shillings, or bee whipped, the 1st. Moth.
Capt. Williams, Richardson.	Capt. Williams was p'ssed, & promised to endeavo', & doe what in him lay to bring backe John Richardson.
Richards fined.	Walthian Richards was vpon his p'sentment fined 5lb., & enjoyned to pay the witnesses, which were Edward Bennet, & his wife; Richard Silvester, & his wife; Arthur Warren, Thomas Rawlings, Thomas Penny, Mr. Waltham, & Mary Smith, after 2s. p day, & to make a Publique.
ffinch his wife ill.	Samuel ffinch his wife was certified to bee ill.
Braintree.	The Inhabitants of Braintree, for the bridge over Minotocot River are respited till the Generall Court.
Hingham.	Hingham hath time till the first of the 3d. Moth. to finish the bridge over Layfords-liking, which they are doe by that time vpon paine of 5lb.
Barnes.	Thomas Barnes about lace, was admonished, & discharged.
Jobson.	John Jobson for vnadvised exp'ssions, was admonished, & discharged.
Hands discharged.	Marke Hands for want of proofe was discharged.
Dorchester fined.	Dorchester for defective wayes was fined 5s., & had ‖ time ‖ till the 2d. Moth.
Marklin recompence Pen.	It was referred to indifferent men to judge, what recompence Marklin knight should returne to James Pen.
Davies fined, bound.	William Davies for keeping an house of disorder, by giveing entertteinement against Order, was fined 20s., & bound in 10lb. not to sell ale, strong beare, wine, or strong-water.
Chidley.	Mr. Chidley was gone out of the Countrey before Co'rt.
Hawkins fined.	Thomas Hawkins for makeing bread to light was fined 5s. and enjoyned to give one witnesse, Edward Bates, 2s. 6d

Boston fined.	Boston for defective [ways] towards Roxbury is fined 10ˢ, & enjoyned to mend them, by the 24ᵗʰ. of the 2ᵈ. Moᵗʰ., vpon paine of five pounds.
Cambridge fined.	Cambridge for a defective way to Charlestowne is fined 5ˢ.
ffuller.	ffuller was respitted till the next Quarter Coʳt.
Knight. Carters wife.	John Knights Cause to be tryed by Action, Carters wife was admonished, & discharged.

[278]   At a Coʳt at Boston the 27ᵗʰ. 11ᵗʰ. Moᵗʰ. 1641.

Present. The Governoʳ. Mʳ. Winthrop.
Mʳ. Dudley. Increase Nowell.

Knowers estate. Stitson	The administration of the estate of Thomas Knower is graunted to James Browne & William Gosse, & his wife, to bee brought to the next Coʳt, to answer things objected against them.
Wilsmore.	Elizabeth Wilsmore had warrant to the Constable of Watertowne, to provide hir a place in service, or otherwise.
Williams. Read.	David Wᵐˢ hath put himselfe to John Read for 4 yeares, from the 12ᵗʰ. of this pʳsent Moᵗʰ.
ffox. Everell.	John ffox hath put himselfe Appʳntise to James Evrell, for 6 yeares, from this pʳsent day.

At a Quarter Coʳt at Boston yᵉ 1ˢᵗ. of the 1ˢᵗ. Moᵗʰ. $\frac{1641}{1642}$.

Present. Mʳ. Governoʳ. Mʳ. Winthrop.
Mʳ. Dudley. Increase Nowell. Mʳ. Bradstreet.

Mʳ. Ballards estate.	Mʳ. Timothy Tomlins, & Thomas Elington were graunted administration of the estate of Mʳ. Ballard, & they are to dispose of the Children, & their estates.
Story comitted. &c.	George Story vpon his miscarriage was comitted, & after vpon his submission, & acknowledgement of his fault, hee was discharged.
Charlestowne. Sudbury. Dedham Lands.	Charlestowne delivered in a transcript of their Lands. Sudbury dd in a transcript of their Lands. Dedham delivered in a transcript of their Lands.

Browne. Perry. Malachy Browne had six shillings 8. pence Costs graunted against ffrancis Perry, for warning him to appeare, & not prosecuting him.

Mr. Trerice fine rem. Mr. Nicholas Trerice ‖ his fine ‖ of forty shillings is remitted him.

Thatcher, Collaine, Allen, Barton, whipt. Peter Thatcher for plotting Piracy was comitted, & to bee whipt; Matthew Collaine, Robert Allen, & Marmaduke Barton, were whipped for concealing the plot of Piracy.

Shermans fine remit. Samuel Sherman is remitted his fine of 20^s.

Singleman, ffuell, bound. Henry Singleman is bound in 20^{lb}. to bee of good behavio^r & to appeare at the Quarter Co^{r}t in the 7th. Moth. 1642. & Samuel ffuell is bound in 10^{lb}. for the good behavio^r & appearance of Singleman.

Hawkins whipt. James Hawkins for prophaining the Sabbath hee was censured to bee whipt, & bound with his Brother Thomas Hawkins in 40^{lb}. to appeare at the Generall Co^{r}t, & answer for venting his corrupt Opinions, & to bee of good behavio^r till then.

Sedgwicke for theft, whipt. &c. Elizabeth Sedgwicke for hir many theftes, & lyes was censured to bee severely whipt, & condemned to slavery, till shee have recompenced double for all hir thefts.

Pesons banished. Pesons, or George the Indian, was banished not to come among the English after a weeke.

Mincarry admonisht. &c. Mincarry, the blackmore was admonished, & dismissed.

Smith admonisht. John Smith was admonished & dismissed.

Coles restitution. Susan Cole was enjoyned to make double restitution.

At a Co^{r}t at Boston 28th. 2^d. Moth. 1642.

Present. The Governo^r. M^r. Winthrop. M^r. Dudley. M^r. Stoughton. Increase Nowell.

Barton comitted. Marmaduke Barton for his theft, & running away, was comitted to the keeper, as a slave, till the next Generall Co^{r}t.*

Briant whipt. Thomas Briant for concealing Thatchers Plott, & consenting to it, was censured to bee severely whipped.

---

* See Mass. Col. Records, Vol. II., p. 21.

OF THE MASSACHUSETTS BAY. 119

Jackson.   Elisha Jackson was with his owne consent turned over for his time, from George Barrell, to John Millam.

The 12th. 3d. Moth. 1642.
Present. The Governor.
Mr. Winthrop.   Increase Nowell.

Woodcocke whipt.   John Woodcooke for his many miscarriages was censured to bee whipped.

[See below after the next four courts for records of courts from June 7 to Dec. 6, 1642, misplaced in the Library copy.]

At a Cort at Boston 20th. 12th. Moth. 1642.
Present. The Governor.   Mr. Dudley.
Mr. Bellingham.   Increase Nowell.

Chadwickes fine discharged.
Whittney fined.   Charles Chadwicke is discharged of his fine of 3s. 4d. & John Whitney the Constable is fined 2d. for not warning him.

Story discharged.   George Story appearing is discharged of his Bond for appearance to answer Capteine Keayne this Cort.*

Charlestownes Constables allowed.   It was ordered that the Constables of Charlestowne should bee allowed 9lb. 12s. 8d. for the charge of ∧

Mr. Ruck. Stow.   Mr. Thomas Rucke, & John Stow appearing, were appointed to appeare at the next Generall Cort, to give in their finall answer about the 50lb. comitted into their hands.

[279]
Davis. Kempe.   It was Ordered James Davies should have 3lb. 12s. for keeping of John Kempe for 12. weekes, at six shillings p weeke.

Hoare. Read.   Mary Hoare was Ordered to pay John Read 10s for hir theft, & trouble of him.

Chapman payd.   It was Ordered that Jacob Chapman should bee allowed 15s. for 9 dayes travell, & 2s. 6d. layd out of purse.

Mrs. Strainge Hinghā.   Order was sent to the Constables of Hingham, that Mrs. Strainge & hir child should bee supplied

---

* See Mass. Col. Records, Vol. II., p. 51; also Winthrop II. p. 69.

according to their necessity that they may bee comfortablie mainteined by the helpe of such worke, as shee is able to doe, & hereof not to faile, as they will answer it.

Stiles allowance.

It is conceived John Stiles should be allowed nine pound per annum for the time hee [time hee] hath served, & twenty shillings, for being turned away in winter, vnprovided.

Marvin allowance.

It is conceived that Thomas Marvin should bee allowed nine pound p annum for the time he served, & twenty shillings, for being turned away in winter, vnprovided, & 40^s. for the 8. wolves killed.

The 16th. of the 12th. Moth. 1642.
Present. The Governo^r.
M^r. Bellingham.   Increase Nowell.

Owles Willoughby fined.

Daniel Owles comeing before vs, for drinking part of severall pints of wine, with William Willoughby was fined ten shillings.

Willoughby comitted.

William Willoughby for beeing distempered with wine, & mispending his time, & neglecting both publique, & private Ordinances, was comitted to Prison to bee kept to worke there.

At a Quarter Co^{r}t at Boston 7th. 1st. Moth.
p^{r}sent. The Governo^r.
The Dep^{tie}. Govr.   M^r. Dudley.
M^r. Bellingham.   M^r. Bradstreet.
M^r. fflint.   Increase Nowell.

Briscoe fined.

M^r. Nathaniel Briscoe for certeine mutinous speeches, & writings was fined 10^{lb}.*

Pescot.
Winter dism.

John Pescot was dismissed with an admonition.
John Winter is discharged wth an admonition.

M^r. Collecot payd.

M^r. Richard Collecot his bill of 21^{lb}. 8^s. 10^d. was assigned to bee paid him, & for himselfe for 18. days, 2^{lb}. 14^s. & for M^r. Holeman, for 18. dayes, 2^{lb}. 14^s.

---

* See Winthrop II. 92, 93.

M^r. Richard Browne beeing questioned for vnmeete & filthy dalliance, with Sarah now wife of Thomas Boylston, for want of full evidence, they were dismissed with an admonition.

<small>Browne, Boylston's wife dismissed.</small>

Willm Bull, & Blith now his wife, were fined 20^s. for fornication comītted before marriage.

<small>Bulls, Bliths fornic. fined.</small>

John Stowers for reading to divers offensive passages (before comp^a) out of a booke, against the Officers, & Church of Watertowne, & for making disturbance there, was fined forty shillings.

<small>Stowers fined.</small>

Sarah Bell for hir theft, stealing money from hir master, was censured to bee whipped, except shee behave hir selfe well, betwixt this, & the next Co^rt, & soe as the Co^rt see cause to remit it.

<small>Bells theft.</small>

John Cornish was comitted, & after was ordered to bee released vpon his owne bond, for his good behavio^r, & appearance, &* the next Co^rt.

<small>Cornish comitted &c.</small>

Susan Hewet, & others which sold Sarah Pell* goods were Ordered to take their goods backe, & repay the money to M^r. Newgate.

<small>Hewet repay.</small>

T[eagu] Ocrimi for a foule, & divilish attempt to bugger a cow of M^r. Makepeaces, was censured to bee carried to the place of execution, & there to stand with an halter about his necke, & to bee severely whipped.

<small>Ocrimi punished.</small>

Robert Wyar, & John Garland beeing indited for ravishing two yong girles, the fact confessed by the girles, & the girles both vpon search found to have bin defloured, & filthy dalliance confessed by the boyes; the Jury found them, not guilty, wth reference to the Capitall Law. The Co^rt judged the boyes to bee openly whipped at Boston, the next market day, & againe to bee whipped at Cambridge on the Lecture day, & each of them to pay 5^{lb}. a peece to their master in service.

<small>Wyar. Garland whipt, & fined.</small>

It was also judged that the two girls Sarah Wythes, & Ursula Odle beeing both guilty of that wickednes, shall bee severely whipped at Cambridge in the p^rsence of the Secretary.

<small>Wythes. Odle. whipt.</small>

The 15th. 2^d. Mth. M^r ffrancis Norton, & John Pentecus, beeing formerly chosen Constables of Charlestowne, by the Towne, did take their Oathes to discharge that Office.

<small>Mr. Norton. Penticus. Charlestowne constables.</small>

---

* So in the Library copy.

At a Co^{rt} at Boston, the 27th. 2^d. Moth. 1642.*
Present. The Governo^r. M^r. Deputie. M^r. Dudley.
M^r. Bellingham. M^r. fflint. Increase Nowell.

Woods Inventory. An Inventory of the estate of Edward Wood deceased, was delivered in, & an account how the Children are disposed of, which the Co^{rt} doth approve.

Taylor admonished & dismissed. Richard Taylo^r beeing enjoyned to appeare at the next Co^{rt} to answer for his rude & vnmeete speeches, hee was dismissed with an admonition.

Hobson freed. Neal to pay witnesses. Henry Neale appearing, his servant Henry Hobson was freed from him, and put [280] to another, & Henry Neale was enjoyned to pay all the witnesses, & deliver vp all bonds, & soe all things were ended betweene them.

Hobson to Meakins. Henry Hobson is put to Goodman Thomas Meakins for the rest of his time, for 4^{lb}. p̄ annū and vpon his good behavio^r to have 2^s. 8^d. at the end of his time.

Stone, Armitage costs graunted. John Stone, & Joseph Armitage, vpon a warrant from Joshuah Hubbard had ten shillings cost graunted them, against Joshua Hubbard for not prosecuting.

Owles servant to ffrench. Daniel Owles is put to Serjeant William ffrench for a yeare, & then to bee brought againe to the Co^{rt}, to have further consideration had of the case, whether Serj^t ffrench had sufficient recompense for the losse of his servant, Edward Walldo, whom Owles concealed, plotting to run away, & councelled thereto.

Smith bound. Richard Smyth concealing his knowledge of Edward Waldo his intent of running away, is bound in ten pound to appeare at the next Co^{rt}.

Wyar to Bowtle. Robert Wyer is put to Leonard Bowtle, with his Masters consent for the rest of his time.

Browne whipt. William Browne for running away, deriding an Ordinance of God, refusing to give account what hee had learned, & refusing to obey [his] master, was censured to be severely whipped.

Mindam discharged. Robert Mindam appearing haveing bin imprisoned vpon an attachement by M^r. Campian, vpon pretence

---

* This should be 1643. Bellingham was Governor 27 April, 1642. Thomas Flint was first chosen an Assistant 18 May 1642.

<small>Quick whipt.</small> The 16th. 3d. Moth. Richard Quick for beeing distempered by drinking wine, & for his idlenes, stubbornes, & dalliance, was censured to bee whipped.

of a debt of 35lb. to Mr. Trerice, he was discharged, because noe action is entered, nor none appeareth to prosecute.

<small>Roberts fined 12d.</small> Edward Roberts was appointed to pay 12d. for drinking to Richard Quick.

<small>Perry Whipt.</small> John Perry for running away was censured to bee whipped 17th. 3d. Moth.

<small>Harding. Hollister. Weymouth Constables.</small> John Harding, & John Hollister beeing chosen Constable of Weymouth, did take their oath to that place apperteining. 23. 3d. Moth.

<small>Baker Ordinary keep.</small> Mr. Baker of Ipswich is allowed to keepe an Ordinary insteed of Goodm. Andrews.

<small>Goodnow Clarke of ye Band.</small> Edward Goodnow beeing chosen Clearke of the Band did take his Oath 5th. 4th. Moth.

<small>Mr. Tomlins Ensigne.</small> Mr. Edward Tomlins beeing chosen is allowed Ensigne at Linn.

<small>Mr. Tory Ensigne.</small> Mr. William Tory is appointed Ensigne at Weymouth.

<small>Johnson.</small> Edward Johnson is appointed to traine the Company at Wooborne.

The 7th. day of the 4th. Moth. 1642.*

p'sent. The Governor. The Deputie. Mr. Dudley. Mr. Bellingham. Mr. Bradstreet. Mr. Stoughton. Mr. fflint. Increase Nowell.

<small>Dedham Lands.</small> Dedham delivering in a transcript of their lands, the Co't gave Mr. Allen leave to have the transcript backe againe.

<small>Forbearance.</small> The other Townes, to wit Boston, Dorchester, Braintree, & Watertowne, had time graunted them till the 4th. Moth. 1643.

<small>Mr. Paine discharged. Costs graunted.</small> Mr. Edward Paine vpon his appearance was discharged there beeing noe Action entered by Clement Campion, and Mr. Paine was graunted 6s. 6d. costs against Clement Campion.

---

* This and the four following records were misplaced in the Library copy. See above under 12th 3d Mo. 1642.

Wood fined.

Edward Wood was fined 8ˢ. for baking wheat meale contrary to order.

Scott & his wives punishment for fornicacon.

Thomas Scot, & his wife for comitting fornication before marriage, were enjoyned to stand an hoᵣe vpon the 16ᵗʰ. pʳsent, in the market place, with each of them a paper with great letters, on their hatts.

Morrice will delivered, &c.

Thomas Morrice his will was delivered [in] vpon oath testified by Edward Woolastone, & William Hudson.

Whitmore* dismissed.

Thomas Whittamore because of his sore leg was dismissed with an admonition.

Concord transcript imperfect.

Concord delivered in a transcript of their Lands, but vnsubscribed, which not beeing according to Order, was delivered backe againe to them to perfect.

Keayne Comitted, &c.

Anne Keayne for hir grosse failing in not testifying the truth, when shee was called vpon oath shee was comitted to the Keeper, & vpon hir petition, & confession of hir fault, she was released.

Bosworth bound, & to find suretyes.

Jonathan Bosworth for discountenancing a wittnesse, was comitted till hee find sureties; Samuel Ward, & Nicholas Jacobs were bound in 10ˡᵇ. a peece for Jonathan Bosworth his good behavioʳ, & appearance at the next Quarter Coʳt, & Jonathan Bosworth himselfe was bound in 20ˡᵇ.

Eliz: Strainge dismis.

Eliz: Strainge vpon acknowledgment of hir sincere, with an jnjunction to acknowledge hir sin publiquely at Hingham, & that to bee certified by the Constable, shee was dismissed with an admonition.

Jones dismissed.

William Jones vpon his acknowledgment here, beeing enjoyned to acknowledge the like Publiquely at Hingham, with an admonition, & an injunction to pay the witnesses 5ˢ. a peece, he was dismissed.

Richards fine abated.

Mʳ. Richards is abated twenty shillings of his fine.

[281]

Mr. Long fined.

John Long Gent. for his misdemeanoʳ, distemper in drinke, swearing & cursing was fined twenty pound, & to put in sureties before his departure.

Wilsons fine respited.

Thomas Wilson his fine is respited till the end of the second Moneth 1643. and Anthony Staniard

---

* So in the Library copy.

is bound in twenty pound for the payment of Thomas Wilsons fine.

Morrell fined.
Isaac Morrell was fined 5ˢ for his absence, which hee is to pay to the rest of the Jury.

Powell Surveyor of Armes.
Nicholas Powell is appointed Surveyoʳ of the Armes for Dedham.

Mʳ. Longs damage.
It was Ordered that Mʳ. Stodder should have three pound of Mʳ. John Long, foɪ himselfe, & ten shillings for the rest of his Company, for the trouble, & danger they susteined by Mʳ. Long.

At a Small Coʳt at Boston, the 28ᵗʰ. of the 5ᵗʰ. Moᵗʰ. 1642.
    pʳsent.
The Governoʳ. Mʳ. Dudley. Mʳ. Stoughton. Increase Nowell.

Smith.
Henry Smith not appearing (beeing warned by the Governoʳ.)

Stephenson liberty graunted.
Margeret Stephenson is judged at liberty to be married to Benjamin Scott.

Kempe cared for.
The Constable of Roxbury was Ordered to take care of John Kempe, servant formerly to Isaac Morrell, both for his maintenance, & cure, till the next Quarter Coʳt, and then further order should bee setled.

Matthew to worke.
The Coʳt thought meet Dermondt Matthew should bee set to worke by such, as have occasion to imploy him, vntill his Mʳ. shall appeare, & take coʳse about him.

Bradley Administracon &c.
Katherin Bradley is graunted administration of hir husbands estate, who gave hir all his estate, only some cloathes, & tooles to his brother.

At a Quarter Coʳt the 6ᵗʰ. of the 7ᵗʰ. Moᵗʰ. 1642.*
    pʳsent.
The Governoʳ. The Deputie Govʳ. Mʳ. Dudley. Mʳ. Bellingham. Mʳ. Saltonstall. Mʳ. Stoughton. Mʳ. Bradstreet. Mʳ. ﬄint. Increase Nowell.

Roberts comitted.
George Roberts was comitted to the keeper for his ill carriage, but after had leave, to goe take care of his corne, beeing it lay vpon spoyling.

---

* See below, Part III., for a record of this date.

Cooper. Hubbard.	Thomas Cooper, & Joshua Hubbard Constables of Hingham.
Converse constable.	Edward Converse Constable of Wooborne.
Bosworth discharged.	Jonathan Bosworth is discharged from his bond.
Sever fined.	Robert Sever for his miscarriage in neglecting the watch, is fined twenty pound which the Co^{r}t doth respite.
The Elders advice desired.	Severall of the Members of Hingham, vpon admonition of the Co^{r}t, did refer it to the Co^{r}t, to speake to the Elders to consider the case, & to send

some of themselves to see, if it may please the Lord by advise to helpe to reconsile their differences, and settle them in a way of Christ.

Wooldrige fined.	M^r. John Wooldrige was fined 3^{lb}., & enjoyned vpon paine of 5^{lb}. to acknowledge his offence, at Boston,

Charlestowne, & Cambridge, reading an acknowledgment written for his drunkenesse, & swearing.

Batter costs graunted.	M^r. Edmund Batter had six shillings, eight pence cost graunted him, against M^r. John Humphrey for serving him to appeare, & not prosecuting.
Lewis whipt.	John Lewis for running away, and breaking an house, was censured to bee whipped, & sent home to his Master.
Cole to worke.	Richard Cole was comitted to worke for his liveing, till a master bee found for him.
Walcot Whipt.	William Walcot was censured to bee whipped, & kept in Prison, till further Order, for his idlenesse, &

abuse of his friends.

White comitted. releas.	Richard White beeing comitted for refusing to watch, vpon his submission he was released.
Het. Whipt, &c.	Anne Hett for attempting to drowne hir child was censured to bee whipped, and kept to hard labo^r, & spare diet.
Cotcree whipt.	Thomas Cotcree was censured to bee severly whipped, for his vnmeet dalliance with two or three girles.
Juryes verdict returned.	The Jury returned verdict about the death of Richard Silvester his child.*

See Winthrop II. 77.

Part of Mo. Thyeryes estate.	The Governo^r hath in his hands about 4^{lb}. of the estate of one Mountsier Thyery, a ffrench man, that dyed here.
[282] Watts fined.	George Watts is appointed to give ten shillings in cotton woole for swearing.
Cole put to Haward.	Richard Cole is put to William Haward for a yeare, vpon such wages as shall bee suteable to his yearnings.

At a Co^rt at Boston the 27th. 8th. Moth. 1642.*

p^rsent.
The Governo^r. M^r. Dudley. M^r. Bellingham. Increase Nowell.

ffinch Gorton excused. Vnions fine respited.	Samuel ffinch, & John Gorton, for not appearing vpon the Alarme, their excuses were accepted, and they freed. Robert Vnnion not appearing vpon the Alarme, his fine of 5^{lb}. is respited, till the Generall Co^rt.
Widdow Merriam administracon graunted.	Widdow Merriam is graunted administration of hir late husband Merriam his estate.
Web fined.	William Web for his neglect, in not carefully attending the Order of Co^rt about his bread, is fined ten shillings.
Comittee appointed.	Vpon Consideration (severall Petitions p^rferred to this Co^rt) It was Ordered that M^r. John Smith, M^r. William Bacon, togeather with M^r. John Oliver, Leivt^t Lusher, & Anthony ffisher, these, or any three of them whereof the said M^r. John Smith, & M^r. John Oliver to bee two, shall have power to take into their custody all the bookes, & writings of the said† Edward Allen, to cast vp, & to cleare the accounts, for deviding of the interests of the severall Parties, & to pay, & receive all debts and to certify the Co^rt with what speed they may.
M^r. Oliver's sume.	The Treasuro^r had order to pay M^r. Oliver the sume of 12^{lb}. for his paines about Mansfeild.
Administracon graunted.	John Newton, & Edward Allen are graunted the Administraçon of the estate of M^r. Edward Allen.
Conway whipt.	Davyd Conway servant to Wm Beamsley, for resisting his master was censured to be whipped.

---

* See Winthrop II. 73, 74, for mention of a civil suit at this Court.
† So in the Library copy.

Neale comitted.

John Neale servant to M^r. Cockram was comitted vpon suspition of felony.

Hudson costs graunted.

William Hudson was graunted six shillings, eight pence against Symon Kempthorne, for attaching, & causing him to attend, & not prosecuting.

M^r. Allens gift testified.

ffrances Pembrooke tooke hir oath, that M^r. Allen, vpon his death bed gave his estate to John Newton, & Edward Allen his kinsman, & that he was then, & after in good memory, & vnderstanding.

Mansfeild to Denux.

The 14th. of the 9th. Mo^th. 1642. Daniel Mansfeild is put to William Denux for five yeares from this p^rsent day.

At a Quarter Co^rt at Boston, the 6th. of the 10th. Mo^th. 1642.*

p^rsent.

The Governo^r. M^r. Dudley. M^r. Bellingham. M^r. fflint. Increase Nowell.

Chadwicke. Holmes fined.

Charles Cadwicke,† & Robert Holmes, are fined three shillings, foure pence a peece, for beeing absent, being warned.

Searchers appointed.

Edward Lewis,   Williams, John Shearman, & George Munnings, are appointed to view the leather which is tanned in Watertowne, & to certify vpon their oathes, (& in perticular leather tanned by John Winter, for which hee was p^rsented, which John Warren can testify) at the next Quarter Co^rt.

Shepheard fined.

William Shepheard for covenanting for 15^lb. wages p annum, is fined two pound.

Copeland fined.

Laurence Copeland for covenanting for 15^lb. wages p annum is fined 2^lb., beeing both released one halfe of the time, which was ordered to bee stayed in John Mowers hand, and by him, to bee payd two shillings to Martin Saunders, & 3^lb. 18^s. to the Treasuro^r.

Watertowne p^rsentm^t.

Watertowne p^rsentment is referred to the next Quarter Co^rt.

M^r. Hibbins allowed.

It was ordered that M^r. Hibbins should bee allowed twenty pounds for his horse killed in Pu[bl]ique service.

---

* See below, Part III., for record of this date.   † So in the Library copy.

M^r. Bartholomew his cause, vpon his brothers vndertaking to bee surety to answer for his brother, at the next Quarter Co^rt, it was referred to the next Quarter Co^rt: And Capteine Keaynes Action is deferred by consent, till M^r. Bartholomew doe come.

Mr. Bartholomew cause refered.

Capt. Keaynes Action defer.

David Weane by consent put himselfe to Hugh Gunnison for 3^lb. 15^s. till that bee wrought out.

Weane to Gunnison.

Isaac Addington did depose that Timothy Higgenson had 6. gallons of M^r. Eldreds wine, Robert Gillam had 5. gallons, William Pearce as hee thinketh had 5. gallons, & himselfe had 5. gallons.

Addington deposition.

Dearmant Matthew is put to Thomas Dexter for the rest of his time, Dexter promiseth to pay what wages Dearmant proveth to bee due, and all is referred to M^r. Sadler, & goodman Armitage to heare, & end all businesses, & the 3 attachments are discharged.

Matthew to Dexter.

It was Ordered that M^r. Walton should have his goods againe, which were vnjustly taken and the Arbitrato^rs to end the businesse of the sow, if they can.

Walton have his goods againe.

[283]

John Lee is graunted six shillings 8. pence against Richard Lettin, for somoning him to appeare, causing him to attend, & not prosecuting.

Lee costs graunted.

Martin Saunders vndertooke the Bridges, p^rsented, should bee repaired, soe Braintree was fined three shillings, foure pence, & discharged.

Braintree fined.

It was Ordered that M^r. Ruck, & Goodman Stow, should bee sent vnto, to come in at the next Co^rt, & should shew how they have disposed of the 50^lb., or bring it in, or shew why they should not.

M^r. Ruck. Stow called.

William Davies was fined 5^lb for his contempt, in keeping victualling against Order of Co^rt.

Davies fined.

Hingham vpon oath given, that the way is made out, is discharged.

Hingham discharged.

Boston is discharged, the way to Charlestowne being made good.

Boston discharged.

The other p^rsentments are respited till the next Quarter Co^rt because of the weather.

p^rsentments respited.

The 11th. Mo^th. 1642. 5. day. Elizabeth Hasnet is put to William Wilson, for 50^s. wages, for the yeare.

El. Hasnet put to Wilson.

Wicks Constable. The 12th. day. George Wicks beeing chosen Constable of Dorchester tooke his Oath.

At a Quarter Co^r at Boston the 10th. of the 4th. Moth. 1643.*

p^rsent.

The Governo^r. The Deputie. M^r. Dudley.
M^r. Bellingham. M^r. Saltonstall. M^r. Bradstreet.
M^r. Hibbens. M^r. fflint. Increase Nowell.

Ridway payd. It was Ordered that forty five shillings of the estate of M^r. William Bladen, should bee payd to James Riddway, who was his servant for his yeares provision.

Boston p^rsented. The Towne of Boston beeing p^rsented for defect of their highwaies, they had bin p^rsented for

M^r. Oliver payd. It was Ordered that M^r. Oliver should have for his paines, & charge about the Saylo^r three pound, about Mansfeild twenty shillings, about Kemp seaven pounds; togeather eleven pounds.

Heathersby discharged. Robert Heathersby appearing is discharged of his bond, & graunted 10^s. costs against

Brittaine respited &c. James Brittaine beeing p^rsented, & traversing the p^rsentment was respited to the next Co^rt, and bound himselfe in twenty pounds to appeare then, & answer. William Brandon to appeare for a witnesse.

Layton discharged. Thomas Layton appearing was discharged.

Smith comitted. Richard Smyth beeing convented, for beeing privy to Edward Waldo his intent to run away, which was wittnessed by Blith Bull, hee was comitted to.

Mills fined. George Mills for a Battery is fined ten shillings.

Willis fined com. Richard Willis for a foule Battery is fined 2^{lb}. 10^s., & comitted till hee pay or give sufficient security.

Chadborne. Low. Butcher. Affeild. Woodward &c. fined. William Chadborne, senio^r, John Low, Robert Butcher, William Affeild, John Woodward, Ambrose Leach & Sacheas Bosworth were fined 10^s. apeece, for drinking too much.

Golthrope fined. Ralph Golthrope is fined 10^s. for beeing distempered with wine.

---

* For previous courts in 1643 see above after the court of the 12th of the 3d month, 1642.

William ffilpot was admonished to take heed of suffering drinking in his house.

ffilpot admonished.

Anker Ainsworth beeing p^rsented for taking excessive wages, it did not appeare, & soe hee was discharged.

Ainsworth discharged.

M^r. Draytons Cause against M^r. Wannerton is transmitted to the Co^rt at Piscataqua.

Mr. Draintons cause transm.*

M^r. Stodder beeing p^rsented for selling cloth at an excessive rate, it appeared noe excesse in him, soe hee promising to satisfy M^r. Paine was discharged.

Mr. Stodder p^rsented, disch.

Henry Leake, & his wife for fornication were enjoyned to appeare the next Lecture day, at Dorchester after the Lecture, and to acknowledge their fault.

Leake & his wife, for fornication to acknowledge.

John Smyth Clarke of the Band at Dorchester.

Smyth Clarke of the Band.

ffrancis Pemble bound him in 20^lb. to appeare at the next Co^rt, to answer for his lewd, & reproachfull speaches.

Pemble bound.

The 27th. of the 5th. Mo^th. 1643.

p^rsent.
M^r. Governo^r. M^r. Dudley. M^r. Bellingham. M^s. Hibbens. Increase Nowell.

Nicholas Rogers for beeing distempered with wine, or strong drinke, was fined 2^lb. who being imprisoned is remitted to ten shillings.

Rogers fined.

William Scutt for selling powder, & shot to the Indians was fined 10^lb. to pay the halfe, when corne is payable, & the other halfe a 12. Mo^th. after, & Thomas Spaule is surety.

Scutt selling powder to Indians, fined.

Samuel Bacon for stealing wine, & other thinges, was censured to be severely whipped, & to make double restitution, to M^rs. Hull, & his Dame.

Bacon stealing, whipt. &c.

Robert Rogers was, for receiving stolen wine, being consenting in it, enjoyned to pay M^r. Manning 32^s. & fined to the Countrey 40^s.

Rogers consenting to theft, fined &c.

Miles Tompson for drinking with them, & beeing privy, was to pay M^r. Manning 16^s.

Tompson.

Toby Davies beeing privy, & drinking with them was to pay M^r. Manning 10^s.

Davies.

---

* So in the Library copy.

[284]

Wyar.
Cooper.

Robert Wyar for drinking with Bacon, beeing privy to the taking of it, was enjoyned to pay M^r. Manning 4^s., Thomas Cooper for drinking, beeing privy to the manner of taking it, to pay M^r. Manning 4^s.

Tapping for theft, whipt.

Nathaniel Tappin for breaking, breaking into severall houses, and stealing severall thinges was censured to be whipped, & put to Goodman Gillam.

Langley Lin Constable.

William Langley beeing chosen Constable of Linn, tooke his Oath.

At a Quarter Co^rt at Boston the 5th. of the 7th. Mo^th. 1643.

p^rsent.

M^r. Deputie Govr. M^r. Dudley. M^r. Bellingham. M^r. Saltonstall. M^r. Pinchon. M^r. Bradstreet. M^r. fflint. M^r. Symons. M^r. Hibbens. Increase Nowell.

Clough fined.

John Clough is fined 6^s. 8^d. for his absence when the Jury was called.

Golthrop fined.

Ralph Golthrop was fined 3^s. for his distemp in drinke, & if he fayle in that againe, to have Corporall punishment.

Legacyes payd.

It is Ordered that vpon the Letter of Atturney shewed heare in Co^rt, the Legacyes should bee payd by M^r. Smyth of Springfeild to John Porter.

Wilson fornicacon fined.

Gawen Wilson is fined twenty shillings for fornication, which M^r. Bozoon Allen vndertooke to satisfy in cotton-woole by M^r. Coitmore.

Napper discharged.

George Napper was discharged, & comitted to his Master, and to stay with him, soe much longer for the time hee hath bin absent.

Bairstow discharged.

William Bairstowe appearing was discharged.

Eliz. Vane comitt. releas.

Elizabeth Vane, for hir miscarriage in abuseing one of the Magistrates, & M^rs. Newgate, was comitted at the pleasure of the Co^rt, & vpon hir humble Petition, & acknowledgment, was released.

Jeames Hingham Const.

ffrancis James chosen Constable of Hingham, tooke his Oath.

Gell whipt. runing away.

Richard Gell servant to ffrancis ffellingham of Salem, for running away was censured to be whipped, & sent to his Master, whom hee is to serve for the time hee hath lost.

Bartlet whipt. fined. Day comitted. Gamage whipt.
John Bartlet for his swearing, theft, & drunkenes was comitted to Prison, & censured to bee whipped, & fined twenty shillings. Stephen Day for his defrauding severall men was comitted. John Gammage for his swearing, drunkenes, & other prophanes, & disorder, was censured to bee well whipped.

Arbitrators.
Mr. Symons, Mr. ffowle, Mr. Smyth, Mr. Dan, & Goodman Bendall, are appointed by consent to arbitrate betweene Mr. Humphrey & Mr. Robert Saltonstall.

Anker fined.
Thomas Anker payd 5ˢ for his distemp in drinke which.

Mr. Pendleton Sudbury.
Mr. Briant Pendleton is appointed to exercise the Company at Sudbury.

Watts fined.
George Watts for his distemp in drinke, swearing, & abusing the watch was fined 10ˡᵇ. & to pay or give sufficient security before hee bee released.

Serjt. Wardall Exeter.
Serjt. Wardall is appointed to traine the Company at Exeter.

Lewis enjoyned. [Lewis*] freed.
Lewis is enjoyned not to strike his servant John Lowe, & to set the said John Lowe free the 24ᵗʰ. of the 4ᵗʰ. Moneth 1644.

Administration graunted.
Andrew Allen is graunted administration of his Brother Edward Allen his estate, who was killed the fourth of this pʳsent Moneth.

Rogers whipt.
The eighth Moᵗʰ twelfth. Nicholas Rogers for his drunkenes, and makeing others drunke with his strong-water, was censured to bee whipped. Swiniard

Lewis fined.
Lewis for his beeing drunke, was fined ten shillings which hee paid.

Hart fined.
The 19. day. Israel Hart is fined twenty shillings for neglecting the watch, and enjoyned allsoe to pay the two witnesses, and the officer.

Wood Ordinary keep.
The 20. day. Richard Wood is allowed to keepe an Ordinary at Roxbury.

Burges admonisht.
Thomas Burges for his distemper, was dismissed with an admonition to take heed of the like fayling.

White costs graunted.
Thom. White is graunted 13ˢ. 4ᵈ. against Andrew Belcher, for the 5ˡᵇ. of powder, & trouble he hath put him to.

---
*Lowe?

Bauldwin comitted.   Thomas Bauldwin for his miscarriage to his master, and striking him was comitted to prison.

Wright fined.   Robert Wright is fined twenty shillings for beeing twice distempered in drinke, or to sit an houre in the stocks, the next Market day at Boston.

Barnes fined.   William Barnes for swearing is fined ten shillings.

Kinloah discharged.   James Kinloah appearing for want of proofe hee was discharged.

Lightfoot payd.   It was Ordered that ffrancis Lightfoot should have paid him, by M^r. Edward Gately ten shillings, and by Joseph Armitage foure shillings, for the trouble, & attendance they caused to him.

[285]   At a Co^{r}t at Boston the 26. of the 8th. 1643.

p^{r}sent. The Deputie Governo^r. M^r. Thomas fflint. Increase Nowell.

ffryar fined.
ffryar, Nelme, Wayne, bound to appeare.   Leonard ffryar was fined 10^s. Leonard ffryar James * Nelme, & David Wayne, all 3. are bound in 40^s. apeece to appeare at the next Quarter Co^{r}t to answer for excessive drinking, & distemper.

Garland to make restitution.   John Garland for stealing severall thinges to the value of 3^s 6^d was enjoyned to make double restitution.

Arnold Watertowne Const.   Thomas Arnold beeing chosen Constable of Watertowne, tooke the Constables Oath.

ffryes will recorded.   The will, & Inventory of William ffry, to the Recorder was delivered the ninth of the ninth Moneth, the widow beeing Executrix, and the wittnesses Thomas Bayly, & John Burges tooke their Oaths.

Dauling. Audley. Jeffrey. whipt.   David Dauling, Mary Audley, & Jane Jeffrey, for their filthy, & vncleane practise, were censured to bee severely whipped.

At a Co^{r}t at Boston the 5th. of the 10th. Moth. 1643.

p^{r}sent. The Governo^r. M^r. Dudley. M^r. Winthrop Junr.
M^r. Stoughton. M^r. Hibbens. M^r. fflint. Increase Nowell.

So in the Library copy.

OF THE MASSACHUSETTS BAY. 135

Capt. Chadwicke fined.
Capteine John Chadwicke for swearing many oathes, and other disorder is fined twenty pounds.*

Capt. Williams fined.
Capteine Aaron Williams for distemp in drinke, is fined ten shillings, which hee paid.

Souldiers charges disbursed.
It was Ordered that John Johnson the Surveyo^r should take out of the Cattell which came from Providence, the money disbursed for that Company, & vndertaking, which is twenty five pounds three shillings, & nine pence, as p pticulers.

Sudbury Mill fined.
The owners of Sudbury Mill are fined 3^s. 4^d. for want of Scales, & Weights, and they are to provide them, by the next Quarter Co^{r}t in paine of twenty shillings.

Dedham transcript accepted.
Dedham delivered in a transcript of their Lands, and was discharged; and for the way betweene Dedham and Cambridge, they have time till the fourth moneth next.

Painter stockt.
Thomas Painter for disturbing the Church of Hingham, was censured to bee sett in stocks a Lecture day, at Lecture time, except hee humble himselfe, and give the Church satisfaction.

Ardway accused, dismissed.
Abner Ardway beeing accused for dallying with Mary Giles for want of proofe he was dismissed with an admonition.

Read dismissed. Williams whipt. Porter considered of.
John Read for refusing to watch hee was dismissed, and the thing to bee considered. David Williams for assaulting the watch was censured to be whipped at Braintree, and warrant to George Read, to stop out of the wages, to pay the witnesses. William Porter for refusing to watch to bee considered of.

Archers whipping respited.
John Archer for resisting his Master was censured to bee whipped, which is respited.

Too much wages considered of.
James Loranson, John Callwell, Thomas Danfort, John Gill, and his wife, with John Pope beeing p^{r}sented, for taking too much wages, to bee considered of.

Johnson chosen Leivtenant.
Edward Johnson beeing chosen Leivt^t of Wooborne is allowed of.

Merryfeild respited. Beamis fined.
Henry Merryfeild beeing p^{r}sented for lewd speeches, is respited. John Beamis for freeing his

---

* See Winthrop II. 149, 150. See also Mass. Hist. Socy. Coll. 5th Ser., Vol. 1, p. 492.

<small>Mr. Broughton dismissed.
Barnard fined.</small>
servant against Order, was fined ten shillings. M^r. Broughton is dismissed, hee beeing not respondent for it. John Barnard for his daingerous well, is fined 10^s. and enjoyned to make it safe with [in] 28. dayes, vpon paine of 40^s.

<small>Adams Braintree Constab.</small>
Henry Adams beeing chosen Constable of Braintree, tooke his Oath.

<small>Golthrop whipt, or fined.</small>
Ralph Golthrop for beeing againe distemped with drinke, was censured to bee whipped, which if hee bring sureties for his good behavio^r and pay twenty shillings, hee is discharged.

<small>Campi[a]n costs graunted.</small>
Clement Campion is graunted three pounds 6. shillings, & 8. pence against John Rogers, for attaching him, & not prosecuting.

<small>Killmaster fined.
Betts discharged.</small>
John Killmaster for beeing twice distempered with drinke was fined twenty shillings. John Betts appearing, for want of proofe was discharged. Thomas

<small>Weatherly fined.</small>
Weatherly for swearing, & quarrelling was fined twenty shillings, and to pay the wittnesses five shillings.

<small>Hudson Ordinary Keep.</small>
William Hudson Junio^r is allowed to keepe an house of enterteinment.

<small>M^r. Stileman discharged.</small>
M^r. Stileman appearing about the way, for want of wittnesses, was discharged.

<small>ffryar. Nelme. Waine. forfeit.</small>
Leonard ffryar, Jasp Nelme, & David Wayne forfeited forty shillings a peece for not appearing.

<small>Wright bound.</small>
George Wright for his attempt to vncleaness with a married woman, is bound to his good behavio^r in forty pound, & to appeare at ye Quarter Co^rt the first Moneth, and to pay the wittnesses.

<small>Knop ordinary keep.</small>
William Knops wife is allowed to keepe an house of enterteinment.

<small>Osborne costs graunted.</small>
Richard Osborne was graunted six shillings, 8. pence, against Thomas Turner for warning him to appeare, & not prosecuting.

<small>Capt. W^{ms} discharged from Capteine Chadwicke.</small>
Capteine Aaron Williams is discharged from Capteine John Chadwicke, in regard hee swore hee would kill him, as was testifyed.

<small>Attachm^{ts} graunted.</small>
Attachments were graunted against such as beeing warned did not appeare, as, Carew Latham, Richard Quick, Samuel ffinch his wife &c.

M^r. Dunsters Petition is graunted him, & any two of the ffeofees to have power to dispose of thinges, and to receive, & pay the debts.

Mr. Dunsters Petition graunted.

At a Co^rt at Boston the 25th. of the 11th. Moth. 1643.
p^rsent.
The Governo^r. M^r. Dudley. M^r. Hibbens. M^r. fflint. Increase Nowell.

Boston Const. fined. Grubs fine discharged. Moulton bound.

The Constable of Boston is fined ten shillings for not returning his warrant. Thomas Grub not appearing upon the Jury is fined 5^s. this is discharged. Thomas Moulton for his light carriage, is bound in ten pound to bee of good carriage, and to appeare at the next Co^rt.

[286]

Barnard stealing.

Bridget Barnard for stealing from M^r. Stodder yards of ribben 3^s. 24. douzen of buttons, 4^s. from William Knop senior ½ yard of bayes 1^s. 6^d. from Goodw. Button a peece of callico, 8^d. & from John Trotman 2. paire of shooes 6^s.

fflint fornication fined.

William fflint beeing a married man haveing gotten a slutt with child is fined 20^{lb}. whereof 10^{lb}. is left to the Toune of Salem to bring vp the child with, and the other ten pound to the Publique, and to lye in Prison till hee pay it, or give security.

Co^rt Charges.

M^r. Treasuro^r was desired to cast vp Goodm. Turners bill, & if it be found right 53^{lb}. 15^s. 6^d. to allow it.

Weanes, Nelmes fine in part remitted.

David Weane is remitted 20^s. of the 40^s. forfeited for non appearance, to pay the other 20^s which George Burden vndertook to pay, within a Month. Jasp Nelme is remitted 20^s. of his forty shillings forfeited, to pay the other twenty shillings.

Chadborne. Shaw.

William Chadborne appearing to answer John Shaw is discharged for the p^rsent.

Watertowne Lands. transcript respited.

The transcript of Watertowne Lands is respited till the Quarter Co^rt in the 4th. Moth. next.

Bentley stealing. Restitution.

Mary Bentley for stealing [for stealing] Mr Waltons jewell of 11^s. price, hee haveing the jewell againe and 9^s. 6^d. of hir wages shee is to pay 18^d. more.

Parker. Kendal. John Parker appearing vpon suṁons from John Kendall, & Kendall not prosecuting, John Parker is graunted six shillings, eight pence against Kendall.

Mason. Munnings, sealers. Bayly to Hill. The 2ᵈ. of yᵉ 12ᵗʰ. Moᵗʰ. Hugh Mason, and George Munnings, beeing pʳsented for sealers, & searchers of leather ^. Richard Bayly put himselfe for 4. yeares to Abraham Hill, from the 13. of yᵉ 11. Moᵗʰ. past.

At a Quarter Coʳt. at Boston the 5ᵗʰ. of yᵉ 1ˢᵗ. Moᵗʰ $\frac{1643}{1644}$:

pʳsent.

The Governoʳ. The Deputie Govʳ. Mʳ. Dudley. Mʳ. Bellingham. Mʳ. Winthrop junʳ. Mʳ. Bradstreet. Mʳ. Hibbens. Mʳ. fflint. Mʳ. Symonds. Increase Nowell.

ffrost distempered fined. George ffrost beeing distempered with wine was fined ten shillings.

Hart distempered fine. John Hart beeing distempered with wine was fined twenty shillings.

Cooper Gillam } fined. Thomas Cooper beeing absent from the Grand Jury, when it was called, is fined six shillings, eight pence. Benjamin Gillam beeing absent from the Jury of Tryalls is fined five shillings.

Halsteeds Inventory. his eldest son Administratoʳ. The Inventory of Nathaniel Halsteed amounting to 213ˡᵇ. 13ˢ. 2ᵈ. was pʳsented, & it was ordered the eldest son should have 106ˡᵇ 10ˢ & the other 2. children, 106ˡᵇ 10ˢ, & the eldest son William is graunted to bee administratoʳ.

ffryars forfeiture remitted for distemp fined. Leonard ffryar his forfeiture is remitted, & hee is fined 15ˢ. for distemper in drinke, & disorder.

Latham. Johnson. Bauldwin. fined. Carew Latham is fined 10ˢ. for his disorder, & dismissed. Edward Johnson junʳ for iṁoderate drinking was fined 5ˢ., & dismissed. John Bauldwin for excessive drinking, was fined 5ˢ., & dismissed.

Anne Clarke divorced. Anne Clarke beeing deserted by Denis Clarke hir husband, & hee refusing to accompany with hir, she is graunted to bee divorced, his refusall was vnder his hand, & seale, which hee gave before Mʳ. John Winthrop junʳ Mʳ. Emanuel Downing, Mʳ. Nehemiah Boʳne, & Richard Babington, alsoe hee confesseth hee liveth in adultry with one, by whom hee hath had 2. & refuseth hir which hee had 2 children by.

Wright discharged. George Wright appearing & testimony of his good carriage hee was discharged.

Milam discharged. John Milam appearing, & declaring hee had the cloth of Mr Stoughton for 9^s. hee was discharged.

M^r. Dutchfeild fined. M^r. Thomas Dutchfeild for distemper in drinke is fined 10^s. & admonished, & dismissed.

Amedowne. Harris. Roger Amedowne was enjoyned to pay 2^s. 6^d. fees. admonished, & discharged. John Harris to pay two^s. 6^d. fees, was admonished, & discharged.

Brittaine. Latham for adultery condemned. James Brittaine beeing found guilty of adultery with Mary Latham, he was condemned to death. Mary Latham beeing found guilty of adultery with James Brittaine, she was condemned to death.*

Taylo^r Rebecka the wife of John Taylo^r

Betson. Stephen Betson for his sinfull attempt hee was bound to his good behavio^r, & enjoyned to appear ye next Co^rt.

Smith theft fined. Nathaniel Smith for his theft was ordered to pay Capt. Sedgwicke 49^s. & fined 20^s. for his intempate drinking.

Stow, Concord 222 acres. Vpon releasment of John Stow, Concord men are graunted Power to seize the 222. acres of Land, & hay, & debts due by any rent of the said Land.

Moulton discharged. Thomas Moulton appearing was discharged.

Richardson sequestred from ffryar. It was Ordered that John Richardson should be sequestred from Elizabeth ffryar, to whom he was married, ye 12th. of the 8th. Moth., & neither to meddle with hir Person, nor estate, till thinges bee cleared by advice from England, & Christop. Lawson is to keepe 5^s. p weeke out of his yearnings, when his debts are paid.

Co^rt Charges. ffrancis Smith is graunted his bill of 2^{lb}. 3^s. 11^d. for ferridge, & horse pasture, of Magistrates, & Deputies horses from the 25th. of y^e 2^d. Moth. 1642, to the 5th. of the 1st. Moth. $\frac{1643}{1644}$.

[287]

Merrickes fined. James, & John Merricke for drinking intemperately, and suffering others to drinke at their house, & selling wine, are fined 10^s. apeece, & to pay 2^s. 6^d. apeece, fees. Thomas Orton for intempate drinking is fined 5^s. & 2^s. 6^d. fees. Thomas Sheepe for intempate drinking is fined 5^s. & 2^s. 6^d. fees.

Orton. fined. Sheep.

---

* See Winthrop II. 157.

ffawer. Dorchester Constable.	The 23. of the 3ᵈ. Moᵗʰ. Barnabas ffawer tooke the oath for Constable for Dorchester for the yeare ensueing.
Richards. Read Waymouth Cō.	The 30ᵗʰ. day. Thomas Richards, & William Read beeing chosen Constables of the Toune of Waymouth did take their oathes.
Johnson. Parks. Comittee Mʳ. Cookes estate.	John Johnson, & William Parks are appointed a Comittee to examine, by the former Commissionoʳˢ or otherwise, to find out, gather vp, & receive into their custody, which hereby they are Authorized to doe, & to certify how they find thinges about Mʳ. Samuel Cooke his estate.

INDEX.

INDEX.

	PAGE
ABBOT	
Daniel, "departed to New Providence"	85
John, death of, Mathewe Bridge to answer for,	66
ABEL or **ABELL**	
Joane, discharged (presented for drunkenness)	105
Robert, discharged for want of witness.	79
business of, referred to Mr. Stoughton	94
ABUSES, power of Justices of Peace for reformation of,	3
ABUSIVE LANGUAGE. (*See* CRIMES, &c.)	
ACCIDENTAL DEATH, jury's verdict as to death of Austen Bratcher	7
ACTION or **ACTIONS**	
civil, order as to,	2
of Battery, jury impanneled to inquire concerning, (Dexter against Endicott)	15
civil, Court of Assistants for, referred to in note.	40
libel, Angell Hollard fined for,	72
molestation, unjust, damages to Richard Cooke against Thomas Robinson,	86
ADAMS	
Edward, enjoined to return to his wife.	105
Ferdinando, discharged.	84
Henry, sworn constable of Braintree	136
Richard, &c., Grand Jury	70
ADDINGTON, ISAAC, deposition by, as to Mr. Eldred's wine	129
ADULTEROUS CARRIAGE } (*See* CRIMES, &c.)	
ADULTERY	
AFFEILD, WILLIAM, &c., case of, (drinking too much)	130
AGGAWAM	
warrant to be sent to, (Order as to Plantations)	4
Sagamore of, banished from coming into any Englishman's house for the space of one year	17
no person shall plant or inhabit at, without leave, &c. except, &c.	31
Tho: Sellen granted leave to plant at,	32
John Shotswell fined for drunkenness at,	34
assessed to defray public charges.	37
to send in their money for three days work towards the Fort,	38

	PAGE

AGGAWAM, *continued*.
    to be called Ipswich 47
    Sagamore of, complaint by, as to damage in his corn by the swine of Charlton   49
    (*See also* IPSWICH.)
AINSWORTH, ANKER, case of, (taking excessive wages) 131
ALCOCK or }
ALCOCKE   }
    ———, Mr. &c., difference between Newton and Charlestown referred to,   29
    George, &c., agreement signed by, (as to bounds of Charles Towne and Newe Towne)   23
        Mr., &c., gift towards the Sea Fort 42
        will of, given in, &c. 102
ALEWIVES, order as to selling 43
ALEWORTH
    ———, Mr., &c., to be sent to England as "unmeet to inhabit here," . 10
        Lieutenant, granted liberty to return to England . . . 28
    Frauncis, Mr., chosen lieutenant unto Capt. Southcoate . . . 18
ALLEGIANCE, oath of, (*See* OATH.)
ALLEIN. (*See* ALLEN.)
ALLEN or ALLEIN
    ———, Mr., his strong water to be delivered to the Deacons of Dorchester for the benefit of the poor   26
        ment^d (case of Mr. Barnard) 94
        Mr., to have the Dedham transcript back 123
        Mr., oath by Frances Pembrooke as to estate of, . . . 128
    Andrew, granted administration on estate of his brother Edward . 133
    Bozoon, Mr., to satisfy for Gawen Wilson's fine 132
    Edward, committee appointed as to affairs of, ... 127
        &c., granted administration on estate of Mr. Edward Allen . 127
        Mr., administration on estate of, &c. 127-8
        a kinsman, &c., Mr. Allen gave his estate to, (Oath by Frances Pembrooke)   128
        administration on estate of, ... 133
    Henry, fined for drunkenness 94
    Joane, and Clem^t. Briggs, Mr. Tho. Stoughton fined for taking upon himself to marry them   10
    Ralfe, fined for releasing a servant before time 84
    Robert, fined for absenting himself from Court as a witness . . 33
        and Margaret Seale, indicted for adultery 66
        found guilty of adultery 70
        &c., whipped for concealing a plot of piracy 118
    Thomas, Mr., discharged 90
    William, land of, ment^d. (grant to Mr. Skelton) 24
ALLERTON or ALLIRTON
    Isaack, Mr., to make a payment to Mr. W^m. Dennison . . 47
ALLIRTON. (*See* ALLERTON.)

INDEX.

	PAGE

ALMY
    William, fined for taking Mr. Glover's canoe without leave . . 16
        fined for not appearing at Court, and to bring inventory of goods of Edw. Johnson 46
        Ensign Jennison &c. to make a payment to, and Robert Way to serve him 61
        and David Johnson, judgment in suit 61
AMEDOWNE, ROGER, to pay fees, admonished and discharged . . . 139
AMMUNITION } (*See* MILITARY AFFAIRS.)
ANCIENT }
ANDERSON
    Robert, fined and imprisoned for contempt 66
    Mr., order as to goods of, in hands of Samuel Maverick . 68
ANDREWE }
ANDREWES }
ANDREWS }
ANDROWS }
    ———, Mr., sale of Mr. Gurling's land to, confirmed 73
    Goodman, Mr. Baker of Ipswich allowed to keep an Ordinary instead of, 123
    Joseph, &c., judgment against Thomas Bushrode for not prosecuting, 82
    Robert, of Ipswich, debt due from, ment^d. (Inventory of goods &c. of Joseph Avery) 58
    Tho: &c., sentenced to be whipped, for assisting in stealing from the Indians, 19
    William, to be whipped and delivered up as a slave for assaulting his master, conspiring &c. 78-79
    Willi:, who was committed to slavery, released, to make a payment to Henry Coggan, and to serve Mr. Endecott, 87
ANKER, THOMAS, case of, (distemper in drink) 133
APLEGATE
    ———, who owned the canoe from which three persons were drowned, to appear in Court 78
    Elisabeth, wife of Thomas, to stand with her tongue in a cleft stick, for swearing, &c. 64
    Thomas, his wife Elizabeth to stand with her tongue in a cleft stick, for swearing, &c. 64
    &c., discharged with an admonition as to too many in a boat, 81
    to receive a payment for his canoe, ... 81
APLETON
    ———, Mr., Richard Saltonstall, &c., order as to agreement between . 64
    &c. accounts between, ment^d. . . 65
APPRENTICE
    Lucy Smith bound an, ... 17
    Sarah Morley apprenticed to Mr. Nathanaell Turner 22
    John Smithe bound an apprentice to Mr. John Wilson . . . 25
    Joshua Harris apprenticed to Frauncis Weston 41
    John Fox apprenticed to James Evrell 117

	PAGE
ARCHER	
Henry, &c., referred to Ipswich Court	83
John, case of, (resisting his master)	135
ARCHIVES, STATE,	
Records of Colony of the Massachusetts Bay in,	1
Records in,	115
ARDWAY, ABNER, dismissed with an admonition (dallying with Mary Giles)	135
ARMITAGE	
———, Goodman, case referred to, (Dearmant Matthew and Thomas Dexter)	129
Joseph, &c., costs against Joshua Hubbard for not prosecuting,	122
to pay four shillings to Francis Lightfoot	134
ARMS. (*See* MILITARY AFFAIRS.)	
ARNOLD or ARNOLL	
Richard, of Wenetsem^t, adm^n. on goods &c. of, granted to William Stitson	35
Thomas, sworn constable of Watertown	134
ARNOLL. (*See* ARNOLD.)	
ARTIFICERS, &c. order as to wages of,	12
ASPINWALL or ASPYNWALL	
———, Mr. &c. gift towards the Sea Fort	42
and Sir W^m. Brewerton, dep^{ns}. to be taken in case between,	48
William, &c. jury, as to death of Austen Bratcher	6
ASSAULT. (*See* CRIMES, &c.)	
ASSESSMENT, RATE, TAX, PUBLIC CHARGES &c.	
houses to be built for ministers at the public charge	1
allowance made to Mr. Patricke &c. at the public charge	4
for maintenance of Mr. Pattricke, &c.	6
Mr. Wilson, &c.	9
for making the Creek at Newe Towne	16
Governor, &c. to let all Islands to help towards public charges	17
for palisade about the Newe Towne	20
any planter trading with Indians for beaver to pay towards the public charges	23
for maintenance of Capt. Underhill, &c.	31
Cart Bridges	34
Public Charges	57
order as to rate on Mr. Dumer's estate in Rocksbury and Saugus	39
rate for cattle of Mr. Downing	40
constable of Dorchester fined for not returning his warrant for the last levy	50
rate to be repaid to Robert Moulton by the town of Salem	65
ASSISTANT or ASSISTANTS	
to direct the Beadle to issue summons &c. in Civil Actions, order as to,	2
justices shall not inflict corporal punishment without consent of,	3

INDEX.   147

ASSISTANT or ASSISTANTS, *continued.*

	PAGE
Capt. Endicott took the oath of an assistant, 7 Sept., 1630	3
any, not present at opening of the Court (8 A.M.) to be fined	4
no person shall plant within the limits of this pattent without leave from the Governor, &c.	4
license from the, as to selling corn, &c.	6
and Justice of the Peace, Isaack Johnson, Esq.,	7
Sir Rich: Saltonstall fined for whipping persons without the presence of another Assistant	9
resident at Boston, business concerning Mr. George Ludlowe to be referred to the, (order as to)	10
order in regard to number of Assistants	12
license from, ment^d. (Order as to travellers)	15
(Order as to persons buying corn &c.)	16
&c., to let &c. all Islands to help towards public charges,	17
every Assistant shall have power to grant warrants &c.	17
Capt. Endicott took the oath of an Assistant	24
any, shall have power to give orders as to levying fines (Order as to use of tobacco)	28
no wood shall be felled for palings but such as shall be allowed by the Assistant	28
Mr. Endicott takes oath as Assistant	33
certificate from, ment^d. (Order as to Military Affairs)	36
Idlers to be taken before the,	37
advice of, ment^d. (Order as to surveying houses, &c.)	45
Mr. John Winthrop, jun^r. took oath of an Assistant	46
John Humfry, Esq. " " " " "	47
&c., case heard by, 2 June 1636, referred to in note	62
oath of, taken by Mr. Richard Saltonstall	66
Mr. John Winthrope, jun^r.	77
Thomas Flint chosen an Assistant, 18, May, 1642	122

(*See also* MAGISTRATES.)

ASSISTANTS, COURT OF, or QUARTER COURT
       { PARTICULAR COURT }
       { SMALL COURT }

Records,	1
23 Aug. 1630,	1
to be held at the Governors house, 7 Sept. 1630	2
the first Tuesday in every month (question propounded)	2
to estimate charges for entertainment by the Governor (mem^o.)	3
7 Sept. 1630	3
7 Sept. 1630 Capt. Endicott took the oath of an Assistant in,	3
to be held every third Tuesday at the Governors house	4
fines imposed upon members absent at opening of the Court,	4
28 Sept., 1630	5
absence from, Sr. Rich: Saltonstall fined for,	6
19 Oct. 1630, (Walter Palmer to answer for manslaughter)	7
9 Nov. 1630	8

ASSISTANTS, COURT OF, *continued.*

	PAGE
30 Nov. 1630	9
meeting of Assistants in December, 1630, mentioned in note	10
1 March 1630–31	10
no Indian to be servant without license from,	11
8 March 1630–31	11
number of Assistants necessary to hold a Court &c.	12
22 March 1630–31	12
12 April 1631	13
3 May 1631	14
John Norman, sen[r]., fined for not appearing in,	14
3 Nov. 1635. ment[d]. in note	15
14 June 1631	15
5 July 1631	16
Acts of, to be authentic if they pass only under the secretary's hand	17
26 July 1631	17
16 Aug. 1631	18
6 September 1631	19
27 September 1631	19
18 October 1631	19
meeting of Assistants, 3 Feb. 1631–2	20
meeting of Assistants Feb. 17 & March 5, 1631–2, mentioned in note	21
6 March 1631–2	21
to be held on the first Tuesday in every month	21
Tho. Knower punished for threatening the Court	21
3 April 1632	21
5 June 1632	23
3 July 1632	24
meeting of Assistants August 3, 1632, mentioned in note	25
7 August 1632	25
4 Sept. 1632	26
3 October 1632	27
7 November 1632	28
meeting of Assistants December 4, 1632, mentioned in note	30
4 March 1632–3	30
finding fault with, Thomas Dexter sentenced for,	30
meeting of Assistants, 4 Dec. 1632 referred to in note,	30
1 April 1633	31
11 June 1633	32
2 July 1633	33
6 August 1633	34
3 September 1633	34, 57
1 October 1633	36
5 November 1633	38
meeting of Assistants, 17 Jan. 1633 (cancelled)	38
4 March 1633–4,	39
record of, in civil actions, referred to in note	40
1 April [1634]	42

INDEX.

ASSISTANTS, COURT OF, *continued*.

	PAGE
3 June 1634,	45
1 July 1634	46
at Newe Towne, 5 August 1634	47
6 October 1634	48
upbraiding of, by Ensign Jennison, mentioned	48
speaking reproachfully of, John Lee punished for	49
7 November 1634	50
meeting of Assistants, Nov. 27, 1634, mentioned in note	50
3 March 1634	50
meeting of Assistants, 27 Nov. 1634, referred to in note	50
7 April 1635	52
2 June 1635	54
7 July 1635	55
4 August 1635	55
1 September 1635	57
3 Nov. 1635	58
action of, in case of John Pratt, referred to in note	58
6 October 1635	59
meeting of the Magistrates Jan., 1635-6 referred to in note	61
1 March 1635-6	61
5 April 1636,	62
7 June 1636. (Quarter Court)	62
[2 June 1636] (note)	62
6 Sept. 1636. Quarter Court	63
6 Dec. 1636 "	64
7 March 1636-7 "	65
6 June 1637. (Quarter Court)	66
5 Sept. 1637. "	69
particular Courts to be kept the last Tuesday in Oct., 1637,	69
19 Sept. 1637. (Quarter Court)	69
5 Nov. 1637. "	71
6 March 1637-8. "	72
5 June 1638	74
4 Sept. 1638	76
4 Dec. 1638. (Quarter Court)	77
5 March 1638-9. "	81
4 June 1639. "	82
3 Sept. 1639. "	85
drawing a knife in, (Case of Thomas Gray)	87
31 Oct., 1639, Court for small causes	88
3 Dec. 1639	89
3 March 1639-40	91
30 April, and 29 Oct., 1640, Court for small causes	92, 93
2 June 1640. (Quarter Court)	93
20 May 1640	95
30 July 1640	95
1 Sept. 1640. (Quarter Court)	96

	PAGE

ASSISTANTS, COURT OF, *continued.*
    1 Dec. 1640. (Quarter Court) 99
    28 Jan. 1640–1 102
    2 March 1640–1. (Quarter Court) 103
    29 April 1641 104
    1 June 1641. (Quarter Court) 105
    29 July 1641 107
    7 Sept. 1641. (Quarter Court) 108
    28 Oct. 1641, record of, referred to 109
    3 Nov. 1635. (Case of John Pratt) 109
    Records of, ... 115
    28 Oct. 1641 115
    7 Dec, 1641. (Quarter Court) 115
    27 Jan. 1641–2 117
    1 March 1641–2. (Quarter Court) 117
    28 April 1642 118
    12 May 1642 119
    20 Feb. 1642–3 119
    16 Feb. 1642–3 120
    7 March 1642–3. (Quarter Court) 120
    27 April 1642 (1643?) 122
    7 June 1642. (Quarter Court?) 123
    28 July 1642 . (Small Court) 125
    6 Sept. 1642. (Quarter Court) 125
    27 Oct. 1642 127
    6 Dec. 1642. (Quarter Court) 128
    10 June 1643   " 130
    27 July 1643 131
    5 Sept. 1643. (Quarter Court) 132
    26 Oct. 1643 134
    5 Dec. 1643 134
    25 Jan. 1643–4 137
    5 March 1643–4. (Quarter Court) 138
ASSURANCE OF LANDS, order as to 45
ATTACHMENTS, every Assistant shall have power to grant attachments, &c. . 17
AUDELEY or }
AUDLEY   }
    Edmond, granted administration on goods of Francis Dent . . . 82
        referred to Court at Salem 83
    Mary, &c., case of, (filthy and unclean practise) . . . 134
AVERY, JOSEPH, Mr., administration and inventory of estate of, . . . 58

BABINGTON, RICHARD, ment^d. (Divorce of Anne Clarke) 138
BACHILER. (*See* BATCHILER.)
BACON
    Daniell, costs against Rich. Neve for not prosecuting, . . . 101
    Mighill, sen^r., discharged 105

INDEX. 151

BACON, *continued.*
 Nicholas, attachment against cattle of, for payment of rent to John Coggan   104
  Samuel, case of, (theft) 131
   Robert Wyar, &c., fined for drinking with, . . . 132
  William, Mr., &c., committee as to affairs of Edward Allen . . 127
BAGGERLY or BEGGARLY, BAGULEY
  ———, Mrs., consent by, to division of goods &c. of Mr. Skelton . 74
  Rich^d. and wife, case between, for divorce, referred to in note . . 62
  Thomas, case of, (seeking to get a maid without her friends consent) 97
   (selling his servants time) 105
BAGNALL, WALTER, order as to inquiry concerning the murder of, . . 25, 26
BAGULEY. (*See* BAGGERLY.)
BAIRSTOW } or BAYRSTOW.
BAIRSTOWE }
  Willi:, &c., sentenced to be whipped for drunkenness 63
  William, discharged 132
BAKER
  ———, Mr., of Ipswich, allowed to keep an Ordinary, . . . 123
  John, Mr. Clearke, ordered to make a payment to, . . . 4
   &c., inquisition on body of Willm. Bateman upon oaths of, . 7
   to be whipped for shooting at fowls on the Sabbath Day . . 9
   damage against John Pemberton for not prosecuting, . . 86
  Natha:, &c., witnesses, grant to, ... 98
  Robert, death of, (case of Richard Hollingworth) 103
  (or BARKER) William, &c., to be whipped for running away from their masters, &c. 59
   sentenced to be whipped for theft . . . 62
BALDWIN or BAULDWIN
  John, case of, (excessive drinking) 138
  Richard, allowed an executor of the will of his father . . . 77
  Sarah, allowed an executor of the will of her husband . . . 77
  Silvester, will of, presented, his wife Sarah and son Richard exec^{rs}. 77
  Thomas, case of, (miscarriage to his master) 134
BALLARD
  ———, Mr., administration on estate of, ... 117
  Willi:, hiring none but such as had lots was discharged . . . 79
BALSHE, JOHN, &c., jury (Case of Walter Palmer) 9
BALSTON or BAULSTON
  William, &c., jury (Case of Walter Palmer) 9
   fined for selling beer, ... 68
   Willi:, licensed to keep a house of entertainment and to sell claret, &c. 68
BAND. (*See* MILITARY AFFAIRS.)
BANISHMENT. (*See* PUNISHMENT.)
BARCROFTE
 Jane, wife of John, to be of good behavior towards all persons, (recognizance) 36

152 INDEX.

	PAGE
BARCROFTE, *continued*.	
John, Mr., recognizance by, for good behavior of his wife Jane,	36
BARKER	
(or BAKER) William, &c., sentenced to be whipped for running away from their masters, &c.	59
William, to be whipped for theft	62
BARLOW	
George, sentenced to be whipped for idleness	70
"Barlow Copy" in Boston Public Library, mentioned	115
BARNARD	
———, Mr., case of, (giving strong water to certain persons)	94
Bridget, case of, (theft)	137
John, case of, (distempered with wine)	95
fined for being distempered with wine	105
case of, (distemper in drinking)	107
fined for his dangerous well	136
Joshua, apprenticed to Mr. Paine	26
Thomas, admonished and discharged about lace	116
William, fined for swearing	134
BARRELL, GEORGE, Elisha Jackson "turned over for his time from," to John Millam	119
BARSHAM	
William, &c., viewed the body of Austen Bratcher	7
Willi:, &c., jury of life and death	70
BARTHOLMEW }	
BARTHOLMEWE }	
BARTHOLOMEW }	
———, Mr., his servant Mary sentenced to be whipped for running away	57
cause of, referred, mentions Capt. Keayne	129
Will:, &c., Grand Jury	70
BARTLET or }	
BARTLETT }	
John, case of, (swearing, theft and drunkenness)	133
Robert, sentenced to have his tongue put in a cleft stick for swearing, &c.	74
summons for,	99
discharged,	103
Thomas, servant to Mr. Pelham, to be whipped for unjust selling of his master's tools	14
William, case of, (drunkenness and lying)	83
Willi:, discharged	99
BARTON,	
Marmaduke, &c., whipped for concealing a plot of piracy	118
case of, (theft and running away)	118
BASSE	
Samuell, fined for contempt	78
Samu:, fine remitted to,	92

INDEX. 153

	PAGE

BATCHELER }
BATCHILER } or BACHILER,
————, Mr. silenced as a pastor, &c., for contempt of authority . . 27
    act restraining him from gathering a Church within this
        pattent, reversed 30
  William, &c., respited until the next Court 88

BATEMAN
————, Sergeant, goods sold by him to Mr. Pinchon, W^m. Parke to
        make satisfaction for, 25
  William, inquisition on body of, 18 Sept. 1630 7
  &c., inquisition upon oaths of, ... 7
  was set on shore near Pullen Point (Oaths by Walter Nor-
        ton &c.) 8

BATES
  Edward, &c. of Weymouth, difference referred to, (Welthia[n]
        Richards and Henry Waltham) 102
    witness, (Case of Thomas Hawkins) 116
BATTE, CHRISTOPHER, case of, (selling his servant his time) 100
BATTER, EDMUND, Mr., costs against John Humphrey for not prosecuting, . 126
BATTERY. (*See* ACTIONS AND CRIMES.)
BAULDWIN. (*See* BALDWIN.)
BAULSTON. (*See* BALSTON.)
BAY, THE. (*See* MASSACHUSETTS.)
BAYLY
————, &c., order to apprehend 69
  Jno. &c., sent for 69
  John, case of, (buying land of the Indians) 83
  Richard, put himself to Abraham Hill 138
  Thomas, &c., witnesses, oath by, (Will of William Fry) . . . 134
BAYRSTOW. (*See* BAIRSTOWE.)
BEADLE, THE,
  James Peñ's employment to be as a beadle (Order as to ministers) . 2
  summons, &c., by, in Civil Actions (Order as to) . . . 2
  James Peñ took oath of, ... 4
  goods of the Company of husbandmen to be inventoried by the beadle 23
  House for the beadle to be built at Boston 27
  agreement as to his salary 27
  process for the warning of jurors to be directed to the beadle . 38
  allowance to James Peñ to build a house and order as to, . . 38
BEAMIS, JOHN, fined for freeing his servant 135
BEAMSLEY, WILLIAM, his servant, David Conway, to be whipped . . 127
BEAVER
  order as to rates for, ... 8
  articles of agreement as to a general trade in beaver, order as to, &c. . 15
  Chickatabut fined a skin of beaver for shooting a swine . . 16
  corn shall pass for payment of all debts except money or beaver be ex-
        pressly named 20
  no planter returning to England shall carry money or beaver with him
        without leave from the Governor 21

BEAVER, *continued.*
  any planter who trades with the Indians for beaver shall pay twelve pence   23
  order as to Mr. Treasurers beaver trade   27

BECK or }
BECKE   }
  Alex:, Joyce Bradwicke to pay him twenty shillings for refusing to marry him   32
  Alexander, to have corn &c. for Mary Joanes   102
    granted corn for his trouble with Mary Joanes . . .   107

BEECHER, THOMAS, Mr., &c., differences referred to   47

BEGGARLY. (*See* BAGGERLY.)

BELCHER, ANDREW, Thom. White granted costs against, . . .   133

BELL
  Sarah, case of, (theft from her master)   121
  Thomas, respited   94
  Will:, non appearance of, (Case of John Morecroft)   103

BELLINGHAM
  ———, Mr., or Deputy, &c., present at Court, 65, 71, 72, 74, 76, 82, 85, 88, 89, 91–93, 119, 120, 122, 123, 125, 127, 128, 130–132, 138
    Deputy, Mr., &c., to examine accounts between Mrs. Walcott and Edmond White   100
    Governor, presentment of, referred to in note   103
    Mr., was Governor 27 April 1642, referred to in note . .   122
  Richard, Mr., &c., present at Court, ... 62–64, 66, 69
    &c. to examine witnesses &c. concerning Mr. White and Mrs. Wolcott   74
    ment^d. (Order as to estate of Joane Drake) . . .   77
    &c., (Court of Assistants) order by, (Case of John Pratt)   112
  Samuell, ment^d. (Will of Joane Drake)   72

BENDALL
  ———, Goodman, &c., to arbitrate between Mr. Humphrey and Robert Saltonstall   133
  Edward, fined "40s. to the Company"   62

BENEFEILD. (*See* BINFEILD.)

BENJAMIN
  ———, Mr., &c., land of Mr. Gurling sold by, ...   73
  John, Mr., &c., dismissed from training by reason of age, &c. . .   50
    to sell Mr. Gurling's land to satisfy creditors . .   71
    account by, as to estate of Richard Gurling . . .   85

BENNET or }
BENNETT   }
  Edward, and wife witnesses, (Case of Walthian Richards) . . .   116
  Elisa:, case of, (unchaste miscarriage)   95
  John, fined for drunkenness   33
    attachment against, ...   73
    &c., referred to Salem for drunkenness   75

INDEX.

	PAGE
BENTLEY, MARY, case of, (stealing Mr. Walton's jewel)	137
BERES, RICHARD, &c. certificate by, (Case of Mighill Bacon)	105
BETS. (*See* BETTS.)	
BETSCOMBE, RICHARD, &c., jury of life and death	70
BETSON, STEPHEN, case of, (sinful attempt)	139

BETTS or BETS
  John, discharged for want of evidence to prove his overselling . . 80
    discharged 136
BICKERSTAFFE, JOHN, to be whipped for fornication 79
BIGGS, JOHN, &c., at Aggawam, ment^d. 31
BILBOES. (*See* PUNISHMENT.)
BILLS, assignment of, to be good debt 18
BILLS, ROBERT, administration on estate of, granted to John Knowles . . 77
BINCKS, BRYAN, &c., bond by, (to answer when called upon to give an account
    of their company goods) 25
BINFEILD (or BENEFEILD), JOHN, deceased, order as to children of, . . 67
BIRCHWOOD, land near Salem so called granted to Capt. Jo: Endicott . . 24
BIRD, SIMON, sentenced to be whipped &c. for running away from their
    masters &c. 59
BISHOPP, RICHARD, on behalf of his wife, granted administration on goods &c.
    of Richard King 54

BLACKESTONE
  ———, Mr., Nahanton ordered to give him two skins of beaver for
    damage done his swine 52
  William, Mr., ground near his house in Boston set out to, . . . 31
BLACKMORE, The, (Mincarry) mentioned 118
BLADEN, WILLIAM, Mr., payment to his servant, James Riddway, mentioned . 130

BLANTON
  William, &c., who were in a canoe from which three persons were
    drowned to appear in Court 78
  Willi: , &c., discharged with an admonition as to too many in a boat . 81
BLASPHEMY. (*See* CRIMES, &c.)

BLUMFEILD
  John, administration on estate of, granted to his son Thomas and order
    as to his estate 91
  Thomas, appointed adm^r. to his father John Blumfeild &c. . . . 91

BOARDS
  whoever buys boards of William Knopp or his son, shall pay one half
    of the price to Sir Richard Siltonstall, 9
  &c., order for preservation of, ... 17

BOATS
  order as to, ... 3
  William Blanton &c. admonished as to too many in a boat . . . 81
BOCKING, John Smitheman &c. of, mentioned 96

BOGGUST
  John, &c., to sit in the stocks at Salem 6
    notice to creditors of, ... 15
BONITO, ———, Capt., his master Henry Laurence discharged . . . 82

	PAGE
BO^RNE. (*See* BOURNE.)	
BOSTON, Town of,	
ordered that Trimountaine shall be called Boston	4
ment^d. (Order as to levy for maintenance of Mr. Patricke &c.)	6
order as to payment for building a ferry between Boston and Charlton	8
ment^d. (Rates for maintenance of ministers)	9
Assistants resident at, business concerning Mr. George Ludlowe to be referred to,	10
John Legge to be whipped in, for striking Richard Wright	14
and Charlton, Edw. Converse to keep the ferry between,	16
ment^d. (Order as to levy for the creek at Newe Towne)	16
a watch of six and an officer shall be kept every night at,	17
&c., Capt. Underhill's Company to train at,	18
part of Mr. Shepheard's fine to be used for paying for ferrying the watch from Boston to Charlton	20
assessed (Order as to levy for making a palisade)	20
House of Correction and a house for the beadle to be built at Boston	27
chosen as the fittest place for public meetings of any place in the Bay.	28
neck of land between Powder Horne Hill and Pullen Point to belong to Boston	29
inhabitants of, to have liberty to fetch wood from Dorchester Neck &c.	29
and Rocksbury, agreed that bounds formerly set out between, shall continue	31
assessed for maintenance of Capt. Underhill &c.	31
to fetch wood from Noddle's Island	31
ground set out to William Blackestone near his house in Boston	31
and Rocksbury, to pay charges for cart bridges over Muddy River and Stony River	34
order as to finishing Fort at,	35
assessed to defray public charges	37
market to be kept at Boston every Thursday	40
and Rocksbury, Ensign Stoughton &c. to settle bounds between	41
Mr. John Wilson pastor of the Church of Boston, grant to,	43
Long Island, Deere Island and Hogg Island granted to Boston for twenty one years	44
constable of, fined for not returning his warrant for the last levy	50
Rich. Cokar sentenced to be whipped at, for enticeing servants to run away, &c.	51
William James to be set in the bilboes at, for incontinency,	65
John Coggeshall of, merchant, ment^d.	67
James Browne to be set in the bilboes at, for drunkenness	68
in New England mentioned (Will of Joane Drake)	72
Nicholas Busbey to appear at, (attachment)	73
traverses their presentment	75
constable of, fined for not returning his jury warrant	76
fined for defective highways and for want of a watch house	79
fined for defective highways	84

INDEX. 157

BOSTON, Town of, *continued*.
 Town of Roxbury fined for damming up the nearest way from Dorchester to Boston   84
 fined for defect of their ways between Powder Horn Hill and the written tree   90
 chose William Hudson to keep an ordinary   93
 &c. to pay charges for Muddy River Bridge   93
 had time to repair their ways between Powder Horn Hill and the written tree   99
 enjoined to mend their ways   106
 Henry Webbe &c. constables of, granted power as to estate of Paul Yonge   107
 to bring in rates of wharfage &c.   108
 Church of, ment^d. (Case of Francis Hutchinson) . . .   109
 fined for defective ways towards Roxbury   117
 Robert Wyar &c. to be whipped at, ...   121
 time granted to, ...   123
 John Wooldridge to acknowledge his fault at, ...   126
 discharged, the way to Charlestown being made good . . .   129
 presented for defective highways   130
 Robert Wright to sit in the stocks at Boston for being distempered with drink   134
 the constable of, fined for not returning his warrant   137
 Court at, ... 20, 86, 88, 91, 92, 98, 102, 107, 125
 Court of Assistants holden at,   8–10, 12–91, 23–28, 30–34, 36, 38, 39, 42, 76, 89, 91, 104, 117–119, 122, 127, 134, 137
 Quarter Court held at,   .   62–66, 69, 77, 81, 82, 85, 90, 93, 96, 99, 103, 105, 108, 115, 117, 120, 128, 130, 132, 138
 Small Court at, 28 July 1642   125
 Public Library, copy of record in, ment^d. 1, 115

BOSWORTH
 ———, Widow, and her family, order as to payment of money for maintenance of   48
 Benjamin, ordered to make a payment to Mr. Seawall   55
 Edward, and family order as to reimbursing Henry Sewall for money spent for,   55
 Jonathan, to make a payment to Mr. Seawall   55
  case of (discountenancing a witness)   124
  bond for appearance &c.   124
  discharged from his bond   126
 Nathanaell, to make a payment to Mr. Seawall   55
 Sacheas, &c., case of (drinking too much)   130

BOURNE (or BORNE), NEHEMIAH, Mr., ment^d. (divorce of Anne Clarke) .   138

BOWEN
 George, case of (not serving on the jury)   107
 Griffin, &c., jury (case of Marmaduke Peirce)   89

BOWLER, MARY, to make double restitution for things stolen by her . .   66

BOWMAN, ———, Rich. Williams fined for drunkenness at house of, . .   40

BOWTLE or BUTTOLPH
 Leonard, case of (neglecting to obey a warrant) 93
  Robert Wyer put to, with his masters consent . . . 122
BOYLSTON
 Sarah, wife of Thomas Boylston ment^d. (case of Richard Browne) . 121
 Thomas, his wife Sarah mentioned (case of Richard Browne) . . 121
BOYSE, THOMAS, case of, (attempting a rape with Sarah Jusall) . . . 81
BRADLEY, KATHERIN, granted admr. on her husband's estate and order as to said estate 125
BRADSTREET or }
BRADSTREETE }
 ——, Mr., &c., present at Court . 3, 5, 8–14, 48, 50, 54, 55, 57, 62
  to examine accounts (Richard Saltonstall and Edward Dillingham) 63
  ment^d. (accounts of Richard Saltonstall, Mr. Apleton &c.) 65
  &c., present at Court 74, 76, 82, 86, 91, 96, 103, 105, 108, 117, 120, 123, 125, 130, 132, 138
 Simon, (or Symon,) secretary, record in handwriting of, . . . 1
  &c., present at Court 1, 15–21, 23, 24
  insolent carriage and speeches to, Thomas Dextor fined for, . 24
  &c., present at Court 25–27
  sixty acres of meadow granted to, in the marsh against the Oyster Bank 28
  &c., present at Court . 28, 30–34, 36, 38, 39, 42, 45, 46, 47, 50
  &c., to take charge of writings left by the husband of Ruth Lockwood 51
  to dispose of the estate, &c. of Edmond Lockwood if necessary, 52
  &c., present at Court 52, 58, 59, 61, 63, 64, 77
  secretary, writing by, referred to 109
  &c., (Court of Assistants) order by (case of John Pratt) . . 112
BRADWICK or }
BRADWICKE }
 Joyce, to pay Alex: Becke twenty shillings for refusing to marry him 32
BRAINTREE, TOWN OF,
 enjoined to make their pound, stocks, and watch house . . . 99
 inhabitants of, respited as to bridge over Minotocot River . . . 116
 time granted to, ... 123
 fined 129
 David Williams to be whipped at, ... 135
 Henry Adams sworn constable of, ... 136
BRANDING. (*See* PUNISHMENT.)
BRANDON, WILLIAM, to appear as a witness (case of James Brittaine) . . 130
BRATCHER
 Austen, or Austin, jury impanneled to inquire concerning death of, 28 Sept. 1630 6
  who died at Mr. Cradock's plantation, his body viewed before burial 7

INDEX.   159

BRATCHER, *continued*.
 Austen, death of, by strokes inflicted accidentally by Walter Palmer (jury's verdict) . . . 7
  Walter Palmer to answer for death of, ... 7
  jury impanneled concerning the death of, ... 9
BREAD
 making bread too light [weight] (case of Thomas Hawkins) . . 116
 Edward Wood fined for baking contrary to order 124
 neglecting an order as to, (case of William Web) 127
BRECKE, EDWARD, &c., jurymen, fined for not appearing 102
BRENTON, ———, Mr., &c., to settle difference between John Coggeshall and Phebe Seales 67
BRERETON. (*See* BREWERTON.)
BREWAR
 Daniell, granted adm^n. on estate of John Greene 81
 &c., jury, (case of Hugh Buett) 101
BREWERTON (or BRERETON), William, Sir, Baronet, and Mr. Aspinwall dep^{ns}.
  of witnesses to be taken in case between 48
BRIANT, THOMAS, case of, (concealing and consenting to piracy) . . . 118
BRIBE in case of Walter Palmer ment^d. (sentence of Tho. Foxe) . . . 12
BRICKLAYERS, order as to wages of 3, 5, 36
BRIDG or }
BRIDGE }
 ———, Goodman, &c., to lay out Mr. Gurling's land 73
  to hear business between John Smith and Jeremy Norcross 100
 John, bond by, (case of Matthew Bridge) 66
 &c., to lay out Mr. Gurling's land 73
  to hear business between John Smith and Jeremy Norcross 100
 Mathewe, or Mathew, bond for appearance to answer for death of John Abbot 66
  acquitted for lack of evidence 71
BRIDGES
 Saugus plantation to make and repair a foot bridge 27
 agreement as to a cart bridge over Muddy River and over Stony River 34
 Israel Stoughton allowed to build a bridge over Neponset River . . 43
 ment^d. (Dorchester presentment) 84
 Town of Hingham fined for defective ways and bridge . . . 94
 ment^d. (order as to Roxbury and Dorchester) 99
 over Minotocot River, inhabitants of Braintree respited as to, . . 116
 Hingham granted time to finish the bridge over Layfords liking . . 116
 in Braintree, Martin Saunders to repair, ... 129
BRIGGS or BRIGS
 Clement, and Joane Allen, Mr. Tho: Stoughton fined for taking upon himself to marry them 10
  fined for entertaining an Indian without leave, &c. . . 49
  bond for his wifes appearance 72
  wife of, mentioned (case of Arthur Warren) . . . 72

	PAGE
BRIGGS or BRIGS, *continued.*	
Clement, wife of, enjoined not to accompany Arthur Warren	75
found not guilty of extortion and discharged	79
BRIGHAM, THOMAS, &c., jury, (case of Marmaduke Peirce)	89
BRIGHT	
Henry, sentenced to be set in the bilboes for swearing	50
dismissed	73
took oath as surveyor of arms in Watertown	95
BRIGS. (*See* BRIGGS.)	
BRISCOE, NATHANIEL, Mr., case of, (mutinous speeches, &c.)	120
"BRISTOWE MARCHANT," Ship, William Waltham fined for being drunk aboard	91
BRITTAIN or BRITTAINE	
James, &c., Robert Tucker sentenced for upbraiding	94
&c., bond by, (case of Gawen Wilson)	115
&c., bond for appearance, &c.	130
condemned to death for adultery with Mary Latham	139
BROOKE, THOMAS, sworn constable of Concord 8 Dec. 1638	80
BROUGHTON, ———, Mr., dismissed	136
BROWNE	
———, Mr., &c., payment from John Simpson for not prosecuting,	86
James, &c., witnesses, ment^d (inquisition on body of William Bateman)	8
Ja., ment^d (case of William Almy)	16
James, &c., bond by, (case of William Dixon)	57
to be set in the bilboes at Boston for drunkenness	68
fined for selling strong water to the Indians	68
company keeping &c. with, Benjamin Hubbard admonished for,	68
&c., jury, (case of Hugh Buett)	101
adm^n. granted to, on estate of Thomas Knower	117
Malachy, costs against Francis Perry for not prosecuting,	118
Richard, &c., jury, as to death of Austen Bratcher	6
&c., inquisition upon oaths of, on body of William Bateman	7
evidence by, as to debt of W^m. Knopp to Sir Richard Saltonstall	13
jury, (Dexter against Endicott)	15
Mr., allowed to keep a ferry over Charles River against his house	38
&c., to take an inventory of goods &c. of Mr. Craford of Watertowne, to receive a payment from William Curtis for John Jesop	48 / 71
Mr., case of, (unmeet dalliance with Sarah Boylston)	121
William, case of, (obscene speeches)	104
(running away, deriding an Ordinance of God &c.)	122
BROWNING, ———, Mr., case of, (selling strong water)	93
BRUMFEILD, WILLIAM, case of, (stealing from his master &c.)	70

INDEX. 161

	PAGE

BUCKLAND
    William, &c. to be whipped for assisting in stealing from the Indians . 19
        to make a payment to Mr. Seawall 55
BUCKMASTER, THOMAS, being in distress is granted money and corn . . 92
BURT ⎫
BUETS ⎬
BUETT ⎭
    Hugh, banished for heresy 101
BUGGERY. (See CRIMES, &c.)
BULGAR
    Richard, testimony as to wages paid to, ... 56
        &c., to make payment towards the discharge of their forfeits 57
BULKELEY
    Peter, Mr., granted the corn of Alexander Thwayte 94
        &c., witnesses to answer by John Pratt 111
BULL
    ———, ten pounds paid to Lt. Mason for taking of, ... 84
    wife of, John White not to go into company of, . . . 95
    Blith, and her husband William, case of, (fornication before marriage) 121
    ment^d (case of Richard Smyth) 130
    William, and his wife Blith, case of, (fornication before marriage) . 121
BULLETS. (See MILITARY AFFAIRS.)
BUNELL or ⎫
BUNNELL ⎭
    William, &c., jury, as to death of Austen Bratcher 6
BUNTING, ANN, will of, given in 102
BURDEN, GEORGE, ment^d (as to David Weane) 137
BURGES
    John, &c., witnesses, oath by, (will of William Fry) . . . 134
    Thomas, dismissed with an admonition 133
BURGLARY. (See CRIMES, &c.)
BURKBEE, THOMAS, watchman, imprisoned for drinking and set in the stocks 87
BURNING GROUND. (See FIRES.)
BURR
    Jehu, &c., chosen for Rocksbury (order as to cart bridge over Muddy
                                    River &c.) 34
    and Mr. Dumer, difference between, referred to a committee . 61
BURROWS, JOHN, case of, (going into mens houses on the Lords Day &c.) . 98
BURSLIN ⎫
BURSLYN ⎬ or BUSLIN
    ———, Mr., referred to Court at Salem 107
    John, order as to his late servant Thomas Lane 45
    &c., jurymen, fined for absence from Court 74
BURT
    Hugh, wife of, fined for swearing &c. 83
    part of fine remitted to, &c. 86
BURTON
    Edward, fined for contempt of authority and drunkenness . . 27

INDEX.

	PAGE
BURTON, *continued.*	
Edward, to keep Robert Way who was assigned to him by Ensign Gennison	48
&c., to make a payment to William Almy	61
BURWOOD or } BURWOODE	
Ales, to be whipped for yielding to John Bickerstaffe &c.	79
William Gurtridge enjoined to take care of,	87
BUSBEY or } BUSBY	
Nicholas, attachment against, for non appearance	73
Willi:, presented for drunkenness found to have the falling sickness	75
BUSHRODE	
Thomas, judgment against, in favor of David Phippen &c. for not prosecuting	82
case of, (defaming the Government)	86
BUSLIN. (*See* BURSLIN.)	
BUSSACKER or } BUSSAKER	
Peter, to be whipped for drunkenness and fined for slighting the magistrates	64
&c. referred to Court at Salem for fighting &c.	80
BUTCHER, ROBERT, &c., case of, (drinking too much)	130
BUTTERWORTH, MARY, and Thomas Clifton, James Parker allowed to marry	102
BUTTOLPH. (*See* BOWTLE.)	
BUTTON	
———, Goodman, ment^d. (allowance to Evan Thomas)	97
allowed charges with Tho: Evans	101
Goodwife, theft from, (case of Bridget Barnard)	137
John, &c., jury, (case of Marmaduke Peirce)	89
BYFORD (or PYFORD), PETER, &c. to be whipped &c. for running away from their masters &c.	59
BYRAM, NICHOLAS, &c., granted adm^n. on goods of Abraham Shawe	98
CABLE, JOHN, &c., sentenced to be whipped for stealing	13
CADWICKE. (*See* CHADWICKE.)	
CAKEBREAD, THOMAS, Grand Jury	70
CALLWELL, JOHN, &c., presented for taking too much wages	135
CAMBRIDGE, Town of,	
Court of Assistants at, 5 June 1638	74
fined &c.	75
constable of, fined for not returning his jury warrant	76
fined for want of a watch house, pound and stocks	80
pound	85
discharged from presentment about stopping fish	85
fined for defective highways	85
enjoined to repair highways at Long Swamp and Vine Brook	85
fined for want of stocks and for neglect of a constant watch	90

INDEX. 163

	PAGE
CAMBRIDGE, Town of, *continued*.	
fined for defective way at Vine Brook and Long Swamp	90
to pay charges for Muddy River bridge	93
discharged of fine as to way at Vine Brook &c.	99
certified to having repaired the way toward Concord	106
enjoined to repair the way between Watertown and Roxbury	106
give Squa Sachim corn &c.	106
fined for a defective way to Charlestown	117
Robert Wyar &c. to be whipped at,	121
John Wooldrige to acknowledge his fault at,	126
and Dedham, order as to the way between	135
(*See also* New Town, Town of)	
CAMPIAN or CAMPION	
———, Mr., attachment by, against Robert Mindam	122
Clement, Mr. Edward Paine granted costs against,	123
costs against John Rogers for not prosecuting	136
CANNONEER. (*See* MILITARY AFFAIRS.)	
CANOES	
order as to,	3
taken from the Indians, (order as to punishment of Thomas Morton)	4
belonging to Mr. Glover, William Almy fined for taking,	16
order as to using canoes at ferries &c.	78
CAPIAS ment^d. (order as to civil actions)	2
CAPING, ———, Goodman, ment^d. (will of John Russell)	57
CAPITAL PUNISHMENT. (*See* PUNISHMENT.)	
CAPTAIN. (*See* MILITARY AFFAIRS.)	
CARDS, all persons that have cards dice or tables in their houses shall do away with them	12
CARPENTER, WILLIAM, took oath as constable of Weymouth	102
CARPENTERS	
order as to wages of	3
master carpenters	5
order as to wages of,	12
master carpenters &c.	36
CART BRIDGE. (*See* BRIDGES.)	
CARTER	
———, wife of, admonished	117
Richard, wife of, admonished	107
Thomas, sen^r. took oath as constable of Charlestown	104
constable of Charlestown fined for not warning the jury in time	108
CASTLE, the, ment^d. (order as to Richard Osborne)	67
CASTLE ISLAND, Fort at, ment^d. (order as to Richard Long)	60
CATTLE	
bought of merchants of Dorchester ment^d.	5
owners of, to make satisfaction for damage done by them	14

164　　　　　　　　　　　INDEX.

                                                                                   PAGE

CATTLE, *continued*.
    ment^d. (order as to Islands) 17
    neglecting to provide houseing &c. for, ment^d. (order as to Thomas Coleman) 58–59

CAYRIES. (*See* CHAIRYES.)

CHADBORNE
    William, sen^r., &c., case of, (drinking too much) . . . 130
        discharged (John Shaw ment^d.) 137

CHADWELL, RICHARD, to receive witness fees from George Woodward . . 68

CHADWICKE or CADWICKE
    Charles, fine remitted to, ... 119
        &c., fined for being absent being warned 128
    John, Capt., case of, (swearing and disorder) 135
        Capt. Aaron Williams discharged from, ... 136

CHAIRYES (or CAYRIES), JOHN, presentment of his wife ment^d. . . . 85

CHALKLEY. (*See* CHAULKLEY.)

CHAPMAN
    Henry, case of, (not obeying a press) 94
    Jacob, allowance to, for travel &c. 119
    John, fined for selling boards contrary to an order of Court and fine remitted upon promise &c. 40
        &c., gift towards the Sea Fort 42
        meadow mowed by, ment^d. (order as to accomodations to Newe Towne), 47

" CHARLES " (ship)
    Willi: Tynge &c. to examine the books about the goods which came in, 97
    bond by Samuel Maverick for the company of, ... 97

CHARLES RIVER
    ordered that the town upon the Charles River be called Watertown . 4
    Mr. John Maisters hath undertaken to make a passage from Charles River to the Newe Towne 16
    land on west side of, granted to Thomas Dudley Esq. . . . 23
    land up Charles River granted to Mr. Phillips 30
    ferry over, Mr. Richard Browne allowed to keep. . . . 38
    land above the Falls on, granted to Thomas Dudley &c. . . 42
    land near Mount Feakes on, granted to John Oldham . . . 43
    ment^d. (agreement as to bounds of Watertown and Newton) . . 53

CHARLESTOWN ⎫
CHARLESTOWNE ⎬ Town of,
CHARLTON ⎭
    Court of Assistants holden at, 23 Aug. 1630 1
                       7 Sept. 1630 3
                       28 Sept. 1630 5
    ment^d. (order as to levy for maintenance of Mr. Patricke &c.) . . 6
    inquisition at, on body of William Bateman 18 Sept. 1630 . . 7
    order as to payment for building a ferry between Boston and Charlton 8
    ment^d. (order as to maintenance of ministers) 9
    Thomas Walford of, case of, ... 14

INDEX.

CHARLESTOWN
CHARLESTOWNE
CHARLTON } Town of, *continued*.

	PAGE
and Boston, Edw. Converse to keep ferry between,	16
ment^d. (order as to levy for the creek at Newe Towne)	16
(order as to a watch of six)	17
(order as to training of Capt. Underhill's Company)	18
part of Mr. Shepheard's fine to be used for paying for ferrying the watch from Boston to Charlton,	20
assessed, (order as to levy for making a palisade)	20
Robert Coles fined for being drunk at Charlton	21
and Newe Towne, agreement as to setting out bounds of,	22
ordered that the difference between, be referred to Mr. Mavericke &c.	29
agreement as to bounds of,	30
assessed for maintenance of Capt. Underhill &c.	31
to fetch wood from Noddle's Island	31
Ezekiell Richardson chosen constable of,	31
grant to inhabitants of, near North River	33
assessed to defray public charges	37
Robert Moulton chosen constable of,	43
inquiry as to damage done by swine of,	46
inhabitants of, to satisfy the Indians for damage done to corn by swine	46
complaint as to damage done by swine of, in corn of the Sagamore of Aggawam	49
Edmond Hubbard, sen^r., chosen constable of,	51
Henry Harwood of, ment^d.	72
Tho. Ewar chosen and sworn constable of,	73
fined &c.	75
for want of a watch house	80
Elisabeth Chaulkley of, ment^d.	83
discharged about Richard Lowden's lot	83
Meeting House in, to be a watch house	90
chose Robert Longe to sell wine	93
allowed to use the Meeting House as a watch house	99
Thomas Carter, sen^r., &c., took oath as constables of,	104
Edward Johnson of, ment^d.	105
Thomas Carter, sen^r. constable of, fined	108
fined for defective way to town of Cambridge	117
delivered in a transcript of their lands	117
allowance to constables of,	119
Francis Norton &c. sworn constables of,	121
John Wooldrige to acknowledge his fault at,	126
way to, being made good, Boston is discharged	129

CHAULKLEY or CHALKLEY

———, wife of Robert Chaulkley, attachment for,	81–82
Elisabeth, of Charlestown, case of, (stealing)	83
Robert, attachment for wife of,	81–82

	PAGE
CHEATING. (*See* CRIMES, &c.)	
CHEBACCO, Willi: Lampson allowed to fell trees on the other side of,	108
CHEESBRO or } CHEESBROUGH }	
Will:, &c., inquisition on oaths of, upon body of William Bateman	7
William, &c., jury, (case of Walter Palmer)	9
to settle the bounds between Dorchester and Rocksbury	29
Willi:, &c., appraisers (estate of Joane Drake)	72
ment^d. (order as to estate of Joane Drake)	77
CHEESHOLME, THOMAS, his servant Richard Wilson sentenced for abusing him	104
CHENY, ——, Goodman, ment^d. (case of Willi: Pilsberry)	107
CHESTER	
——, Mr., bond for appearance	43
case of, (for selling contrary to order)	44
CHICKATABUT } CHICKATAUBOTT } CHICKATAUBUT }	
fined a skin of beaver for shooting a swine	16
land sold by, to Mr. Pinchon ment^d.	55
CHIDLEY	
——, Mr., case of, (confederating and concealing)	109
was gone out of the country before Court	116
CHILDE	
Ephraim, &c., evidence by, as to debt of William Knopp to Sir Richard Saltonstall	13
comm^{rs}. to take an inventory of Mr. Crispe's estate &c.	20
to take an inventory of goods &c. of Mr. Craford	48
CHRIST, "in a way of Christ" ment^d. (order as to Hingham members)	126
CHUBB, THOMAS, shall be freed from the service of Mr. Samuel Maveracke	14
CHURCH or CHURCHES	
gathering of, by Mr. Batchel^r.	80
of Boston, grant to Mr. John Wilson pastor of,	43
Waterton, to dispose of the children and estate Edmond Lockwood	52
&c., consent by, as to estate of Edward Lockwood	54
of Salem, ment^d. (order as to settlement of Mr. Skelton's estate)	74
Mary Oliver punished for disturbing	80
opinion against singing in the Churches (case of Edward Tomlins)	105
of Boston, ment^d. (case of Francis Hutchinson)	109
Watertown, offensive passages against (case of John Stowers)	121
of Hingham, Thomas Painter sentenced for disturbing	135
CHURCH	
Garrett, &c., gift towards the Sea Fort	42
bond by, (case of Mr. Chester)	43
(case of Christopher Grant)	103
CHURCHES. (*See* CHURCH.)	
CIVIL ACTIONS. (*See* ACTIONS.)	

INDEX. 167

	PAGE

CLAPBOARD-RYVERS &c. order as to wages of, ... 36
CLARE, JOHN, case of, (drunkenness) 92
CLARKE or CLEARKE, CLERKE
    ———, Mr., to make a payment to John Baker (for fraudulent dealing) 4
        bond by, as to his good behavior &c. 8
        prohibited cohabitation with Mrs. Freeman . . . 8
        &c., at Aggawam ment^d. 31
    Anne, granted a divorce from her husband Denis Clarke for desertion &c. 138
    Daniell, referred to Ipswich Court 83
        case of, (immoderate drinking) 86
    Denis, Anne Clarke granted a divorce from, for desertion, &c. . . 138
    James, and Joane Clarke suspected of fornication 63
    Joane, and James Clarke suspected of fornication 63
    Thomas, Mr., his man sold shot to an Indian 101
    William, &c., jury, (Dexter against Endicott) 15
    Will:, sentenced for theft 64
CLAY, THOMAS, charges to John Baker for not prosecuting . . . 98
CLEARKE. (*See* CLARKE.)
CLEFT STICK. (*See* PUNISHMENT.)
CLERK OF THE BAND. (*See* MILITARY AFFAIRS.)
CLERKE. (*See* CLARKE.)
CLIFTON, THOMAS, and Mary Butterworth, James Parker allowed to marry, 102
CLOIS, JOHN, admonished to use his servant, Peter Tylls, well, &c. . 88
CLOTHING &c. order as to price of, ... 39
CLOUGH
CLOUGHE }
CLUFFE
    John, fined for his absence when the jury was called 132
    Richard, order as to seizing strong waters belonging to, . . . 5
        fined and bound to good behavior for saying " shall I pay 12^d.
        for the fragments which the grandjury rogues have left ? " 97
COASTERS, common, &c., ment^d. (order as to idlers) 37
COBBETT
    ———, Mr., &c. to be sent to England " as unmeet to inhabit here " . 10
    house of, and Wanottymies River, ground between granted to
        Govr. John Winthrop, Esq. 29
COCKRAM ———, Mr., his servant, John Neale, committed on suspicion of felony 128
CODDINGTON
    ———, Mr., &c., present at Court,   3, 5, 8–12, 32–34, 36, 38, 39, 42, 47, 65
        &c. chosen for Boston (order as to cart bridge over Muddy River, &c.) 34
        ment^d. (case of John Woolrige) 88
    William, Mr., &c., present at Court 63–64
        &c. (Court of Assistants) order by, (case of John Pratt) . 112

	PAGE
COGAN, COGGAN or COGGIN	
———, Mr., &c., granted adm^n. on goods &c. of John Tilley	43
testimony as to wages paid to James Hawkins	56
Henry, and John Tylley, difference between, referred to John Winthrop, sen^r. &c.	47
his servant, W^m. Androws, punished for assaulting him &c.	78–79
&c., judgment against Thomas Bushrode for not prosecuting	82
Willi: Androws to make a payment to,	87
John, Mr., &c., gift towards the Sea Fort	42
and John Tylley, difference between, referred to John Winthrop, Esq. &c.	47
&c., difference between, as to ship "Thunder," referred to a committee	54
discharged because those whom he hired were other mens servants	79
Mr., to receive a payment from Mr. Willi: Tyng	92
attachment against Nicholas Bacon's cattle for payment of rent to,	104
COGGESALL, COGGESHALL or COXEALL, COXESHALL	
———, Mr., John Sayle and his daughter bound to	32
his servant, John Sayles, to be whipped for running away	40
&c., gift towards the Sea Fort	42
business of, referred to Mr. Pinchon &c.	53
John, of Boston, order as to his apprentice, Phebe Seales,	67
COGGIN. (*See* COGGAN.)	
COITMORE, ———, Mr., ment^d. (case of Gawen Wilson)	132
COKAR, RICHARD, to be whipped for enticeing servants to run away &c.	51
COLBRAN or COLEBRAN, COLEBRON	
———, Mr., &c., chosen for Boston (order as to cart bridge over Muddy River &c.)	34
to lay out Mr. Gurlings land	73
Thomas, Mr., &c., to settle estate of Mr. Mellows	97
William, &c., appointed to lay out bounds between Waterton and Newe Towne, return by,	53
COLCHESTER or COLECHESTER, Town of,	
Samuel Winsley sworn surveyor of the arms at,	98
presentments discharged	100
COLE or COLES	
Clement, &c., to be whipped &c. for running away from their masters	59
John, to be whipped for stealing	59
Richard, to work for his living until a master be found for him	126
put to William Haward for one year	127
Robert, &c., fined for drinking	18
confessed his fault and his fine for drunkenness was remitted	21
of Rocksbury, fined for being drunk	21
Mr., &c., at Aggawam ment^d.	31

INDEX. 169

        PAGE

COLE or COLES, *continued.*
- Robert, fined for drunkenness &c. 34
    - sentenced for drunkenness 41
    - damages to be paid by Mr. Fawne 59
    - enjoined to pay witnesses and discharged 76
- Samuell, forfeited twenty shillings for selling beer . . . 59
    - &c., testimony by, (case of John Hathaway) . . . 66
    - licensed to sell claret and white wine 67
    - fined for selling beer 67
- Susan, to make double restitution 118

COLEBRAN ⎱
COLEBRON ⎰ (*See* COLBRAN.)
COLECHESTER. (*See* COLCHESTER.)
COLEMAN
- Andrewe, letter of attorney to John Haynes ment^d. 96
    - and Willi: Swift order in case between 96
- Thomas, keeper of cattle, order as to, ... 58
    - Anthony Emery to pay charges to, ... 80

COLES. (*See* COLE.)
COLLAINE, MATTHEW, &c., whipped for concealing a plot of piracy . . 118
COLLECOT. (*See* COLLICOTT.)
COLLEGE, the, ment^d. (case of Thomas Symonds) 88
COLLENS
- ——, Mr., &c., to hear business between John Smith and Jeremy Norcross 100
- Henry, fined for not serving on the Grand Jury 76
- William, Mr., case of, (seducing) 109

COLLICOT ⎱
COLLICOTT ⎰ or COLLECOT
- ——, Sergeant, house of, to be used as a watch house by the town of Dorchester 84
- Richard, &c., difference between John Cogan, John Tylley &c. referred to 54
    - &c. jurymen, fined for absence from Court 74
    - case of, (mending Indians guns) 101
    - Mr., bill paid to, ... 120

COLLIER, THOMAS, &c., bond by, (as to things taken from John Hardies wreck), 105
COLONIAL SOCIETY OF MASSACHUSETTS, Transactions of, referred to . 103, 115
COLONY, THE. (*See* MASSACHUSETTS.)
COMMODITIES
- no servant shall give sell or truck any commodity without license from their masters 5
- no person shall buy corn or any other provisions of any ship that comes into the Bay without license 16
- order as to price of, ... 39
- selling, contrary to order, by Mr. Chester, Garett Church, &c. bound to appear to give testimony as to, 44

INDEX.

	PAGE

COMMONWEALTH, THE. (*See* MASSACHUSETTS.)
COMPANY. (*See* MILITARY AFFAIRS.)
CONAMABSQNOONCANT RIVER or DUCK RIVER
    land near Salem bounded on the south by, granted to Mr. Samuel Skelton . . . 24
    land near Salem bounded on the north by, granted to Capt. Jo. Endicott . . . 24
CONANT or CONNANT
    ———, Mr., &c., to settle the bounds between Rocksbury and Dorchester . . . 29
    Christopher, &c., jury, (case of Walter Palmer) 9
    Roger, &c., bond by, (case of John Ellford) 11
    to set out land to John Humfry, Esq. 30
CONANT'S ISLAND
    &c. shall be appropriated to the public benefit &c. 16
    with privileges of fishing &c. demised to John Winthrop Esq. Govr. for life and to be called Governors Island . 22
CONCORD, Town of,
    fined for want of a pair of stocks and a watch house 79
    Thomas Brooke sworn constable of, 8. Dec. 1638 80
    Willi: Fuller who kept the mill at, ment^d. 85
    discharged as to lot of Robert Edwards 85
    fined for want of a watch house 85
    highways leading to, to be repaired by town of Cambridge . . . 85
    fined for not giving in a transcript of their lands and for neglecting their watch . 90
    deferred until the Quarter Court 100
    Walter Edmonds took oath as constable of, ... 103
    town of Cambridge certified to having repaired the way toward, . . 106
    fined for neglecting the watch and non appearance . . . 106
    ment^d. (answer by John Pratt) 110
    delivered in an imperfect transcript of their lands &c. . . . 124
    men of, granted power to seize land &c. 139
CONECTICUT. (*See* CONNECTICUT.)
CONFEDERACY. (*See* CRIMES, &c.)
CONFRONTING. (*See* CRIMES, &c.)
CONNANT. (*See* CONANT.)
CONNECTICUT, Colony of,
    Thomas Marshfeild of, ment^d. 100
    ment^d. (answer by John Pratt) 110
CONSTABLE, ———, Mr., Simon Voysey fined for striking . . . 115
CONSTABLES
    John Woodbury chosen constable of Salem 5
    Thom[as] Stoughton chosen constable of Dorchester 5
    John Woodbury took the oath of constable 5
    allowance for killing of wolves &c. to be levied by the constables of the plantations . 8
    Mr. Thomas Stoughton, constable of Dorchester, fined for "taking upon him to marry" . 10

CONSTABLES, *continued.*
 of the several plantations, order to, as to creditors of Capt. Levett &c. . 15
  Dorchester, William Phelpes chosen 19
  Rocksbury, Mr. Shepheard's fine returned by, ... 20
  Saugus, Mr. Turner chosen, ... 26
  Dorchester, George Dyar chosen, ... 28
  Charlton, Ezekiel Richardson chosen, ... 31
  plantations to publish order as to selling liquor . . . 33
 and two inhabitants to name wages of inferior workmen . . 36
 to use special care &c. as to idlers 37
 of Rocksbury, Mr. William Dennison chosen, ... 40
  Charlton, Robert Moulton chosen, ... 43
  plantations to whip runaways and send them home . . . 43
 and four inhabitants of every town to make a survey of houses &c. . 45
 of Dorchester, Eltwood Pumery sworn, ... 45
  Waterton, Samuel Hosier chosen and sworn, ... 48
  Dorchester and Boston fined for not returning their warrants for the last levy 50
  Charlton, Edmund Hubbard, sen^r. chosen, ... 51
  Dorchester, Steven Terry sworn, ... 55
   John Philips chosen, ... 63
 Richard Osborne to give a weekly account to, of how he spends his time 67
 of Newbury, to apprehend Schooler &c. 69
  Charlestown, Thomas Ewar chosen and sworn, . . . 73
  Cambridge and Boston fined for not returning their jury warrants 76
  Dedham, John Haward sworn, 5 Dec. 1638 80
  Concord, Thomas Brooke sworn, 8 Dec. 1638 80
 John Dunvard to make a payment to the constable for witnesses . 93
 neglecting to obey warrant served by, (case of Leonard Bowtle) . 93
 John Porter and Henry Tuttle took oath as constables of Hingham . 97
 of Weymouth, William Carpenter sworn, ... 102
  Concord, Walter Edmonds sworn, ... 103
  Charlestown, Thomas Carter, sen^r. &c. sworn, . . . 104
  Watertown, John Whitney sworn, ... 105
  Charlestown, Thomas Carter sen^r., fined for not warning the jury in time &c. 108
  Watertown to provide a place of service for Elizabeth Wilsmore . 117
 John Whitney fined for not warning Charles Chadwicke . . 119
 of Charlestown, allowance to, ... 119
  Hingham, order sent to, as to Mrs. Strainge and her child . 119
  Charlestown, Francis Norton &c. sworn, ... 121
  Weymouth, John Harding &c. sworn, ... 123
 ment^d. (case of Eliz: Strainge) 124
 of Roxbury, to take care of John Kempe 125
  Hingham, Thomas Cooper, &c., ment^d. 126
  Woburn, Edward Converse, ment^d. 126
  Dorchester, George Wicks sworn, ... 130

	PAGE
CONSTABLES, *continued*.	
of Lynn, William Langley sworn,	132
Hingham, Francis James sworn,	132
Watertown, Thomas Arnold sworn,	134
Braintree, Henry Adams sworn,	136
Boston, fined for not returning his warrant	137
Dorchester, Barnabas Fawer sworn,	140
Weymouth, Thomas Richards and William Read sworn,	140
CONTEMPT. (*See* CRIMES, &c.)	
CONVERSE	
Edward, &c., jury, as to death of Austen Bratcher	6
(Dexter against Endicott)	15
hath undertaken to set up a ferry between Boston and Charlton	16
allowance to, for ferrying officers over the water	31
&c., bond by, (case of William Dixon)	57
appraisers, (estate of Henry Harwood)	72
bond for appearance of Edward Fuller	88
case of, (neglecting the ferry)	94
constable of Woburn ment^d.	126
CONVEYANCES to be recorded	45
CONWAY, DAVYD, case of, (resisting his master W^m. Beamsley)	127
COOKE	
Richard, grant against Thomas Robinson for unjust molestation	86
Samuel, Mr., committee appointed as to estate of,	140
COOLEY, WILLIAM, fined for drunkenness	40
COOPER	
Anthony, forfeited his bond for non appearance	61
John, jun^r., committed to his father for correction	80
Thomas, &c., constables of Hingham ment^d.	126
fined for drinking with Samuel Bacon	132
absence from the Grand Jury	138
COPE, Willi:, case of, (concealing)	109
COPELAND, Laurence, case of, (covenanting for wages)	128
COPPERAS thrown into a man's yard (case of Thomas Davenport)	91
CORN	
owners of cattle to make satisfaction for trespass in,	14
burning ground for, ment^d. (order for preservation of houses &c.)	17
to pass for payment of all debts except money or beaver be expressly named	20
Sagamore John promised to fence his corn against all kinds of cattle	26
every person shall satisfy for the damage done by his swine in the corn of another	28
order as to price of,	31
fencing corn &c.	33
price of corn and as to giving it to swine	38
price of,	43
surveying cornfields &c.	45
allowance of corn to Evan Thomas	97

INDEX.

CORNALL
CORNEHILL
CORNELL
    Thomas, being licensed was discharged 79
          fined for selling wine &c. 84
CORNISH or
CORNISHE
    John, bond for appearance 121
    Katherine, wife of Richard, suspected of incontinency, seriously admonished 74
          respited, &c. 79
    Richard, recognizance by, for appearance of his wife 47
          his wife, Katherine, admonished 74
COTCREE, THOMAS, case of (dalliance with girls) 126
COTTON WOOL
    fine to be paid in, ment^d. (case of George Watts) 127
    ment^d. (case of Gawen Wilson) 132
COUNCIL, The,
    &c., oaths for. ment^d. in note 15
    meeting of, Nov. 23, 1632, referred to in note 30
    &c., case heard by, 2 June 1636, referred to in note 62
    the "Counsell Table" ment^d. (case of Thomas Miller committed for seditious speeches) 63
COURT OF ASSISTANTS. (*See* ASSISTANTS, COURT OF.)
    GENERAL. (*See* GENERAL COURT.)
    QUARTER. (*See* ASSISTANTS, COURT OF.)
    PARTICULAR, or SMALL COURT. (*See* ASSISTANTS, COURT OF.)
    at Boston, Salem, &c. (*See* under name of place)
COW HOUSE RIVER, or SOEWAMAPENESSETT RIVER, near Salem ment^d., grant to Capt. Jo. Endicott 24
Cows, ment^d. (order as to trespasses in corn) 14
COXEALL
COXESHALL } (*See* COGGESHALL.)
CRABTREE, JOHN, &c., bond by, as to overpayment 98
CRADOCK or
CRADOCKE
    ———, Mr., plantation of, Austen Bratcher died at, ... 7
        order as to his servant, Tho. Foxe 12
        to care for one of the children of John Binfield, deceased . 67
        George Pye to remain with, &c. 76
    Mathewe, Mr., fined for his men being absent from training . . 29
        of London, &c. weir at Misticke granted to, . . . 41
CRAFORD ——— Mr., goods of, inventoried 48
CREDITORS of Ralfe Glover to demand their debts (order as to his estate) . 46
CRIBB, BENJAMYN, &c., sentenced to be whipped for stealing 13
CRIMES, MISDEMEANORS, &c.
    absence from Court, Mr. Ludlowe &c. fined for, ... 4
    wrong done to Indians, Thomas Morton punished for, . . . 4

	PAGE

CRIMES, MISDEMEANORS, &c., *continued.*

fraudulent dealing, Mr. Clearke to pay for,	4
planting without leave, order as to,	4
Indians using firearms, order as to,	5
servants selling commodities, order as to,	5
wages fixed	5
absence from Court, Sr. Richard Saltonstall fined for,	6
selling corn without license, order as to,	6
felony, John Goulworth &c. sentenced for,	6
manslaughter, death of Austen Bratcher (jurys verdict)	7
misdemeanor towards his master, Richard Diffy to be whipped for,	8
manslaughter, the jury finds Walter Palmer not guilty of manslaughter	9
whipping contrary to order, Sr. Richard Saltonstall fined for,	9
stealing a loaf of bread, Bartholmewe Hill to be whipped for,	9
shooting at fowl on the Sabbath Day, John Baker punished for,	9
Thomas Moulton to pay for wrong done to Mr. Glover	10
Thomas Stoughton fined for marrying persons unlawfully	10
selling money to an Indian, order as to,	10
Indians as servants, order as to,	11
Nich. Knopp fined for undertaking to cure the scurvy	11
Sr. Richard Saltonstall to pay for wigwams burnt by his servant	11
malicious and scandalous speeches, Thomas Foxe to be whipped for,	12
cards, dice or tables, order as to,	12
stealing, Benjamin Cribb, John Cable and Morris Trowent to be whipped for,	13
shooting after the watch is set, order as to,	13
assault, John Legge whipped for striking Richard Wright	14
contempt of authority and confronting officers, Thomas Walford sentenced for,	14
Thomas Bartlett whipped for unjustly selling &c.	14
not appearing at Court, John Norman, sen^r. fined for,	14
running away from master, Phillip Swaddon punished for,	16
malicious and scandalous speeches against the Government, &c Philip Ratliffe sentenced for,	16
buying corn without leave, order as to,	16
shooting a swine, Chickataubott fined for,	16
taking away a canoe, William Almy fined for,	16
burning ground till first of March, order as to,	17
misbehavior &c. towards his master, Francis Perry sentenced for,	18
drunkenness, Mr. Shepheard &c. fined for,	18
writing falsely, &c., against the Government, Henry Lyñ sentenced for,	19
enticing an Indian woman to lie with him, John Dawe sentenced for,	19
whether adultery either with English or Indian shall not be punished with death (question propounded)	19
drunkenness, &c., Mr. Alex. Wignall sentenced for,	19
stealing corn from the Indians, Josias Plastowe punished for,	19

INDEX. 175

PAGE

CRIMES, MISDEMEANORS, &c., *continued*.
stealing corn from the Indians, Wm. Buckland and Tho. Andrewe sentenced for aiding Josias Plastowe in, 19
adultery, if any man shall have carnal copulation with another man's wife both shall be punished with death 19
drunkenness, Robert Coles fined for, ... 21
      remitted by the Court . . 21
threatening the Court, Tho. Knower was set in the bilbowes for, . 21
insolent carriage and speeches to S. Bradstreete, Thomas Dexter fined for, 24
drunkenness, Mr. James Parker, &c., fined for, ... 25
murder of Walter Bagnall, order as to inquiry concerning, . . . 25, 26
drunkenness, James Woodward to be set in the bilbowes for, . 26
cursing, swearing, &c., Robert Shawe sentenced to be whipped for, . 26
refusing to watch, John Stickland fined for, ... 26
drunkenness, William Hamon sentenced to be set in the bilbowes for, 26
selling firearms, powder and shot to the Indians (case of Rich^d. Hopkins) 27
contempt of authority, &c., Mr. Batchel^r. silenced for, . . 27
      Edward Burton fined for, ... 27
running away from his master, &c., James Woodward sentenced for, 27
drunkenness, &c., Edward Burton fined for, ... 27
drunkenness and fornication, Nicholas Frost sentenced for, . 28
taking tobacco publicly, forbidden, ... 28
absence from training and wanting arms, John Finch &c. fined for, . 29
fornication, Robert Huitt and Mary Ridge, sentenced for committing, 30
seditious words against the Government, Thomas Dexter sentenced for, 30
drunkenness, Thomas Wincall fined for, ... 31
planting at Aggawam without leave, order as to, ... 31
feloniously taking away corn and fish, (case of John Sayle) . . 32
drunkenness, William Dixon sentenced for, ... 32
fornication with Eliz. Marson, John Pemberton sentenced for, . 32
absenting himself from Court as a witness, Robert Allen fined for, . 33
drunkenness, James White fined for, ... 33
    John Bennett fined for, ... 33
selling strong water, order as to, ... 33
drunkenness, John Woolridge fined for, ... 34
drunkenness, John Shotswell fined for, ... 34
drunkenness, enticing &c. Robert Coles sentenced for, . . 34
confronting of authority, assault on Mr. Ludlowe, &c., Capt. John Stone sentenced for, 35
absence from the Jury, Mr. Palmer fined for, ... 35
contempt of authority &c. Alex. Wignall fined for, . . . 35
drunkenness, &c , Alex. Wignall fined for, ... 35
drunkenness, Sergeant Perkins sentenced for, ... 36
    Thomas Dexter fined for, ... 36
absence from training, order as to, ... 36

PAGE

CRIMES, MISDEMEANORS, &c., *continued.*
idleness, order as to punishment of idlers 37
extortion, order as to, ... 39
running away from his master (case of John Sayles) 40
buying land of any Indian without leave, order as to, ... 40
stealing and running away from his master, &c., Christopher Tarling sentenced for, 40
selling boards contrary to an order of Court, John Chapman fined for, 40
drunkenness, Richard Williams fined for, ... 40
William Cooley fined for, ... 40
Timothy Hawkins &c. fined for, ... 40
selling strong water contrary to order, Edward Howe fined for, . . 41
drunkenness, Robert Coles sentenced for, ... 41
abusive language, John Lee punished for, ... 43
non appearance, Thomas Foxe fined for, ... 43
Wm. Almy fined for, ... 46
taking too high wages (case of James Rawlens) 47
unchaste &c. behavior with Thomas Elkyn, Katherine Gray sentenced for, 48
upbraiding the Court with injustice, &c., Ensign Jennison fined for, . 48
entertaining an Indian without leave Clement Briggs fined for, . . 49
speaking reproachfully of the Governor and enticing, &c., John Lee sentenced for, 49
drunkenness, Samuel Hall fined for, ... 49
swearing, Henry Bright set in the bilbowes for, ... 50
defacing the colors (case of Ensign Damford) 50
swearing, bond for appearance of Wm. Knopp for, ... 50
drunkenness, Christ. Graunt fined for, ... 50
not returning his warrant, constable of Dorchester fined for, . . 50
enticing servants to run away, Rich. Cokar sentenced for, ... 51
Samuel Johnson sentenced for, . . 52
stealing, Griffin Montague sentenced for, ... 53
swearing and stealing, John Hayward sentenced for, ... 53
absenting himself from court, Mr. Humfry fined for, ... 54
misdemeanor, Francis Toby sentenced for, ... 55
drunkenness, John Love fined for, ... 55
threatening to sink a boat, &c., Mr. Thomas Wonnarton sentenced for, 55, 56
taking too high wages, Arthur Holbidge, &c., sentenced for, . . 56
felony, William Wills sentenced for, ... 56
contempt, Arthur Holbidge sentenced for, ... 56
running away from his master Andrew Storyn to be whipt for, . . 57
Robert Scarlett to be whipt for, . . 57
her master Mr. Bartholmewe's servant to be whipt for, 57
misdemeanor, John Pease sentenced for striking and deriding his mother, &c. 59
stealing, John Cole sentenced for, ... 59
returning after banishment, Nich. Frost to be tried for, . . . 59

INDEX. 177

CRIMES, MISDEMEANORS, &c., *continued*.

	PAGE
selling beer at 2ᵈ a quart, Samuel Cole sentenced for,	59
liquor, Mr. Nowell, &c., fined for selling wine, &c.	59
stealing, &c., Clement Cole &c., servants, sentenced for,	59
stealing, Daniel White sentenced for,	60
felony, Robert Scarlett, a known thief sentenced for,	60
contempt of authority, &c., Richard Long fined for,	60
extortion in selling knives, &c., (case of Joshua Huyes)	60
carnally knowing their wives before marriage, Edward Gyles &c., fined for	60
drunkenness, Richard Phelps fined for,	61
non-appearance, Anthony Cooper forfeited his bond for,	61
Henry Joslyn &c. forfeited their bonds for,	61
non-appearance, bond forfeited by Griffin Montague for,	61
drunkenness, James Luddam fined for,	61
stealing victuals from his master, &c., Wᵐ. Shepheard sentenced for,	62
drunkenness, &c., Wᵐ. Perkins sentenced for,	62
striking his master, George Ropps sentenced for,	62
theft, Wᵐ. Barker sentenced for,	62
drunkenness, John Whitele &c., sentenced for,	63
seditious speeches, Thomas Miller committed for,	63
swearing, Robert Shorthose sentenced for,	63
drunkenness, Peter Bussaker sentenced for,	64
attempting a rape, swearing, house-breaking, &c., Edward Woodley sentenced for,	64
swearing, revileing, &c., Elizabeth Aplegate sentenced for,	64
theft, Will: Clarke sentenced for,	64
fornication, Anthony Robinson sentenced for	64
light carriage, Capt. Lovell admonished to take heed of,	65
incontinency, knowing his wife before marriage, Wᵐ. James sentenced for,	65
slander, idleness, &c., Thomas Pettet sentenced for,	65
theft, Mary Bowler to make restitution for things stolen by her	66
shooting a wolf dog, John Sweete fined for,	66
contempt, Robert Anderson sentenced for,	66
Will: Powell to answer for,	66
adultery, John Hathaway indicted for,	66
Robert Allen and Margaret Seale indicted for	66
drunkenness, Edward Seale sentenced for,	67
entertainment, keeping a house of, &c., without license, George Munnings fined for,	67
liquor, selling, &c., without license, George Munnings fined for,	67
selling beer at 2ᵈ., Robert Longe &c. fined for,	68
drunkenness and selling strong water to the Indians without license, James Browne sentenced for,	68
speeches against Mr. Vaine, Wᵐ. Knop to answer for,	68
murder of John Hobbey, John Williams found guilty of,	69
murder, Wᵐ. Schooley found guilty of,	69

INDEX.

CRIMES, MISDEMEANORS, &c., *continued*.

	PAGE
adultery, John Hathaway found guilty of,	70
Robert Allen found guilty of,	70
Margaret Seale " " "	70
stealing, idleness, &c., W^m. Brumfeild sentenced for,	70
receiving stolen money, George Spencer " "	70
idleness, George Barlow sentenced for,	70
drunkenness, John Hogges fined for,	71
speaking contemptuously of the magistrates, John Green sentenced for,	71
lending a gun to an Indian, Mr. John Stretton fined for,	71
theft and running away, Luke Henbury sentenced for,	72
liquor, Joseph Faber fined for selling wine	72
libell, Angell Hollard fined for,	72
keeping company with another man's wife Arthur Warren fined for,	72
drunkenness, &c., John Woolridge admonished, &c. for,	73
drinking, &c., Christopher Grant fined for,	73
speaking against the law about swine, Thomas Starr fined for,	73
absence from the Jury, Rich^d. Collicot fined for	74
swearing, &c., Robert Bartlet sentenced for,	74
John Smith sentenced for,	74
contempt, Edward Lambe fined for contempt	75
dancing, wife of Laurence Waters, &c., admonished for dancing	75
drunkenness, John Bennet, &c., referred to Salem for,	75
leaving a pit or well open, Thomas Ewar and Edmond Hubberd, Senr., fined for,	75
absence from the Jury, Henry Collens fined for,	76
speaking against the Magistrates, Elders and Churches, Katherine Finch punished for,	76
drunkenness, George Horne fined for,	76
swearing, George Walton fined for,	77
drawing wine contrary to order, contempt, &c., (case of John Holgrave)	78
taking above double toll, Thomas Wilson fined for,	78
contempt, Samuel Basse fined for	78
drunkenness, Richard Turner fined for,	78
murder, Dorothy Talbie to be hanged for,	78
assault upon his master, conspiracy &c., William Androws sentenced for,	78, 79
stealing and breaking into houses, John Haslewood sentenced for	79
stealing and house breaking, Gyles Player sentenced for,	79
fornication, John Bickerstaffe sentenced for,	79
extortion, Clement Brigs found not guilty of,	79
abusing his servant, John Poole fined for,	80
disturbing the Church of Salem, case of Mary Oliver	80
quarrelling and fighting, Richard Greaves, &c., referred to Court at Salem for,	80
prophaning the Sabbath, case of Rich^d. Hollingsworth	80

INDEX.

CRIMES, MISDEMEANORS, &c., *continued*.

	PAGE
pound breach, Anthony Emery fined for,	80
lying, Thomas Savory referred to Ipswich Court for lying	80
lewdness, John Davies to be whipped &c. for attempting,	81
rape, Thomas Boyse sentenced for attempting a rape with Sara Jusall.	81
stealing, Isaack Deesbury fined for,	81
tempting to uncleanness, Richard Ibrooke fined for,	81
swearing, &c., John Hogges fined for,	81
selling strong water, Richard Silvester fined for,	81
speeches against the magistrate, Robert Shorthose sentenced for,	81
speaking against the law about hogs, &c., Richard Silvester fined for,	82
speaking against ministers, Samuel Norman sentenced for,	82
non appearance, Mr. John Harrison fined for, and admonished against gaming	83
drinking and lying, William Bartlet fined for,	83
cursing, &c., Ellen Peirce fined for,	83
stealing, Elizabeth Chaulkley to make double restitution for things stolen by her	83
selling strong water, Mr. Goouch fined for,	83
buying land of the Indians without leave, John Bayly fined for,	83
swearing, &c., Hugh Burt's wife fined for swearing, &c.	83
liquor, Thomas Cornell fined for selling wine, &c.	84
idleness & disorderly living, Nicho. Ellen fined for,	84
giving his man his time, Capt. Stoughton fined for,	84
want of scales and weights, Mr. Waltham &c. fined for,	84
taking too much toll, Mr. Waltham fined for,	84
giving a servant his time, Ralfe Allen fined for,	84
taking too much toll, Wm Fuller fined for,	85
common railing, John Gosse sentenced for,	85
drinking, John Stacy, jun^r. set in the stocks for,	85
excessive drinking, Ralfe Warriner fined for,	85
liquor, Nicholas Merry fined for selling strong water	86
running away and stealing, John Neale sentenced for,	86
stealing, Richard Wilson sentenced for,	86
drunkenness, Richard Turner fined for,	86
sundry drinkings at his house, Willi: Dawes fined for,	86
defaming the Government, Thomas Bushrode fined for,	86
murder, suspicion of, (case of Marmaduke Peirce)	86
drinking, Daniel Clarke fined for immoderate drinking	86
being in company of drunkards, John Wedgwood sentenced for,	86
unclean attempts, John Kempe sentenced for,	86
Matthew Edwards sentenced for misdemeanor	87
selling strong water, Thom. Knore fined for,	87
swearing, Nicholas Davison fined for swearing	87
drunkenness, John Hogg fined for,	87
John Kitchen fined for showing books he was to bring to the Governor	87
defileing his wife before marriage, John Joanes fined for,	87

INDEX.

CRIMES, MISDEMEANORS, &c., *continued.*

	PAGE
drunkenness, profanity &c., Thom. Gray sentenced for,	87
quarrelling, Richard Redman, &c., fined for,	87
going to, and pleading with the jury, case of Thomas Lechford	87
Thomas Millard, &c., watchmen, imprisoned for drinking strong water	87
drunkenness, Burkbee set in the stocks for,	87
John Woolrige fined for,	88
cheating, Richard Joanes sentenced for,	88
Willi: Powell fined for resisting the surveyor	88
Edward Fuller, &c. to appear at the next court for being distempered with wine	88
swearing, ——— Tacye fined for,	88
extortion, Richard Pepper fined for,	89
bigamy, James Luxford sentenced for having two wives	89
murder, Marmaduke Peirce found not guilty of,	89
light behavior, Elnor Peirce sentenced for,	89
——— Quick " "	89
extortion, Lewes Hewlet fined for and bound over for contempt	89
disorderly house and drunkenness, Jane Robinson sentenced for,	89
ill behavior, Margaret Hindersham sentenced for,	90
unclean attempt, &c., Robert Penyar sentenced for,	90
drunkenness, William Waltham fined for,	91
defileing and refusing to marry, John Vaughan committed to prison for,	91
Thom. Davenport admonished for causing balls of paste with copperas, to be thrown into a yard	91
extortion, money paid to the Govr. by one guilty of, ment^d.	91
contemptuos speeches, &c., Mr. Henry Seawell punished for,	92
drunkenness, John Clare fined for,	92
unchaste attempt, stubbornness, &c., John Pope sentenced for,	92
uncleanness, John Danvard accused of,	93
George Palmer punished for committing folly	93
enticing, Margery Rugs sentenced for,	93
scandalous speeches, Nathaniell Travell admonished for,	93
neglecting to obey a warrant, Leonard Bowtle fined for,	93
selling strong water, Mr. Browning fined for,	93
insolent carriage, George Hyrne sentenced for,	93
unquietness with his wife (case of James Davies)	93
not obeying a press, Henry Chapman fined for,	94
upbraiding James Britain, Robert Tucker fined for,	94
getting his wife with child before marriage, Willi: Powell fined for,	94
drunkenness, &c., Thom. Gray sentenced for,	94
breaking a house in the time of exercise, and theft, Thom. Savory sentenced for,	94
drunkenness, Henry Allein, &c., fined for,	94
giving strong water, Mr. Barnard fined for,	94
immodest expressions, Elizabeth Lovel admonished for,	94

INDEX. 181

                                         PAGE

CRIMES, MISDEMEANORS, &c., *continued*.
  getting his wife with child before marriage, John Downham fined for, 94
  neglecting the ferry, Edward Converse fined for, 94
  want of weights and scales, Mr. Rich^d. Dummer fined for, 94
  disturbing the peace, John Tower fined for, 95
  insolent carriage, two indian women sentenced for, 95
  unchaste miscarriage, Elisa Bennet whipped for, 95
  drunkenness, John Hogges fined for, 95
  Hope, an Indian, to be whipped for running away, &c. 95
  getting his master's daughter with child (case of Joell Jenkin) 95
  drunkenness, &c., Henry Illery fined for, 95
      John Barnes fined for being distempered with wine 95
  not attending the jury, Thomas Tylestone, &c., fined for, 97
  speaking against the grand jury, Richard Cluffe fined for 97
  pilfering, Edmond Mathewe admonished for, 97
  running away, two servants of Walter Merries to be whipped &c. for, 97
  going into men's houses on the Lord's day, &c., John Burrows sentenced for, 98
  drunkenness, &c., John Knight sentenced for, 98
  being distempered with wine, Benjamin Pauly fined for, 98
  swearing, stealing, &c., John Dutton sentenced for, 98
  for taking a boat, &c., from the deputy Governor, &c., Giles Player sentenced 99
  fireing the barn of his master, Henry Stevens punished for, 100
  heresy, Hugh Buet found guilty of, and banished 101
  not appearing as jurymen, John Holland, &c., fined for, 102
  swearing, lying, theft and unclean speech, Samuel Haukes sentenced for, 102
  drunkenness, idleness, wastefulness, &c., John Hogg punished for, 102
  cruel usage of his servant, Christopher Graunt fined for, 103
  not appearing as juryman, Robert Stedman fined for, 103
  causing death by negligence, Richard Hollingworth fined for, 103
  unfit carriage, John Morecroft fined for, 103
  rude & contemptious speeches, Walter Knight fined for, 104
  abusing his master, Richard Wilson sentenced for, 104
  distemper in drinking and obscene speeches, Joseph Kinge sentenced for, 104
  obscene speeches and distemper in drinking (case of Henry Pitts) 104
  obscene speeches, William Browne admonished for, 104
  selling his servant his time, Thomas Baguley fined for, 105
  being distempered with wine, John Barnes fined for, 105
  not serving on the jury, Edward Johnson fined for, 105
  making an Indian drunk, James Dane fined for, 105
  distemper in drinking, &c. John Longe fined for, 105
  dishonoring the name of God, the wife of Robert Lewes whipped for, 106
  extortion, Enoch Hunt fined for, 106
  Jonathan Thing punished for ravishing Mary Greenfield 106
  selling strong water to Indians, John Skidmer fined for, 106

182   INDEX.

	PAGE
CRIMES, MISDEMEANORS, &c., *continued.*	
selling his servant his time, Abraham Morrell fined for,	106
Samuel Sherman fined for,	106
gross misdemeanor, David Hickbourne sentenced for,	107
selling beer, Willi: Knop fined for,	107
distemper in drinking, John Barnes fined for,	107
absence from the jury, George Bowen fined for,	107
James Laurence sentenced for leaving his master's house, and for keeping company with a lewd woman	107
William and Dorothy Pilsberry sentenced for defileing their master's house	107
giving her husband quicksilver, &c., Mary Osborne sentenced for,	108
theft, Mary Felton punished for,	108
defect in warning the jurymen, Thomas Carter Senr., constable fined for,	108
Nicholas Trerice fined for his miscarriage in Court	108
adulterous practices, Thomas Owen sentenced for,	108
miscarriage, Sara Hales sentenced for,	108
affronting the governor, Anthony Stoader fined for,	108
distemper, John Kilmaster &c. sentenced for,	108
confederacy with Thomas Owen, to break prison, &c., Samuel Mavericke fined for,	108, 109
confederating and concealing Mr. Chidley, &c. fined for,	109
Thomas Owen, &c., fined for escaping	109
William Collens sentenced for being a seducer	109
corrupt speeches, Francis Hutchinson punished for,	109
writing letters against the country to England (case of John Prat)	109–112
striking Mr. Constable, Symon Voysey fined for,	115
unadvised expressions, John Jobson admonished for,	116
keeping a house of disorder, William Davies fined for,	116
making bread too light (case of Thomas Hawkins)	116
miscarriage, George Story committed for,	117
plotting piracy, and concealing the plot (case of Peter Thacher &c.)	118
prophaning the Sabbath (case of James Hawkins)	118
theft and lying, Elizabeth Sedgwicke sentenced for,	118
theft and running away (case of Marmaduke Barton)	118
concealing piracy plot, Thomas Briant punished for,	118
miscarriages, John Woodcocke whipped for,	119
John Whitney, constable, fined for not warning	119
theft, Mary Hoare punished for,	119
drinking, Daniel Owles fined for,	120
William Willoughby sentenced for being distempered with wine, neglecting public and private ordinances	120
mutinous speeches and writings, Nathaniel Briscoe fined for,	120
unmeet dalliance with Sarah Boylston (case of Richard Browne)	121
fornication before marriage, William Bull and his wife fined for,	121
reading offensive passages against the Church of Watertown, John Stowers fined for,	121

INDEX.

CRIMES, MISDEMEANORS, &c., *continued.*

	PAGE
stealing money from her master (case of Sarah Bell)	121
foul attempt to bugger a cow, (case of T[eagu] Ocrimi)	121
ravishing two young girls (case of Robert Wyar &c.)	121
wickedness with Robert Wyar, &c., Sarah Wythes, &c. whipped for,	121
running away, deriding an Ordinance of God, &c., William Browne whipped for,	122
being distempered by drinking, idleness, &c. Richard Quick whipped for,	123
drinking to Rich^d. Quick, Edward Roberts fined for,	123
running away, John Perry whipped for,	123
baking wheat meal contrary to order, Edward Wood fined for,	124
fornication before marriage, Thomas Scott & his wife punished for,	124
distemper in drink, swearing, &c., John Long fined for,	124
absence from the jury, Isaac Morrell fined for,	125
George Roberts committed for his ill carriage	125
neglecting the watch, Robert Sever fined for,	126
drunkenness and swearing, John Woolridge fined for,	126
running away and breaking into a house, John Lewis sentenced for,	126
idleness and abuse of his friends, William Walcot sentenced for,	126
refusing to watch, Richard White committed for,	126
attempting to drown her child, Anne Hett sentenced for,	126
unmeet dalliance with girls, Thomas Cotree sentenced for,	126
swearing, George Watts fined for,	127
not appearing upon the alarm (case of Samuel Finch, &c.)	127
neglecting an order as to bread, William Web fined for,	127
resisting his master, David Conway sentenced for,	127
suspicion of felony, John Neale committed upon,	128
Charles Cadwicke, &c., fined for being absent, being warned	128
covenanting for wages, William Shepheard fined for,	128
Laurence Copeland fined for,	128
keeping victualling against order of the Court (case of William Davies)	129
being privy to Edward Waldo's intention of running away (case of Richard Smyth)	130
battery, George Mills fined for,	130
Richard Willis fined for,	130
drinking too much, William Chadborne, &c., fined for,	130
being distempered with wine, Ralph Golthrope fined for,	130
fornication, Henry Leake and his wife punished for,	131
Francis Pemble to answer for his lewd and reproachful speeches	131
being distempered with wine, Nicholas Rogers fined for,	131
selling powder, &c. to the Indians, William Scutt fined for,	131
stealing wine, &c., Samuel Bacon punished for,	131
receiving stolen wine (case of Robert Rogers)	131
Miles Tompson and Toby Davies fined for drinking with others	131
Robert Wyar and Thomas Cooper fined for drinking with Samuel Bacon	132
breaking into houses and stealing, Nathaniel Tappin sentenced for,	132

INDEX.

CRIMES, MISDEMEANORS, &c., *continued.*

	PAGE
absence from Jury, John Clough fined for,	132
distemper in drink, Ralph Golthrop fined for,	132
fornication, Gawen Wilson fined for,	132
abusing a magistrate (case of Elizabeth Vane)	132
running away from his master, Richard Gell whipped for,	132
swearing, drunkenness, and theft, John Bartlet sentenced for,	133
defrauding several men (case of Stephen Day)	133
swearing, drunkenness, &c., John Gammage sentenced for,	133
distemper in drink, Thomas Anker fined for,	133
swearing and abusing the watch, George Watts fined for,	133
drunkenness, &c. Nicholas Rogers sentenced for,	133
Swiniard Lewis fined for,	133
neglecting the watch, Israel Hart fined for,	133
miscarriage to, and striking his master, Thomas Bauldwin committed for,	134
being distempered with drink, Robert Wright sentenced for,	134
swearing, William Barnes fined for,	134
excessive drinking, &c. (case of Leonard Fryar, &c.)	134
stealing, John Garland to make double restitution for things stolen by him	134
David Dauling &c., whipped for their unclean practise	134
swearing and disorder, Capt. John Chadwicke fined for,	135
distemper in drink, Capt. Aaron Williams fined for,	135
scales & weights, owners of Sudbury Mill fined for want of,	135
disturbing the Church of Hingham, Thomas Painter punished for,	135
assaulting the watch, David Williams punished for,	135
freeing his servant against order, John Beamis fined for,	135, 136
dangerous well, John Barnard fined for,	136
being distempered with drink, Ralph Golthrop punished for,	136
being distempered with drink, John Killmaster fined for,	136
swearing and quarrelling, Thomas Weatherly fined for,	136
non appearance, Leonard Fryar, &c. forfeited forty shillings for,	136
not returning warrant, Constable of Boston fined for,	137
light carriage (case of Thomas Moulton)	137
stealing from Mr. Stodder, &c. (case of Bridget Barnard)	137
having gotten a slut with child (case of William Flint)	137
theft from Mr. Walton (case of Mary Bentley)	137
being distempered with wine, George Frost fined for,	138
being distempered with wine, John Hart fined for,	138
being absent from the Grand Jury, Thomas Cooper fined for,	138
absence from the jury of trials, Benjamin Gillam fined for,	138
distemper in drink, &c., Leonard Fryer fined for,	138
disorder, Carew Latham fined for,	138
immoderate drinking, Edward Johnson jun^r. fined for,	138
excessive drinking, John Bauldwin fined for,	138
distemper in drink, Thomas Dutchfield fined for,	139

INDEX.

	PAGE
CRIMES, MISDEMEANORS, &c., *continued.*	
adultery, James Brittaine and Mary Latham condemned to death for,	139
sinful attempt (case of Stephen Betson)	139
theft and intemperate drinking, Nathaniel Smith sentenced for,	139
drinking and selling wine, &c., James Merrick, &c., fined for,	139
intemperate drinking (case of Thomas Orton, &c.)	139
(" " Thomas Sheepe)	139
CRISPE, ———, Mr., estate of, & his Company to make a payment to John Kirman	20
CROFTE, GRIFFIN, &c., jury (case of Hugh Buett)	101
CROSBEY, DOROTHY, bond for appearance, &c.	107
CROSSE	
John, warned to appear as to his servant Clement Manning, discharged	76
Robert, remitted to Ipswich Court	100
CRUGOTT, JAMES, &c., viewed the body of Austen Bratcher	7
CURSING. (*See* CRIMES, &c.)	
CURTIS	
Henry &c., bond by (case of George Richardson)	99
Willi:, &c., jury of life and death	70
William, of Roxbury, ment^d. (order as to Richard Brown)	71
CUTLER, ROBERT, &c., jury (case of Marmaduke Peirce)	89
CUTSHAMACHE, to pay charges to James Ludden for not prosecuting	82
DADE, WILLI: &c., jury (case of Marmaduke Peirce)	89
DALTON, TYMOTHY, Mr., &c., were made free	69
DAMERILLS COVE, thefts from the Indians at, &c. Nicholas Frost sentenced for,	28
DAMFORD ⎫	
DAMFORT ⎬ (*See* DAVENPORT.)	
DAMPORT ⎭	
DAN, ———, Mr., &c., arbitrators (Mr. Humphrey & Robert Saltonstall)	133
DANE, JAMES, case of, (making an Indian drunk)	105
DANFORT, THOMAS, &c., presented for taking too much wages	135
DANVARD or DUNVARD	
John, bond for appearance	92, 93
DAULING, DAVID, &c., case of, (filthy and unclean practise)	134
DAVENPORT or DAMFORD, DAMFORT, DAMPORT	
———, Mr., &c., to lay out Mr. Gurling's land	73
(or DAVIES), ———, Sergeant, testimony by, (administration on goods of Francis Dent)	82
———, Lt., John Kempe committed to, as a slave	86
Jonathan Hatch committed to, as a slave	97
Giles Player committed to him until he satisfy for his theft	99
John Hogg committed to,	102
Rich., Ensign, to be sent for, for defacing his colors	50
Thom, case of, causing balls with copperas in them to be cast into a man's yard	91

	PAGE
DAVIES or } DAVIS	
(or DAMPORT) ———, Sergeant, testimony by, (Administration on goods of Francis Dent)	82
Ephraim, widow of, married John Knowles, mentd.	77
Isaack, to be sent home to his wife in England	67
James, case of, (unquietness with his wife)	93
allowance to, for keeping John Kempe	119
John, &c., discharged	77
to be whipped and to wear the letter V upon his breast for gross offences	81
discharged from wearing the letter V	87
bond for appearance	98
Nico:, bond for appearance	89
Toby, fined for drinking with others	131
Willi:, case of (drinkings at his house)	86
William, case of (keeping a disorderly house)	116
(keeping victualling against order of the Court)	129
DAVISON or } DAVYSON	
———, Mr., &c., to examine accounts between Mr. Joanes & Mr. Mayhewe	93
Nicolas, to bring Edward Saunders into Court	80
Mr., forfeited his bond (case of Edward Saunders)	82
case of (swearing)	87
bill of, delivered by Sill, to be kept by the secretary	98
DAWE, JOHN, sentenced to be whipped for enticing an Indian woman to lie with him	19
DAY, STEPHEN, case of (defrauding)	133
DEACONS OF DORCHESTER, Mr. Allen's strong water to be delivered to	26
DEARE,	
Philip, attachment against,	73
&c., referred to Salem for drunkenness	75
DEATH. (*See* PUNISHMENT.)	
DEAWY. (*See* DEWAY.)	
DEBTS	
any bill assigned to another shall be good debt, &c.	18
corn shall pass for payment for all debts	20
Margery Mathew, widow, allowed to sell her husband's house &c., to pay debts	109
DEDHAM, Town of,	
John Howard sworn constable of, 5 Dec. 1638	80
fined for want of a pair of stocks	84
weights and measures	90
delivered in a transcript of their lands	117, 123
Nicholas Powell appointed surveyor of arms at Dedham	125
delivered in a transcript of their lands, &c., and order as to a way	135
DEED in 1636, by Willi: Swift to John Haynes, mentd.	96

INDEX.

	PAGE
DEERE ISLAND, &c., granted to Boston for twenty one years	44

DEESBRO or }
DEESBURY }
    Isaack, fined for stealing at Pecoit 81
    Isaac, bond for appearance at Salem Court and Boston Court . . 90
        forfeited his recognizance 92
DENNE, WILLI:, to satisfy for fine imposed on his servant George Horne . 76
DENNISON
    Daniell, [Mr.], &c., land above the Falls on Charles River granted to, 42
    William, Mr. chosen constable of Rocksbury 40
        &c., gift towards the Sea Fort 42
        Isaack Allerton to make a payment to, in a suit for debt . 47
    Willi:, &c., had liberty until the next Court 84
DENT, FRANCIS, administration on goods of, granted to Edmund Audley . 82
DENUX, WILLIAM, Daniel Mansfield put to, for five years, 14 Nov. 1642 . 128
DEPUTY or }
DEPUTY GOVERNOR }
    creditors to repair to, (adm^n. on goods, &c. of Robert White) . . 56
    to direct the Beadle to issue summons &c. in Civil Actions . . . 2
    shall always be a Justice of the Peace 3
    &c., present at Court, 3, 5, 8–21, 23–28, 30–34, 36, 39, 42, 45–48, 50, 52, 54,
        55, 57–59, 61–67, 69, 71, 72, 74, 76, 77, 81, 82, 85,
        88, 89, 91–93, 95, 96, 98, 99, 102–105, 107, 108,
        120, 122, 123, 125, 130, 132, 134, 138
    business concerning Mr. George Ludlowe to be referred to . . 10
    &c., license from, ment^d. (order as to travellers) 15
    no person shall sell wine &c. without leave from 33
    and inhabitants of Dorchester, to receive three pounds for caring for
        Thomas Lane 46
    &c., to examine witnesses (Mr. Hough against Mr. Maveracke) . . 58
    to settle difference between John Coggeshall and Phebe Seales . 67
DERIDING. (*See* CRIMES, &c.)
DESBRE, THOMAS, John Moody granted administration on goods, &c. of, . 35
DEWAY (or DEAWY), THO., &c., witnesses, (will of John Russell) . . 57
DEXTER or }
DEXTOR }
    Thomas, against Capt. Endicott (action of battery) 15
        bound to his good behavior, and fined for speeches, &c., to
        S. Bradstreete 24
        part of his fine forgiven him 30
        sentenced to be set in the bilbowes, disfranchised, &c., for
        seditious words 30
        John Dillingham, &c., difference between, referred to Mr.
        Endicott, &c. 35
        fined for drunkenness 36
        forfeited his recognizance (case of Walter Knight) . . 102
        Dearmant Matthew put to, ... 129

INDEX.

	PAGE
DICE, order against cards, dice or tables in houses	12
DICKERSON or DICKINSON	
Thomas, sentenced to be whipped and condemned to slavery . .	90
discharged from slavery and committed to Ensign Richard Walker	97
DIFFY, RICH., servant to Sr. Richard Saltonstall, to be whipped . . .	8
DILLINGHAM	
———, Mr., to be rated for the cattle of Mr. Downing's . . .	40
Edward, and Richard Saltonstall, order as to accounts between . .	63
Mr. Richard Saltonstall, &c., order as to agreement between	64
Mr. Apleton, &c., accounts between, ment^d. . . .	65
John, &c., jury (Dexter against Endicott)	15
Richard Wright, &c., differences between, referred to Mr. Endicott, &c.	35
and wife, deceased, comt^{ee}. to report as to estate of, . . .	63
DINELY, WILLI:., George Woodward granted damages against, for not prosecuting	72
DISTRINGAS, ment^d. (order as to Civil Actions)	2
DISTURBANCE. (See CRIMES, &c.)	
DIVORCE, case between Richard Beggarly & his wife referred to in note .	62
Anne Clarke granted a divorce from Denis Clarke . . .	138
(See also HUSBAND and WIFE.)	
DIXON	
William, sentenced to be set in the bilbowes for drunkenness . .	32
forfeited his bond and goods attached	57
DORCHESTER, Town of,	
ordered that Mattapan shall be called Dorchester	4
order as to "those of Dorchester who bought cattle of the merchants of Dorchester"	5
Thom[as] Stoughton chosen constable of Dorchester	5
ment^d., order as to levy for maintenance of Mr. Patricke, &c. . .	6
Mr. Tho. Stoughton, constable of, fined "for taking upon him to marry"	10
ordered that a watch of four shall be kept every night at Dorchester, &c., to begin at sunset	13
William Gayllerd of, ment^d.	14
ment^d. (order as to levy for the creek at Newe Towne) . . .	16
William Phelpes chosen constable of, ...	19
assessed (order as to levy for making a palisade)	20
Mr. Allen's strong water to be delivered to the Deacons of Dorchester	26
George Dyar chosen constable of, ...	28
as to land at Dorchester Neck	29
and Rocksbury, Capt. Traske, &c. to settle bounds between, . .	29
John Russell of, ...	35
assessed to defray public charges	37
Eltweed Pumery sworn constable of, ...	45
ment^d. (order as to Thomas Lane)	45, 46

INDEX. 189

PAGE

DORCHESTER, Town of, *continued*.
 inhabitants of, to receive three pounds for caring for Thomas Lane . 46
 constable of, fined for not returning his warrant for the last levy . 50
 Steven Terry sworn constable of, ... 55
 Church of, Mr. John Warham, pastor of, ment^d. (Will of John
  Russell) 57
 old people of, ment^d. (Will of John Russell) 57
 John Russell, merchant, died at, 26 August 1633 57
 John Philips chosen constable of, ... 63
 Nicholas Upsall of, ment^d. 68
 fined &c. 75
 fined for a defective highway 79
 town of Roxbury fined for damming up the nearest way from Boston
  to Dorchester 84
 presentments of, as to highways &c. discharged 84
 to use Sergeant Collicot's house for a watch house . . . 84
 fined for not bringing in a transcript of their lands . . . 90
 &c., to pay charges for Muddy River Bridge 93
 way of, presented 94
 discharged, the " bridge and way being repaired " . . . 99
 way to be mended 106
 fined for defective ways, ... 116
 time granted to, ... 123
 George Wicks sworn constable of, ... 130
 Henry Leake and his wife to acknowledge their fault at, . . 131
 John Smyth, clerk of the band at Dorchester, ment^d., . . . 131
 Barnabas Fawer sworn constable of, ... 140
DORCHESTER BROOK, presentment of bridge at, discharged for want of proof, 84
DORCHESTER MILL, way toward, ment^d. (order as to town of Roxbury) . . 106
DORCHESTER NECK, inhab^{ts}. of Boston to have liberty to fetch wood from, &c. 29
DOWNEING. (*See* DOWNING.)
DOWNES, WILLIAM, etc., sentenced to be whipped for running away from
 their masters, &c. 59
DOWNHAM, JOHN, case of, (getting his wife with child before marriage) . 94
DOWNING or DOWNEING
 ——, Mr., rate on cattle of, in possession of Mr. Dillingham . . 40
 Emanuel, Mr., &c., ment^d. (divorce of Anne Clarke) 138
DRAINTON or DRAYTON —— Mr., his cause against Mr. Wannerton trans-
 mitted to Piscataqua Court 131
DRAKE
 Joane (or Jane) will &c. of, presented 72
  order as to legacy by, to her nephew, John Nott . 77
DRAYTON (or DRAINTON) ——, Mr., his cause against Mr. Wannerton trans-
 mitted to Piscataqua Court 131
DRINKING, excessive, or drinking to another. (*See* CRIMES, &c.)
DRIVER, ROBERT, case of, ... 88
DRUNKENNESS. (*See* CRIMES, &c.)
DUCKE RIVER, or Conamabsqnooncant River, ment^d. (grant to Capt. Jo:
 Endicott) 24

190 INDEX.

	PAGE
DUCKET ——, Mr., case of, (confederacy & concealing)	109

DUDLEY

——, Mr., &c. present at Court 54, 55
    difference referred to 56
    &c., present at Court 57–59, 61, 62
    to examine accounts between Rich^d. Saltonstall and Edward Dillingham 63
    ment^d. (Accounts of Richard Saltonstall, Mr. Apleton &c.) 65
    &c., present at Court, 65, 105, 107, 108, 115, 117–120, 122, 123, 125, 127, 128, 130–132, 134, 137, 138
 Samuel, Mr., fined for drunkenness 25
    land above the Falls on Charles River granted to, . . 42
 Thomas, Mr., Deputy Govr., &c. present at Court 1
   Esq., Deputy Governor, two hundred acres of land near Newe Towne, granted to, 23
    &c. land above the Falls on Charles River granted to, 42
   Mr., sen^r., &c., present at Court 62–64
   &c. (Court of Assistants) order by, (case of John Pratt) . 112

DUGLAS ——, " sister," ment^d. (will of Joane Drake) . . . 72

DUMER }
DUMER }
DUMMER }

——, Mr., rate placed on estate of, in Rocksbury and Saugus . . 39
  &c., gift towards the Sea Fort 42
  &c., present at Court . . . 54, 55, 57, 58, 61–64
  and Jehu Burr, difference referred to a committee . . 61
 Richard, Mr., &c., present at Court, ... 64
    fined for want of weights & scales . . . 94
    fine remitted to, ... 104

DUNCAN ——, Lt., to take an inventory of goods of Sarah Lishe &c. . 91
DUNKIN, SAMUEL, discharged 100
DUNSTER ——, Mr. petition of, granted &c. 137
DUNVARD. (*See* DANVARD.)
DUTCHFIEL'D

——, Mr. &c., admonished to take heed of concealment . . . 109
 Thomas, Mr. case of, (distemper in drink) 139
DUTCH PLANTATION, THE, enticing servants to run away to, &c. Rich. Cokar sentenced for, 51
DUTTON, JOHN, case of, (drunkenness &c.) 98
DYAR
 George &c. jury, as to death of Austen Bratcher . . . 6
  chosen constable of Dorchester 28

EASTWARD, THE,
 Plantation to, commission, as to murder of Walter Bagnall . . 26
 Lt. Mason to receive ten pounds for his voyage to, . . . 84
 testimony by John Holland at, ... 55

		PAGE
EATON ———, Mr., house of, ment^d. (case of Thomas Symonds) . . .		88

EATON ———, Mr., house of, ment^d. (case of Thomas Symonds) . . . 88
EDMONDS
    Walter, took oath as constable of Concord 103
    Willi: bond by, for his wife's appearance 76
EDWARDS
    Henry &c. discharged from their recognizance 98
    Mathewe, to be whipped for misdemeanor 87
    Robert, town of Concord discharged as to lot of, ... 85
ELDERS, The, advice of, desired by members of Hingham . . . 126
ELDRED
    ———, Mr., theft from his man (case of Mary Felton) . . . 108
            deposition by Isaac Addington as to his wine . . . 129
ELFORD } (*See* ELLFORD.)
ELFORDS }
ELINGTON, THOMAS, &c , granted admⁿ. on estate of Mr. Ballard . . . 117
ELIOT, JACOB, deposed to the will and inventory of John Tee . . . 115
ELKYN, THOMAS, unchaste behavior with, Katherine Gray sentenced for, . 48
ELLEN, NICHO., fined for idleness & disorderly living 84
ELLFORD or ELFORD, ELFORDS
    John, bond by, to answer for the death of Thomas Puckett . . . 11
    &c. had respite until the next Court 83
ELLIS, ARTHUR, &c., viewed the body of Austen Bratcher 7
ELLWELL }
ELWELL }
    ———, and Kibbe, capias granted to bring them before the Governor . 65
    Roberte, &c., testimony by, (case of Thomas Wonnarton) . . 56
EMERSON
    John, accused by Edith Pitts, forfeit by, ... 65
    of Scituate, evidence against, ... 74
    bond for appearance, and bound to his good behavior, . . 76
    discharged of his recognizance 82
EMERY
    Anthony, fined for a pound breach, and to pay charges to Thomas Coleman 80
    John, carpenter, debt due from, ment^d. (inventory of goods of Joseph Avery) 58
ENDECOT }
ENDECOTT }
ENDICOT }
ENDICOTT }
    ———, Capt., took the oath of an Assistant, 7 Sept. 1630 . . . 3
    Mr. or Capt., Col., &c., present at Court, 3, 5, 8, 10, 14, 15, 17,
            19, 20, 21, 24, 26, 27,
            30, 31, 33, 39, 42, 46–
            48, 50, 63, 64, 66, 69,
            74, 76, 77, 81, 82, 85,
            89, 93, 96, 103
    Mr. &c., to be Justices of Peace 3

INDEX.

ENDICOTT, *continued*.

	PAGE
———, Capt., Thomas Dextor against, (action of battery)	15
ment^d. articles concerning a general trade of beaver	15, 16
took the oath of an Assistant	24
ground of, ment^d. (grant to Mr. Skelton)	24
Mr., takes oath as Assistant	33
&c., to settle differences between John Dillingham, &c.	35
&c., to examine accounts (Richard Saltonstall & Edward Dillingham)	63
ment^d. (accounts of Mr. Richard Saltonstall, Mr. Apleton, &c.)	65
Col., John Sweete sentenced for shooting his dog	66
Mr., Willi: Androws to serve Mr. Endecott	87
ment^d. (case of Thom. Gray)	94
Thomas Patience referred to,	105
Jo: Capt., three hundred acres of land near Salem granted to,	24
John, Esq., &c., to determine &c. all matters of difference concerning estate of Willust	52
to see correction given to George Ropps	62
Mr. or Col., &c., present at Court	63, 64, 66, 69, 77
&c., agreement as to estate of John and William Fiske	77

ENGLAND

Power of Justices of the Peace in,	3
Thomas Morton sent a prisoner to,	4
Mr. Aleworth &c. to be sent to, "as unmeet to inhabit here"	10
petition sent from, as to Mr. George Ludlowe	10
Assistants going to,	12
Capt. Southcoate granted liberty to go to England	18
writing falsely to, ment^d. (sentence of Henry Lyn)	19
order as to planters who intend returning to,	21
Tho. Knower said he would have his case tried in,	21
Lt. Aleworth granted liberty to return to,	28
cost of provisions &c. in, ment^d.	39
ment^d. (order as to Thomas Coleman)	58
Isaack Davies to be sent home to,	67
Old England ment^d. (will of Joane Drake)	72
(case of John Woolridge)	73
ment^d. (order as to George Pye)	76
James Luxford sent to,	89
ment^d. (Andrew Coleman and Willi: Swift)	96
(as to John Hogg)	103
reports made to, ment^d. (answer by John Pratt)	110–112
advice from, ment^d. (order as to John Richardson)	139

ENGLISH or ENGLISHMAN

order as to selling corn &c. to the English and Indians	6
whether adultery with English or Indian shall not be punished with death	19

INDEX.   193

	PAGE

ENGLISH or ENGLISHMAN, *continued*.
    grain not prospering in our land, ment^d. (answer by John Pratt) . . 111
    Pesons, or George, the Indian, banished not to come among the English after a week . 118
    John Winthrop, Esq., Governor of the English Colony in the Massachusetts, great lot of land of, ment^d. 22
    order as to paying any Englishman that kills a wolf 8
    no Englishman shall entertain or give houseroom to Thomas Graye 20
    no Englishman shall receive any reward for killing wolves . . 29
ENTERTAINMENT, House of. (*See* ORDINARY.)
ENTICING. (*See* CRIMES, &c.)
EVANS, THO., Button allowed charges with, ... 101
EVAR. (*See* EWAR.)
EVRELL, JAMES, John Fox apprenticed to, ... 117
EWAR or EVAR
    ———, [widow], allowed executrix of her husband 80
    Thomas, chosen constable of Charlestown 73
        fined for leaving his pit or well open 75
        deceased, his widow allowed his exec^x. 80
EXETER, Sergt. Wardall to train the company at Exeter . . . 133

FABER, JOSEPH, fined for selling wine 72
FALLS ON CHARLES RIVER, land above the falls on the Easterly side of Charles River granted to Thomas Dudley, &c. 42
FARMS, order as to improvement of, within three years 43
FARRINGTON
    John, bond for appearance 90
    forfeited his recognizance 92
FAWER, BARNABAS, sworn constable of Dorchester 140
FAWNE, ———, Mr., to pay damages to Robert Coles 59
FEAKES or FEKE
    ———, Lt., &c., to take an inventory of goods &c. of Mr. Craford . 48
    Robert, Mr., &c., comm^{rs}. to take an inventory of Mr. Crispe's estate, 20
        chosen Lieutenant to Capt. Patricke 27
        &c., to audit accounts, &c. (Edward Howe & William Knopp) 52
FEARNES, ———, Mr., of ship "Hector," ment^d. (case of Thomas Miller) . 63
FEKE. (*See* FEAKES.)
FELLINGHAM or ⎰
FELMINGHAM   ⎱
    Francis, discharged for want of witness 80
    of Salem, his servant, Richard Gell, whipped for running away, 132
FELONIOUSLY taking away, &c. (*See* CRIMES, &c.)
FELONY. (*See* CRIMES, &c.)
FELPES. (*See* PHELPES.)

	PAGE
FELTON	
Benjamin, brought Robert Scarlett into this country	60
case of his wife Mary Felton (theft)	108
Mary, wife of Benjamin Felton, case of, (theft)	108
FEN, ROBERT, to take John Twogood to Connecticut	100
FENCES or FENCING	
order as to corn fence	33
town of Hingham fined for not making sufficient fences, &c.	91
FERRY	
between Boston and Charlton, order as to payment for building,	8
Charlton and Boston, Edw. Converse to keep,	16
allowance to Edward Converse for ferrying, &c.	31
over Charles River, Mr. Richard Browne allowed to keep,	38
order as to canoes used at,	78
town of Lynn to lay a ferry	83
Edward Converse fined for neglecting the ferry	94
allowance to Francis Smith for ferriage	139
FIBBIN, ROBERT, freed, and debt to John Russell forgiven by consent of William Gallerd	46
(*See also* PHIPPEN.)	
FILPOT, WILLIAM, case of (allowing drinking in his house)	131
FINCE } or FYNCH FINCH }	
———, Gooddy, sentenced to be whipped	94
Daniell, &c., jury	15
comm^rs. to take an inventory of Mr. Crispe's estate, &c.	20
John, fined for wanting arms for his man and for being absent from training	29
Laurence Waters' wife, &c. to make a payment to,	75
Katherine, wife of Samuel, to be whipped, &c. for speaking against the magistrates, &c.	76
case of, to carry herself dutifully towards her husband	82
Samuell, &c. jury of life & death	70
his wife, Katherine to be whipped, &c.	76
case of his wife Katherine Finch	82
wife of, attachment against,	89
certification that his wife is ill	116
&c., case of, (not appearing upon the alarm)	127
wife of, &c., attachment against,	136
FINES. (*See* PUNISHMENT.)	
FIRES, order as to burning any ground, &c.	17
FISH. (*See* FISHING.)	
FISHER, ANTHONY, &c., committee, as to affairs of Edward Allen	127
FISHING or FISH	
Conant's Island, with liberties of fishing &c. demised to John Winthrop, Esq., Govr, for the term of his life	22
order as to swine in fishing time at Marble Harbor, &c.	32

INDEX.

	PAGE

FISHING or FISH, *continued.*
    town of Cambridge discharged from the presentment about fish . 85
    trade of, ment^d. (answer by John Pratt) 110
FISKE
    John, Mr., and his brother, William, agreement as to division of estate, approved &c. 77
    William, and his brother, John, agreement as to division of estate, approved &c. 77
FITCH, JOHN, &c., discharged with an admonition as to too many in a boat . 81
FLETCHER, ROBERT, discharged 85
FLINT, ———, Mr., &c., present at Court, 120, 122, 123, 125, 128, 130, 132, 134, 137, 138
    Thomas, was chosen an Assistant, 18 May, 1642, referred to in note . 122
    Mr., &c., present at Court 134
    William, case of, (fornication) 137
FOOT BRIDGE. (*See* BRIDGE.)
FORD, THO , &c., to set out bounds between Boston and Roxbury . . . 41
FORNICATION. (*See* CRIMES, &c.)
FORT, THE, or THE SEA FORT
    at Boston, order as to finishing 35
    ment^d., order as to Sergeant Perkins 36
    plantations in the Bay to do two days work apiece at the Fort . . 38
    John Chapman to give three hundred of four inch planks towards the sea fort 40
    newcomers to contribute towards (cancelled) 40
    as to collecting money for the Moving Fort 41
    money given for the Sea Fort 42
    shingles for the Fort at Castle Island, ment^d. (order as to Richard Long) 60
FOSDITCH, STEVEN, &c., jury (case of Marmaduke Peirce) 89
FOSTER, ———, Goodman, &c., referred to Ipswich Court . . . 83
FOULE. (*See* FOWLE.)
FOWL or FOWLING, FOWLERS
    no person shall shoot at fowl on Pullen Point or Noddle's Island . . 21
    Conant's Island with liberties of fishing and fowling demised to Govr. John Winthrop, Esq. for the term of his life 22
    unprofitable fowlers &c. ment^d. (order as to idlers) 37
FOWLE or FOULE
    ———, Mr., &c., arbitrators, (case of William Tynge and Tompson . 104
    (Mr. Humphrey and Saltonstall) . . 133
    Thomas, attachment against Thomas Owen 99
Fox }
FOXE }
    John, apprenticed to James Evrell 117
    Thomas, servant to Mr. Cradocke to be whipped for malicious speeches 12
        fined for not appearing to give evidence against John Lee . 43
        fined 104
FREEDOM. (*See* FREEMEN.)

INDEX.

PAGE

FREEDOM. (*See* SERVANT.)
FREE INHABITANTS. (*See* FREEMEN.)
FREEMAN
    ——, Mr., bond by, (case of Mr. Clearke) 8
        Mrs., Mr. Clearke prohibited from cohabitation with, . . 8
    Samuel, damages against John Gay for not prosecuting . . . 72
FREEMEN or FREE INHABITANTS, FREEDOM
    list of those desiring to be made freemen ment^d. 8
    admitted from 1631 to 1634 list of, mentioned in note 15
    assurance of land to, ment^d. 45
    lists of, 1634–5 referred to 45
    list of, 1635, 1636 referred to 54
        May 1636 to March 1638–9 referred to 66
    Mr. George Moxham and Mr. Timothy Dalton were made free . . 69
    list of, for May and June 1639 referred to 82
        May and Sept. 1640 referred to 93
    order as to Watertown Freemen 99
FRENCH
    Willi: &c., jury, (case of Marmaduke Peirce) 89
    William, Sergeant, Daniel Owles put to, for one year 122
FRESH POND ment^d. (agreement as to bounds of Watertown and Newton) . 53
FRIENDSHIP (ship) ment^d. (order as to fine of Mr. Shepheard &c.) . . 18
FROST
    George, case of, (being distempered with wine) 138
    Nicholas, case of, (theft, fornication and drunkenness) . . . 28
        tried for returning after banishment 59
        &c., of Paskataqua, forfeited their bonds for non appearance 61
        discharged of his recognizance, and bond for appearance . 62
FRY, WILLIAM, will and inventory of, delivered in 134
FRYAR
    Elizabeth, John Richardson to be sequestered from her &c. . . 139
    Leonard, fined and bond for appearance 134
        forfeited forty shillings for not appearing . . . 136
        his forfeiture remitted 138
        fined for distemper in drink 138
FUELL, SAMUEL, bond by, (case of Henry Singleman) . . . 118
FULLER
    ——, respited 117
    Edward, attachment for, ... 79
        bond for appearance 88
        bond by Edward Converse for appearance of, . . 88
        &c., to appear at Court for being distempered with wine . 88
    Willi:, who kept the mill at Concord fined for taking too much toll . 85
FYNCH. (*See* FINCH.)

GAGE, JOHN, &c., at Aggawam ment^d. 31
GAGER, ——, Mr., maintenance of, ment^d. (order as to ministers) . . 2

INDEX. 197

	PAGE

GALARD
GALLARD } or GAYLARD, GAYLLARD, GAYLLERD
GALLERD

  William, &c., jury, (case of Walter Palmer) 9
    of Dorchester, Thomas Chubb to become his servant . . 14
    &c., granted adm.^{n} on goods &c. of John Russell . . . 35
     to set out bounds between Boston and Roxbury . . 41
    adm^r of John Russell &c. Robert Fibbin freed by consent of, 46
    &c., to determine &c. as to damage by swine . . . 49
     exec^{rs}., exhibited an inventory of goods of John Russell, 55
GALLEY, JOHN, fined for knowing his wife carnally before marriage . . 60
GALLOWS. (*See* PUNISHMENT.)
GAMBLING. (*See* CRIMES, &c.)
GAMMAGE, JOHN, case of, (swearing drunkenness &c.) 133
GARDNER, CHRISTOPHER, S^r., &c., to be sent prisoners to England . . 10
GARFORD, ———, Mr., George Ropps to be whipped for striking him . 62
GARLAND
  John, &c., case of, (ravishing two young girls) 122
    (stealing) 134
GARRET
GARRETT }
  James, &c., jury, (case of Marmaduke Peirce) 89
  Richard, &c., inquisition upon oaths of, on body of William Bateman 7
    exec^{rs}. of, to make a payment to Henry Harwood . . . 18
GATELY, EDWARD, Mr., to make a payment to Francis Lightfoot . . . 134
GAY, JOHN, charges to Samuel Freeman for not prosecuting . . . 72
GAYLARD
GAYLLARD } (*See* GALLARD.)
GAYLLERD
GEAVES
  (or GRAVES), ———, &c., witnesses, grant to, ... 98
  Richard, &c., referred to Court at Salem for fighting &c. . . . 80
GEEPIN, JOHN, &c., jury of life and death 70
GELL, RICHARD, servant of Francis Fellingham, case of, (running away) . 132
GENERAL COURT
  to be held on the last Wednesday in every term (question propounded) 2
  19 Oct. 1630 record of, mentioned 8
  order passed in June 1641, reference to, in note 13
  18 May 1631 record of, ment^d. in note 15
  order passed by, in Nov. 1639 reference to, in note . . . 17
    in Sept. 1638 reference to, in note 18
  Robert Coles enjoined to confess to being drunk before, . . . 21
  9 May 1632 record of, referred to 23
  March 1635 order of, referred to, in note 23
  Capt. Endicott chosen an assistant at, ... 24
  Thomas Dexter ordered to confess his fault at, (insolent carriage &
    speeches to S. Bradstreete) 24
  rent for Noddle's Island to be paid yearly at, ... 31

198 INDEX.

        PAGE

GENERAL COURT, *continued.*
- 29 May 1633 record of, referred to 32
- Mr. Endicott chosen an Assistant ment^d. 33
- order as to Fort at Boston ment^d. 35
- record of, May 14, 1634, referred to 45
  - March 4, 1634–5 referred in note 45
- Mr. John Winthrop, Junr. chosen an Assistant at, ment^d . . . 46
- John Humfry Esq. chosen an Assistant at, ment^d. 47
- record for Sept. 1634 referred to 48
  - 4 March 1634–5 referred to 52
  - for May, June and July 1635 referred to 54
- 1 Sept. 1635 first Grand Jury at, referred to in note . . . 57
- record of, for Sept. 1635 referred to 59
- 3 March 1635–6 record of, referred to 61
- records of, from March 3, 1635–6 to May 25, 1636 referred to, . . 62
- record Sept. 8 to Oct. 28, 1636 referred to, ... 64
  - 7 Dec. 1636 to 18 April 1637 referred to 64
  - 17 May 1637 referred to 66
- Mr. Richard Saltonstall chosen an Assistant at, ment^d. . . . 66
- record 1 Aug. 1637 referred to 69
- 26 Sept. 1637 by adjournment 69
- record 26 Sept. 1637 to 20 Nov. 1637 referred to 71
  - for March and May 1638 referred to 74
- ment^d. (banishment of William South) 76
- record for Sept. 1638 referred to 77
  - March, May and June 1639 referred to 82
  - Sept. and Nov. 1639 referred to 88
- 13 May 1640 referred to 93
- for Oct. 1640 referred to 98
  - July 1641 referred to 107

GENESON
GENISON } (*See* JENNISON.)
GENNISON

GEORGE
- (or PESONS), ——, an Indian, banished 118
- John, put to John Winthrope, Senr. for eight years 104

GERMANY &c. Churches of God in, ment^d. (order as to a day of public thanksgiving) 23

GIBBINGS } or GIBONES, GIBONS.
GIBBONS
- ——, Mr., his servant, James Woodward, whipped for running away, 27
- &c., to take an inventory of goods &c. of Alex. Wignall . 33
- Capt., &c., arbitrators, (case of William Tynge and Robert Tompson) 104
- Edw^{ard}, &c., fined for drinking 18
- Mr., &c., comm^{rs}. to take an inventory of Mr. Crispe's estate, 20
- John, fined 83
- (or Wilbore), Samuel, &c., Grand Jury 70

INDEX.   199

	PAGE
GIBBS, GYLES, to receive a payment from W^m. Wills, for felony	56
GIBONES } (*See* GIBBONS.) GIBONS	
GIBSON, CHRISTOPHER, &c., jury, (case of Hugh Buett)	101
"GIFTE" (ship) Thomas Morton sent a prisoner to England in,	4
GILBERD, NICHOLAS, a servant, Christopher Graunt fined for cruel usage of,	103
GILES. (*See* GYLES.)	
GILHAM. (*See* GILLAM.)	
GILL, JOHN, and his wife &c. presented for taking too much wages	135

GILLAM or GILHAM

	PAGE
———, Goodman, Nathaniel Tappin put to,	132
Benjamin, &c., witnesses, allowance to, (case of Richard Lambert)	49
fined for absence from jury of trials	138
Robert, had wine of Mr. Eldred	129
GILLOW, ———, action against, 4 Sept. 1688, referred to in note	76
GINNER, ——— Mr., &c. to settle things between John Turner and William Richards	97

GLOVER

	PAGE
———, Mr., canoe of, William Almy fined for taking,	16
Ralfe, Mr., &c., William Bateman was left with, at Pullen Point ment^d. (inquisition on body of William Bateman)	7
witnesses, ment^d. (inquisition on body of William Bateman)	8
Thomas Moulton to pay forty shillings to,	10
Benjamin Cribb &c. sentenced for stealing pigs of,	13
admⁿ. granted to Mr. Mayhewe on goods &c. of,	34
inventory and order as to estate of,	46

GOATS

	PAGE
order as to allowance for weaned goats &c.	8
&c. owners of, to make full satisfaction for damage done by them	14
order restraining ram goats	34
GOBLE, THOMAS, &c., jury, (case of Hugh Buett)	101
GODSON, FRAUNCIS, bond for appearance	48
GOILTHAYT, THOMAS, Mr. Pelham to pay him five pounds	16
GOLD, FRANCIS, &c., watchmen, imprisoned for drinking strong water	87
GOLDSTON, HENRY, &c., dismissed from training by reason of age &c.	50

GOLTHROPE

	PAGE
Ralph, case of, (being distempered with wine)	130
(distemper in drink)	132
(being distempered with drink)	136
GOODNOW, EDWARD, sworn clerk of the band 5 June 1643	123
GOOSE, WILLI:, Mr., respited	80
GOOUCH, ———, Mr., of Newberry, case of, (selling strong water)	83
GORTON, JOHN, &c., case of, (not appearing upon the alarm)	127
GOSPEL, the, ment^d. (answer by John Pratt)	111

GOSSE

	PAGE
John, &c., jury, (Dexter against Endicott)	15
case of, (common railing)	85

INDEX.

GOSSE, *continued*.

	PAGE
John, etc., fine remitted to,	98
William, and his wife to answer things objected against them	117

GOULDSWORTH }
GOULDWORTH }

John, to be whipped and set in the stocks	6

GOVERNOR

&c. present at Court 1, 3, 5, 6, 8–21, 23–28, 30–34, 36, 38, 39, 42, 45–48, 50, 52, 54, 55, 57, 59, 61–66, 69, 71, 72, 74, 76, 77, 81, 82, 85, 88, 89, 91, 92, 95, 96, 98, 99, 102–105, 107, 108, 115, 117, 118–120, 122, 123, 125, 127, 128, 130, 131, 134, 137, 138

Mr., ment^d (order as to ministers)	2
James Peñ appointed a Beadle to wait upon	2
Court of Assistants to be held at the Governors house 7 Sept. 1630	2
to direct the Beadle to issue summons in Civil Actions	2
shall always be a Justice of the Peace.	3
entertainment of public persons by, charges for, to be estimated (mem^o.)	3
House of, Court of Assistants to be held every third Tuesday at	4
ordered that no person shall plant within the limits of this pattent without leave from the Governor &c.	4
license from, as to selling corn &c.	6
Mr., time for building the ferry between Boston and Charlton to be appointed by,	8
petition sent out of England to, as to Mr. George Ludlowe	10
business concerning Mr. George Ludlowe to be referred to,	10
&c., oaths for, mentioned in note.	15
license from, ment^d. (order as to travellers)	15
&c., no person shall buy corn &c. from any ship that comes into the Bay without license from,	16
&c., ordered that all the Islands within this pattent are to remain in the power of,	17
grant to Govr. Winthrop of land near his house at Misticke	19
Mr., to have part of Mr. Shepheard's fine to pay for ferrying the watch from Charlton to Boston	20
no planter returning to England shall carry money or beaver with him without leave from,	21
for the time being, rent for Conant's Island to be paid to,	22
bond by Bryan Bincks &c. that they will not depart out of the limits of this pattent without leave from,	25
inquiry concerning the murder of Walter Bagnall referred to	26
great lot of, ment^d. (agreement as to bounds of Charlestown and Newton)	30
for the time being, rent to be paid to, (Noddle's Island granted to Mr. Samuel Mavericke)	31
committee chosen to take an account of debts due to,	33
salary of, order as to	33

INDEX. 201

GOVERNOR, *continued*.
 no person shall sell wine &c. without leave from, ... 33
 John Lee punished for speaking reproachfully of, ... 49
 &c., to dispose of the estate &c. of Edmond Lockwood, if necessary . 52
 &c., to dispose of the estate &c. of Edward Lockwood 54
 return to be made to, as to bounds of land sold by Chickataubut to Mr.
  Pinchon 55
 &c., case heard by, 2 June 1636, referred to, in note 62
 mentioned (case of Thomas Miller) 63
 Moses Maverick paid rent to, for Noddle's Island 63
 had leave to keep a Naviganset Indian and his wife 91
 money delivered to, by one who had taken "too great prices" . . 91
 "the Court gave way to," "to free his servant Thomas Philips" . . 92
 affronting, (case of Anthony Stoader) 108
 Mr. Bellingham was Governor 27 April, 1642, referred to in note . 122
 part of estate of Monsieur Thyery, deceased, in hands of, . . . 127
GOVERNORS GARDEN, name of Conants Island changed to, . . . 22
GRAMES, SAMUEL, &c., goods of John Hogg secured to, . . . 103
GRAND JURY. (*See* JURY.)
GRANT or GRAUNT
 Christopher, fined for drunkenness 50
  fined for drinking &c. 73
  to satisfy for John Clare's fine 92
  case of, (cruel usage of his servant Nicholas Gilberd) . 103
  discharged 106
GRANTS of Farms to be improved within three years 43
GRAUES. (*See* GRAVES.)
GRAUNT. (*See* GRANT.)
GRAVES or GRAUES
 ———, Mr., neck of land whereon he dwells to belong to the Newe
  Towne (agreement) 22, 30
  &c., to take an inventory of goods &c. of Alex: Wignall . . 33
  drinking aboard ship of, John Woolridge fined for, . . . 84
 (or GEAVES) ——— &c., witnesses, grant to, ... 98
 Thomas, &c., viewed the body of Austen Bratcher 7
GRAY }
GRAYE }
 Katherine, to be whipped for unchaste behavior with Thomas Elkyn . 48
 Thomas, enjoined to attend Court to answer &c. and to remove out of
  the limits of this pattent 6
  house of, at Marble Harbor to be pulled down &c. . . 20
  sentenced to be whipped and banished 76
  house of, at Marblehead ment[d]. (case of Ralph Warriner) . 85
  case of, (drunkenness profanity &c.) 87
  case of, (drunkenness &c.) 94
GREAT POND and land above the Falls on Charles River granted to John
  Haynes Esq. &c. 42

202 INDEX.

	PAGE

GREEN }
GREENE }
 John, Mr., of New Providence, fined and banished from this jurisdiction for speaking contemptuously of the magistrates   71
 adm^n. on estate of, granted to Daniel Brewar in whose house he died   81

GREENFIELD
 Mary, Jonathan Thing sentenced for ravishing her 106
 Samuel, payment to, (case of Jonathan Thing) 106

GREENLIFFE
 Edmond, referred to Ipswich Court 83
     charges to Willi: Hamond for not prosecuting . . . 98

GRUB, THOMAS, fined for not appearing upon the jury 137
GUNNISON, HUGH, David Weane put himself to, ... 129

GURLIN }
GURLING }
 ———, Mr., land of, to be sold to satisfy creditors 71
    sale of land of, confirmed &c. 73
    land of, Mr. Willard &c. appointed as to, . . . 74
    widow, ment^d. (account as to estate of Richard Gurling) . . 85
 Richard, account as to estate of, by John Benjamin 85

GURTRIDGE. (See GUTRIGE.)
GUTRIGE (or GURTRIDGE), WILLIAM, enjoined to take care of Ales Burwood . 87

GYLES or GILES
 Edward, fined for knowing his wife carnally before marriage . . 60
 Mary, dallying with, Abner Ardway accused of, ... 135

HAINES. (See HAYNES.)
HALE }
HALES }
 ———, Mr., &c., admonished to take heed of concealment . . . 109
 Robert, &c., appraisers, (estate of Henry Harwood) 72
 Sara, wife of Willi: Hales, case of, (miscarriage) 108
   case of, (escaping) 109
 (or HALL), Thomas, referred to Ipswich Court 83
 Willi: , case of his wife Sara Hales (miscarriage) 108

HALFORD, WILL: , &c., difference between John Cogan, John Tylley &c. referred to,   54

HALL or HAUL, HAULE
 Edward, &c., referred to Salem 76
 John, case of, (correcting his boy) 83
  &c., jury, (case of Hugh Buett) 101
 (or HALE), Thomas, referred to Ipswich Court 83

HALSTEED
 Nathaniel, inventory of, presented and order as to estate . . 138
 William, appointed adm^r. of estate of his father Nathaniel Halsteed . 138

INDEX.

	PAGE
HAMMON, HAMON, HAMOND	
William, to be set in the bilboes for drunkenness	26
Thomas, &c., Grand Jury,	70
Willi:, attachment for,	85
charges against Edmond Greenliffe for not prosecuting	98
HAMPTON, Town of,	
presentments discharged	100
fined for want of weights and measures	106
HANDS, MARKE, discharged	116
HANDWRITING	
of Increase Nowell, secretary, record in,	1
of Secretary Simon Bradstreet, record in,	1
of Edward Rawson, secretary,	1
marginal note in, mentioned in note	20
of Increase Nowell, entry in, referred to in note	30
record in, referred to,	62
of the secretary referred to in note	96
of Thomas Lechford record in,	115
HARBOR RIVER (Salem) land upon, granted to Mr. Skelton	24
HARDIE. (See HARDY.)	
HARDING, HARDINGE	
—— Mr., &c., gift towards the Sea Fort	42
John, &c., sworn constables of Weymouth, 23 May 1643	123
Robert, &c., inquisition upon oaths of,	7
grand jury	70
HARDY or HARDIE	
John, things taken from wreck of, (bond by Thomas Turner, &c.)	105
Thomas, &c., at Aggawam, ment^d.	31
HARLAKENDEN. (See HERLAKENDEN.)	
HARRIS	
John, to pay fees, admonished and discharged	139
Josiah (or Josuah), apprenticed to Frauncis Weston	41
HARRISON	
John, gentleman, attachment for,	80, 81, 82
Mr., fined for non appearance, and admonished as to gaming	83
HART	
Isaack, bound to his good behavior	95
Israel, case of, (neglecting the watch)	133
John case of, (being distempered with drink)	138
HARVEST, plentiful, &c., Day of Thanksgiving for,	37
HARVY, JOSEPH, will and inventory of estate of, delivered into Court	85
HARWOOD	
Henry, exec^{rs}. of Rich: Garrett to pay him the sum of twenty nobles	18
of Charlstowne, inventory of estate of, presented to the Court	72

	PAGE
HASLEWOOD, JOHN, to be whipped, and delivered up as a slave, for breaking into houses, &c.	79
HASNET, ELIZABETH, put to William Wilson, 5 Jan. 1642-3	129
HASTINGS, THOMAS, &c., certificate by, (case of Mighill Bacon)	105

HATCH }
HATCHE }
    Jonathan, to be whipped and committed as a slave to Lt. Davenport . 97
    Will:, &c., bond forfeited by, (case of John Emerson) . . . 65

HATHAWAY
    John, indicted for adultery with Margaret Seale 66
          found guilty of adultery 70

HATHORNE or HAYTHORNE
    William, Mr., &c., to determine, &c. as to damage by swine . . 49
          &c., difference between John Cogan, John Tylley, &c., referred to, 54
    Willi:, &c., agreement made by, as to estate of John and William Fiske 77

HAUGH. (*See* HOUGH.)

HAUKES
    Adam, referred to Court at Salem 83
    Samuell, case of, (swearing, lying, &c.) 102

HAUL }
HAULE } (*See* HALL.)

HAWARD
    John, sworn constable of Dedham, 5 Dec., 1638 80
    William, Richard Cole put to, for one year 127

HAWKENS }
HAWKINS }
    James, forfeits to be levied on, ... 56
          testimony as to wages paid to, ... 56
          &c., to make a weekly payment towards their forfeits . . 57
          case of, (profaning the Sabbath) 118
    Thomas, case of, (scurrilous speeches) 102
            (making bread too light [weight]) 116
          bond by, (case of James Hawkins) 118
    Tymothy, &c., fined for company keeping, drinking, &c. . . . 40

HAY, &c., order for preservation of, ... 17
HAYDEN (or HEYDEN), JAMES, servant, freed from his master . . . 65

HAYNES or HAINES
    ———, Mr., &c., gift towards the Sea Fort 42
          present at Court 45-48, 50, 52
          committee as to estate of Mr. Ouldam 63
          present at Court. 65
          ment^d. (order as to release of Edward Woodley . . . 65
    John, Esq., land and Great Pond granted to, ... 42
          &c., to take charge of writings left by the husband of Ruth Lockwood, 50, 51
          to audit accounts, &c. (Edward Howe & William Knopp) 52

HAYNES or HAINES, *continued*.
    John, Esq., &c., to dispose of the estate, &c. of Edmond Lockwood, if necessary   52
        Mr., &c., present at Court 63, 64
        Esq., letter of attorney from Andrew Coleman, ment^d. . . 96
        Willi: Swift mortgaged his house and lands to, &c., ment^d. . 96
        Governor, &c. (Court of Assistants), order by, (case of John Pratt)   112
    Richard, &c., bond by, (case of Daniel Hutchins) 95
HAYTHORNE. (*See* HATHORNE.)
HEATHERSBY, ROBERT, discharged of his bond, &c. 130
HECTOR (ship), Thomas Miller, pilot & mate of, committed for seditious speeches   63
HEFFORD (or HOFFORD), SAMUEL, freed from his master, Jonathan Wade, and put to John Johnson   101
HENBURY (or HENBERRY), LUKE, to be whipped, for theft, and for running away   72
HERESY. (*See* CRIMES, &c.)
HERLACKINGDEN ⎫
HERLAKENDEN   ⎬ or HARLAKENDEN
HERLAKENDON ⎭
    ———, Mr., &c., committee as to estate of Mr. Ouldam . . . 63
                present at Court . . . 65, 71, 72, 74, 76
    Roger, Mr., &c.,   "   "   " 63, 66, 69
               Capt. Lovell's business &c. referred to, . . . 77
HETT, ANNE, case of, (attempting to drown her child) 126
HEWARD. (*See* HEYWARD.)
HEWES. (*See* HUGHES.)
HEWET or HUET, HUITT
    Robert, to be whipped for committing fornication 30
    Susan, &c., who sold goods to Sarah Pell, order as to 121
    Willi:, &c. appraisers (estate of Joane Drake) 72
HEWLET
    Lewes, case of, (extortion, &c.) 89
        forfeited his recognizance 92
HEYDEN. (*See* HAYDEN.)
HEYWARD (or HEWARD), JOHN, sentenced to be whipped for swearing, &c. . 53
HIBBENS ⎫
HIBBINS ⎬
    ———, Mr., ment^d. (bond by John Crabtree, &c.) 98
        allowance to, for his horse killed in public service . . 128
        &c., present at Court . . . 130–132, 134, 137, 138
HICKBOURNE, DAVID (or DAVY), case of, (gross misdemeanors) . . . 107
HIGGENSON
    ———, Mrs., land of, ment^d. (grant to Mr. Skelton) 24
    Timothy, had wine of Mr. Eldred 129
HIGHWAYS or WAYS
    town of Lynn enjoined to mend their ways 75

INDEX.

	PAGE
HIGHWAYS or WAYS, *continued*.	
town of Weymouth fined for,	79
Dorchester " "	79
Boston " "	79
Ipswich " "	80
presentment of town of Ipswich for, mentioned	83
town of Lynn fined for,	83
Boston " "	84
&c., ment^d. (Dorchester presentment).	84
town of Weymouth fined for,	84
to the mill, town of Watertown discharged as to,	85
town of Watertown fined for,	85
Cambridge " "	85
at Long Swamp, &c., town of Cambridge enjoined to repair	85
attachment against town of Ipswich for,	90
town of Cambridge fined for, at Vine Swamp, &c.	90
Boston fined for,	90
Hingham fined for,	91
way of Dorchester presented	94
town of Hingham fined for,	94
set out by town of Ipswich, ment^d.	97
town of Boston to repair the ways between Powder Horn Hill and the Written Tree	99
Lynn enjoined to repair their ways	100
Roxbury enjoined to make a sufficient way between the burial place and the gate	105
enjoined to repair the way over the swamp toward Dorchester Mill	106
Ipswich enjoined to repair their ways	106
Cambridge enjoined to repair the way between Watertown and Roxbury	106
Weymouth's defective way certified to be mended	106
Salem enjoined to repair their ways,	106
Boston " " " " "	106
Salisbury " " " " way .	106
Rowley " " " " ways .	106
Dorchester way to be mended	106
fined for,	116
Boston fined for defective ways towards Roxbury .	117
Cambridge fined for a defective way to Charlestown	117
Boston presented for,	130
Dedham granted time as to a way between Dedham and Cambridge	135
HILL	
Abraham, Richard Bayly put himself to,	138
Bartholomewe, case of, (stealing a loaf of bread)	9
John, &c., bond by, as to overpayment	98
Säm^ll., fined for drunkenness	49

	PAGE
HILL, *continued.*	
Willm̃, Mr., &c., to determine &c. as to damage by swine	49
John Cogan, &c., difference between, as to ship "Thunder" referred to a committee	54
HILTON, WILLIAM, Mr., debt due from, ment^d. (inventory of goods &c. of Joseph Avery)	58
HINDERSHAM (or HINDERSAM), MARGARET, case of (ill behavior)	90
HINGHAM, Town of	
fined, &c.	75
to use the meeting house for a watch house	84
acquitted from the presentment about Thom. Turner's lot	84
fined for not making sufficient fences, for defective highways & for not keeping constant watch	91
fined for defective ways and bridge	94
John Porter & Henry Tuttle took oaths as constables of Hingham	97
meeting house in, to be used as a watch house	100
granted time to finish the bridge over Layford's liking	116
constables of, order sent to, as to Mrs. Strainge & her child	119
William Jones and Eliz: Strainge to acknowledge their fault publicly at,	124
Thomas Cooper, &c., constables of Hingham, ment^d.	126
members of, desire advice of the elders to settle their differences	126
discharged, the way being made out	129
Francis James sworn constable of Hingham	132
church of, Thomas Painter sentenced for disturbing	135
HITCHCOCK } HITCHCOCKE }	
Richard bond for appearance	48
HOARE, MARY, case of, (theft)	119
HOBBE } HOBBEY } JOHN, murder of, John Williams found guilty of	69
HOBSON	
Henry, servant of Henry Neale, freed from his master	122
put to Goodman Thomas Meakins	122
HOFFE. (*See* HOUGH.)	
HOFFORD. (*See* HEFFORD.)	
HOGG } HOGGE }	
John, fined for drunkenness	87
case of,	93
(drunkenness, &c.)	102
goods of, secured to Samuel Grames, &c.	103
HOGGES or HOGGS	
John, fined for drunkenness	71
swearing and cursing his servant	81
Mr., fine remitted to,	89
case of, (drunkenness)	95
HOGG ISLAND, &c., granted to Boston for twenty one years	44
HOGGS. (*See* HOGGES.)	

208 INDEX.

	PAGE
HOLBIDGE	
Arthur, testimony by Mr. Hutchingson as to wages paid to,	56
bound to his good behavior, &c., for contempt, &c.	56
&c., to make weekly payments in discharge of their forfeits	57
HOLEMAN, ———, Mr., payment for,	120
HOLGRAVE	
John, &c., grand jury	70
referred to Salem	75
presented for drawing wine, and fined for contempt, &c.	78
HOLLAND	
John, testimony by, as to Thomas Wonnarton	55
&c., jury of life & death	70
jurymen, fined for not appearing	102
HOLLARD, ANGELL, fined for libel	72
HOLLINGSWORTH }	
HOLLINGWORTH }	
Richard, to be set in the stocks at Salem, for profaning the Sabbath	80
case of, (causing the death of Robert Baker)	103
HOLLISTER, JOHN, &c., sworn constables of Weymouth, 23 May, 1643	123
HOLLOWAY	
———, bond for appearance	76
Thomas, discharged	78
HOLMAN	
John, &c., Nicholas Frost sentenced to pay a fine to,	28
jury of life & death	70
HOLMES, ROBERT, &c., fined for being absent, being warned	128
HOLTE, NICHOLAS, of Newbury, ment^d. (inventory of goods, &c., of Joseph Avery)	58
HOOKER, THOMAS, &c., witnesses to answer by John Pratt	111
HOPE, an Indian, to be whipped for running away, &c.	95
HOPKINS, RICHARD, sentenced to be whipped and branded on one cheek for selling " peeces " to the Indians	27
HORN } or HURNE	
HORNE }	
George, fined for being distempered with drink	76
case of, insolent carriage	93
HORSES, &c., owners of, to make full satisfaction for damage done by them	14
HOSIER	
Samuel, &c., to return tools to Mr. Pelham or the price of them	14
jury (Dexter against Endicott)	15
chosen and sworn constable of Waterton	48
to pay William Almy for service of Robert Way	61
HOSKINS	
John, &c., jury (case of Walter Palmer)	9
stealing a loaf of bread from, (Bartholmewe Hill to be whipped)	9
Senr., goods &c. of Christopher Ollyver to satisfy,	50
HOUCHENS. (*See* HUTCHINS.)	

INDEX.

	PAGE
HOUGH ⎫ or HAUGH, HOFFE	
HOUGHE ⎭	
——, Mr., &c., present at Court	54, 55
ment^d. (difference about two heifers)	56
&c., present at Court	57, 58
against Mr. Maveracke, witnesses to be examined by Mr. Winthrop, &c.	58
present at Court	59, 61, 62
Atherton, Mr., &c., to settle estate of Mr. Mellows	97
Atterton, &c. (Court of Assistants) order by (case of John Pratt)	112
HOUSE. (*See* HOUSES.)	
HOUSEHOLDERS ⎫	
HOUSEKEEPERS ⎭	
&c. to take the oath of allegiance	44
none but housekeepers to hire any person for a servant, &c.	15
HOUSE OF CORRECTION to be built at Boston	27
HOUSE OF ENTERTAINMENT. (*See* ORDINARY.)	
HOUSES OR HOUSE	
to be built for ministers	1
James Pen (order as to ministers)	2
Mr. Gayer " " " "	2
ment^d. (allowance &c. to Mr. Patricke & Mr. Underhill)	4
&c., order for preservation of,	17
of Thomas Graye at Marble Harbor to be pulled down, &c.	20
Mr. Rich. Browne allowed to keep a ferry over Charles River against his house	38
&c., order as to surveying, &c.	45
HOW ⎫	
HOWE ⎭	
——, Lt., bond for appearance	73
Edward, fined for selling strong water	41
and William Knopp, John Haynes &c. to audit accounts between, &c.	52
HOWLETT, THOMAS, &c., at Aggawam, ment^d.	31
HUBBARD ⎫	
HUBBERD ⎬	
HUBBERT ⎥	
HUBBURD ⎭	
Benjamin, admonished for drinking strong water, &c.	68
&c., bond for appearance, &c. of Robert Shorthose	78
Edmond, Senr. chosen constable of Charlton	51
&c. grand jury	70
fined for leaving a pit open	75
James, discharged	100
Joshua, costs to John Stone, &c. for not prosecuting	122
&c., constables of Hingham, ment^d.	126
HUDSON	
——, widow, discharged	84

	PAGE
HUDSON, *continued.*	
Ralph, &c., jury of life & death	70
William, chosen by town of Boston to keep an ordinary	93
Willi: &c., bond by, as to overpayment	98
discharged from their recognizance	98
William, &c., will of Thomas Morrice testified to by,	124
costs against Symon Kempthorne, for not prosecuting	128
Junr., allowed to keep a house of entertainment	136
HUES. (*See* HUGHES.)	
HUET. (*See* HEWET.)	
HUGHES or HEWES, HUES, HUYES	
Josuah, &c., gift towards the Sea Fort	42
fined for taking too much profit	60
HUITT. (*See* HEWET.)	
HULL	
———, Mr., &c., to determine &c. as to damage by swine	49
Mrs., Samuel Bacon to make restitution to,	131
HUMFREY ⎫	
HUMFRY ⎬	
HUMPHREY ⎪	
HUMPHRY ⎭	
———, Mr., ordered that his servant John Legge shall be whipped	14
&c., present at Court	47
fined for absenting himself from Court	54
Mr., ment^d. (difference about two heifers)	56
&c., present at Court, 58, 65, 72, 85, 89, 91, 93, 96, 99, 103–105, 107, 108	
and Robert Saltonstall, arbitrators between	133
John, Esq., land in Saugus to be set out for,	30
took oath of an Assistant	47
&c., to take depositions (Aspinwall & Brewerton)	48
to take depositions as to will of William Payne	49
&c., to determine &c. all matters of difference concerning estate of Willust	52
Mr., &c., present at Court.	63, 64, 69, 102
firing barn of, (case of Henry Stevens)	100
&c. (Court of Assistants) order by, (case of John Pratt)	112
Mr., costs to Edmund Batter for not prosecuting	126
HUNT, ENOCH, case of, (extortion)	106
HURNE. (*See* HORNE.)	
HUSBAND and WIFE	
order as to Henry Seawall and wife	60
case between Rich^d. Beggarly and wife referred to in note	62
divorce of James Luxford	89
Edward Adams enjoined to return to his wife	105
Anne Clarke granted a divorce from Dennis Clarke	138
John Richardson to be sequestered from Elizabeth Fryar, &c.	139

INDEX. 211

	PAGE
HUSBANDMEN	
company of, goods of, to be inventoried by the beadle &c.	23
ment^d. (order as to John Kirman)	52

HUTCHINGSON. (*See* HUTCHINSON.)
HUTCHINS or HOUCHENS
    Daniell, bond for appearance 95
        freed from attendance at Court 98
HUTCHINSON or HUTCHINGSON
    ———, Mr., testimony by, as to wages paid Arthur Holbidge &c. . . 56
        &c., committee, as to debts &c. of Mr. Ouldam . . 63
    Francis, case of, (corrupt speeches) 109
HUYES. (*See* HUGHES.)
HYATT, THOMAS, " brother," ment^d. (will of John Russell) . . . 57

IBROOKE
    ———, &c., attachment for, ... 79
    Richard, fined for tempting maids to uncleanness 81
IDLENESS. (*See* CRIMES, &c.)
IGNOMINIOUS PUNISHMENT. (*See* PUNISHMENT.)
ILLERY, HENRY, case of, (drunkenness, &c.) 95
IMPRESSMENT (case of Henry Chapman) 94
IMPRISONED. (*See* PUNISHMENT.)
INCENDIARISM. (*See* CRIMES, &c.)
INDIANS
    canoe taken from, ment^d. (order as to punishment of Thomas Morton) 4
    order as to permitting use of fire arms to, ... 5
        selling Indian Corn &c. to the English &c. 6
        selling corn to the Indians &c. 6
    all persons forbidden to trade in money with, ... 10
    any person employing, shall discharge him or her . . . 11
    none to entertain any Indian as a servant without a license . . 11
    Sir Richard Saltonstall to satisfy the Indians for wrongs done them by his servant 11
    wigwams ment^d. (order as to training of Capt. Underhill's Company) . 18
    John Dawe sentenced for enticing an Indian woman . . . 19
    Josias Plastowe sentenced for stealing from, ... 19
    as to punishment with death for adultery with English or Indian . 19
    trucking houses to be appointed in every plantation . . . 23
    every planter who trades with for beaver, shall pay twelve pence . 23
    selling powder, shot &c. to, Richard Hopkins sentenced for, . . 27
    at Damerills Cove, Nicholas Frost sentenced for theft from, . . 28
    not to receive any reward for killing wolves 29
    no man shall give or sell strong waters to, ... 33
    no person to buy land from, without leave &c. 40
    inquiry as to damage done by swine in Indian barns of corn . . 46
    entertaining an Indian without leave &c. Clement Briggs fined for . 49
    to set out the bounds of land sold by Chickataubut to Mr. Pinchon . 55
    stealing beans from, &c. William Shepheard sentenced for, . . 62

INDEX.

	PAGE
INDIANS, *continued*.	
selling strong water to, James Browne fined for,	68
lending a gun to an Indian, John Stretton fined for,	71
an Indian released, and to make satisfaction for a cow.	78
John Bayly fined for buying land of,	83
the Governor allowed to keep a Naviganset Indian and his wife	91
two Indian women to be whipped for abusing Mrs. Weld &c.	95
Hope an Indian, to be whipped for running away &c.	95
selling gunpowder to, (case of Richard Parker)	101
(case of Roger Tole)	101
selling shot to an Indian (case of John Stowe)	101
(Mr. Thomas Clarke's man)	101
mending Indians guns (case of Richard Collecot)	101
making an Indian drunk (case of James Dane)	105
John Skidmer fined for selling strong water to,	106
Pesons or George an Indian, banished.	118
selling powder and shot to, (case of William Scutt)	131
INQUISITION	
a jury to enquire concerning the death of Austen Bratcher.	6, 7
inquisition on the body of William Bateman	7
IPSWICH, Town of,	
Aggawam to be called,	47
John Pyke brought from, as a witness.	56
Robert Andrewes of, ment^d.	58
Richard Kent of, ment^d.	58
fined and to repair defects &c.	75
fined for defective highways.	80
John Davies to be whipped at, for attempting lewdness with women.	81
presentment of, for defective highways	83
John Wedgwood set in the stocks at, for being in the company of drunkards	86
attachment against, for defective ways.	90
paid its attachment	97
enjoined to repair their ways	106
Jonathan Thing to be whipped at,	106
Mr. Baker of, ment^d.	123
(*See also* AGGAWAM.)	
IPSWICH COURT	
J^{no}. Bayly &c. to be brought before,	69
Henry Sewall to answer for beating his wife	74
Thomas Savory referred to, for lying.	80
Edmond Greenliffe referred to,	83
Thomas Hall referred to,	83
Goodman Foster &c. referred to,	83
Mr. Henry Seawall to acknowledge his fault publicly at,	92
Robert Crosse remitted to,	100
Christopher Batte referred to,	100
case of Richard Nicoles referred to,	101

INDEX 213

ISLANDS
    order as to Islands within the limits of this pattent 16
    "his island" ment^d. (case of Samuel Maverick), ... 109
IVER, MICHA: forfeited his recognizance 92

JACKSON
    Elisha, turned over from George Barrell to John Millam . . . 119
    Samuell, &c., evidence by, (case of John Emerson) 74
JACOBS, NICHOLAS, &c., bond by, (case of Jonathan Bosworth) . . 124
JAMES
    Francis, sworn constable of Hingham 132
    Will: to be set in the bilboes &c. for incontinency 65
    Willi: &c., respited until the next Court 83
JARVIS, JOHN, &c., viewed the body of Austen Bratcher 7
JEANISON. (*See* JENNISON.)
JEFFREY, JANE, &c., case of, (filthy and unclean practise) . . . 134
JENKIN
    Joel, case of, (getting his masters daughter with child) . . . 95
    discharged 99
JENNISON OR JEANISON, GENNISON, GENESON, GENISON
    ———, Mr., &c., to take an inventory of Goods &c. of Alex: Wignall 33
    Anchient, goods of Thomas Walford to remain in hands of, . 35
    Ensign, Robert Way to remain with, ... 46
    order as to Robert Way who was assigned by him to Edward Burton 48
    fined for upbraiding the Court &c. 48
    fine remitted to, ... 52
    &c., to require the Indians to set out bounds . . 55
    to make a payment to William Almy . . 61
    Capt., payment from John Simpson for not prosecuting . . 86
    William, Mr., chosen anchient to Capt. Pattricke 18
    line between Roxbury and Newton laid out by, . . . 53
JESOP, JOHN, payment to, ment^d. (order as to Richard Brown) . . 71
JOANES OR JONES
    ———, Mr., and Mr. Mayhewe, accounts between to be examined . 93
    Edward, &c., sworn constables of Charlestown, ... 104
    John, case of, (defileing his wife before marriage) 87
    Mary, corn &c. granted to, ... 102
    corn granted to Alexander Becke for his trouble with, . . 107
    Richard, &c., Grand Jury, ... 70
    case of, (cheating) 88
    William, to acknowledge his fault publicly &c. 124
JOBSON
    John, shipmaster, bond by, (case of Francis Tobey) 62
    case of, (unadvised expressions) 116
JOCELY. (*See* JOSLYN.)
JOHN, SAGAMORE,
    &c., complaint by, as to having two wigwams burned . . . 11

	PAGE

JOHN, SAGAMORE, *continued.*
    promised to fence his corn against all kinds of cattle 26
    Richard Saltonstall to give him a hogshead of corn for damage done by his cattle 29

JOHNSON
    ――――, Mr., &c., to be Justices of the Peace 3
                  present at Court 3
        widow, to make a payment to William Almy 61
    David, and William Almy, judgment in suit 61
    Edward, goods received of, William Almy to bring in an inventory of . 46
        of Charlestown, case of, (not serving on the jury) . . 105
        appointed to train the Company at Woburn 123
        chosen Lieutenant of Woburn 135
        Junr., case of, (immoderate drinking) 138
    Fraucis, &c., gift towards the Sea Fort 42
    Isaack, Esq., Assistant and Justice of the Peace, &c., inquisition before, on body of William Bateman 7
        &c., jury, (case of Hugh Buett) 101
    John, &c., jury, as to death of Austen Bratcher 6
        (Dexter against Endicott) 15
        difference between Newton and Charlestown referred to, . 29
        chosen for Rocksbury, (order as to cart bridge over Muddy River, &c.) 34
        gift towards the Sea Fort 42
        return as to bounds between Watertown and Newe Towne . 53
    freed from training and to make payment to the Company . 88
    Samuel Hefford to serve, ... 101
    of Roxbury, freed from training 104
    surveyor, order to, mentions cattle from Providence . . . 135
    &c., committee, as to estate of Mr. Samuel Cooke . . . 140
    Peter, &c., bond by, (to give an account of their company goods) . 25
    Richard, acknowledged a debt to Sir Richard Saltonstall . . 13
        those who employ him are to pay out of his wages to Sir Richard Saltonstall 13
    Samuell, to be whipped for enticing servants to run away &c. . . 52
JOINERS, order as to wages of, ... 3, 5, 12, 36
JONES. (*See* JOANES.)
JOSLYN or JOCELY
    Henry, gentleman, &c., of Paskataqua, forfeited their bonds for non-appearance 61
                  discharged from their recognizance . . 62
JOYNERS. (*See* JOINERS.)
JUDGMENT against Joseph Twitchwell, five pounds of, to be abated . . 40
JUDSON, WILLI: discharged 81
JURISDICTION
    as to number of Assistants within this, ... 12
    no man within this, to hire a servant for less than year . . 15
    banishment from, ... 16, 60, 71, 101

INDEX. 215

JURISDICTION, *continued*.
    order as to planters within the limits of, ... 21
    Nicholas Frost tried for coming into this jurisdiction after banishment 59
    (*See also* PATENT, MASSACHUSETTS.)
JURY or GRAND JURY, Jury of Trials
    impannelled to inquire concerning the death of Austen Bratcher 28 Sept., 1630 . 6
    verdict of, in case of Walter Palmer 7
    present that William Bateman died by God's visitation . . . 8
    impannelled for the trial of Walter Palmer 9
    finds Walter Palmer not guilty of manslaughter 9
    impannelled to inquire concerning an action of battery . . . 15
    Mr. Palmer fined for absenting himself being warned to serve on a jury 35
    jurors to be warned by the beadle fourteen days before the Court . 38
    first Grand Jury referred to, in note 57
    of life and death, list of, ... 70
    Grand Jury, list of, ... 70
    absence from Court (case of Richard Collicot &c.) 74
    Henry Collens fined for not serving on, ... 76
    John Holgrave fined for sending a paper to a juryman . . . 78
    to appear, (case of Marmaduke Peirce) 86
    part of fine paid to the jury (case of Daniel Clarke) . . . 86
    pleading with the jury out of Court (case of Thomas Lechford) . 87
    list of jurymen (case of Marmaduke Peirce) 89
    Thomas Tylestone &c. fined for not attending the jury . . . 97
    calling the Grand Jury rogues (case of Rich. Cluffe) . . . 97
    found Hugh Buett guilty of heresy 101
    grant to the jury (case of Hugh Buett) 101
    John Holland &c. jurymen, fined for not appearing . . . 102
    Robert Stedman juryman, fined for not appearing . . . 103
    Robert Rendall found not guilty 103
    not serving on the jury (case of Edward Johnson) . . . 105
    absence from the jury (case of George Bowen) 107
    not warning the jury correctly (case of Thomas Carter, sen^r.) . 108
    not serving on the jury (case of Edward Larkin) . . . 108
    found Robert Wyar &c. not guilty with reference to the capital law . 121
    absence from the jury (case of Isaac Morrell) 125
    verdict as to death of Richard Silvester's child 126
    John Clough fined for his absence when the jury was called . 132
    Thomas Grub fined for not appearing upon the jury . . . 137
    Thomas Cooper fined for absence from, ... 138
    Benjamin Gillam fined for absence from, ... 138
JURY OF TRIALS. (*See* Jury.)
JUSALL, SARA, Thomas Boyse sentenced for attempting a rape with, . . 81
JUSTICE OF THE PEACE
    to direct the Beadle to issue summons &c. in civil actions . . 2
    the Governor and Deputy Governor shall always be, . . . 3
    power of, (S^r. Richard Saltonstall &c. appointed) 3
    Isaack Johnson, Esq. Assistant and Justice of the Peace . . 7

216 INDEX.

	PAGE
KEAYNE	
———, Capt., George Story discharged of his bond to answer to,	119
his action deferred until Mr. Bartholomew comes	129
Anne, case of, (testifying falsely)	124
KELLY, WILLIAM, mentioned in note	67
KEMBALL, HENRY, &c., allowance to, for cloth	105
KEMP } KEMPE }	
———, ment^d. (order as to a payment to Mr. Oliver)	130
John, case of, (unclean attempts with three young girls)	86
allowance to James Davis for keeping,	119
former servant of Isaac Morrell, to be cared for by the constable of Roxbury	125
KEMPTHORNE, SYMON, costs to William Hudson for not prosecuting &c.	128
KENDALL, JOHN, costs to John Parker for not prosecuting	138
KENDRICK, GEORGE, &c., bond forfeited by, (case of John Emerson)	65
KENT	
Richard, costs to John Kirman for not prosecuting	49
of Ipswich, debt due from, ment^d. (inventory of goods &c. of Joseph Avery)	58
KETCHAM, HESTER, freed from service with her master John Woolrige	92
KEYES, ROBERT, bond for appearance	76
KIBBE, ———, and ELWELL, capias to bring them before the Governor	65
KILCUP, WILLI:, &c., bond by, (case of Daniel Hutchins)	95
KILLMASTER } KILMASTER }	
John, &c., admonished for their distemper	108
case of, (being distempered with drink)	136
KING, The, &c., (recognizance by Mr. John Barcrofte)	36
KING } KINGE }	
John, &c., discharged	77
Joseph, Mr., case of, (obscene speeches, drinking &c.)	104
Richard, adm^r. on goods &c. of, granted to Richard Bishopp	54
KINGMAN	
Henry, of Weymouth, licensed to keep a house of entertainment	69
&c., Grand Jury	70
KINLOAH, JAMES, discharged	134
KIRKMAN } KIRMAN }	
John, to receive a payment from the estate of Mr. Crispe	20
costs against Richard Kent for not prosecuting	49
Capt. Traske to pay to, as his share in a plow patent	52
KITCHEN, JOHN, case of, (showing books he was to bring to the Governor)	87
KNIGHT	
———, a witness, order as to, (case of James Luddam)	61
John, admⁿ. on goods &c. of, granted to Roger Ludlowe, Esq.	30
of Newbury, ment^d. (inventory of goods &c. of Joseph Avery)	58

INDEX. 217

	PAGE

KNIGHT, *continued.*
    John of Newberry, licensed to keep an Ordinary &c. 68
        bond for appearance 92
        case of, (drunkenness &c.) 98
        &c., admonished for their distemper 108
        committed 115
        cause of, to be tried by action 117
    Marklin, to recompense James Pen 116
    Richard, of Newbury, ment^d. (inventory of goods &c. of Joseph Avery) 58
    Walter, forfeited his recognizance 102
        case of, (rude and contemptuous speeches) . . . 104

KNOP
KNOPE
KNOPP
    ———, fine remitted to, ... 26
    John, &c., admonished for their distemper 108
    Nicholas, fined for taking upon him to cure scurvey . . . 11
        Mr. William Pelham &c. promised to pay five pounds for, . 11
    William, or his son, whoever employs, to pay one half of their wages
                                to S^r. Richard Siltonstall 9
        owes debt to S^r. Richard Saltonstall 13
        bond for appearance 50
        and Edward Howe, John Haynes &c. to audit accounts be-
                                tween, &c. 52
    Will: to answer for speeches about our late Governor Mr. Vaine . 68
    Willi: &c., bond by, (case of George Richardson) . . . 99
        case of, (selling beer) 107
    William, wife of, allowed to keep a house of entertainment . . 136
        theft from, (case of Bridget Barnard) 137

KNORE
KNOWER
    Thomas, bond for appearance 20, 21
        set in the bilbowes for threatening the Court . . . 21
        fined for selling strong water 87
        adm^n. on estate of, granted to James Browne . . . 117
KNOWLES, JOHN, who married the widow Davies, granted adm^n. on estate of
                                          Robert Bills 77

LABOURERS, order as to wages of, ... 6, 36
LACE, Thomas Barnes admonished about lace 116
LAMBE
    Edward, attachment against, ... 73
        fined for contempt, to make a payment to John Finch and ad-
                            monished for dancing 75
    Thomas, slate demised to, in Slate Island 34
LAMBERT
    Richard, bond for appearance forfeited by, ... 49
        &c., referred to Salem 76

INDEX.

	PAGE
LAMPSON, WILLI: allowed to fell trees on the other side of Chebacco	108

LANDS
    no person to buy land of any Indian without leave &c. . . . 40
    assurance of, to free inhabitants ment^d. 45
    sale or grant of houses and lots to be entered in survey book . . 45
    all towns had respite to bring in a transcript of their lands . . . 83
    town of Concord fined for not giving in a transcript of their lands &c. 90
    town of Lynn   fined for not giving in a transcript of their lands &c. 90
          Dorchester " " " " " " " " " " " " 90
          Weymouth " " " " " " " " " " " " 90
    Charlestown, Sudbury and Dedham delivered in a transcript of their lands 117
    transcript of their lands delivered in by town of Dedham ment^d. . . 123
    Concord delivered in an imperfect transcript of their lands . . . 124

LANE
    Thomas, late servant to John Burslyn, order as to, ... 45, 46
        inhab^s. of Dorchester to receive three pounds for caring for, 46

LANGE, RICHARD, and town of Weymouth, Mr. Stoughton to hear business between, 99

LANGLEY, WILLIAM, sworn constable of Lynn 132

LARKIN, EDWARD, fined for not serving on the jury, and fine remitted . . 108

LASCIVIOUS ACTIONS. (*See* CRIMES, &c.)

LATHAM
    Carew, &c., attachment against, ... 136
        fined for his disorder 138
    Mary, condemned to death for adultery with James Brittaine . . 139

LAURENCE or LAWRENCE
    Henry, case of, (as to his servant Capt. Bonito) 82
    James, case of, (leaving his masters house &c.) 107

LAUSON. (*See* LAWSON.)

LAW
    Bibliographical Sketch of the Laws of the Colony referred to, . 115
    capital law ment^d. (case of Robert Wyar &c.) 121

LAWRENCE. (*See* LAURENCE.)

LAWSON or LAUSON
    Christopher, order as to, ... 139
    Henry, &c., notice to creditors of, ... 15

LAYFORD, "Layfords Liking" ment^d. 116

LAYTON, THOMAS, discharged 130

LEACH
    Ambrose, &c., case of, (drinking too much) 130
    Laurence, &c., jury, (case of Walter Palmer) 9

LEAKE, HENRY, and his wife, case of, (fornication) 131

LEATHER. (*See* SEALERS, &c.)

LECHFORD
    Thomas, copy by, ment^d. 1, 13, 15, 42, 115
        note book of, referred to . 80, 82, 84, 86, 87, 89, 94, 96, 99, 103
        Mr., case of, (pleading with the jury out of Court) . . 87
            dismissed 99

INDEX. 219

	PAGE

LECTURE DAY
    no lecture to begin before one o'clock in the afternoon . . . 37
    at Salem, ment^d. (case of Francis Weston's wife) 75
        (case of Richard Hollingsworth) 80

LEE
    John, Thomas Foxe fined for not appearing as a witness against . . 43
    to be fined and whipped for calling Mr. Ludlowe a false hearted knave &c. 43
    whipped &c. for speaking reproachfully of the Governor . . 49
    part of his fine remitted 50
    discharged of his fine 87
    costs against Richard Lettin for not prosecuting . . . 129

LEG }
LEGGE }
    John, servant to Mr. Humfry, to be whipped for striking Richard Wright 14
        bond by, for his wifes appearance 76

LETTIN, RICHARD, costs to John Lee for not prosecuting . . . 129
LEVENS. (*See* LEVINS.)
LEVERET, THOMAS, Mr., &c., to settle Mr. Mellows estate . . . 97
LEVETT, ———, Capt., &c., notice to creditors of, ... 15
LEVINS or LEVENS
    John, and Mr. Coxeall &c., business between referred to Mr. Pinchon 53
        of Roxbury, ment^d. (order as to Phebe Seales) 67

LEWES or LEWS
    Robert, discharged 106
    wife of, to be whipped for dishonoring the name of God . . 106

LEWIS
    ———, enjoined not to strike his servant John Lowe, and to set free 133
    Edward, &c., to view the leather tanned in Watertown &c. . . . 128
    John, case of, (running away and breaking into a house) . . . 126
    Swiniard, case of, (drunkenness) 133

LEWS. (*See* LEWES.)
LIBEL. (*See* ACTIONS.)
LICENSE. (*See* LIQUOR and ORDINARY.)
LIEUTENANT. (*See* MILITARY AFFAIRS.)
LIGHT behavior. (*See* CRIMES.)
LIGHTERAGE, rates of, referred to the General Court 108
LIGHTFOOT, Francis, Edward Gatly to pay ten shillings to, . . . 134
LIN. (*See* LYNN.)
LINEN, order as to sale of, ... 39
LINN. (*See* LYNN.)
LIQUOR
    Samuel Cole licensed 67
    Robert Longe licensed 68
    William Baulston licensed to sell claret &c. 68
    Robert Longe chosen by town of Charlestown to sell wine . . 93
    giving strong water to certain persons (case of Mr. Barnard) . . 94

	PAGE
LIQUOR, *continued.*	
William Davies bound not to sell ale, wine &c.	116
(*See also* STRONGWATER.)	
LISHE, SARAH, inventory of goods of, to be taken by Lt. Duncan	91
LOCKEWOOD } LOCKWOOD	
Edmond, Mr., &c., jury for trial of Walter Palmer	9
promised to pay five pounds for Nicholas Knopp	11
children and estate of, to be disposed of by the Church of Watertown	52
Edmond, (?) order as to estate of, &c.	54
Edward (Edmond?), order as to estate of, &c.	54
Robert, exec^r. of Edmond Lockwood, consent by, to disposition of estate &c.	52
Ruth, widow, ordered to bring writings left by her husband	50, 51
LONDON, Mr. Mathewe Cradocke of,	41
LONG } LONGE	
John, Mr., case of, (distemper in drinking &c.)	105
bond for appearance	107
gentleman, case of, (distemper in drink &c.)	124
Mr., to make a payment to Mr. Stodder and Company	125
(or LOUGE), Richard, confessed a debt to Mr. Ludlowe	13
fined for contempt of authority &c.	60
Robert, fined for selling beer and licensed to sell claret	68
&c., appraisers, (estate of Henry Harwood)	72
discharged for want of proof	83
chosen to sell wine by town of Charlestown	93
LONG ISLAND &c. granted to Boston for twenty one years	44
LONG SWAMP, &c. town of Cambridge fined for defective way at,	90
LOOMAN, ANN, Mrs., goods &c. of. to be inventoried &c.	51
LORANSON, JAMES, &c., presented for taking too much wages	135
LORDS DAY. (*See* SABBATH DAY.)	
LOUGE	
(or LONGE), Richard, confessed owing a debt to Mr. Ludlowe	13
(LONG or LONGE), Richard, fined for contempt of authority &c.	60
LOVE, JOHN, fined for drunkenness	55
LOVEL } LOVELL	
———, Capt., admonished to take heed of light carriage	65
his wife Weybro, presented for light behavior	65
business &c. of, referred to Roger Herlakenden	77
Elisabeth, case of, (immodest expressions)	94
Weybro, wife of Capt. Lovell presented for light behavior	65
LOW or LOWE	
John, &c., case of, (drinking too much)	130
to be freed from his master	133
LOWDEN, RICHARD, town of Charlestown discharged about his lot	83

INDEX.   221

                                                       PAGE
LOWE. (*See* LOW.)
LUDAM }
LUDDAM }
    James, fined for drunkenness 61
        to make a payment to William Almy 61
        a servant, suit as to, (David Johnson and William Almy) . 61
LUDDEN, JAMES, costs against Cutshamache for not prosecuting . . . 82
LUDLOWE
  ——, Mr., &c., to be Justices of the Peace 3
      present at Court, 1, 3, 5, 8-21, 23-28, 30-34, 35, 36, 38, 39,
                                                                 42
        fined for absence from Court 4
        Richard Louge confessed owing money to, . . . 13
        &c., committee, to take an account of debts due to the
                                            Governor &c. 33
        Capt. John Stone sentenced for abusing, &c. . . . 35
        John Lee sentenced for calling him a false hearted
                                        knave &c. 43
        granted adm^n. on goods &c. of Mr. John Tilley . . 43
    George, Mr., order as to business concerning, ... 10
    Robert, (or Roger), Mr., &c., present at Court 1
    Roger, Mr., Lucy Smyth bound an apprentice to, ... 17
        one hundred acres of land granted to, ... 29
        Esq., granted adm^n. on goods &c. of John Knight . . 30
LUSHER, ——, Lt., &c., committee as to affairs of Edward Allen . . 127
LUXFOARD }
LUXFORD }
    James, &c., bond for appearance &c. of Robert Shorthose . . . 78
        case of, (having two wives) 89
        to be delivered to his creditors 115
LYING. (*See* CRIMES, &c.)
LYNN, or LINN, Town of,
    witness from, called by George Woodward 68
    fined and enjoined to mend the highways 75
    fined for bad highways and to lay a ferry 83
    fined for not keeping constant watch, for want of sealed weights, and
                for not giving in a transcript of their lands 90
    enjoined to repair their ways 100
    allowed to use the meeting house as a watch house . . . 100
    discharged 106
    Mr. Edward Tomlin. allowed Ensign at Lynn 123
    William Langley sworn constable of Lynn 132
    (*See also* SAUGUS.)
LYNN or LIN, LINN,
    Henry, to be whipped for committing felony 6
        to be whipped and banished from the plantation for writing
                falsely against the government &c. 19
        fined for absenting himself from training . . . 29

	PAGE
LYNTON, RICHARD, &c., viewed the body of Austen Bratcher	7
LYON (Ship)	
Mr. Aleworth &c. to be sent to England in, ...	10
Lt. Aleworth granted liberty to return to England in, ...	28
MADOX, JOHN, discharged	106
MAGISTRATES	
excepted, (order as to providing inhab^s. of towns with fire arms) .	12
(order as to building a Fort at Boston)	35
(order as to work on Fort)	38
meetings of, Jan. 1635–6 referred to in note	61
slighting, Peter Bussaker sentenced for, ...	64
speaking contemptuously of, John Green sentenced for, . . .	71
&c. speaking against, Katherine Finch punished for, . . .	76
ment^d. (case of Robert Shorthose)	78
slighting, Robert Shorthose sentenced for, ...	81
abusing, (case of Elizabeth Vane)	132
(*See also* ASSISTANTS.)	
MAISTER, JOHN, Mr., to make a passage from Charles River to the New Town	16
MAKEPEACE, ———, Mr., his cow ment^d. (case of T[eagu] Ocrimi) . .	121
MALLOWS, ABRAHAM, Mr., will of, delivered into Court . . .	85
MANNERING, JOSEPH, judgment paid by, ment^d.	40
MANNING	
———, Mr., to be paid, (case of Robert Rogers &c.) . . .	131, 132
Clement, his master John Crosse warned to appear . . .	76
MANSFIELD	
———, Mr. Oliver to be paid for his pains about, . . .	127
ment^d. (payment to Mr. Oliver)	130
Daniel, put to William Denux for five years, 14 Nov. 1642 . .	128
MANSLAUGHTER. (*See* CRIMES, &c.)	
MARBLE HARBOR	
assessed, (order as to levy for making a palisade) . . .	20
house of Thomas Graye at, to be pulled down &c. . . .	20
stage at, ment^d. (order as to swine)	32
MARBLEHEAD, Town of,	
James White fined for drunkenness at, ...	33
John Bennett " " " "	33
house of Thomas Graye at, ment^d. (case of Ralph Warriner) . .	85
Thomas Gray sentenced for drunkenness &c. at, . . .	94
Hope an Indian, to be whipped at, for running away &c. . .	95
MARKET to be kept at Boston every Thursday	40
MARRIAGE	
Mr. Thomas Stoughton fined for "taking upon him to marry" persons	10
refusing to keep promise of, Joyce Bradwicke fined for, . . .	32
seeking maid without friends consent (case of Thomas Baguley) . .	97
Margaret Stephenson at liberty to marry	125

INDEX.

	PAGE

MARRINER }
MARRYNER }
    ———, Mr., &c., and John Tilley, difference between, referred to
                                  John Winthrop, sen^r. &c.   47
    Thomas, formerly servant to Robert Smyth, discharged . . . 88
MARSH, MARY, Richard Ibrooke fined for tempting her to uncleanness . 81
MARSHFIELD
    Thomas, of Connecticut, John Twogood a servant to be sent to his wife 100
MARSON, Eliz: John Pemerton sentenced for committing fornication with, . 32
MARTEN }
MARTIN }
    John, &c., jury, (case of Hugh Buett) 101
    Robert, &c., to view the land beyond Monotoquid River &c. . . 63
MARVIN, THOMAS, allowance to, for time he served and for killing wolves . 120
MARY, servant of Mr. Bartholomewe, to be whipped &c. for running away . 57
MASON
    ———, Lt., to receive ten pounds for his voyage to the Eastward . 34
            Capt., Sergt. Stoughton chosen Ensign to, . . . 38
    Hugh, &c., certificate by, (case of Mighill Bacon) . . . 105
               presented for sealers and searchers of leather . . 138
MASONS, &c. order as to wages of, ... 5, 36
MASSACHUSETTS (or MASSACHUSETTS BAY, COLONY OF MASSACHUSETTS,
                          COMMONWEALTH OF MASSACHUSETTS)
    records of, referred to 1
    Pullen Point in, mentioned 7
    records of, referred to in note 13
    John Winthrop, Esq., Governor of, mentioned 22
    prisoners to be brought into the Bay 26
    the Bay mentioned (order as to public meetings) . . . 28
                         (order as to Thomas Walford) . . . 35
                         (order as to work at the Fort) . . . 38
                         (order as to swamps) 39
    defence of the Colony mentioned (order as to the "moveing fort") . 41
    the Bay mentioned (order as to goods of Mr. John Tilley) . . . 43
    land about Massachusetts, order as to bounds of, . . . 55
    the Bay mentioned (case of Thomas Wonnorton) . . . 56
    John Trumble fined to the Commonwealth 66
    the Commonwealth mentioned (case of Wm. Andrews) . . 78–79
                                 (case of John Tower) 95
    Colonial Society of Massachusetts, transactions of, referred to in note 103
    Colony records referred to 109
    the Commonwealth mentioned (answer by John Pratt) . . . 110
    copy of Colony records mentioned 115
    laws of Massachusetts Colony mentioned 115
    Colonial Society of Massachusetts, transactions of, referred to . . 115
    records of, referred to in note 118, 119
    (*See also* JURISDICTION, PATENT.)

	PAGE

MASSACHUSETTS HISTORICAL SOCIETY
    Collection, 4th. series vol. 7 page 308 referred to in note . . . 103
                   5th. series vol. 1 page 402 referred to in note . . . 135
MASSEY, GEOFFREY (or JEFFREY), &c., agreement made by, as to estate of
                             John and William Fiske 77
MASTER Carpenter &c. order as to wages of, ... 5
MASTERS
    John, Mr., &c.. comm^{rs}., to take an inventory of Mr. Crispe's estate &c. 20
        discharged, having license 85
MASTER TAILORS. (*See* TAILORS.)
MATCH. (*See* MILITARY AFFAIRS.)
MATHEW
MATHEWE   } (*See* MATTHEW.)
MATHEWS
MATTACHUSETTS. (*See* MASSACHUSETTS.)
MATTAPAN
    ment^d. (allowance to Mr. Wilson) (order as to ministers) . . . 2
    to be called Dorchester 4
MATTHEW or MATHEW or MATHEWE, MATHEWS
    Dearmant, put to Thomas Dexter 129
    Dermondt, to be set to work until his master appears 125
    Edmond, admonished to take heed of pilfering 97
    Margery, widow of Thomas Mathew, allowed to sell her husbands
                                 house, land &c. 109
    Thomas, Margery Mathew widow of, allowed to sell her husbands
                                   house &c. 109
MAVERACK
MAVERICK   }
MAVERICKE
    ———, Mr., drinking at house of, ment^d. (order as to fine of Mr.
                                   Shepheard &c.) 18
        Senr., &c., to inquire &c. as to estate of Josias Plastowe . 23
        Junr., &c., difference between Newton and Charlestown re-
                                 ferred to, 29
        creek near " Mr. Mavericks " ment^d. 33
        Mr. Hough against, witnesses to be examined 58
    Elias, &c., witnesses, ment^d. (inquisition on William Bateman) . 8
    Moses, Mr., paid rent for Noddle's Island 63
    Samuel, Mr., Thomas Chubb to be freed from service of, &c. . . 14
        Noddle's Island granted to, ... 31
        &c., (recognizance by Mr. John Barcrofte) . . . 36
        order as to goods of Robert Anderson . . . 68
        to bring James Meadecalfe into Court 81
        forfeited his bond (case of James Meadcalfe) . . 82
        payment by, ... 89
        bond by, for the company of the " Charles " . . . 97
        case of, (confederacy with Thomas Owen &c. and his
                               Island ment^d.) 108, 109

INDEX.

	PAGE
MATHEWE	
———, Mr., granted adm^n. on goods &c. of Mr. Ralfe Glover	34
&c., committee, as to debts &c. of Mr. Ouldam	63
to examine witnesses &c. concerning Mr. White and Mrs. Wolcott	74
and Mr. Joanes, accounts between, to be examined	93
Thomas, &c., agreement signed by, (as to bounds of Charles Towne and Newe Towne)	23
Mr., to examine what hurt the swine of Charlton have done	46
adm^r. of Mr. Ralfe Glover, inventory exhibited by,	46
&c., to examine accounts (Saltonstall, Apleton &c.)	65
to examine accounts between Edmond White and Mrs. Wolcott	100
MEADCALFE } MEADECALFE }	
James, "to be brought in"	81
case of, (bond forfeited by Samuel Maverick)	82
ment^d. (case of Samuel Maverick)	89
MEADFORD, or MEDFORD, Town of,	
ment^d. (order as to levy for maintenance of Mr. Patricke &c.)	6
(order as to maintenance of ministers)	9
assessed, (order as to levy for making a palisade)	20
assessed for maintenance of Capt. Underhill &c.)	31
" to defray public charges	37
land near, granted to Mr. John Wilson	43
John Smith of, ment^d.	74
MEAKINS, THOMAS, Goodman, Henry Hobson put to,	122
MEASURES. (*See* WEIGHTS.)	
MEDFORD. (*See* MEADFORD.)	
MEDICAL, Nicholas Knopp fined for taking upon himself to cure scurvey	11
MEETING HOUSE	
in Hingham to be used as a watch house	84
Charlestown " " " " " "	90, 99
Salem " " " " " "	100
Lynn " " " " " "	100
Hingham " " " " " "	100
MELLOWS, ———, Mr., order as to estate of,	97
MERRIAM	
———, widow, granted adm^n. on estate of her husband	127
———, adm^n. on estate of, granted to his widow	127
MERRICKE	
James, &c., case of, (drinking intemperately, selling wine, &c.)	139
John " " " " " " " "	139
MERRIES. (*See* MERRY.)	
MERRIMACK } MERRIMAK } or MERRYMACK RIVER	
Mr. John Winthrop, Junr. &c., to set up a trucking house up Merrymak River	85
Jno. Bayly, &c., dwelling beyond Merrimack, order to apprehend	69

	PAGE
MERRY or MERRIES	
Nicholas, fined for selling strong water	86
Walter, Henry Illery fined for calling him a knave	95
his servants to be whipped for running away	97
MERRYFIELD, HENRY, respited (lewd speeches)	135
MERRYMACK. (*See* MERRIMACK.)	
MESSENGER, HENRY, bond for appearance	98
MILAM or MILLAM	
John, Elisha Jackson turned over to, from George Barrell	119
discharged, as to cloth of Mr. Stoughton	139
MILITARY AFFAIRS	
order as to permitting Indians to use "any peece," &c.	5
Jost Weillust chosen surveyor of the Ordinance and Cannoneer	11
ordered that the inhabitants of every town within this pattent be provided with arms	12
order as to punishment of persons who shoot off any "peece" after the watch is set	13
order as to muskets, powder, bullets & match	13
ordered that every Captain shall train his company on Saturday in every week	13
ordered that persons travelling between these plantations and Plymouth shall carry arms	14
order as to training of companies	18
Mr. Francis Aleworth chosen Lieutenant unto Capt Southcoate	18
Mr. William Gennison chosen anchient to Capt. Patricke, &c.	18
order as to providing single persons with arms	21
order as to searching pieces and charging with bullets	25
Captains shall be maintained by their several companies	26
order for payment to Capt. Underhill, &c.	27
Mr. Robert Feakes chosen Lieutenant to Capt. Patricke	27
Alex: Miller, &c. punished for wasteful expense of powder, &c.	27
John Finch fined for wanting arms for his man and for being absent from training	29
Henry Lynn, &c., fined for being absent from training	29
Mr. Mathewe Cradocke fined for his men being absent from training	29
ordered that Captains shall train their companies only once a month	29
Boston, &c., assessed for maintenance of Capt. Underhill, &c., also choice of ancient to Capt. Underhill	31
order as to punishment of trained soldiers who absent themselves from training, &c.	36
Mr. Thomas Mooteham chosen an Ensign in place of Ensign Morris discharged	38
Sergeant Stoughton chosen an Ensign to Capt. Mason	38
Mr. Nathaniel Turner chosen Captain of the military company at Saugus	40
Richard Morris chosen Lieutenant to Capt. Underhill	40
money to be collected for building a Moving Fort	41
Ensign Damford to be sent for about defacing the colors	50

INDEX.

MILITARY AFFAIRS, *continued*.

	PAGE
Mr. John Benjamin &c. dismissed from training by reason of age, &c.	50
John Johnson freed from training, and to make a yearly payment to the Company	88
Henry Bright took oath as surveyor of arms in Watertown . . .	95
Mr. Samuel Winsley sworn surveyor of the arms at Colchester . .	98
John Johnson freed from training	104
Edward Goodnow chosen clerk of the Band and sworn . . .	123
Mr. Edward Tomlins allowed Ensign at Lynn	123
Mr. William Tory appointed Ensign at Weymouth	123
Edward Johnson appointed to train the Company at Woburn . .	123
Nicholas Powell appointed surveyor of arms at Dedham . . .	125
Mr. Stodder and his Company to be paid by Mr. Long	125
allowance to Mr. Hibbins for his horse killed in the public service .	128
John Smyth, Clerk of the Band at Dorchester	131
Mr. Briant Pendleton to exercise the company at Sudbury . . .	133
Sergt. Wardall to train the company at Exeter	133
Edward Johnson allowed lieutenant of Woburn	135

MILITARY COMPANY. (*See* MILITARY AFFAIRS.)

MILL

&c., Mr. Israel Stoughton granted liberty to build a mill, &c. on Neponset River	43
of Mr. Waltham, &c., ment^d.	84

MILLAM. (*See* MILAM.)

MILLARD, THOMAS, &c., watchmen, imprisoned for drinking strong water . 87

MILLER

Alex:, &c., to make a payment for their wasteful expense of powder,	27
Thomas, pilot and mate of the "Hector," committed for seditious speeches	63

MILLS, GEORGE, case of, (battery)	130
MINARD, THOMAS, &c., witnesses, grant to, ...	98
MINCARRY, the blackmore, admonished & discharged	118
MINDAM, ROBERT, discharged (attachment by Mr. Campian) . .	122

MINISTERS

proposition as to maintenance of, ...	1, 2
excepted (order as to providing inhabs. of towns with fire arms) .	12
(order as to building a fort at Boston)	35
(order as to work on Fort)	38
Meeting of, 19 Jan., 1634–5, referred to in note	50
Samuel Norman sentenced for saying "if ministers will but rail against England," &c.	82

(*See also* PASTOR.)

MINOTOCOT RIVER, inhabs. of Braintree respited as to the bridge over, . . 116

MISTICKE

ment^d. (order as to training of Capt. Underhill's Company) . .	18
six hundred acres at, near his house, granted to Govr. Winthrop .	19
Weir at, granted to John Winthrop, Esq., &c.	41
inquiry as to damage done by swine in the Indian corn on the north side of Mystic	46

228   INDEX.

                                                                                    PAGE
MOLESTATION. (*See* ACTIONS.)
MONEY
        corn shall pass for payment of all debts except money or beaver be ex-
                                                        pressly named   20
        no planter returning to England shall carry money or beaver without
                                                leave from the Governor   21
MONOTOQUID RIVER, John Olyver, &c. to view land beyond   63
MONTAGUE or MOUNTAGUE
        Griffin, to be set in the bilbowes for stealing boards, &c., and enjoined
                                                to remove from Muddy River   53
                forfeited his bond for non appearance   61
MOODY, JOHN, Mr., administration granted to, on goods, &c. of Thomas
                                                                    Desbre 35
MOOR
        George Pye, " a more," order as to, ...   76
        Mincarry " the blackmore," order as to   118
MOORE
        John, &c., witnesses (will of John Russell)   57
        Thomas, &c., witnesses (will of John Russell)   57
MOOTEHAM, THOMAS, Mr., chosen an Ensign   38
MORECROFT, JOHN, Mr., case of, (unfit carriage)   103
MORELL. (*See* MORRELL.)
MORGAN, ROBERT, &c., referred to Salem   76
MORLEY, SARAH, apprenticed to Mr. Nathanaell Turner   .   .   .   22
MORRELL or MORELL
        Abraham, case of, ...   88
                        (selling his servant his time)   106
        Isaack, &c., grand jury   70
        Isaac, case of, (absence from the jury)   125
                order as to his former servant, John Kempe   .   .   .   125
MORRICE }
MORRIS }
        ———, Sergeant, chosen ancient to Capt. Underhill   31
                Ensign, discharged   38
        Richard, &c , jury (case of Walter Palmer)   9
                Mr., chosen Lieutenant to Capt. Underhill   40
        Thomas, will of, delivered in upon oath by Edward Woolastone, &c. . 124
MORTON
        ——— of Mount Woolison, order that he be sent for by process   .   3
        Thomas, of Mount Wolliston (or Wollaston) punishment of,   .   .   4
MOULTON
        Robert, chosen constable of Charlton   43
                Goodman, to be repaid his rate by town of Salem   .   .   65
        Thomas, to pay forty shillings to Mr. Ralfe Glover   .   .   .   10
                bond for appearance and bound to his good behavior   .   . 137
                discharged   139
MOUNTAGUE. (*See* MONTAGUE.)
MOUNT FEAKES, on Charles River, land near, granted to John Oldham .   .   43

INDEX. 229

	PAGE
MOUNT WOLLASTON ⎫	
MOUNT WOLLISTON ⎬	
MOUNT WOOLISON ⎭	
——— Morton of, order that he be sent for by process	3
Thomas Morton of,	4
MOVING FORT. (*See* FORT.)	
MOWERS, &c., order as to wages of,	36
MOWERS, JOHN, ment^d. (case of Laurence Copeland)	128
MOWING Ground, &c., order as to surveying, &c.	45
MOXHAM, GEORGE, Mr., &c. were made free	69
MUDDY RIVER	
&c., agreement as to a cart bridge over,	34
line between Roxbury and Newton to run south west from,	53
Griffin Mountague to remove his habitation from, for stealing	53
town of Roxbury fined for a defective bridge at,	84
Bridge, order as to charges for,	93
MUDGE	
Jarvice, attachment for,	80
Jarvise, ment^d.	86
MULLINDER, ———, dismissed	73
MUNINGS ⎫	
MUNNINGS ⎭	
George, fined for selling beer and keeping a house of entertainment without license	67
&c., to view the leather tanned in Watertown, &c.	128
presented for sealers and searchers of leather	138
MUNT ⎫	
MUNTE ⎭	
Thomas, testimony as to wages paid to,	56
&c., to make a weekly payment towards their forfeits	57
goods of John Hogg secured to,	103
MURDER. (*See* CRIMES, &c.)	
MUSKETS. (*See* MILITARY AFFAIRS.)	
MUSQUANTUM Chappell and the mouth of Naponsett, land lying between, granted to Mr. Roger Ludlowe	29
MUSTLEWHITE, JOHN, allowance of fee to John Pyke, a witness against,	56
NAHANTON, to give two skins of beaver to Mr. Blackestone for damage done his swine	52
NAPONSETT RIVER	
Mouth of, and Musquantum Chappell, land lying between, granted to Mr. Roger Ludlowe	29
Israel Stoughton granted liberty to build a bridge. &c., over,	43
NAPPER, George, discharged	132
NARHIGANSETT or NAVIGANSET, NAVIGAN	
to make satisfaction for a cow	78
Indian, and his wife, the Governor allowed to keep	91

230 INDEX.

	PAGE
NATASCETT	
ment^d. (order as to levy for maintenance of Mr. Patricke, &c.)	6
(order as to levy for the creek at Newe Towne)	16

NATT. (*See* NOTT.)

NAVIGAN.   } (*See* NARHIGANSETT.)
NAVIGANSET.

NEALE
    Henry, &c., discharged with an admonition as to too many in a boat . 81
        his servant, Henry Hobson freed from him, &c. . . . 122
        to be whipped and kept chained by his master for running away & stealing 86
        servant of Mr. Cockram, committed on suspicion of felony . 128

NEGLIGENCE causing death. (*See* CRIMES, &c.)

NEGUS, JONATHAN, &c., jury (case of Hugh Buett) 101

NELME
    James, &c., bond for appearance 134
    Jasper, forfeited forty shillings for not appearing . . . 136
        fine remitted to, ... 137

NEVE, RICHARD, costs to Daniel Bacon for not prosecuting . . . 101

NEWBERRY }
NEWBURY } or NEWEBERRY, Town of,
    Richard Knight, &c. of, ment^d. 58
    John Knight of, ment^d. 68
    constable of, to apprehend Schooler, &c. 69
    town of, fined, and enjoined to repair defects, &c. . . . 75
        for want of a pair of stocks 80
    Mr. Goouch of, ment^d. 83
    fined for want of town weights and measures 95
    ment^d. (answer by John Pratt) 110

NEW COMERS to contribute towards the Sea Fort (cancelled) . . 40

NEWEBERRY. (*See* NEWBURY.)

NEWEMAN. (*See* NEWMAN.)

NEW ENGLAND
    landing of the Governor in, ment^d. (mem^o.) . . . 3
    service in, ment^d. (release of Robert Fibbin) . . . 46
    John Stanley died on his way to, order as to estate of, . . 51
    Boston in, ment^d. (will of Joane Drake) 72

NEWE TOWNE. (*See* NEW TOWN.)

NEWGATE
    ———, Mr. money to be repaid to, (case of Susan Hewet, &c.) . 121
    Mrs., abusing, (case of Elizabeth Vane) 132

NEWMAN or NEWEMAN
    ———, Mr., &c., of Weymouth, difference referred to (Welthia[n] Richards and Henry Waltham) 102
    advice of, ment^d. (order as to goods taken from a wreck) 105

NEW PROVIDENCE
    Mr. John Greene of, ment^d. 71
    "Daniel Abbot departed to," 85

INDEX. 231

                             PAGE

NEWTON (Town of). (*See* NEW TOWN.)
NEWTON
  John, &c., granted administration on goods of Mr. Edward Allen . 127
      Mr. Allen gave his estate to, (oath by Frances Pembrooke) 128
NEW TOWN or NEWE TOWNE, NEWTON, Town of,
  passage from Charles River to the, Mr. John Maister hath undertaken
      to make 16
  order as to levy for making of the creek at the New Town . . . 16
  ment^d. order as to training of Capt. Underhill's Company . . . 18
  levy for making a palisade about the, ... 20
  assessed (order as to levy for making a palisade) 20
  and Charles Towne, agreement as to setting out bounds of, &c. . . 22
  two hundred acres of land near, granted to Thomas Dudley, Esq. . 23
  James Woodward sentenced for being drunk at the Newe Towne . 26
  and Charles Towne, order as to the difference between, as to bounds . 29
  agreement as to bounds of, ... 30
  assessed for maintenance of Capt. Underhill, &c. . . . 31
     to defray public charges 37
  swamp within the Newe Towne pale excepted (order as to fetching
      wood from swamps) 39
  Court holden at, 3 June, 1634 45
    of Assistants holden at, ... 46, 47
  inhabitants of, to enjoy the meadow on the north side of the Pond . 47
  Court of [Assistants] holden at, 6 Oct., 1634 . . . . 48, 50, 52
  and Roxbury, line between, to run south west from Muddy River . 53
    Waterton, agreement as to bounds between, (mentions the Weir) . 53
  Court of [Assistants] holden at, 7 July, 1635 . . 55, 57, 59, 61, 62
  Synode at, for settling differences, ment^d. 69
  Quarter Court held at, 7 Sept. 1637 . . . . . 69, 71, 72
  John Smith to appear at, (attachment) 73
  John Prat of, ment^d. 112
  (*See also* CAMBRIDGE, Town of)
NICOLES, RICHARD, case of, referred to Court at Ipswich . . . 101
NODDLE ISLAND }
NODDLES ISLAND }
  &c. shall be appropriated to the public benefit, &c. 17
  no person shall shoot at fowl on, ... 21
  granted to Mr. Samuel Mavericke 31
  rent paid for, by Mr. Moses Maverick 63
NON APPEARANCE. (*See* CRIMES, &c.)
NORCROS, JEREMY, and John Smyth, Mr. Collens, &c. to examine accounts, &c. 100
NORMAN
  John, sen^r., fined for not appearing at Court when summoned . . 14
  Richard, &c., inquisition upon oaths of, upon body of William Bate-
      man 7
  Samuell, to be whipped for saying "if ministers will but rail against
      England," &c. 82

	PAGE
NORTH RIVER	
land near, ment^d	33
or Three Mile Brook, land on, granted to Mr. Increase Nowell . .	43
NORTON	
——, warrant sent to, as to bill by Goodman Perkins . . .	54
Francis, Mr., &c., sworn constables of Charlestown, 15 April, 1642-3	121
Walter, Esq., &c., inquisition on body of William Bateman upon oaths of,	7
NOTT or NATT, NUTT	
—— Goodman, &c., allowance to, ...	105
John, ment^d. (will of Joane Drake)	72
(order as to estate of Joane Drake)	77
NOWELL	
—— Mr., &c., present at Court, ... 3, 5, 9-19	
present at meeting of Assistants	20
present at Court . . . . · 21, 23-28, 30-33	
committee to take an account of debts due to the Governor, &c.	33
present at Court	34
to settle differences between John Dillingham, &c. .	35
present at Court 36, 38, 39, 42	
gift towards the Sea Fort	42
land granted to, ment^d. (grant to Mr. John Wilson)	43
&c., present at Court 45-48	
to hear witnesses as to damage done by swine of Charlton	49
&c., present at Court 50, 52	
bridge of, ment^d. (line between Roxbury and Newton)	53
&c., present at Court 54-55	
&c., difference as to heifers kept by Richard Wright referred to	56
&c. present at Court 57-59	
fined for selling wine	59
mentioned in short hand note	61
&c. present at Court 61, 62	
Increase, Mr., &c., present at Court	1
secretary, record in handwriting of	1
mentioned in note	15
writing by, reference to in note	19
entry in handwriting of, referred to in note . . .	30
I[ncrease], Mr., land on North River granted to, . . .	43
&c, to take dep^{ns}. (Aspinwall & Brewerton) . .	48
record in handwriting of, referred to, ...	62
&c., present at Court	63
committee, as to estate of Mr. Ouldam . . .	63
secretary, &c., present at Court	64
&c., present at Court	65

NOWELL, *continued*.
 I[ncrease], to examine accounts (Saltonstall, Appleton, &c.) . . 65
    present at Court 66, 69, 71, 72, 74
    &c., to examine witnesses, &c.. concerning Mr. White and
               Mrs. Wolcott 74
    present at Court 76
    Capt. Lovell's business, &c., referred to, ... 77
    present at Court 78, 81, 82, 86
    part of fine paid to, (case of Daniel Clarke) . . . 86
    fine paid to, (case of John Woolrige) 88
    &c., present at Court . . . 88, 89, 91, 92, 93, 95, 96, 98, 99
    to examine accounts (Edmond White and Mrs. Wolcott) . 100
    present at Court 102–105, 107, 108
    &c. (Court of Assistants), order by (case of John Pratt) . 112
    present at Court, 115, 117–120, 122, 123, 125, 127, 128, 130, 131,
               132, 134, 137, 138
NUNCUPATIVE will of John Russell 57
NUTT. (*See* NOTT.)

OATELEY, ———, Mr., case of, (concealing) 109
OATH
 of an Assistant taken by Capt. Endicott 3
 Constable taken by John Woodbury 5
 for the Governor and the Council, ment[d]. in note . . . 15
 of an Assistant, taken by Capt. Endicott 24
 Constable, taken by Mr. Turner 26
     George Dyar 28
 an Assistant, taken by Mr. Endicott 33
 of allegiance, to be taken by householders, &c. 44
 Constable, taken by Eltweed Pumery 45
 an Assistant taken by John Winthrop, jun[r]. 46
     John Humphey Esq. 47
 Constable, taken by Samuel Hosier 48
     Steven Terry 55
 an Assistant taken by Mr. Richard Saltonstall 66
 Constable taken by Tho. Ewar 73
 an Assistant taken by Mr. John Winthrope, jun[r]. . . . 77
 Constable taken by John Haward 80
     Thomas Brooke 80
 as constables of Hingham taken by John Porter & Henry Tuttle . . 97
 of constable of Weymouth taken by William Carpenter . . 102
    Concord " " Walter Edmonds . . 103
 Thomas Carter, sen[r]., &c., took oaths as constables of Charlestown . 104
 John Whitney took oath as constable of Watertown . . . 105
 Francis Norton, &c., sworn constables of Charlestown . . 121
 John Harding, &c., sworn constables of Weymouth, 23 May, 1643 . 123
 Edward Goodnow sworn clerk of the band, 5 June 1643 . . 123
 George Wicks sworn constable of Dorchester 130

	PAGE
OATH, *continued.*	
William Langley sworn constable of Lynn	132
Francis James sworn constable of Hingham	132
Thomas Arnold sworn constable of Watertown	134
Henry Adams sworn constable of Braintree	136
Barnabas Fawer sworn constable of Dorchester	140
Thomas Richards, &c., sworn constables of Weymouth	140
OBOLUS, or half penny, ment^d. (allowance for killing a woolf)	8
OCRIMI, T[EAGU], case of, (buggery)	121
ODLE, URSULA, &c., to be whipped (case of Robert Wyar, &c.)	121
OFFICERS. (*See* MILITARY AFFAIRS.)	
OKAM, THOMAS, &c., goods &c. of Christopher Ollyver in hands of	50
OLDAM } or OULDAM OLDHAM	
———, Mr., committee as to estate of,	63
Jo[hn], Mr., grant to, of land near Mount Feakes on Charles River	43
OLIVER } OLLYVER OLYVER	
———, Mr., to be paid for his pains about Mansfield	127
order as to a payment to,	130
Christopher, goods &c. of, to be sequestered for debt	50
John, &c., to view the land beyond Monotoquid River, &c.	63
committee, as to affairs of Edward Allen	127
Mary, wife of Thomas, committed for disturbing the Church of Salem	80
Thomas, his wife, Mary, committed to prison	80
ORDERS or ACTS made by any number of the Assistants in Court shall be legal	12
ORDINANCE. (*See* MILITARY AFFAIRS.)	
ORDINANCES. (*See* SABBATH DAY.)	
ORDINARY or HOUSE OF ENTERTAINMENT	
John Knight of Newbury licensed to keep	68
license to keep, granted to Nicholas Upsall of Dorchester	68
William Baulston licensed to keep	68
Henry Kingman licensed to keep	69
William Hudson chosen by town of Boston to keep	93
Mr. Baker of Ipswich allowed to keep	123
Richard Wood to keep an ordinary at Roxbury	133
William Hudson, jun^r., allowed to keep a house of entertainment	136
wife of William Knop allowed to keep a house of entertainment	136
ORKHUSSUNT RIVER, or Wooleston River, land near Salem bounded on the east by, granted to Capt. Jo: Endicott	24
ORRICE, GEORGE, &c., bond by, (case of John White)	95
ORTON, THOMAS, case of, (intemperate drinking)	139
OSBORN } OSBORNE	
———, Mary, wife of, case of,	70
Mary, case of (about death of her daughter)	70
(giving her husband quicksilver, &c.)	108

OSBORN, *continued.*
 Richard, enjoined to give a weekly account of how he spends his time,
   to the constable . . . 67
  costs against Thomas Turner, for not prosecuting . . . 136
OTTIS, JOHN, &c., witnesses, grant to, ... 98
OULDAM. (*See* OLDHAM.)
OWEN
 Thomas, attachment against, granted to Thomas Fowle . . . 99
  case of, (adulterous practises) 108
  confederating with, to break prison (case of Samuel Maverick) 108, 109
  case of, (escaping from prison) 109
OWLES
 Daniel, case of, (drinking) 120
  put to Sergt. William French, for one year, &c. . . . 122
OYSTER BANK, sixty acres of meadow granted to Simon Bradstreet in the marsh against, 28
PAGE
 Edward, servant, freed 104
 John, &c., jury (case of Walter Palmer) 9
  to return tools to Mr. Pelham or the price of them . . 14
  fined for turning the way about 79
  town of Watertown fined for a bad highway at John Page's 85
PAINE or PAYNE
 ———, Mr., Josuah Barnes apprenticed to, ... 26
  satisfaction to, ment^d. (case of Mr. Stodder) . . . 131
 Edward, Mr., discharged, and granted costs against Clement Campion 123
 William, John Humfry, Esq., to take depositions of witnesses of will of William Payne 49
PAINTER. (*See* PAYNTER.)
PALFLIN (or PAULFLIN) JOHN, fined, and part of fine remitted . . 83
PALFRY
 Peter, &c., jury, as to death of Austen Bratcher 6
  to set out land to John Humfry, Esq. 30
PALISADE about the Newe Towne, levy placed for making . . . 20
PALLATTINATE, Churches in, ment^d. (order as to a day of public thanksgiving) 23
PALMER
 ———, Mr., fined for absenting himself from jury service . . . 35
 Abraham, &c., jury, as to death of Austen Bratcher . . . 6
  appointed to lay out bounds between Waterton and Newe Towne, return by, 53
  grand jury 70
 George, set in the stocks for committing folly with Margery Rugs . 93
 Henry, bond for his wife's good behavior &c. 103
 John, granted costs against George Woodward for not prosecuting . 67
 Walter, strokes given by, accidentally caused the death of Austen Bratcher (jury's verdict) 7
  bond by (death of Austin Bratcher) 7

PALMER, *continued.*
    Walter, jury impannelled for trial of 9
        the jury find not guilty of manslaughter 9
        case of, ment^d. (sentence of Tho: Foxe) 12
PANTRY, WILLIAM, &c., dismissed from training by reason of age, &c. . . 50
PAPER on clothing. (*See* PUNISHMENT.)
PARISH, JOHN, ment^d. (case of Thomas Davenport) 91
PARKE. (*See* PARKS.)
PARKER
    ———, Mr., of Rocksbury, &c., gift towards the Sea Fort . . 42
    &c. of Weymouth, difference referred to (Welthia[n]
        Richards and Henry Waltham) 102
        theft from (case of Mary Felton) 108
    James, Mr., fined for drunkenness 25
        is allowed to marry Thomas Clifton & Mary Butterworth 102
    John, charges against Thomas Clay for not prosecuting . . 98
        costs against John Kendall " " " . . 138
    Richard, Mr., case of (selling gunpowder to an Indian) . . . 101
PARKES } or PARKE
PARKS }
    William, promise by, to satisfy Mr. Pinchon, for goods bought from
        Sergeant Bateman 25
        his servant John Webb set at liberty from, ... 32
        &c., difference referred to, (Mr Dumer and Jehu Burr) . 61
        to settle difference between John Coggeshall & Phebe
        Scales 67
        &c., grand jury 70
        committee, as to estate of Samuel Cooke . . . 140
PASCATAQUA. } (*See* PISCATAQUA.)
PASKATAQUA. }
PASTOR or TEACHER, Mr. Batchel^r to forbear as a pastor or teacher &c. . 27
    (*See also* MINISTERS.)
PATENT or PATTENT
    order as to persons planting within the limits of the pattent . . 4
    Thomas Gray ordered to remove out of the limits of this pattent . 6
    order as to selling, &c. corn within limits of this pattent . . . 6
    money to be paid for killing wolves within the limits of this
        pattent 8
    no person within the limits of this pattent shall trade &c. in money with
        the Indians 10
    ordered that the inhab^{ts}. of every town within this pattent be provided
        with fire arms 12
    Tho: Walford and his wife ordered to depart from the limits of this
        Pattent for contempt of authority, &c. 14
    order as to persons travelling out of this pattent 15
        Islands within the limits of this pattent 16
    no person within the limits of this pattent shall burn any ground any
        year before March first 17

INDEX. 237

	PAGE
PATENT or PATTENT, *continued.*	
plantations within the limits of this pattent ment[d].	20
order as to planters within this pattent trading beaver with the Indians	23
bond by Bryan Bincks, &c. that they will not depart out of the limits of the pattent without leave from the Governor	25
Mr. Batchel[r]. silenced as a pastor or teacher in this pattent	27
Nicholas Frost banished out of the pattent, &c. for thefts from the Indians, &c.	28
act restraining Mr. Batchel[r]. from gathering a Church within this pattent reversed	30
Capt. John Stone prohibited from coming into the pattent without leave &c. on pain of death	35
the, ment[d]., (answer by John Pratt)	110
(*See also* JURISDICTION, MASSACHUSETTS.)	
PATIENCE, THOMAS, referred to Mr. Endecot	105
PATRICK } or PATTRICKE	
PATRICKE }	
———, Mr., allowance to,	4, 5
(or Capt.), order as to levy for maintenance of,	6
Capt. William Gennison "chosen anchient to,"	18
&c., to be paid a quarters exhibition	27
Mr. Robert Feakes chosen his Lieutenant	27
&c., Boston &c. assessed for maintenance of,	31
PATTENT. (*See* PATENT.)	
PATTRICKE. (*See* PATRICKE.)	
PAULFLIN. (*See* PALFLIN.)	
PAULY, BENJAMIN, fined for being distempered with wine	98
PAYNE. (*See* PAINE.)	
PAYNTER or PAINTER	
Thomas, &c., viewed the body of Austen Bratcher	7
punished for disturbing the Church of Hingham	135
PEARCE. (*See* PEIRCE.)	
PEASE, JOHN, sentenced to be whipped and bound to his good behavior for striking his mother, Mrs. Weston	59
PECK, ———, Mr., minister, advice of, ment[d]. (order as to goods taken from a wreck)	105
PECOIT, Isaack Deesbury fined for stealing at,	81
PEIRCE or PEARCE	
Ellen, case of, (cursing)	83
Elnor " " (light behavior)	89
&c., admonished to see better order kept	107
John " " " " " " "	107
Marmaduke, case of, (suspected of murder)	86
(murder)	89
discharged	92
William, Mr. &c., differences referred to,	47
Willi: Mr. &c. to examine as to goods which came in the "Charles"	97
had wine of Mr. Eldred	129

PAGE

PELHAM
——, Mr., his servant, Thomas Bartlett, to be whipped for unjust selling of his master's tools 14
John Page, &c., to return to him the tools bought of Thomas Bartlett or their price 14
ordered to pay five pounds unto Thomas Goilthayt 16
William, Mr., &c., have promised to pay five pounds for Nicholas Knopp 11
PELL, SARAH, order as to Susan Hewet, &c., who sold goods to, 121
PEMBERTON or PEMERTON
John, sentenced to be whipped, bound to his good behaviour, &c. for fornication 82
charges to John Baker for not prosecuting 86
PEMBLE, FRANCIS, bond for appearance, &c. 131
PEMBROOKE, FRANCES, oath by, as to estate of Mr. Allen 128
PEMERTON. (See PEMBERTON.)
PEÑ
James, allowance to, his employment to be as a Beadle (order as to ministers) 2
took the oath of Beadle 4
the beadle, allowed thirty pounds to build a house 38
&c., gift towards the Sea Fort 42
testimony by, (case of John Hathaway) 66
Marklin Knight to recompense him 116
PENDLETON
——, Mr., &c., to take an inventory of goods, &c. of Mr. Craford 48
Brian, &c., grand jury 70
Briant, Mr., to exercise the company at Sudbury 133
PENIARS. (See PENYER.)
PENNE. (See PENNY.)
PENNIMAN, JAMES, &c., appraisers (estate of Joane Drake) 72
PENNY or PENNE
Richard, forfeited his recognizance 88
Thomas, &c., witnesses (case of Walthian Richards) 116
PENTECUS, JOHN, &c., sworn constables of Charlestown, 15 April, 1642-3 121
PENYAR ⎫
PENYER ⎬ or PENIARS
Robert, bond for appearance 86
attachment against, and his surety discharged 88
to be whipped for non appearance and his unclean attempt 90
PEPPER
Richard, case of, (extortion) 89
fine remitted to 91
PERKINS
——, Sergeant, to carry forty pieces of turf to the fort, as a punishment for drunkenness 36
Goodman, bill by, to Thomas Wade to be brought into Court 54
John, to take fowls with nets on Pullen Point and Noddle's Island 21

INDEX. 239

	PAGE

PERKINS, *continued*.
    John, &c., to settle the bounds between Dorchester and Rocksbury . 29
    William, &c., at Aggawam, ment^d. 31
            sentenced to stand one hour in public view with a large D on
                his breast for drunkenness 62

PERRY
    Francis, referred to Court at Salem 83
            costs to Malachy Browne for not prosecuting . . . 118
    Frauncis, to be whipped for misbehavior, &c., toward his master . 18
    John, case of, (running away) 123
    Richard, jun^r. granted damages 87

PERSONAL INJURY. (*See* CRIMES, &c.)
PESCOT, JOHN, dismissed with an admonition 120
PESONS, or George, an Indian, banished 118
PESTER, WILLI:, discharged for want of witness 80
PETER, SAGAMORE, &c., complaint by, as to having two wigwams burned . 11
PETERS, HUGH, Mr., delivered into the Court a deed of Mr. Saltonstall, 71
PETET ⎫
PETTET ⎭
    Thomas, to be whipped, &c. for idleness, &c. 65
            Will: Powell to answer to, ... 66

PHELP ⎫
PHELPES ⎭ or FELPES
    Richard, fined for drunkenness 61
    William, &c., jury (case of Walter Palmer) 9
            chosen constable of Dorchester 19
            &c., to set out bounds between Boston and Roxbury . . 41

PHILIPS ⎫
PHILLIPS ⎭
    ———, Mr., maintenance of, ... 1
            house to be built for, (order as to ministers) . . . 1, 2
            allowance to, (order as to ministers) 2
            rates on plantations for maintenance of, ... 9
            land upon Charles River granted to, ... 30
    John, chosen constable of Dorchester 63
    Thomas, "the Court gave way to the Governor to free his servant
                                Thomas Philips" 92

PHIPPEN,
    David, &c., judgment against Thomas Bushrode for not prosecuting 82
    Rebecca, Richard Ibrooke fined for tempting her to uncleanness . 81
    (*See also* FIBBIN.)

PICKRIN, or PICKRING, PICKRYN
    John, &c., to sit in the stocks at Salem, for felony 6
            of Paskataqua, forfeited their bonds for non appearance . 61
            discharged from their recognizance (case of Nicholas Frost) 62

PICKRING ⎫
PICKRYN ⎭ (*See* PICKRIN.)
PIECES. (*See* MILITARY AFFAIRS)

240   INDEX.

	PAGE
PILOT, Thomas Moulton to pay Mr. Ralfe Glover xl^s. for "leaving him without a pylot"	10

PILSBERRY
    Dorothy, case of, (uncleanness, defiling her master's house) . . 107
    Willi: bond for appearance, &c., and put to service 107
    William, case of, (defiling his master's house) 107

PINCHION }
PINCHON }
    ———, Mr., &c., present at Court, 3, 5, 8–19, 21, 23, 24, 25, 45, 46–48, 50, 52, 54, 55, 58, 59, 61, 62, 132
        fined for absence from Court 4
        &c., present at meeting of Assistants 20
            to inquire &c. as to estate of Josias Plastowe . . 23
        goods sold by Sergt. Bateman to, William Parks to make satisfaction for, 25
        to appoint men to take an inventory of the goods &c. of Ann Looman 51
        &c., to prepare the business of Mr. Coxeall &c. . . 53
        land sold to, by Chickataubut, ment^d. 55
    William, Mr., &c., present at Court 1
        chosen treasurer for one year 26
        treasurer, order as to his beaver trade . . . 27
            on committee to take account of debts due to the Governor 33
        &c., present at Court 63
        &c., (Court of Assistants) order by, (case of John Pratt) 112

PINES, the "first Pines" ment^d. (grant to Mr. Phillips of land up Charles River) 30

PIRACY. (*See* CRIMES, &c.)

PISCATAQUA or PASCATAQUA, PASKATAQUA
    Henry Joslyn &c. of, ment^d. 61
    ment^d. (case of James Meadecalfe) 81
    (case of Edward Saunders) 81
    Court at, cause transmitted to, (Mr. Drayton against Mr. Wannerton) 131

PIT. (*See under* WELL.)

PITS }
PITTS }
    Edith, accusation by, (case of John Emerson) 65
        &c., evidence by, (case of John Emerson) 74
    Henry, Mr., case of, (obscene speeches and distemper in drink) . . 104

PLAISTOW. (*See* PLASTOWE.)

PLANTATIONS
    order as to planting in any place 4
    warrant to be sent to Aggawam to command those that are planted there to come away 4
    levy placed on the several plantations for the maintenance of Mr. Patricke and Mr. Underhill 6
    of Mr. Cradock ment^d 7

INDEX. 241

PLANTATIONS, *continued*.

    order as to allowance for wolves killed &c. in any plantation . . 8
    rates on, for maintenance of ministers 9
    no person shall travel single between these plantations and Plymouth nor without arms 14
    owners of cattle to make full satisfaction for damage done by them in any plantation 14
    order to the constables of the several plantations as to creditors of Capt. Levett &c. 15
    order for levy for making the creek at New Towne 16
    Henry Lyñ to be whipped and banished from the plantation . . . 19
    Mr. Alexander Wignall ordered to remove to some settled plantation &c. 19
    levy to be placed on the several plantations towards the making of a palisade 20
    trucking houses to be appointed in every plantation where the Indians may trade 23
    to the Eastward, commission as to murder of Walter Bagnall . . 26
    order as to Aggawam 31
    constables of, to publish order as to license for selling liquors . . 33
    October 16, 1633 to be observed as a day of public thanksgiving in the plantations 37
    assessment placed on the several plantations to defray public charges . 37
    in the Bay to do two days work apiece at the Fort 38
    order as to the number of swine to be kept in, ... 38
    ment^d. (answer by John Pratt) 110

PLANTERS

    order as to Planters returning to England carrying money or beaver with them 21
    order as to planters trading beaver with the Indians 23

PLANTING without leave, order as to, ... 4

PLASTOW } or PLAISTOW
PLASTOWE }

    ———, Mr., &c., to be sent to England " as unmeet to inhabit here " . 10
    Josias, to give the Indians corn in return for corn stolen by him and shall not be called Mr. &c. 19
    Mr. Pinchon &c. to enquire concerning estate of, . . . 23

PLAYER

    Gyles, to be whipped and delivered up for a slave for stealing &c. . 79
    Giles, case of, (taking a boat &c.) 99

PLIMOUTHE. (*See* PLYMOUTH.)

PLOW PATENT, John Kirman to receive a payment as his share in a plow patent 52

PLYMOTH }
PLYMOUTH } or PLIMOUTHE, Town of,
PLYMOUTHE }

    William Bateman was brought from Plymouth in a shallop ment^d. (inquisition on body of William Bateman) 7

INDEX.

PLYMOUTH, *continued.*

    coming from, ment^d. (order as to Thomas Moulton) 10
    order as to persons travelling between these plantations and Plymouth 14
    letter from, as to murder of Walter Bagnall 25

PONOMENEUHCANT RIVER, land near Salem abutting on, granted to Mr. Samuel Skelton 24

PONTON, RICHARD, put to John Reade for eight years 104
POOLE, JOHN, fined for abusing his servant 80

POOR, THE,
    of Dorchester, Mr. Allen's strong water to be used for the benefit of, . 26
    money and corn granted to Thomas Buckmaster 92
    allowance of corn to Evan Thomas 97
    corn &c. granted to Mary Joanes 102
    (Hingham) order for supply to Mrs. Strainge and her child . . . 119

POPE
    Ephraim, &c., watchmen, imprisoned for drinking strong water . . 87
    John, case of, (stubborn carriage against his master, unchaste attempt &c.) 92
    &c., presented for taking too much wages 135

PORTER
    ―――, Goodman, &c., difference referred to, (Mr. Dummer and Jehu Burr) 61
    John, took oath as constable of Hingham 97
    &c., witnesses, grant to, ... 98
    Mr. Smyth to pay legacies to, ... 132
    William, case of, to be considered (refusing to watch) . . . 135

POTTER
    ―――, Goodman, &c., difference referred to, (Mr. Dummer and Jehu Burr) 61
    Willi: &c., discharged with an admonition as to too many in a boat . 81

POUND
    town of Cambridge fined for want of a pound &c. 80, 85
    Anthony Emery fined for a pound breach 30
    ment^d. (order as to town of Braintree) 99

POWDER. (*See* MILITARY AFFAIRS.)

POWDER HORN HILL
    and Pullen Point, neck of land between, to belong to Boston . . 29
    the written tree, town of Boston fined for defect of ways between, 90
    ment^d. (order as to town of Boston) 99

POWELL
    Nicholas, appointed surveyor of the arms for Dedham . . . 125
    Willi:, attached for contempt and to answer to Thomas Pettet . . 66
    Willi:, fined for resisting the surveyor 88
    case of, (getting his wife with child before marriage) . . 94

PRAT }
PRATT }
    Abraham, &c., jury, as to death of Austen Bratcher 6
    John, "answer of," and action of the Court thereon referred to in note 15

INDEX. 243

	PAGE

PRATT, *continued.*
    John, "questioned" at Court 3 Nov. 1635 referred to in note . . 58
        answer of, and action of the Court thereon referred to . . 109
        answer by 109–112
        of Newe Towne, answer by, to be recorded &c. 112
PRESS. (*See* IMPRESSMENT.)
PRICHARD, WILLIAM, John Smith granted five shillings against, . . . 116
PRISON
    Mary Oliver committed to, for disturbing the Church of Salem . . 80
    breaking prison &c. (case of Samuel Maverick &c.) 109
    William Willoughby committed to, for being distempered with wine &c. 120
PROCESS
    or summons by the beadle in civil actions, order as to, . . . 2
    Morton of Mount Woolison to be sent for by process 3
    for the warning of jurors to be directed by the secretary . . . 38
PROFANITY. (*See* CRIMES, &c.)
PROVIDENCE, cattle from, also "money disbursed for that company" ment^d (order to John Johnson) 135
PROVISIONS
    order as to buying corn &c. 16
    price of, ... 39
PUBLIC CHARGES. (*See* ASSESSMENT.)
PUBLIC LIBRARY, Boston, copy of record in, ... 1, 115
PUBLIC MEETINGS, Boston chosen as the fittest place for, . . . 28
PUBLIC SERVICE, allowance to Mr. Hibbins for, ... 128
PUBLIC WORSHIP. (*See* SABBATH DAY.)
PUCKETT, THOMAS, John Ellford to answer for death of, ... 11
PULLEN POINT
    in Massachusetts Bay, William Bateman was set on shore upon neck of land near, (oaths by Walter Norton &c.) 7
    order as to shooting at fowl on, ... 21
    and Powder Horne Hill, neck of land between, to belong to Boston . 29
PUMERY
    Eltweed, sworn constable of Dorchester 45
    &c., to determine as to damage by swine 49
PUNISHMENT (by death, banishment, imprisonment, whipping, fines &c.)
    Justices of the Peace shall have power to imprison offenders . . 3
    power of justices to inflict corporal punishment 3
    Thomas Morton to be set into the "bilbowes," and to be sent prisoner to England 4
    John Goulworth to be whipped and set in the stocks 6
    John Boggust and John Pickryn sentenced to sit in the stocks at Salem 6
    Henry Lyñ to be whipped for committing felony 6
    Richard Diffy to be whipped for his misdemeanor towards his master . 8
    S^r. Richard Saltonstall fined for whipping two persons contrary to law 9

PUNISHMENT, *continued*.

	PAGE
Bartholmewe Hill to be whipped for stealing	9
John Baker to be whipped for shooting at fowls, on the Sabbath Day	9
Thomas Moulton to be whipped or pay a fine	10
Mr. Thomas Stoughton fined "for taking upon him to marry" persons	10
Nicholas Knopp fined for deceit, to be imprisoned until he pay his fine, or else to be whipped	11
Thomas Foxe to be whipped for uttering malicious speeches	12
Benjamin Cribb &c. to be whipped for stealing	13
John Legge to be whipped for striking Richard Wright	14
Thomas Walford fined and he and his wife to depart the limits of the pattent	14
Thomas Bartlett to be whipped for unjustly selling his masters tools	14
John Norman, Senr., fined for not appearing	14
Phillip Swaddon to be whipped for running away from his master	16
Phillip Ratliffe to be whipped, to have his ears cut off and to be fined and banished for malicious speeches	16
Chickatabut fined a skin of beaver for shooting swine	16
William Almy fined	16
Frauncis Perry to be whipped	18
Mr. Shepheard &c. fined for drinking	18
Henry Lyñ to be whipped and banished from the plantation	19
John Dawe to be whipped	19
adultery to be punished with death (question and order)	19
Mr. Alexander Wignall fined, bound to his good behavior and to remove his dwelling to some settled plantation	19
Josias Plastowe for stealing is to give the Indians eight baskets of corn, to be fined and hereafter to be called Josias and not Mr. as formerly	19
William Buckland and Thomas Andrewe to be whipped	19
Robert Coles fined for being drunk and fine remitted	21
Thomas Knower set in the bilboes for threatening the Court to have it tried in England	21
Thomas Dexter bound to his good behavior and fined for insolent carriage and speeches to S. Bradstreete	24
Mr. James Parker fined for drunkenness	25
Mr. Samuel Dudley " " "	25
Mr. Allen punished for selling strong water	26
James Woodward to be set in the bilboes for being drunk	26
Robert Shawe to be whipped for cursing &c.	26
John Stickland fined for refusing to watch at the Captains command	26
William Hamon to be set in the bilboes for being drunk	,26
Richard Hopkins to be whipped and branded on one cheek for selling powder &c. to the Indians	27
shall selling powder &c. to the Indians be punished with death? (question propounded)	27
James Woodward to be whipped for running away from his master	27
Edward Burton fined for contempt of authority and drunkenness	27

INDEX. 245

PUNISHMENT, *continued.*

	PAGE
Nicholas Frost fined, whipped, branded on the hand and banished for stealing from the Indians	28
Robert Huitt and Mary Ridge to be whipped for committing fornication	30
Thomas Dexter set in the bilboes disfranchised and fined for seditious words	30
Thomas Wincall fined for drunkenness	31
John Sayle to forfeit his estate to be whipped and bound as a servant for theft	32
William Dixon to be set in the bilboes for drunkenness	32
John Pemerton to be whipped &c. for fornication	32
Robert Allen fined for absenting himself from Court as a witness	33
James White &c. fined for drunkenness	33
Mr. John Woolridge fined for drunkenness	34
John Shotswell fined for drunkenness	34
Robert Coles fined and enjoined to stand with a paper on his back with drunkard written on it for drunkenness &c.	34
Capt. John Stone fined and prohibited coming into the pattent without leave &c. on pain of death	35
Mr. Palmer fined for absenting himself from jury service	35
Alexander Wignall fined for drunkenness &c.	35
Sergeant Perkins to carry forty pieces of turf to the fort for drunkenness	36
Thomas Dexter fined for drunkenness	36
John Sayles to be whipped for running away from his master	40
Christopher Tarling to be whipped for stealing from his master and for running away	40
John Chapman fined for selling boards contrary to order	40
Richard Williams fined for drunkenness	40
William Cooley " " "	40
Timothy Hawkins &c. fined for company keeping, drinking strong water &c.	40
Edward Howe fined for selling strong water	41
Robert Coles to be disfranchised and to wear the letter D on his garments for one year for drunkenness	41
John Lee to be whipped and fined for calling Mr. Ludlowe a false hearted knave &c.	43
Thomas Foxe fined for not appearing as a witness	43
William Almy fined for not appearing at Court when summoned,	46
James Rawlens fined for taking too much for work done by one of his servants	47
Katherine Gray to be whipped for unchaste behavior	48
Ensign Jennison fined for upbraiding the Court &c.	48
Clement Briggs fined for entertaining an Indian without leave &c.	49
John Lee to be whipped and fined for speaking reproachfully of the Governor &c.	49
Samuel Hill fined for drunkenness	49

246 INDEX.

PAGE

PUNISHMENT, *continued.*

Henry Bright to be set in the bilboes for swearing 50
Christopher Graunt fined for drunkenness 50
constables of Dorchester and Boston fined for not returning warrants . 50
Richard Cokar and Samuel Johnson to be whipped for enticing servants to run away &c. 51, 52
Griffin Mountague to be set in the bilboes and to move from Muddy River for stealing 53
John Hayward to be whipped for swearing &c. 53
Mr. Humfry fined for absenting himself from Court 54
John Love fined for drunkenness 55
Frauncis Toby bound to his good behavior for a misdemeanor, . . 55
Arthur Holbidge &c. punished for taking too much wages . . . 56
William Wills punished for felony 56
Arthur Holbidge bound to his good behavior and imprisoned for contempt 56
Andrew Storyn to be whipped for running away from his master . 57
Robert Scarlett to be whipped for running away from his master . 57
Mary servant of Mr. Bartholmewe to be whipped for running away . 57
John Pease to be whipped and bound to his good behavior for striking his mother &c. 59
John Cole to be whipped for stealing 59
Nicholas Frost to be imprisoned and tried for returning after banishment 59
Samuel Cole forfeited twenty shillings for selling beer . . . 59
Mr. Nowell fined for selling wine 59
Clement Cole &c. to be whipped &c. for running away from their masters &c. 59
Daniel White to be fined and whipped for stealing 60
Robert Scarlett to be whipped branded on the forehead with the letter T and banished for felony 60
Richard Long fined for contempt of authority &c. 60
Josuah Huyes fined for taking too much profit 60
Edward Gyles &c. fined for knowing their wives carnally before marriage 60
Richard Phelpes fined for drunkenness 61
Anthony Cooper &c. forfeited their recognizance for non appearance . 61
James Luddam fined for drunkenness 61
William Shepheard to be whipped for stealing 62
William Perkins to stand in public view one hour wearing a large D on his breast for drunkenness &c. 62
George Ropps to be whipped for striking his master Mr. Garford . 62
William Barker to be whipped for theft 62
Edward Bendall fined " 40^s to the Company " 62
John Whitele &c. to be whipped for drunkenness 63
Thomas Miller committed for seditious speeches 63
Robert Shorthose to have his tongue put in a cleft stick for swearing . 63
Peter Bussaker to be whipped for drunkenness and fined for slighting the magistrates 64

INDEX.

PUNISHMENT, *continued.*

	PAGE
Edward Woodley to be whipped imprisoned for one year and to wear a collar of iron for rape, housebreaking &c.	64
Elisabeth Aplegate to stand with her tongue in a cleft stick for swearing &c.	64
Will: Clarke to be whipped committed to prison and sent home for theft	64
Anthony Robinson to be whipped for fornication	64
Weybro Lovell admonished to repent for light behavior . . .	65
William James to be set in the bilboes at Boston and in the stocks at Salem for incontinency	65
Capt. Lovell admonished to take heed of light carriage . . .	65
Mary Bowler to make restitution for things stolen by her . .	66
John Sweete fined and imprisoned for shooting a dog . . .	66
Robert Anderson fined and imprisoned for contempt . . .	66
Edward Seale to be set in the bilboes and whipped for drunkenness .	67
George Munnings fined for selling beer &c. without license . .	67
Samuel Cole fined for selling beer	67
Robert Long &c. fined for selling beer	68
James Browne to be set in the bilboes at Boston for drunkenness and fined for selling strong water to the Indians	68
Benjamin Hubberd admonished for drinking &c.	68
William Brumfeild to be branded, whipped, &c. for theft from his master, &c.	70
George Spencer to be whipped, and to make restitution for receiving stolen money	70
George Barlow to be whipped for idleness	70
John Hogges fined for drunkenness	71
John Greene fined and banished from the jurisdiction for contempt .	71
John Stretton fined for lending a gun to an Indian . . .	71
Luke Henbury to be whipped for theft, &c.	72
Joseph Faber fined for selling wine	72
Angell Howard fined for libel	72
John Woolridge admonished for fraud and drunkenness in Old England, &c.	73
Christopher Grant fined for drinking, &c.	73
Thomas Starr fined for speaking against the law about swine . .	73
Richard Collicot, &c., jurymen, fined for absence from Court . .	74
Robert Bartlet to have his tongue put in a cleft stick, for swearing, &c.	74
John Smith to be set in the bilboes for swearing	74
Laurence Waters' wife &c. admonished for dancing . . .	75
Edward Lambe fined for contempt	75
Thomas Ewar fined for leaving his pit or well open . . .	75
Edmund Hubbard, Senr., fined for leaving a pit open . . .	75
Francis Weston's wife set in the bilboes	75
Thomas Gray to be whipped and banished	76
constables of Cambridge and Boston fined for not returning jury warrants	76

248   INDEX.

PUNISHMENT, *continued*.
                                 PAGE

Henry Collens fined for not serving on the grand jury	76
Katherine Finch to be whipped &c. for speaking against the magistrates, &c.	76
George Horne fined for distemper in drink	76
William South to be whipped and "kept to the General Court, by whom hee was banished to return no more upon paine of death"	76
George Walton fined for swearing	77
Robert Shorthose committed for contempt	78
John Holgrave fined for contempt, &c.	78
Thomas Wilson fined for taking above double toll	78
Samuel Basse fined for contempt	78
Richard Turner fined for drunkenness	78
Dorothy Talbie to be hanged, being guilty of the death of her daughter	78
William Androws to be whipped and delivered up as a slave, for conspiracy, &c.	78
John Haslewood and Gyles Player each to be whipped and delivered up as a slave, for stealing and breaking into houses	79
John Bickerstaffe and Ales Burwoode to be whipped for fornication	79
Isaac Sternes and John Page fined for turning the way about	79
John Poole fined for abusing his servant	80
Mary Oliver committed to prison for disturbing the Church of Salem	80
Richard Hollingsworth to be set in the stocks at Salem for profaning the Sabbath in travelling	80
Anthony Emery fined for a pound breach	80
John Davies to be whipped and to wear the letter V upon his breast, for attempting lewdness with women	81
Thomas Boyse, to be whipped and imprisoned for attempting a rape	81
Isaack Deesbury fined for stealing	81
Richard Ibrooke fined for tempting two maids to uncleanness	81
John Hoggs fined for swearing, &c.	81
Richard Silvester fined for selling strong water	81
Robert Shorthose set in the bilboes for slighting the magistrates	81
Richard Silvester fined for speaking against the law about hogs, &c.	82
Samuel Norman to be whipped for saying "if ministers will but rail against England," &c.	82
Mr. John Harrison fined for non appearance and admonished not to use gaming	83
John Palflin fined	83
John Gibons fined	83
William Bartlet fined for drunkenness & lying	83
Ellen Peirce fined for cursing, &c.	83
Elisabeth Chaulkley to make double restitution for things stolen by her	83
Mr. Goouch fined for selling strong water	83
John Bayly fined for buying land of the Indians without leave	83
Hugh Burt's wife fined for swearing, &c.	83
Thomas Cornell fined for selling wine, &c.	84

PUNISHMENT, *continued.*

Nicholas Ellen fined for idleness, &c.	84
Capt. Staughton fined for releasing his man before time	84
Mr. Waltham and Mr. Richards fined for want of scales, &c., and Mr. Waltham for taking too much toll	84
Ralfe Allen fined for releasing a servant before time	84
William Fuller fined for taking too much toll	85
John Gosse disfranchised, fined, and committed to prison for common railing	85
John Stacy, Jr., set in the stocks for being distempered with drink	85
Ralfe Warriner fined for excessive drinking	85
Nicholas Merry fined for selling strong water	86
John Neale to be whipped and kept chained by his master for running away, &c.	86
Richard Wilson to be put out to service and to wear the letter T upon his clothing for stealing	86
Richard Turner fined for drunkenness	86
William Davies fined for sundry drinkings at his house	86
Thomas Bushrode fined for defaming the government	86
Daniel Clarke fined for immoderate drinking	86
John Wedgwood set in the stocks at Ipswich for being in company of drunkards	86
John Kempe to be whipped and committed as a slave for unclean conduct	86
Mathewe Edwards to be whipped for misdemeanor	87
Thomas Knore fined for selling strong water	87
Nicholas Davison fined for swearing	87
John Hogg fined for drunkenness	87
John Kitchen fined for showing books he was to bring to the Governor	87
John Joanes fined for defiling his wife before marriage	87
John Davies discharged from wearing a V	87
Thomas Gray to be whipped for drunkenness, &c.	87
Richard Redman, &c. fined for quarrelling	87
Mr. Thomas Lechford debarred from pleading any man's cause, &c. for pleading with the jury out of Court	87
Thomas Millard, &c. imprisoned for drinking strong water	87
——— Burkbee set in the stocks for drunkenness	87
John Woolrige fined for drunkenness	88
Richard Joanes to be whipped, and put to the assignee of the party wronged, to make satisfaction for cheating	88
William Powell fined for resisting the surveyor	88
——— Tacye fined for swearing	88
Richard Pepper fined for extortion	89
James Luxford fined, set in the stocks, and sent to England for having two wives	89
Elnor Peirce to stand in the market place with a paper for light behavior	89
——— Quick to stand in the market place with a paper for her light behavior	89

250   INDEX.

PUNISHMENT, *continued.*

	PAGE
Lewes Hewlet fined for extortion	89
Jane Robinson to be whipped for drunkenness, &c.	89
Margaret Hindersham to stand in the market place with a paper for her ill behavior	90
Thomas Dickerson to be whipped & condemned to slavery	90
Robert Penyar to be whipped for his unclean attempt, &c.	90
William Waltham fined for drunkenness	91
John Vaughan committed to prison until he marry her whom he hath defiled, &c.	91
Thomas Davenport admonished for causing copperas to be thrown into a man's yard	91
Mr. Henry Seawall to acknowledge his fault publicly and bound to his good behavior for contemptuous speeches, &c.	92
John Clare fined for drunkenness	92
John Pope to be whipped for dalliance and for stubborn carriage against his master, &c.	92
George Palmer set in the stocks for folly	93
Margery Rugs to be whipped for enticing George Palmer	93
Nathaniell Travell admonished for scandalous speeches	93
Leonard Bowtle fined for neglecting to obey a warrant	93
Mr. Browning fined for selling strong water	93
George Hurne to be laid in irons and whipped for his insolent carriage	93
Henry Chapman fined for not obeying a press	94
Robert Tucker fined for upbraiding James Brittain	94
Willi: Powell fined for getting his wife with child before marriage	94
Thomas Gray to be whipped for drunkenness, &c.	94
Gooddy Finch sentenced to be whipped	94
Thomas Savory to be whipped and sold for a slave for theft, &c.	94
Henry Allein, &c., fined for drunkenness	94
Mr. Barnard fined for giving strong water to certain persons	94
Elisabeth Lovel admonished for immodest expressions	94
John Downham fined for getting his wife with child before marriage	94
Edward Converse fined for neglecting the ferry	94
Richard Dummer fined for want of weights, &c.	94
John Tower fined for disturbing the peace	94
two Indian women to be whipped for abusing Mrs. Weld, &c.	95
Elisa. Bennet to be whipped for her unchaste miscarriage	95
John Hoggs fined for drunkenness	95
Hope, an Indian, to be whipped for running away, &c.	95
Henry Illery fined for drunkenness, &c.	95
John Barnes fined for being distempered with wine	95
Thomas Tylestone, &c. fined for not attending the jury	97
Richard Cluffe fined, and bound to his good behavior for saying "shall I pay 12^d for the fragments which the grand jury rogues have left?"	97
Edmond Mathewe admonished for pilfering	97

PUNISHMENT, *continued.*

	PAGE
Jonathan Hatch to be whipped and committed as a slave to Lt. Davenport	97
two servants of Walter Merries to be whipped for running away	97
John Burrows to be whipped for going into men's houses on the Lord's day, &c.	98
John Knight to be whipped for drunkenness	98
Benjamin Pauly fined for being distempered with wine	98
John Dutton to be whipped for drunkenness, &c.	98
Giles Player committed to Lt. Davenport, &c. until he satisfies for his thefts	99
Henry Stevens to be a servant to John Humfrey, for firing his barn	100
Hugh Buet banished for heresy	101
John Holland, &c., jurymen, fined for not appearing	102
Samuel Haukes to be set in the stocks and have a cleft stick on his tongue for swearing, &c.	102
John Hogg committed to Lt. Davenport for drunkenness, &c.	102
Christopher Graunt fined for cruel usage of his servant	103
Robert Stedman, juryman, fined for not appearing	103
Richard Hollingworth fined for causing the death of Robert Baker by negligence	103
John Morecroft fined for his unfit carriage	103
Walter Knight fined for rude and contemptuous speeches	104
Richard Wilson to be whipped for abusing his master	104
Joseph Kinge fined for distemper in drinking, &c.	104
Henry Pitts fined for obscene speeches, &c.	104
William Browne admonished for obscene speeches	104
Thomas Baguley fined for selling his servant's time	105
John Barnes fined for being distempered with wine	105
Edward Johnson fined for not serving on the jury	105
James Dane fined for making an Indian drunk	105
John Longe fined for distemper in drinking, &c.	105
the wife of Robert Lewes whipped for dishonoring the name of God	106
Enoch Hunt fined, &c. for extortion	106
Jonathan Thing to be whipped and fined for ravishing Mary Greenfield	106
John Skidmer fined for selling strong water to Indians	106
Abraham Morrell fined for selling his servant his time	106
Samuel Sherman fined for selling his servant his time	106
David Hickbourne to be whipped, to wear an iron collar, and to serve his master for a longer time for gross misdemeanors	107
Willi: Knop fined for selling beer	107
John Barnes fined for distemper in drinking	107
George Bowen fined for being absent from the jury	107
James Laurence to be whipped for leaving his master's house, &c.	107
Willi: Pilsberry enjoined to work for Goodman Wiswell, &c.	107
William and Dorothy Pilsberry to be whipped for defiling their master's house	107

INDEX.

PUNISHMENT, *continued.*

	PAGE
Mary Osborne to be whipped for giving her husband quicksilver, &c.	108
Thomas Carter, Senr. fined for not warning the jury in time, &c.	108
Nicholas Trerice fined for his miscarriage in Court	108
Thomas Owen to be sent to the gallows with a rope about his neck, &c. for his adulterous practises	108
Sara Hales to be carried to the gallows with a rope about her neck, and banished for miscarriage	108
Anthony Stoader fined for affronting the Governor	108
John Kilmaster, &c. admonished for their distemper	108
Mr. Samuel Maverick, Mr. Chidley, &c. fined for confederacy with Thomas Owen	108-109
Thomas Owen fined for breaking out of prison	109
Sara Hales to be whipped and banished for escaping	109
Mr. Dutchfield, &c. admonished to take heed of concealment	109
Mr. William Collens fined and banished for being a seducer	109
Francis Hutchinson fined and banished for corrupt speeches	109
Symon Voysey fined for striking Mr. Constable	115
John Vocar to be fined or whipped	116
Walthian Richards fined	116
Thomas Barnes admonished about lace	116
John Jobson admonished for unadvised expressions	116
William Davis fined for keeping a house of disorder, and bound not to sell ale, &c.	116
Thomas Hawkins fined for making bread too light [weight]	116
the wife of ——— Carter admonished	117
George Story committed for his miscarriage	117
Peter Thatcher to be whipped for plotting piracy	118
Matthew Collaine, &c. to be whipped for concealing a plot of piracy	118
James Hawkins whipped for profaning the Sabbath	118
Elizabeth Sedgwicke whipped and condemned to slavery for thefts, &c.	118
Pesons, or George, the Indian, banished	118
Mincarry, the blackmore, admonished & dismissed	118
John Smith admonished and dismissed	118
Susan Cole to make double restitution	118
Marmaduke Barton committed as a slave for theft and running away	118
Thomas Briant whipped for concealing piracy	118
John Woodcocke whipped for his many miscarriages	119
John Whitney, constable fined for not warning Charles Chadwicke	119
Mary Hoare to make a payment to John Read, for theft, &c.	119
Daniel Owles fined for drinking	120
William Willoughby fined and committed to prison for being distempered with wine, &c.	120
Nathaniel Briscoe fined for mutinous speeches, &c.	120
William Bull and his wife Blith fined for fornication before marriage	121
John Stowers fined for disturbing the Church of Watertown	121
Sara Bell to be whipped for theft from her master	121

INDEX. 253

PUNISHMENT, *continued.*

	PAGE
T[eagu] Ocrimi to be whipped, and to stand in the place of execution with a halter about his neck, for a foul attempt to bugger a cow	121
Robert Wyar and John Garland to be whipped, and to make a payment to their master for ravishing two girls	121
Sarah Wythes and Ursula Odle to be whipped, for wickedness with Robert Wyar, &c.	121
William Browne whipped for running away, &c.	122
Richard Quick whipped for being distempered by drinking, &c.	123
Edward Roberts fined for drinking, and for drinking to Richard Quick	123
John Perry whipped for running away	123
Edward Wood fined for baking wheat meal contrary to order	124
Thomas Scott & his wife to stand in the market place with papers on their hats for fornication before marriage	124
John Long fined for distemper in drink &c.	124
Isaac Morrell fined for absence from the jury	125
George Roberts committed for his ill carriage	125
Robert Sever fined for neglecting the watch	126
John Woolridge fined for drunkenness, &c., and to acknowledge his offence	126
John Lewis whipped for running away, &c.	126
William Walcot to be whipped and kept in prison, for idleness, &c.	126
Anne Hett to be whipped and kept at hard labor and on spare diet, for attempting to drown her child	126
Thomas Cotcree to be whipped for unmeet dalliance with girls	126
George Watts fined for swearing	127
William Web fined for neglecting an order as to bread	127
David Conway to be whipped for resisting his master	127
Charles Cadwicke, &c. fined for absence, being warned,	128
William Shepheard fined for covenanting for 15^{lb} wages	128
Laurence Copeland " " " " " "	128
William Davies fined for keeping victualling against order of the Court	129
George Mills fined for battery	130
Richard Willis " " "	130
William Chadborne, &c. fined for drunkenness	130
Ralph Golthrope fined for being distempered with wine	130
William Filpot admonished to take heed of suffering drinking in his house	131
Henry Leake and his wife to acknowledge their fault at Dorchester	131
Nicholas Rogers fined for being distempered with drink	131
William Scutt fined for selling powder and shot to the Indians	131
Samuel Bacon to be whipped, &c. for theft	131
Robert Rogers fined, and to pay Mr. Manning for receiving stolen wine	131
Miles Tompson, &c. fined for drinking with others	131
Robert Wyar and Thomas Cooper fined for drinking with Samuel Bacon	132
Nathaniel Tappin to be whipped, and put to Goodman Gillam for breaking into houses, &c.	132
John Clough fined for his absence when the jury was called	132

254   INDEX.

PUNISHMENT, *continued.*

	PAGE
Ralph Golthrop fined for distemper in drink	132
Gawen Wilson fined for fornication	132
Richard Gell whipped for running away from his master	132
John Bartlet to be whipped and fined for theft, &c.	133
Stephen Day committed for defrauding	133
John Gammage to be whipped for drunkenness, &c.	133
Thomas Anker fined for distemper in drink	133
George Watts fined for distemper in drink, &c.	133
Nicholas Rogers to be whipped for drunkenness, &c.	133
Swiniard Lewis fined for drunkenness	133
Israel Hart fined for neglecting the watch	133
Thomas Bauldwin committed for striking his master, &c.	134
Robert Wright fined, or to sit in the stocks, for being distempered with drink	134
William Barnes fined for swearing	134
John Garland to make double restitution for things stolen by him	134
David Dauling, Mary Audley & Jane Jeffrey whipped for their unclean practice	134
Capt. John Chadwicke fined for swearing, &c.	135
Capt. Aaron Williams fined for distemper in drink	135
owners of Sudbury mill fined for want of scales and weights	135
Thomas Painter to be set in the stocks for disturbing the Church of Hingham	135
David Williams to be whipped for assaulting the watch	136
John Beamis fined for freeing his servant	135-6
John Barnard fined for his dangerous well	136
Ralph Golthrop to be whipped or fined for being distempered with drink	136
John Killmaster fined for being distempered with drink	136
Thomas Weatherly fined for swearing, &c.	136
the constable of Boston fined for not returning his warrant	137
Thomas Grub fined for not appearing on the jury	137
Bridget Barnard fined for stealing	137
William Flint fined for fornication	137
Mary Bentley to make restitution for stealing	137
George Frost fined for being distempered with wine	138
John Hart " " " " " "	138
Thomas Cooper fined for absence from the Grand Jury	138
Benjamin Gillam fined for absence from the Jury of Trials	138
Leonard Fryar fined for distemper in drink &c.	138
Carew Latham fined for his disorder	138
Edward Johnson, Junr fined for immoderate drinking	138
John Bauldwin fined for excessive drinking	138
Thomas Dutchfield fined and admonished for distemper in drink	139
Roger Amedowne to pay fees, admonished &c.	139
John Harris to pay fees, admonished and discharged	139
James Brittaine and Mary Latham condemned to death for adultery	139

INDEX.

	PAGE
PUNISHMENT, *continued.*	
Nathaniel Smith fined for intemperate drinking &c.	139
James Merricke &c. fined for drinking and for selling wine &c.	139
Thomas Orton &c. fined for intemperate drinking	139
PYE, GEORGE, "a more" (moor?), to remain with Mr. Cradock &c.	76
[P]YFORD (or BYFORD), PETER, &c., to be whipped &c. for running away from their masters &c.	59
PYKE, JOHN, allowance of witnesses fee to,	56
PYNES, the. (*See* PINES.)	
PYNNEY, HUMFRY, difference between him and John Cogan &c. referred to a committee	54
QUALITY, safe arrival of persons of, day of thanksgiving for,	37
QUARTER COURT. (*See* COURT OF ASSISTANTS.)	
QUICK	
———, case of, (light behavior)	89
Richard, case of, (distemper in drinking, idleness &c.)	123
Edward Roberts fined for drinking to,	123
&c., attachment against,	236
RAINSFORD, EDWARD, &c., jury, (case of Hugh Buett)	101
RAPE. (*See* CRIMES, &c.)	
RATES	
(*See* ASSESSMENT.)	
(*See* WAGES.)	
(*See* WHARFAGE.)	
RATLIFFE, PHILLIP, case of, (malicious speeches against the government)	16
RAWLENS or }	
RAWLINGS }	
James, fined for taking too much for work done by one of his servants	47
Thomas, &c., witnesses, (case of Walthian Richards)	116
RAWSON	
———, Secretary, numbering of pages by, ment^d in note	15
marginal entry in handwriting of, referred to in note	82
Edward, Secretary from 1650 to 1686, handwriting of, mentioned	1
marginal note in handwriting of, ment^d in note	20
RAYE, DANIELL, &c. Grand Jury,	70
READ or }	
READE }	
George, warrant to, (case of David Williams)	135
John, Richard Ponton put to, for eight years	104
David Williams put himself to,	117
Mary Hoare to make a payment to, for theft &c.	119
dismissed, (as to refusing to watch)	135
Thomas, &c., viewed the body of Austen Bratcner	7
gift towards the Sea Fort	42
William, &c., sworn constables of Weymouth	140

	PAGE
REAL ESTATE	
sale or grant of town lots &c. to be recorded	45
authority to sell to pay debts	109
RECORDS	
of the Court of Assistants, ment[d].	1
Colony of the Massachusetts Bay, ment[d].	1
General Court, 19 Oct. 1630 ment[d].	8
Massachusetts Colony, reference to, in note	13
General Court 18 May 1631 ment[d]. in note	15
for 5 June 1632 referred to in note	30
of the General Court 29 May 1633 referred to	32
of the Court of Assistants in civil actions referred to in note	40
town book for surveys and assurance of lands to be written at length and not in figures and sales or grants to be recorded	45
of the Court of Assistants ment[d].	115
of Massachusetts Colony ment[d].	115
REDMAN, RICHARD, &c., fined for quarrelling,	87
REEVES, WILLI: &c., discharged	77
RENDALL	
Robert, deferred until the next Quarter Court	99
found not guilty by the Grand Jury	103
RICHARDS	
———, Mr., &c., fined for want of weights &c. in their mill	84
fine remitted to,	124
George, attachment for,	79
Thomas, order as to damage by swine in corn of,	49
of Weymouth, difference between his wife and Henry Waltham referred	102
&c., sworn constables of Weymouth	140
Walthian, fined and enjoined to pay witnesses	116
Welthia[n], wife of Thomas Richards, and Henry Waltham difference between, referred	102
William, and John Turner, Mr. Ginner &c. to settle things between,	97
RICHARDSON	
Elizabeth (error for Ezekiel), &c., jury of life and death	70
Ezekiell, chosen constable of Charlton	31
Ezechi: &c., jury of life and death	70
George, bound to his good behavior	99
costs against James Smyth for not prosecuting	101
John, &c., discharged	116
Capt. Williams promised to bring him back	116
to be sequestered from Elizabeth Fryar	139
RIDDWAY, JAMES, payment to, from estate of his master William Bladen	130
RIDGE, MARY, to be whipped for fornication	30
RIGHT. (*See* WRIGHT.)	
ROBERTS	
Edward, case of, (drinking) !	123
George, case of, (ill carriage)	125

INDEX. 257

	PAGE

ROBINSON
    Anthony, to be whipped for fornication 64
    Jane, case of, (disorder in her house, drunkenness &c.) . . . 89
    Thomas, to pay Richard Cooke for unjust molestation 86
ROCKESBURY. (*See* ROXBURY.)
ROCKEWELL. (*See* ROCKWELL.)
ROCKSBURY. (*See* ROXBURY.)
ROCKWELL or ROCKEWELL
    William, &c., jury, (case of Walter Palmer) 9
        adm^n. granted to, on goods &c. of John Russell . . 35
        exec^{rs}., exhibited an inventory of goods &c. of John Russell 55
ROCSBURY. (*See* ROXBURY.)
ROGERS
    John, costs to Clement Campion for not prosecuting 136
    Nicholas, case of, (being distempered with drink) 131
        (drunkenness and making others drunk) . . . 133
    Robert, case of, (receiving stolen wine &c.) 131
ROPE ABOUT THE NECK. (*See* PUNISHMENT.)
ROPPS, GEORGE, to be whipped for striking his master 62
ROSSITER
    ———, Mr., &c., present at Court 3, 5
        fined for absence from Court 4
    Edward, Mr., &c., present at Court 1
ROWLEY, Town of,
    presentments discharged 100
    enjoined to mend their ways 106
    way to, ment^d. (order as to town of Ipswich) 106
ROXBERRY }
ROXBURY } or ROCKESBURY, ROCKSBURY, ROCSBURY, Town of,
    ment^d. (order as to levy for maintenance of Mr. Patricke &c.) . . 6
    (order as to maintenance of ministers) 9
    (order as to levy for the creek at Newe Towne) . . . 16
    (order as to a watch of six) 17
    &c. Capt. Underhill's Company to train at, ... 18
    constable of, receipt of Mr. Shepheard's fine returned by, . . 20
    assessed, (order as to levy for making a palisade) . . . 20
    Robert Coles of, ment^d., ... 21
    and Dorchester, Capt. Traske &c. to settle bounds between, . . 29
    and Boston, agreed that bounds formerly set out between, shall continue 31
    to enjoy convenience of the creek 31
    assessed for maintenance of Capt. Underhill &c. 31
    and Boston, to pay charges for cart bridges over Muddy River and Stony River 34
    assessed to defray public charges 37
    Mr. Dumer's estate in, rated 39
    Mr. William Dennison chosen constable of, ... 40

ROXBURY, *continued.*
 Robert Coles sentenced for drunkenness at, ... 41
 and Boston, Ensign Stoughton &c. to settle bounds between, . . 41
 Mr. Parker of, ment[d]. (list of gifts to the Sea Fort) . . . 42
 freemen of, to take an inventory of the goods &c. of Mrs. Ann Looman 51
 and Newton, line between, to run south west from Muddy River . . 53
 John Levins of, ment[d]. 67
 John Woolcot of, ment[d]. 71
 William Curtis of, ment[d]. 71
 fined &c. 75
 fined for damming up the nearest way from Boston to Dorchester &c. . . 84
 fined for a defective bridge at Muddy River 84
 &c. John Kempe to be whipped at, ... 86
 fined for neglect of an order about swine 89
 &c. to pay charges for Muddy River bridge 93
 discharged, "the bridge and way being repaired," . . . 99
 John Johnson of, ment[d]. 104
 enjoined to make a sufficient way between the burial place and the gate 105
 enjoined to repair the way over the swamp toward Dorchester Mill . 106
 and Watertown, town of Cambridge to repair the way between, . . 106
 fine remitted to, ... 106
 town of Boston fined for defective ways towards Roxbury . . . 117
 constable of, to take care of John Kempe 125
 Richard Wood to keep an ordinary at Roxbury 133

RUCK or }
RUCKE   }
 ———, Mr., order as to, ... 129
 Thomas, Mr., &c., to appear at the General Court . . . 119

RUGELLS, JOHN, &c., jury, (case of Hugh Buett) 101

RUGS
 Margery, George Palmer sentenced for committing folly with, . . 93
  to be whipped for enticing George Palmer 93

RUNAWAYS, order as to, ... 43

RUNNING AWAY. (*See* CRIMES, &c.)

RUSSELL
 Henry, "brother," ment[d]. (will of John Russell) . . . 57
 John, of Dorchester, adm[n]. on goods &c. of, granted to William Gallard &c. 35
  William Gallerd adm. of, ... 46
  debt due to, forgiven to Robert Fibbin 46
  inventory of goods &c. of, exhibited in Court by his exec[rs]. . 55
  merchant, died in Dorchester August 26, 1633, will of, . . 57

RYE, advice to be sent to, (case of George Pye) 76

SABBATH DAY, or LORDS DAY, PUBLIC WORSHIP, ORDINANCES,
 shooting at fowl on the Sabbath Day, John Baker sentenced for, . 9
 James White fined for being drunk on the Sabbath Day . . . 33

INDEX. 259

SABBATH DAY, *continued.*   PAGE
   Richard Hollingsworth to be set in the stocks at Salem for profaning the Sabbath   80
   Katherine Finch promised to go to the Ordinance 82
   going into mens houses on the Lords Day (case of John Burrows) . 98
   opinion against singing in the churches (case of Edward Tomlins) . 105
   profaning the Sabbath (case of James Hawkins) 118
   neglecting Ordinances (case of William Willoughby) 120
SACKETT (or SUCKET), ISABELL, granted adm[n]. on goods &c. of her husband . 59
SADLER,———, Mr., case referred to, (Dearmant Matthew and Thomas Dexter) 129
SAGAMORE
   of Aggawam is banished from coming into any Englishman's house for one year   17
      complaint by, as to damage done in his corn by the swine of Charlton   49
   John, promised to fence his corn against all kinds of cattle . . . 26
SALE or grants of town lots &c. to be recorded &c. 45
SALEM, Town of,
   ment[d]. allowance to Mr. Wilson, (order as to ministers) . . . 2
   John Woodbury chosen constable of, ... 5
   John Boggust and John Pickryn to sit in the stocks at Salem . . 6
   ment[d]. (order as to levy for maintenance of Mr. Patricke &c.) . . 6
   John Legge to be whipped at, for striking Richard Wright . . . 14
   excepted, (order as to payment for damage done by cattle in any plantation) 14
   Church of, and the Government, Phillip Ratliffe sentenced for malicious speeches against, 16
   ment[d]. (order as to levy for the creek at Newe Towne) . . . 16
   assessed, (order as to levy for making a palisade) 20
   neck of land lying about three miles from, granted to Capt. Jo: Endicott 24
   three hundred acres of land lying about three miles from, granted to Mr. Samuel Skelton 24
   Richard Waterman to be paid for killing a wolf in Salem Plantation . 26
   assessed to defray public charges 37
   &c. to send in their money for three days work towards the Fort . . 38
   George Ropps to be whipped at, for striking his master . . . 62
   to repay his rate to Robert Moulton 65
   William James to be set in the stocks at Salem for incontinency . 65
   care of sending Isaack Davies to England committed to, . . . 67
   Church of, ment[d]. (order as to Mr. Skelton's estate) . . . 74
   John Bennet &c. referred to Salem for drunkenness 75
   Francis Weston's wife to be set in the bilboes at Salem . . . 75
   John Holgrave referred to, ... 75
   Court at, bond for appearance of the wives of John Leg and William Edmonds 76
   Robert Morgan &c. referred to, ... 76

260   INDEX.

                                                                                                              PAGE

SALEM, Town of, *continued.*
    the wife of Josua Verin referred to, ... 79
    Mary Oliver punished for disturbing the Church of Salem . . . 80
    Court at, Richard Geaves &c. referred to, for fighting &c. . . . 80
    Richard Hollingsworth to be set in the stocks at Salem upon a lecture
                                  day for profaning the Sabbath 80
    Court at, Francis Perry referred to, ... 83
        Adam Haukes and Edmond Audeley referred to, . . . 83
    &c. John Kempe to be whipped at, ... 86
    Court at, bond for appearance of Isaac Deesbro, ... 90
    fined for not keeping constant watch 90
        neglecting their watch 93
    allowed to use the meeting house for a watch house . . . 100
    way to, ment^d. (order as to town of Ipswich) . . . 106
    enjoined to repair their ways 106
    Court at, Mr. Burslin referred to, ... 107
    Francis Fellingham of, ment^d 132
    ment^d. (case of William Flint) 137
SALEM PLANTATION. (*See* SALEM.)
SALISBURY or SALSBERRY, Town of,
    enjoined to mend their way 106
    fined for want of weights and measures 106
SALSBERRY. (*See* SALISBURY, Town of.)
SALTONSTALL or SILTONSTALL, SOLTONSTALL
    ———, Mr., &c., present at Court 74, 86, 89, 91–93, 96, 99, 103, 105, 108,
                                                             125, 130, 132
    Mr., contemptuous speeches &c. to, Mr. Henry Scawall punished
                                                               for, 92
    Richard, S^r., ment^d. as to erecting a house at his plantation for use of
                                                                   ministers 1
        Kn^t. &c., present at Court 1, 3
        &c., to be Justices of the Peace 3
        fined for absence from Court 6
        &c., present at Court 8–12
        his servant Richard Diffy to be whipped for his misde-
                                        meanor towards him 8
        fined for whipping two persons without the presence of
                                        another Assistant 9
        to receive one half of the wages of William Knopp and
                                          his son 9
        order as to recompensing Indians for wigwams burned
                                          by his servant 11
        Richard Johnson acknowledged a debt to, . . . 13
        to receive two shillings a week from those persons for
                                    whom Richard Johnson works 13
        William Knopp owes debt to, ment^d. 13
        Chickatabut fined a skin of beaver for shooting swine
                                            belonging to, 16

INDEX. 261

SALTONSTALL, &c., *continued*.
 Richard, S^r., to give Sagamore John a hogshead of corn for damage done by his cattle . . . 29
  ment^d. (order as to Thomas Coleman) 58
  Mr., and Edward Dillingham, committee to settle accounts between, . . . 63
  Mr. Apleton, &c. order as to agreement between, . . 64
   accounts between, ment^d . . . 65
  took oath of an Assistant 66
  &c., present at Court 66, 69, 77, 81, 82
 Robert, Mr., deed to satisfy creditors of, delivered into Court by Hugh Peters 71
  bond by, (case of Isaac Hart) 95
  fine discounted by, (case of Richard Cluffe) . . . 97
  and Mr. Humphrey, arbitrators between, appointed . 133
SAMFORD, ———, Mr., &c., chosen for Boston, (order as to cart bridge over Muddy River &c.) 34
SAMPSON, J^{NO}. attachment against estate of, ... 104
SAUGUS or SAUGUST, Town of, or Plantation of,
 ment^d. (order as to levy for the creek at Newe Towne) . . 16
 assessed, (order as to levy for making a palisade) . . . 20
 Mr. Nathanaell Turner of, ... 22
 Mr. Turner chosen constable of, ... 26
 to have liberty to build a wear upon Saugus River . . . 27
 Mr. Turner &c. to set out land in Saugus to John Humfry, Esq. . . 30
 assessed to defray public charges 37
 &c., to send in their money for three days work towards the Fort . 38
 rate placed on Mr. Dumer's estate in, ... 39
 Mr. Nathaniel Turner chosen Captain of the military company in, . 40
 (or Lynne) witness from, called by George Woodward . . . 68
 (*See* also LYNN, Town of.)
SAUGUST. (*See* SAUGUS, Town of.)
SAUNDERS
 Edward, sick at Pascataqua, "to be brought in" 81
  case of, (bond forfeited by Nicholas Davison) . . . 82
 Martin, ment^d. (case of Laurence Copeland) 128
  to repair bridges in Braintree 129
 Robert, &c., jury, (case of Marmaduke Peirce) 89
SAVORY
 Thomas, referred to Court at Ipswich for lying 80
  case of, (theft, breaking a house &c.) 94
SAWERS. (*See* SAWYERS.)
SAWYERS, order as to wages of, ... 3, 19, 36
SAYLE }
SAYLES }
 ———, ment^d. (order as to business of Mr. Coxeall &c.) . . . 53
 John, for theft of corn &c. to forfeit his estate, to be whipped and bound as a servant for three years 82

INDEX.

	PAGE
SAYLE or SAYLES, *continued.*	
John, bound to Mr. Coxeshall for three years	32
to be whipped for running away from his master	40
SCALES. (*See* WEIGHTS, &c.)	
SCARLETT	
Robert, to be whipped for running away from his master	57
a thief, to be whipped and branded on the forehead with the letter T and banished	60
to be sent out of this jurisdiction by his master Benjamin Felton	60
SCHOLEE } SCHOOLEE } SCHOOLER } SCHOOLEY }	
Mary, murder of, William Schooley found guilty of,	69
William, order to apprehend,	69
found guilty of the murder of Mary Schooley	69
SCITUATE, Town of, John Emerson of, mentd.	74
SCOT } SCOTT } or SCUTT	
Benjamin, Margaret Stephenson is at liberty to marry,	125
Robert, &c., jury, (case of Marmaduke Peirce)	89
Thomas, and his wife, case of,	124
William, case of, (selling powder and shot to the Indians)	131
SCURVEY, Nicholas Knopp fined for taking upon himself to cure scurvey	11
SCUTT. (*See* SCOTT.)	
SEA FORT. (*See* FORT.)	
SEALE or SEALES	
———, Margaret wife of, found guilty of adultery	70
Edward, Margaret wife of, John Hathaway indicted for adultery with,	66
to be set in the bilboes and whipped for drunkenness	67
Margaret, wife of Edward Seale, John Hathaway indicted for adultery with,	66
and Robert Allen indicted for adultery	66, 70
Phebe, apprentice to John Coggesall, order as to	67
SEALERS AND SEARCHERS OF LEATHER, Hugh Mason &c. presented for,	138
SEALES. (*See* SEALE.)	
SEAWALL. (*See* SEWALL.)	
SECRETARY	
Acts of the Court shall be authentic if they pass only under the secretarys hand	17
process for the warning of jurors to be directed by the secretary to the beadle	38
to dispose of the estate &c. of Edward Lockwood	54
signature in hand of the Secretary referred to in note	96
bill of Nicholas Davison to be kept by the Secretary	98
writing by Simon Bradstreet, Secretary, referred to	109

INDEX.

SEDGWICK \
SEDGWICKE /

    ——, Capt., payment to, (case of Nathaniel Smith) 139
    Elizabeth, case of, (theft and lying) 118
SEDITION. (*See* CRIMES, &c.)
SEDUCING. (*See* CRIMES, &c.)
SEELY
    Robert, his servant Phillip Swaddon, to be whipped for running away . 16
                                      to be set free upon payment of ten shillings 18
SELLEN, THOMAS, granted leave to plant at Aggawam 32
SERJEANT, WILLIAM, &c., at Aggawam ment^d. 31
SERVANTS
    order as to giving or selling servants any commodity 5
    employing Indians for servants 11
    &c. to be provided with fire arms 12
    Thomas Chubb shall become servant to William Gayllerd . . . 14
    no person shall hire any person for a servant for less time than a year unless he be a settled housekeeper 15
    Francis Perry whipped for ill speeches &c. towards his master . . 18
    Phillip Swaddon set free from his master 18
    of Mr. Gibbons sentenced for running away 27
    John Sayle to be bound as a servant 32
    John Webb set at liberty from William Parks 32
    John Sayles to be whipped for running away from his master . . 40
    Christopher Tarling sentenced for running away from his master . 40
    order as to servants running away 43
    James Rawlens fined for taking too much for work done by one of his servants 47
    enticing servants to run away &c. Richard Cokar &c. sentenced for, . 51, 52
    William Swifte to pay towards the cure of his servant 53
    Andrew Storyn to be whipped for running away from his master . 57
    Robert Scarlett " " " " " " " " " . 57
    Mary, servant of Mr. Bartholmewe, to be whipped for running away . 57
    Clement Cole &c. to be whipped for running away from their masters &c. 59
    Benjamin Felton to be liable for damage done by his servant Robert Scarlett 60
    Robert Way to serve William Almy 61
    William Shepheard to be whipped for stealing from his master &c. . 62
    Edward Woodley released to his master 65
    James Hayden freed from his master 65
    John Crosse warned to appear as to his servant Clement Manning . 76
    William Denne to satisfy for fine imposed on his servant . . . 76
    William Androws punished for conspiring against the life of his master &c. 78, 79
    John Poole fined for abusing his servant 80
    John Hogges fined for cursing his servant &c. 81

SERVANTS, *continued.*

	PAGE
Capt. Staughton fined for releasing his servant before time	84
Ralfe Allen " " " " " " "	84
John Neale to be whipped and kept chained by his master for running away &c.	86
Thomas Marriner formerly servant to Robert Smyth discharged	88
John Clois admonished to use his servant Peter Tylls well &c.	88
covenant of, ment^d.	88
" the Court gave way to the Governor to free his servant Thomas Philips "	92
Hester Ketcham freed from her master John Woolrige	92
John Pope to be whipped for his stubborn carriage against his master &c.	92
John Woodbridge discharged of his presentment for releasing a servant	94
getting his masters daughter with child (case of Joell Jenkin)	95
two of Walter Merries servants to be whipped for running away	97
selling his servant his time (case of Christopher Batte)	100
John Twogood placed as a servant with Thomas Marshfield	100
Henry Stevens sentenced for firing his masters barn	100
Samuel Hefford freed from his master Jonathan Wade	101
Christopher Graunt fined for cruel usage of his servant Nicholas Gilberd	103
Richard Wilson sentenced for abusing his master Thomas Cheesholme	104
Edward Page freed	104
Thomas Baguley fined for selling his servants time	105
selling his servant his time (case of Abraham Morrell)	106
(case of Samuel Sherman)	106
David Hickbourne to serve his master for a longer time	107
James Laurence sentenced for leaving his masters house at night &c.	107
Willi: Pilsberry bound to service	107
William and Dorothy Pilsberry sentenced for defiling their masters house	107
constable of Watertown to provide a place of service for Elizabeth Wilsmore	117
Elisha Jackson turned over for his time from George Barrell to John Millam	119
theft from her master (case of Sarah Bell)	121
Robert Wyar and John Garland to make a payment to their master	121
Henry Hobson freed from his master Henry Neale	122
put to Goodman Thomas Meakins	122
Daniel Owles put to Sergeant William French &c.	122
Robert Wyar put to Leonard Bowtle with his masters consent	122
William Browne whipped for running away &c.	122
order as to John Kempe former servant of Isaac Morrell	125
Dermondt Matthew to be set to work until his master appears	125
John Lewis sent home to his master	126

INDEX.

SERVANTS, *continued.*

	PAGE
order as to Richard Cole	126
Richard Cole put to William Haward for one year	127
David Conway to be whipped for resisting his master	127
John Neale, a servant, committed on suspicion of felony	128
Daniel Mansfield put to William Denux for five years	128
David Weane put himself to Hugh Gunnison	129
Dearmant Matthew put to Thomas Dexter	129
Elizabeth Hasnet put to William Wilson	129
George Napper to stay with his master so much longer for the time he was absent	132
Richard Gell to be whipped for running away from his master	132
John Lowe to be freed from his master Lewis June 24, 1644	133
resisting his master (case of John Archer)	135
John Beamis find for freeing his servant	135, 136

SERVITUDE, single persons not provided with arms to serve any master &c. . 21
SEVER, ROBERT, case of, (neglecting the watch) 126

SEWALL or SEAWALL

Ellen, wife of Henry Seawall, to be at her own disposal and her husband to make allowance to her . . 60
Henry, Mr., order as to reimbursing him for money used for Edward Bosworth and family . . 55
order that his wife Ellen Seawell " shall be at her own disposal " . . 60
presented for beating his wife, ... 74
Mr., case of, (contemptuous speech &c. to Mr. Saltonstall) . 92

SEXTON

Giles, &c., jury, as to death of Austen Bratcher 6
witnesses, &c., ment^d. (inquisition on body of William Bateman) . . 8

SHARPE

———, Mr., &c., present at Court 3, 10, 12
Thomas, Mr., &c. 1

SHATSWELL or SHOTSWELL

John, fined for drunkenness 34
wife of, Robert Coles sentenced for enticing, ... 35

SHAW }
SHAWE }

Abraham, adm^n. granted on goods of, ... 98
John, ment^d. (case of William Chadborne) 137
Joseph, &c., adm^n. granted to, on goods of Abraham Shawe . . 98
Robert, to be whipped for cursing &c. 26
Roger, &c., jury, (case of Marmaduke Peirce) 89

SHEARMAN. (*See* SHERMAN.)
SHEEPE. (*See* SHEPPE.)
SHEPHEARD

———, Mr., &c., fined for drinking 18
receipt of his fine returned by the constable of Roxbury . 20

INDEX.

	PAGE
SHEPHEARD, *continued.*	
William, servant of William Suffer to be whipped for stealing	62
case of, (covenanting for wages)	128
SHEPPE or SHEEPE	
Thomas, &c., to appear at the next Court for being distempered with wine	88
case of, (intemperate drinking)	139
SHERMAN or SHEARMAN	
John, &c., jurymen, fined for not appearing	102
to view the leather tanned in Watertown &c.	128
Samuel, enjoined to appear at Court	104
case of, (selling his servant his time)	106
fine remitted to,	118
SHIPS	
safely arrived &c. day of Thanksgiving for,	87
&c. arrival of, " " " "	47
SHOOTING. (*See* CRIMES, &c.)	
SHOOTING at fowl on Pullen Point &c. order as to,	21
SHORTHAND	
in margin of record referred to in note	32, 61
referred to in note.	59
SHORTHOSE	
Robert to have his tongue put in a cleft stick for swearing	63
bond for appearance	78
set in the bilboes for slighting the magistrates	91
SHOT. (*See* MILITARY AFFAIRS.)	
SHOTSWELL. (*See* SHATSWELL.)	
SHUT^E., ———, Mr., &c., ordered to be sent to England by the next ship " as persons unmeet to inhabit here "	10
SILL, ———, bill delivered by, to be kept by the Secretary	98
SILTONSTALL. (*See* SALTONSTALL.)	
SIMPSON, JOHN, case of, (not prosecuting)	86
SINGING in the churches, opinion against, (case of Edward Tomlins)	105
SINGLEMAN, HENRY, bond for appearance	118
SINGLE PERSON, ordered that all single persons shall be provided with arms	21
SILVESTER	
Richard, fined for selling strong water	81
case of, (speaking against the law as to hogs &c)	82
fine respited upon his good behavior	87
and wife, witnesses, (case of Walthian Richards)	116
jury's verdict as to death of his child	126
SKELTON	
———, Mr., order as to settlement of estate of,	74
Samuel, Mr., land near Salem granted to, also land upon which his house stands	24
SKIDMER, JOHN, case of, (selling strong water to Indians)	106
SLANDER. (*See* CRIMES, &c.)	

INDEX.   267

                                                                                                                          PAGE

SLATE
    raising slate ment^d. (order as to Islands) 17
    in Slate Island, demised to Thomas Lambe 34
SLATE ISLAND, demise of slate in, ... 34
SLAVE
    William Androws &c. delivered up as slaves 78, 79
    John Kempe committed as a slave to Lt. Davenport 86
    Thomas Savory to be sold as a slave for theft 94
    Jonathan Hatch committed as a slave to Lt. Davenport . . . 97
    Marmaduke Barton committed as a slave for theft and running away . 118
SLAVERY
    Willi: Androws released from slavery 89
    Thomas Dickerson condemned to slavery 90
    Thomas Dickinson discharged from slavery 97
    Elizabeth Sedgwicke condemned to slavery for theft &c. . . . 118
SMALL CAUSES, COURT FOR. (*See* ASSISTANTS, COURT OF.)
SMITH }
SMITHE } or SMYTH, SMYTHE
    ———, Mr., &c., to go with Ensign Jennison &c. as to bounds of land
                                 sold to Mr. Pinchon   55
    of Springfield, to pay legacies to John Porter 132
    &c., arbitrators, (Mr. Humphrey and Robert Saltonstall) . 133
    Francis, &c., jury, as to death of Austen Bratcher 6
    his bill for ferriage granted 139
    Hen: certification by, ment^d. (Hingham presentment) . . 94
    Henry, did not appear 125
    Jacob, discharged for want of evidence 71
    James, costs to George Richardson for not prosecuting . . . 101
    John, bond by, to be accountable for his companys goods . . 25
        apprenticed to Mr. John Wilson 25
        goods sent over with, to remain in Mr. Wilson's hands . . 25
        &c., jury of life and death 70
        (or Thomas), attached for not appearing 73
        of Meadford, to be set in the bilboes for swearing . . . 74
        bond for appearance 76
        and his father, Jeremy Norcross, Mr. Collens &c. to hear busi-
                            ness between, and examine accounts   100
        granted five shillings against William Prichard 116
        admonished and dismissed 118
        Mr., &c., committee, as to affairs of Edward Allen . . . 127
        clerk of the Band at Dorchester 131
    Joseph (Josua or Josiah), surety, ment^d. (bond to make payment to
                                   Andrew Coleman &c.)   96
    Josiah (Josua or Joseph), ment^d. in note 96
    Josua, surety, bond to make a payment to Andrew Coleman ment^d. . 96
    Lucy, bound an apprentice to Mr. Roger Ludlowe for seven years . 17
    Mary, &c., witnesses, (case of Walthian Richards) . . . 116
    Nathaniel, case of, (theft &c.) 139

INDEX.

	PAGE
SMITH, *continued*.	
Ralph, &c., attachment for,	79
discharged	81
Richard, bond for appearance (concealing Edward Waldo's intention of running away),	122
case of, (being privy to Edward Waldo's intent to run away),	130
Robert, his former servant Thomas Marriner discharged	88
Thomas (or John), attached for not appearing	73
SMITHEMAN, JOHN, &c., of Bocking, clothiers, made a payment to Andrew Coleman ment^d.	96

SMYTH }
SMYTHE } (*See* SMITH.)

SOEWAMAPENESSETT RIVER commonly called Cow House River, land near Salem bounded on the south by, granted to Capt. Jo: Endicott   24

SOJOURNERS within this jurisdiction for six months or more to take oath of allegiance   44

SOLDIERS. (*See* MILITARY AFFAIRS.)
SOLTONSTALL. (*See* SALTONSTALL.)

SOUTH, WILLIAM, to be whipped and banished upon pain of death   70

SOUTHCOATE
 ———, Capt., Mr. Francis Aleworth chosen Lieutenant to,   18
  granted liberty to go to England   18

SOUTH RIVER, land in Salem abutting on, granted to Mr. Skelton   24

SPARHAUKE, ———, Mr., &c., to hear business between John Smith and Jeremy Norcross   100

SPAULE, THOMAS, surety, (case of William Scutt)   131

SPENCER
 ———, Mr., &c., appointed as to Mr. Gurlin's land   74
 George, to be whipped and to make double restitution for receiving stolen money   70

SPRAGE
 Ralfe, &c., jury, as to death of Austen Bratcher   6
  inquisition on body of William Bateman upon oaths of,   7
  bond by, (case of Walter Palmer)   7
  Mr., (cancelled), &c., witnesses, ment^d. (inquisition on body of William Bateman)   8
  chosen umpire as to settlement of bounds between Roxbury and Dorchester   29

SPRING, ROGER, principal debtor, bond to make a payment to Andrew Coleman ment^d.   96

SPRINGFIELD, Mr. Smyth of, ment^d.   132

SQUA SACHEM, town of Cambridge enjoined to give her corn &c.   106

SQUIRE, THOMAS, jury of life and death   70

STACY
 John, Junr., set in the stocks for drinking   85
 Willi: Junr., &c., of Bocking, clothiers, made a payment to Andrew Coleman ment^d.   96

INDEX. 269

	PAGE
STAGG, ———, Mr., &c., differences referred to	47
STANIARD, ANTHONY, bond by, (case of Thomas Wilson)	124

STANLEY

John, order as to settlement and division of estate of, (mentions brothers Thomas and Timothy and children Ruth and John)	51
Junr., (son of John) his uncle Thomas Stanley to educate him &c.	51
Ruth, (daughter of John) her uncle Timothy Stanley to educate her &c.	51
Thomas, part of goods &c. of his deceased brother John Stanley put into his hands &c.	51
Tymothy, part of goods &c., of his deceased brother John Stanley put into his hands &c.	51

STAR }
STARR }

Susan, granted admⁿ. on estate of her husband Thomas Starr	103
Thomas, fined &c. for speaking against the law about swine	73
admⁿ. on estate of, granted to his wife Susan Starr	103

STAUGHTON. (*See* STOUGHTON.)

STEBBEN, JOHN, &c., bond by, (for the good behavior of Christopher Grant till the next quarter court)	103
STEDMAN, ROBERT, juryman, fined for not appearing	103
STEPHENSON, MARGARET, is at liberty to marry Benjamin Scott	125
STEPPING STONES, Weymouth, ment^d.	84

STERNES

Isaac, &c., jury, (Dexter against Endicott)	15
Isaack, &c., fined for turning the way about	79

STEVENS

———., Mr., promised ten pounds for his work &c., as to building a Fort	41
Henry, case of, (firing the barn of his master John Humfrey)	100

STICKLAND

JOHN, &c., inquisition upon oaths of, on body of William Bateman	7
jury (Dexter against Endicott)	15
fined for refusing to watch at the Captains command	26
STICKLETT, JOHN, &c., bond by, (case of Walter Palmer)	7

STILEMAN

———, Mr., constable, ment^d. (case of Robert Scarlett)	60
discharged as to a way	136
STILES, JOHN, allowance to,	120

STITSON

William, granted admⁿ. on goods &c. of Richard Arnoll	35
of Robert White	56
&c., to be brought into Court.	117

STOADER. (*See* STODDER.)

STOCKS

town of Concord fined for want of a pair of stocks &c.	79
Watertown " " " " " " " "	79

	PAGE

STOCKS, *continued*.
 town of Cambridge fined for want of stocks &c. 80
  Newbury " " " " a pair of stocks &c. . . . 80
 ment^d. (order as to town of Boston) 84
 town of Dedham fined for want of a pair of stocks 84
  Watertown " " " " " " " " 85
  Cambridge " " " " stocks &c. 90
 ment^d. (order as to town of Braintree) 99
  (*See also* PUNISHMENT.)

STODDER or STOADER
 ———, Mr., &c., theft from, (case of Mary Felton) 108
  and his Company granted charges against Mr. John Long 125
  case of, (selling cloth at an excessive rate) . . . 131
  theft from, (case of Bridget Barnard) 137
 Anthony (or George), &c., constables of Boston, granted power as to estate of Paul Yonge 107
  case of, (affronting the Governor) 108
 George (or Anthony), &c., constables of Boston, granted power as to estate of Paul Yonge 107

STONE
 John, Capt., fined and prohibited from coming into this patent &c. for confronting of authority &c. 35
 &c., costs against Joshua Hubbard for not prosecuting . . 122
STONY RIVER, &c. agreement as to a cart bridge over, ... 34
STOREY }
STORY }
 Andrewe Storey (or Storyn) to be whipped for running away from his master 57
 George, case of, (miscarriage) 117
  discharged of his bond for appearance to answer to Capt. Keayne 119
STORYN, ANDREWE, to be whipped for running away from his master . 57
STOUGHTON or STAUGHTON
 ———, Sergeant, chosen Ensign to Capt. Mason 38
 Ensign, &c., to set out bounds between Boston and Roxbury . 41
 Mr., Robert Way to be taken from, and to serve William Almy 61
 Mr., &c., present at Court . 71, 72, 74, 76, 82, 86, 88, 89, 91–93
 business of Robert Abels referred to, ... 94
 Mr., &c., present at Court 95, 96
  to hear business between Richard Lange and the town of Weymouth 99
  &c., present at Court, 99, 103, 105, 107, 108, 118, 123, 125, 134
  cloth of, ment^d. (case of John Milam) 139
 Israell, his servants Alexander Miller, &c. ordered to make a payment to him for their wasteful expense of powder, &c. 27
 Mr., &c., gift towards the Sea Fort 42
  granted liberty to build a mill, a wear and a bridge over Naponsett River, &c. 43

INDEX.

STOUGHTON or STAUGHTON, *continued*.
    Israell, Mr., goods, &c. of Christopher Ollyver to remain in hands of   50
        &c., present at Court 66, 69, 78, 81
            fine remitted to, ... 88
            &c., present at Court 98
        Thom[as] chosen constable of Dorchester 5
            Mr., constable of Dorchester, fined " for taking upon him to marry " persons   10

STOW }
STOWE }
    ———, Goodman, &c., order as to, ... 129
    John, case of, (selling shot to an Indian) 101
        &c., to appear at the General Court 119
            upon release of, Concord men are granted power to seize land, &c. 139

STOWER or STOWRE
    Nicholas, payment to, for keeping cattle (order as to) . . . 5
        &c., jury, as to death of Austen Bratcher 6
            inquisition on body of William Bateman upon oaths of, 7

STOWERS, JOHN, case of, (reading offensive passages against the officers and Church of Watertown)   121

STOWRE. (*See* STOWER.)

STRAINGE
    ———, Mrs., and her child to be supplied according to their necessity   119
    Elizabeth, dismissed with an admonition, &c. 124

STRETTON
    John, Timothy Tomlins consented to take ten shillings from, . . 65
        capias granted to, against Kibbe, &c. 65
        Mr., fined for lending a gun to an Indian 71
        freed from his bond 82

STRONG WATER
    order as to seizure of, ... 5
    Mr. Allen's strong water to be delivered to the Deacons of Dorchester for the benefit of the poor   26
    selling to such as were drunk with it 26
    &c., no person shall sell strong water without leave from the Governor, and none to sell or give to an Indian   33
    drinking, &c., Timothy Hawkins, &c. fined for, ... 40
    selling, Edward Howe fined for, ... 41
        to the Indians, James Browne fined for, ... 68
    drinking, &c., Benjamin Hubberd admonished for, . . . 68
    (*See also* LIQUOR.)

STUBBORNNESS. (*See* CRIMES, &c.)

SUCKET (or SACKETT), ISABELL, granted administration on goods &c. of her husband   59

SUDBURY, Town of,
    deferred until the Quarter Court 100
    delivered in a transcript of their lands 117
    Mr. Briant Pendleton to exercise the company at, . . . 133

272 INDEX.

	PAGE
SUDBURY MILL, owners of, fined for want of weights & scales . . .	135
SUMER ⎫ SUMMER ⎭ WILLIAM, his servant William Shepheard sentenced to be whipped for stealing	62
SUMMONS	
in Civil Actions (order as to)	2
&c., every Assistant shall have power to grant, ...	17
SURVEYOR, Willi: Powell fined for resisting the surveyor	88
SUTTON, JOHN, &c., bond by (as to things taken from John Hardies' wreck)	105
SWADDON	
Phillip, to be whipped for running away from his master . . .	16
shall be set free from his master, Robert Seely, upon the payment of ten shillings	18
SWAMPS, containing above one hundred acres, order as to, ...	39
SWEET ⎫ SWEETE ⎭	
John, ground of, ment^d. (grant to Mr. Skelton)	24
fined and imprisoned for shooting a dog	66
SWIFT ⎫ SWIFTE ⎭	
William, to pay towards the cure of his servant	53
Willi: mortgaged his house and lands in Watertown to John Haynes, ment^d.	96
surety, bond to make payment to Andrew Coleman, ment^d. .	96
and Andrew Coleman, order in case	96
SWINE	
order as to allowance for weaned swine, &c.	8
found in any man's corn shall be forfeited to the public . . .	14
shooting of, Chickataubott fined for, ...	16
every person shall satisfy for the damages done by his swine in the corn of another	28
at Marble Harbor, order as to, ...	32
it shall be lawful for any man to kill swine that comes into his corn .	34
order as to the kind of corn to be given to swine	38
number of swine to be kept in every plantation . .	38
damage done in corn of Thomas Richards . . .	49
of Charlton, damage by, complained of, ...	49
damage to, by setting traps, order as to, ...	50
town of Roxbury fined for neglect of an order about swine . . .	89
town of Weymouth fined for not looking to the execution of the order about swine, &c.	91
SYMONDS ⎫ SYMONS ⎭	
——, Mr., &c., present at Court	132, 138
arbitrators, (Mr. Humphrey & Robert Saltonstall) .	133
Samuel, copy made by, referred to, ...	103, 115
Thomas, enjoined to appear at the Quarter Court	88
SYNODE at Newetowne for settling differences, ment^d.	69

INDEX. 273

	PAGE
TABLES, all persons that have cards, dice or tables in their houses shall do away with them	12

TABOR
    Phillip, &c., gift towards the Sea Fort 42
                bond by, (case of Mr. Chester) 44
TACYE, ———, case of, (swearing) 88
TAILORS, Master, order as to wages of, ... 36
TALBIE }
TALBYE }
    Difficult, her mother, Dorothy Talbie, to be hanged for causing death of, 78
    Dorothy, wife of John, to be hanged for causing the death of her daughter 78
    John, Dorothy, wife of, to be hanged for causing the death of her daughter 78
TAPPIN, NATHANIEL, case of, (breaking into houses, &c.) 132
TARLING, CHRISTOPHER, to be whipped for stealing from his master, and for running away 40
TAX. (*See* ASSESSMENT).
TAYLOR
    John, Rebecca Taylor, wife of, mentioned 139
    Rebecka, wife of John Taylor, " 139
    Richard, dismissed with an admonition 122
TEACHER. (*See* PASTOR.)
TEE, JOHN, Jacob Eliot deposed to the will and inventory of, ... 115
TERRY
    Steven, sworn constable of Dorchester 55
    Thomas enjoined to appear at Court 80
THACHER. (*See* THATCHER.)
THANKSGIVING DAY
    13 June, 1632, order for, ... 23
    19 " 1633 " as to, ... 32
    16 October, " " " " 37
    20 August, 1634 " " " 47
    15 June, 1637 " " " 68
THATCHER or THACHER
    ———, Thatcher's plot, ment^d. (case of Thomas Briant) . . . 118
    Anthony, Mr., granted administration on goods, &c. of Joseph Avery, and inventory returned by, 58
    Peter, case of, (plotting piracy) 118
THATCHERS, order as to wages of, ... 3
THEALE
    Nicholas or (Richard) attachment against, ... 73
        to make a payment to John Finch, and admonished to avoid dancing 75
    Richard (or Nicholas) attachment against, ... 73
THEFT. (*See* CRIMES, &c.)
THING, JONATHAN, case of, (ravishing Mary Greenfeild) . . . 106
THOMAS, EVAN, allowance of corn to, ... 97

	PAGE
THORNE, ———, Mr., case of, (concealing, hiding, &c.)	109
THORNEDICKE, ———, Mr., &c., at Aggawam, ment^d.	81
THORPE, ROBERT, &c., discharged with an admonition as to too many in a boat	81
THREE MILE BROOK or North River, land on, granted to Mr. Increase Nowell	43
"THUNDER," (ship) difference between John Cogan, John Tylley, &c., as to, referred to a committee	54
THWAYTE, ALEXANDER, corn of, granted to Peter Bulkeley	94
THYERY ———, Monsieur, a Frenchman, who died here, part of estate of, in hands of the Govr.	127
TILERS. (*See* TYLERS.)	
TILLEY or TYLLEY	
John, Mr., administration granted on goods, &c., of,	43
and Mr. Marriner, &c., difference between, referred to John Winthrop, Senr., &c.	47
Henry Cogan, difference between, referred to John Winthrop, Senr., &c.	47
John Coggin, difference between, referred to John Winthrop, Senr., &c.	47
John Cogan, difference between, as to ship "Thunder" referred to a committee	54
TIMBER	
&c., order for preservation of,	17
order as to preservation of,	28
TOBACCO	
no person shall take tobacco publicly	28
tobacco takers, &c., ment^d. (order as to idlers)	37
TOBEY } TOBY	
Francis, bond for, by John Jobson	62
Frauncis, bound to his good behavior for a misdemeanor	55
TOLE, ROGER, Mr. Henry Webbe's man, case of, (selling gunpowder to an Indian)	101
TOLL	
Thomas Wilson fined for taking above double toll	78
Mr. Waltham fined for taking too much toll	84
Willi: Fuller fined for " " " "	85
TOMPKINS, RALFE, theft from, William Baker sentenced for,	62
TOMLINS	
Edward, Mr., case of, (opinions against singing in Churches)	105
allowed Ensign at Lynn	123
Tymothy, consented to take ten shillings of John Stretton	65
Timothy, Mr., &c., granted admⁿ. on estate of Mr. Ballard	117
TOMPSON	
Miles, fined for drinking with others	131
Robert, Mr., & William Tynge difference between referred	104
TOMPSON'S ISLAND, &c., shall be appropriated to the public benefit, &c.	17
TORY, WILLIAM, Mr., appointed Ensign at Weymouth	123

INDEX. 275

	PAGE
TOWER, JOHN, case of, (disturbing the peace)	95
TOWN BOOK OF WEYMOUTH, Mr. Stoughton to have power to call for,	99

TOWNS
 ordered that every Town within this pattent shall provide every person
      with fire arms, before April 5th, 1630-31   12
 order as to fetching wood from swamps belonging to towns . . .   39
 constable and four of the inhab^{ts}. of every town to make a survey of
      the houses, &c.   45
 all towns had respite to bring in the transcript of their lands . .   83
 ment^d. (answer by John Pratt)   110

TRADE
 order as to articles concerning a general trade of beaver agreed upon
      by Capt. Endicott and others   15
      buying corn, &c.   16
 trucking house to be appointed in every plantation where the Indians
      may trade   23
 Mr. John Winthrop, Jr., &c., granted liberty to set up a trucking house
      up Merrimak River   35
 ment^d. (answer by John Pratt)   110

TRADING, order as to trading beaver with Indians   23
TRAINING. (*See* MILITARY AFFAIRS.)
TRANSCRIPT of lands
 delivered in, by Charlestown, Sudbury and Dedham . . .   117
      town of Dedham, ment^d.   123
 Concord delivered in an imperfect transcript of their lands . . .   124
 delivered in by town of Dedham   135

TRASK }
TRASKE }
 ———, Capt., &c. to settle the bounds between Dorchester and Rocks-
      bury   29
  to make a payment to John Kirman, as his share in a
      plow patent   52

TRAVELL, Nathaniell, case of, (scandalous speeches)   93
TRAVELLERS
 ordered that no person shall travel single between this plantation and
      Plymouth, nor without arms   14
 no person shall travel out of this pattent either by sea or land without
      leave from the Governor, &c.   15

TREASURER
 rent to be paid to, (Conant's Island demised to Govr. John Winthrop) .   22
 Mr. William Pinchon chosen   26
 ordered to make a payment to Richard Waterman for killing a wolf .   26
 &c., present at Court, 26-28, 30-34, 36, 38, 39, 42, 45-47, 50, 52, 55, 57-59,
      61, 62
 ordered to pay a quarters " exhibition " to Capt. Underhill, &c. . .   27
 order as to his beaver trade   27
 &c., committee to take an account of debts due to the Governor, &c. .   33
 ordered to pay Lt. Mason for his voyage to the eastward . . .   34

INDEX.

	PAGE
TREASURER, *continued*.	
&c., chosen for Rocksbury (order as to bridge over Muddy River, &c.)	34
to give James Peñ the beadle thirty pounds to build a house	38
rent to be paid to, (Long Island, &c. granted to Boston)	44
to pay three pounds to inhabitants of Dorchester for care of Thomas Lane	46
to pay money for maintenance of widow Bosworth and her family	48
&c., to prepare the business of Mr. Coxeall, &c.	53
creditors to repair to the, (adm^n. on goods of Robert White)	56
Mr. Bel[lingham], &c., present at Court	92
to make a payment to Thomas Buckmaster	92
TREES, William Lampson allowed to fell trees on the other side of Chebacco	108
TRERICE	
———, Mr., to pay Tacye's fine	88
debt to, ment^d., attachment against Robert Mindam	123
Nicholas, Mr., case of, (miscarriage in Court)	108
fine remitted to,	118
TRESPASS in Corn, owners of cattle are ordered to pay for damages done by,	14
TRIMOUNTAINE, ordered that Trimountaine shall be called Boston	4
TROTMAN, JOHN, theft from, (case of Bridget Barnard)	137
TROWENT, MORRIS, &c., sentenced to be whipped for stealing	13
TRUCKING HOUSE. (*See* TRADE.)	
TRUMBLE	
John, fined &c.	66
part of fine remitted to,	67
TRUSDELL, RICHARD, &c., jury (case of Hugh Buett)	101
TUCKER, ROBERT, case of, (upbraiding James Brittain)	94
TURNER	
———, Mr., chosen constable of Saugus	26
&c., difference between Newton & Charlestown referred to,	29
to set out land to John Humfry, Esq.	30
Capt., &c., gift towards the Sea Fort	42
Goodman, the treasurer to cast up his bill, and if it be found right to allow it	137
John, and William Richards, Mr. Ginner &c. to settle things between,	97
Nathanaell, Mr., of Saugus, Sarah Morley apprenticed to,	22
&c., agreement signed by, (as to bounds of Charles Towne & New Towne)	23
Mr., chosen Captain of the military company at Saugus	40
Richard, fined for drunkenness	78
case of, (drunkenness)	86
Robert, discharged for want of proof	84
Thomas, town of Hingham acquitted from the presentment about Thomas Turner's lot	84
&c., bond by, (case of Robert Penyer)	86
(as to things taken from John Hardie's wreck)	105
costs to Richard Osborne, for not prosecuting	136

INDEX. 277

	PAGE
TUTTLE, HENRY, took oath as constable of Hingham	97
TWITCHWELL, JOSEPH, five pounds of the judgment against, to be abated	40
TWOGOOD, JOHN, servant of Thomas Marshfield order as to,	100
TYLERS, &c., order as to wages of,	36
TYLESTONE, THOMAS, &c., fined for not attending the jury	97
TYLLEY. (See TILLEY.)	
TYLLS, PETER, his master, John Clois, admonished to use him well	88

TYNG }
TYNGE }

——, Mr., &c., to examine accounts between Mr. Joanes & Mr. Mayhewe . . 93
Will: Mr., to make a payment to Mr. John Coggan 92
&c., to examine the books about the goods which came in the "Charles" . . 97
William, Mr., & Robert Tompson, difference between, referred . . 104

UNDERHILL
——, Mr., allowance to, ... 4, 5
(or Capt.) order as to levy for maintenance of, . . 6
Capt., order as to training of his Company . . . 18
&c., to be paid a quarters exhibition 27
Boston, &c., assessed for maintenance of, . . 31
Sergeant Morris chosen ancient to, . . . 31
Mr. Richard Morris chosen Lieutenant to, . . 40
John, Capt., acquitted 108
UNDERWOOD, MARTEN, &c., allowance to, ... 105
UNION. (See UNNION.)
UNJUSTLY SELLING, &c. (See CRIMES, &c.)
UNNION (or UNION), ROBERT, fine respited to, ... 127
UPSALL
Nicholas, &c., jury, as to death of Austen Bratcher 6
of Dorchester, licensed to keep an ordinary, &c. . . . 68
&c., jury of life and death 70

VAINE }
VANE }

——, Mr., late Governor, William Knop to answer for speeches against, 68
Elizabeth, case of, (abusing a magistrate, &c.) 132

VAUGHAN }
VAUHAN }

John, &c., fined for company keeping, drinking, &c. 40
to appear at the next Court 90
committed to prison until he marry her whom he hath defiled, & to provide for the child, &c. 91
VERIN, JOSUA, his wife referred to Salem 79
VINE BROOK
&c., town of Cambridge to repair highways at, ... 85
fined for defective way at Vine Brook, &c. . . 90

	PAGE
VIRGINIA, ment^d. (sentence of Phillip Swaddon)	16
(ship) misdemeanor and drunkenness committed aboard, Mr. James Parker fined for,	25
VOCAR, JOHN, sentenced to be fined or whipped	116
VOYSEY, SYMON, Mr., case of, (striking Mr. Constable)	115

WADE
 Jonathan, money given to, ment^d. 54
  &c., Grand Jury 70
  his servant, Samuel Hefford freed 101
  bound to his good behavior 101
 Samuel, his servant, Richard Wilson, sentenced for stealing, &c. . 86
 Thomas, bill by Goodman Perkins to, to be brought into Court . . 54

WAGES
 of Carpenters, &c., order as to, ... 3, 36
  Master Carpenters, &c., order as to, ... 5, 36
 order as to wages for laborers 6, 36
 of William Knopp, order as to, ... 9
 order as to wages of workmen 12
 of workingmen, order as to, ... 36
 of inferior laborers to be referred to the constable, &c. . . 36
  tailors, order as to, ... 36
 John Humfry punished for taking too great wages . . . 47
 Frauncis Godson to answer for taking too great wages . . . 48
 forfeited by Arthur Holbidge, &c. 56
 as to price of, (case of William Shepheard, &c.) 125
 taking excessive wages (case of Anker Ainsworth) . . . 131
 James Loranson, &c. presented for taking too much wages . . 135

WAHQUACK, land near Salem so called granted to Mr. Samuel Skelton . . 24
WAHQUAMESEHCOK, land near Salem so called in the Indian tongue granted to Capt. Jo: Endicott   24
WAKE, WILLI: counselled to go home to his wife and discharged . . . 100
WALCOT }
WALCOTT } (*See* WOLCOTT.)
WALDO or WALLDO
 Edward, servant of William French, Daniel Owles punished for concealing him &c.   122
  concealing his intention of running away, (case of Richard Smyth)   122
  being privy to his intention of running away (case of Richard Smyth)   130
WALES, TYMOTHY, &c., to be whipped for drunkenness 63
WALFORD
 Thomas, of Charlton, fined and he and his wife enjoined to depart out of this pattent   14
  goods of, to be sequestered to pay his debts 35
WALKER
 Richard, Ensign, Thomas Dickinson committed to, ... 97
 Robert, &c., witnesses, allowance to, (case of Richard Lambert)   49

INDEX.

                                                        PAGE

WALLDO. (*See* WALDO.)
WALTHAM
    ———, Mr., fined for taking too much toll 84
        &c., fined for want of weights &c. in their mill . . 84
        witnesses, (case of Walthian Richards) . . . 116
    Henry, Mr., discharged 101
    and Welthia Richards, difference between, as to a mill in Weymouth referred 102
        Mr., &c., bond by, (case of Gawen Wilson) 115
    William, case of, (drunkenness) 91
WALTON
    ———, Mr., to have his goods which were unjustly taken . . . 129
        Mary Bentley to make restitution for stealing his jewel . 137
    George, fined for swearing 77
WANNERTON. (*See* WONNARTON.)
WANOTTYMIES RIVER and Cobbett's House, meadow land lying between, granted to Gov[r]. John Winthrop 29
WARD
    Samuel, &c., bond by, (case of Jonathan Bosworth) . . . 124
    Thomas, &c., viewed the body of Austen Bratcher 7
WARDALL, ———, Sergt., to train the company at Exeter . . . 133
WARE. (*See* WEIR.)
WARHAM, JOHN, Mr., pastor of the Church of Dorchester, &c., witnesses, (will of John Russell) 57
WARNER, THOMAS, &c., fined for quarrelling 87
WARRANTS
    to be sent to Aggawam (order as to plantations) 4
    &c., every Assistant shall have power to grant warrants . . 17
WARREN
    Arthur, found guilty of keeping company with Clement Briggs wife . 72
        wife of Clement Brigs enjoined not to accompany him . . 75
        &c., witnesses, (case of Walthian Richards) 116
    John, ment[d]. as to leather of John Winter 128
WARRINER, RALFE, fined for excessive drinking 85
WATCH
    ordered that a watch of four shall be kept every night at Dorchester and Waterton to begin at sunset 13
    order as to punishment of persons who shoot off fire arms after the watch is set 13
    ordered that a watch of six and an officer shall be kept every night at Boston 17
    part of Mr. Shepheard's fine to be used to pay for ferrying the watch from Charlton to Boston 20
    John Stickland fined for refusing to watch at the Captains command . 26
    town of Boston fined for want of a watch house &c. . . . 79
        Concord " " " " " " " . . . 79
        Cambridge fined " " " " " " . . . 80
        Charlestown " " " " " " " . . . 80

280 INDEX.

PAGE

WATCH, *continued.*
    order as to watch house for town of Dorchester 84
                          at Hingham 84
    town of Concord fined for want of a watch house 85
        Salem fined for not keeping constant watch 90
        Concord fined for neglecting their watch &c. 90
        Cambridge fined for neglect of a constant watch &c. . 90
    order as to watch house at Charlestown 90
    town of Lynn fined for not keeping constant watch &c. . . . 90
        Weymouth fined for want of a watch house &c. . . . 90
                    neglecting to keep a constant watch . 90
        Hingham fined for not keeping a constant watch &c. . . 91
        Salem fined for neglecting their watch 95
    watch house ment^d. (order as to town of Braintree) 99
    town of Charlestown to use the meeting house for a watch house . 99
        Salem " " " " " " " " " . . 100
        Lynn " " " " " " " " " . . 100
        Hingham " " " " " " " " " . . 100
    town of Concord fined for neglecting the watch &c. 106
    neglecting the watch (case of Robert Sever) 126
    refusing to watch (case of Richard White) 126
    George Watts fined for abusing the watch &c. 133
    Israel Hart fined for neglecting the watch &c. 133
    David Williams sentenced for assaulting the watch . . . 135
    refusing to watch (case of William Porter &c.) 135
WATCH HOUSE. (*See* WATCH.)
WATERMAN, RICHARD, to be paid for killing a wolf 26
WATERS
    Lawrence, bond for his wifes appearance 73
        wife of, to make a payment to John Finch and admonished
                for dancing 75

WATERTON ⎫
WATERTOWN ⎬ Town of,
WATERTOWNE ⎭
    ordered that the town upon the Charles River shall be called Water-
                                        town 4
    ment^d. (order as to levy for maintenance of Mr. Patrick &c.) . . 6
        (order as to maintenance of ministers) 9
    Court of Assistants at, 8 March 1630–31 11
    ordered that a watch of four shall be kept every night at Watertown
                                &c. to begin at sunset 13
    ment^d. (order as to a levy for the creek at Newe Towne) . . . 16
    assessed, (order as to levy for making the palisade) . . . 20
    ment^d. (agreement as to bounds of Charles Towne and Newe Towne) . 23
    bounds of, ment^d. (agreement as to bounds of Charlestown and Newton) 30
    assessed for maintenance of Capt. Underhill &c. 31
        to defray public charges 37
    Samuel Hosier chosen and sworn constable of, ... 48

	PAGE
WATERTOWN, Town of, *continued.*	
Church of, to dispose of the children and estate of Edmond Lockwood and Newe Towne, agreement as to bounds between, mentions the Weir	52 53
Church of, &c., consent by, to disposition of estate and children of Edward Lockwood	54
Richard Browne of, ment^d.	71
fined for want of a pair of stocks	79, 85
discharged as to a highway to the mill	85
fined for a bad highway	85
to pay charges for Muddy River bridge	93
Henry Bright took oath of surveyor of arms in,	95
Willi: Swift mortgaged his house and lands in Watertowne to John Haynes ment^d.	96
freemen of, discharged (as to proportion to townsmen)	99
John Whitney took oath as constable of Watertown	105
and Roxbury, town of Cambridge enjoined to repair the way between,	106
discharged	106
constable of, to provide a place of service for Elizabeth Wilsmore	117
Church of, disturbing the, &c., (case of John Stowers)	121
time granted to, as to transcript of lands	123
Edward Lewis &c. to view the leather tanned in Watertown &c.	128
presentment referred to the Quarter Court	128
Thomas Arnold sworn constable of,	134
lands, transcript of, respited	137
WATTS	
George, case of, (swearing)	127
(distemper in drink, abusing the watch &c.)	133
WAY	
———, assigned Robert Way to Ensign Gennison	46
Henry, &c., Nicholas Frost to pay a fine to,	28
debt owned by, ment^d. (case of Thomas Wonnarton)	55
Robert, to remain with Ensign Gennison	46
who was assigned to Edward Burton, order as to,	48
bills &c. about, to be delivered into the Court	61
to be taken from Mr. Stonghton and to serve William Almy	61
WAYMOTH WAYMOTHE WAYMOUTH } (*See* WEYMOUTH.)	
WAYNE. (*See* WEANE.)	
WAYS. (*See* HIGHWAYS.)	
WEANE or WAYNE	
David, put himself to Hugh Gunnison	129
&c., bond for appearance	134
forfeited forty shillings for not appearing	136
fine remitted to,	137
WEAR. (*See* WEIR.)	
WEATHERLY, THOMAS, case of, (swearing &c.)	136

INDEX.

	PAGE
WEAVER or WEVER	
———, Mr., &c., to be sent to England " as unmeet to inhabit here "	10
ment^d. (case of Mr. Barnard)	94
Clement, fined for drunkenness	94
WEB ⎫	
WEBB ⎬	
WEBBE ⎭	
———, Mr., &c., theft from, (case of Mary Felton)	108
Henry, discharged for want of witness	79
Mr., his man, Roger Tole, sold gunpowder to an Indian	101
&c., constables of Boston, granted power as to estate of Paul Yonge	107
John, set at liberty from his master William Parks	32
William, case of, (neglecting an order as to bread)	127
WEDGWOOD, JOHN, case of, (being in the company of drunkards)	86
WEIGHTS AND SCALES, MEASURES, &c.	
in mill of Mr. Waltham &c. ment^d.	84
town of Dedham fined for want of weights &c.	90
Lynn " " " " sealed weights &c.	90
Richard Dummer fined for want of weights &c.	94
town of Newbury " " " " " "	95
Salisbury " " " " " "	106
Hampton " " " " " "	106
ment^d. (order as to Sudbury mill)	135
WEILLUST, or WELLUST, WILLUST	
———, John Humfrey &c. to determine as to estate of,	52
Jost, chosen surveyor of the Ordinance and cannoneer	11
allowance to for his transportation into his own country	24
WEIR or WEAR, WARE	
at Mystic granted to John Winthrop, Esq. &c.	41
Mr. Israel Stoughton granted liberty to build a wear &c. over Neponset River	43
ment^d. (agreement as to bounds of Watertown and Newton)	53
WELD	
———, Mrs., punished for abusing two Indian women	95
Joseph, Mr., &c., to sell Mr. Gurlings land to satisfy creditors	71
Mr. Gurlings land sold by,	73
WELL	
John Barnard fined for his dangerous well	136
Thomas Ewar &c. fined for leaving his pit or well open	75
WELLS, WILLI: to answer for oppression	108
WELLUST. (*See* WEILLUST.)	
WENETSEMET. (*See* WINNETTSEMET.)	
WESSAGUSCUS	
ment^d. (order as to levy for maintenance of Mr. Patricke &c.)	6
(order as to levy for the creek at Newe Towne)	16
assessed, (order as to levy for making a palisade)	20
inhabitants of, to pay to Dorchester for all charges for caring for Thomas Lane	45, 46

INDEX. 283

	PAGE

WESTON
———, Mrs., John Pease sentenced for striking and deriding his mother, Mrs. Weston, . . . 59
    Francis, wife of, to be set in the bilboes at Salem &c. 75
    Frauncis, Josuah Harris apprenticed to, ... 41
WEVER. (*See* WEAVER.)
WEYMOTH }
WEYMOUTH } or WAYMOTH, WAYMOTHE, WAYMOUTH, Town of,
    Richard Long's fine to be used towards building a bridge in Weymouth 60
    riveing trees into clapboards and selling them from Waymothe Town, Richard Long fined for 60
    Henry Kingman of, ment^d. 69
    fined &c.,. 75
        for defective highways 79
            a bad highway at the stepping stones 84
            want of a sufficient watch house, for neglect of keeping constant watch and for not delivering in a transcript of their lands 90
    fined for not looking to the execution of the order about swine . . 91
    ment^d. (case of John Danvard)| 93
    and Richard Lange, Mr. Stoughton to hear business between, . . 99
    Willam Carpenter sworn constable of, ... 102
    Thomas Richards of, ment^d. 102
    Mr. Neweman &c. of, ment^d. 102
    defective way certified to be mended 106
    fine remitted to, ... 106
    John Harding &c. sworn constables of Weymouth . . . 123
    Mr. William Tory appointed Ensign at, ... 123
    Thomas Richardson &c. sworn constables of, ... 140
WHARFAGE and LITRIGE, rates of, referred to the General Court . . . 108
WHEELWRIGHTS, &c., order as to wages of, ... 36
WHETLE (or WHITELE), JOHN, &c., to be whipped for drunkenness . . 63
WHIPPING. (*See* PUNISHMENT.)
WHITE
———, Mr., and Mrs. Woolcot, difference between, referred to Mr. Rich^d. Bellingham &c. 74
    Daniel, to be fined and whipped for stealing. 69
    Edmond, Mr., and Mrs. Woolcott, accounts between, to be examined . 100
    James, fined for drunkenness 33
    John, forfeited his bond 64
        &c., bond by, (case of Robert Penyer) 86
        bound to his good behavior &c. 95
            discharged 106
    Richard, case of, (refusing to watch) 126
    Robert, adm^n. on goods &c. of, granted to William Stitson . . 56
    Thomas, grant to, as a witness 84
        &c., to settle things between John Turner and William Richards 97
        granted costs against Andrew Belcher 133

PAGE

WHITELE (or WHETLE), John, &c., to be whipped for drunkenness . . 63
WHITMORE
    (or WHITTAMORE), Thomas, dismissed with an admonition . . . 124
    W. H., his Bibliographical Sketch of the Laws of the Massachusetts Colony mentioned 115
WHITNEY
    John, &c., allowance of cloth to, ... 105
        sworn constable of Watertown 105
        constable, fined for not warning Charles Chadwicke . . . 119
WHITTAMORE (or WHITMORE), Thomas, dismissed with an admonition . . 124
WICKS, George, sworn constable of Dorchester 130
WIGNALL
    Alex: &c., jury, (Dexter against Endicott) 15
    Mr., fined for drunkenness 18
    case of, (drunkenness) 19
    order as to inventory 33
    fined for drunkenness, quarrelling, breach of a Court order and contempt of authority 35
WIGWAMS, order as to recompensing Indians for two wigwams which were burned 11
WILBEE. (*See* WILBY.)
WILBORE
    ———, Mr., stealing boards &c. from, Griffin Mountague sentenced for, 53
    (or Gibones), Samuel, &c., Grand Jury 70
WILBY or WILBEE
    George, &c. to be whipped for running away from their masters &c. . 59
    Mary, case of, (concealing and consenting to an escape) . . . 109
WILKINSON, BRAY, &c., testimony by, (case of Thomas Wonnarton) . . 56
WILL
    of John Russell sworn to in Court 3 Sept. 1633 57
    Silvester Baldwin presented 77
    George Alcock given in 102
    Ann Bunting " " 102
    Thomas Morrice delivered in &c. 124
    and inventory of William Fry delivered in &c. 134
WILLARD, ———, Mr., &c., appointed as to Mr. Gurlin's land . . . 74
WILLIAMS
    ———, Mr., &c., admonished to take heed of concealment . . . 109
    Capt., promised to endeavor to bring back John Richardson . 116
    &c., to view the leather tanned in Watertown &c, . . . 128
    Aaron, Capt., case of, (distemper in drink) 135
    discharged from Capt. John Chadwicke . . . 136
    David, put himself to John Read 117
    case of, (assaulting the watch) 135
    John, found guilty of the murder of John Hobbe 69
    Richard, fined for drunkenness 40
    Roger, &c., jury, as to death of Austen Bratcher 6

INDEX. 285

	PAGE

WILLIAMS, *continued.*
 Roger, &c., goods &c. of Christopher Ollyver in hands of, order as to,   50
  difference between John Cogan, John Tylley, &c. referred to,   54
 Thomas, &c., inquisition on body of William Bateman upon oaths of,   7
 William, &c., certificate by, (case of Mighill Bacon)   105
WILLIS
 Michael, discharged   101
 Nicholas, &c., jury, (case of Marmaduke Peirce)   89
 Richard, case of, (battery)   130
WILLOUGHBY, WILLIAM, case of, (being distempered with wine, neglecting private and public Ordinances &c.)   120
WILLS, WILLIAM, to make a payment to Gyles Gibbs for felony   56
WILSMORE, ELIZABETH, warrant to constable of Watertown to provide her a place in service   117
WILSON
 ———, Mr., maintenance of,   1
  house to be built for, (order as to ministers)   1, 2
  allowance to, (order as to ministers)   2
  rates on plantations for maintenance of,   9
  goods sent over with John Smythe to remain in hands of,   25
 Edward, inventory of estate of, delivered into Court   77
 Gawen, case of, (bond by Henry Waltham &c.)   115
  and his sureties discharged   116
  case of, (fornication)   132
 John, Mr., John Smithe bound an apprentice to,   25
  &c., gift towards the Sea Fort   42
  pastor of the Church of Boston, land granted to,   43
  &c., witnesses to answer by John Pratt   111
 Richard, case of, (stealing from his master Samuel Wade)   86
  (abuse of his master Thomas Cheesholme)   104
 Thomas, exec^r., delivered an inventory of estate of Edward Wilson   77
  fined for taking above double toll and "presented for standing above six months excommunicate"   78
  &c., had liberty until the next Court   84
  fine respited to,   124
 William, Elizabeth Hasnet put to, 5 Jan. 1642-3   129
WILLUST. (*See* WEILLUST.)
WILY, JOHN, &c., bond by, (case of John White)   95
WINCALL, THOMAS, fined for drunkenness   31
WINE &c., no person shall sell either wine or strong water without leave from the Governor   33
WINETTSEMET. (*See* WINNETTSEMET.)
WINGE, JOHN, testimony by, (adm^n. on goods of Francis Dent)   82
WINNETTSEMET or WINETTSEMET, WENETSEMET,
 ment^d. (order as to maintenance of ministers)   9
  (order as to levy for making the creek at New Towne)   16
 house of Mr. Maveracke in, ment^d.   18

INDEX.

WINNETTSEMET, *continued.*
 assessed, (order as to levy for making a palisade) 20
 Richard Arnold of, ment^d. 35
 assessed to defray public charges 37
WINSHOT, EDWARD, &c., fined for not attending the jury 97
WINSLEW (or WINSLEY), SAMUEL, Mr., sworn surveyor of the arms at Colchester 98
WINTER
 John, discharged with an admonition 120
 Edward Lewis &c. to view leather tanned by, &c. . . . 128
WINTHROP }
WINTHROPE }
 ———, Governor, land granted to, near his house at Misticke . . 19
  Mr. &c. reference to, in case of Richard Wright . . . 56
  present at Court 24, 25, 27, 28, 32–34, 42, 45–48, 50, 50, 52,
   54, 55, 57–59, 61, 62, 105, 107, 108, 115,
   117–119
  Junr. &c. present at Court 23, 30, 45, 48, 86, 89, 91, 93, 99, 103,
   105, 134, 138
  Senr. &c. to examine witnesses (Hough against Maveracke) 58
  present at Court . . . 93, 95, 96, 98, 99, 103, 104
 John, Mr., Esq., or Governor, present at Court 1, 26
  inquisition on body of Wm. Bateman before, 7
  Conant's Island demised to, . . . 22
  his great lot mentioned 22
  grant to, near Wanottymies River . 29
  &c. at Aggawam mentioned . . . 31
  weir at Misticke granted to, . . . 41
 &c. (Court of Assistants) order by, (case of John Pratt) . . 112
 Journal of, referred to in note 10, 13, 15, 16, 18, 19–21, 23, 25, 27, 30,
  32, 33, 35, 37, 39, 40, 41, 44, 47, 50,
  57, 58, 61–63, 69, 76, 78, 80, 86, 89,
  101, 103, 108, 109, 119, 120, 126, 127,
  135, 139
  Junr., Mr., granted liberty to set up a trucking house . . . 35
  took oath of an Assistant 46, 77
  present at Court . . 63, 64, 66, 69, 76, 78, 80, 102
  mentioned (divorce of Anne Clarke) . . . 138
  Senr. Mr., or Esq., differences referred to, ... 47
   marginal note by, referred to in note . . 59
   present at Court 102
   John George put to, for eight years . . 104
WIPPLE, JOHN, &c., to make a payment to their master, Israel Stoughton, for their wasteful expense of powder &c. 27
WISWELL, ———, Goodman, ment^d. (case of Willi: Pilsberry) . . . 107
WITHEREDGE, JOHN, &c., allowance of cloth to, ... 105
WITNESS, Robert Allen fined for being absent from Court as a witness . . 33

INDEX. 287

	PAGE
WOBURN or WOOBORNE, Town of,	
Edward Johnson appointed to train the company at,	123
Edward Converse constable of, ment^d.	126
Edward Johnson chosen Lieutenant of,	135

WOLCOTT or WOLLCOTT, WALCOT, WALCOTT, WOOLCOTE, WOOLCOT, WULCOTT
- ———, Mrs., to bring in an inventory 74
- ——— and Mr. White ment^d. 74
- ——— Edmond White, accounts between, to be examined 110
- Henry, &c., jury, (Dexter against Endicott) 15
- ——— John Cogan, &c., difference between, referred to a committee . 54
- (or Wolridge), John, of Roxbury, ment^d. (order as to Richard Brown) 71
- William, case of, (idleness and abuse of his friends) 126

WOLLASTON. (*See* WOOLASTONE.)
WOLLCOTT. (*See* WOLCOTT.)
WOLRIDGE. (*See* WOOLRIDGE.)

WOLVES
- order as to money to be paid for killing wolves, &c. 8
- Richard Waterman to be paid for killing a wolf 26
- no reward shall be given for killing wolves 29
- allowance to Thomas Marvin for killing wolves 120

WONNARTON or WANNERTON
- ———, Mr., Mr. Drayton's cause against, transmitted to Piscataqua Court 131
- Thomas, Mr., threat by, (testimony by John Holland) . . . 55
- ——— bound to his good behavior &c. 56

WOOBORNE. (*See* WOBURN.)

WOOD
- felled and squared for use of sawyers, order as to, ... 3
- felling, ment^d. (order as to Islands) 17
- order as to felling wood for palings 28
- inhabitants of Boston to have liberty to fetch wood from Dorchester Neck 29
- Boston and Charlestown to fetch wood from Noddle's Island . . 31
- order as to fetching wood from swamps 39

WOOD
- Edward, inventory of estate of, and an account of the disposition of his children delivered in, 122
- ——— case of, (baking wheat meal contrary to order) . . . 124
- Richard, to keep an ordinary at Roxbury 133

WOODBERRY. (*See* WOODBURY.)
WOODBRIDG, JOHN, Mr., case of, (releasing a servant) 94

WOODBURY or WOODBERRY
- John, took the oath of a constable 5
- ——— chosen constable of Salem 5
- ——— &c., bond by, (case of John Ellford) 11
- ——— agreement made by, as to estate of John and William Fiske 77

WOODCOCKE (or WOODCOOKE), JOHN, case of, (miscarriages) . . . 119

288   INDEX.

	PAGE
WOODLEY, WOODLY	
Edward, to be whipped, imprisoned for one year and to wear a collar of iron for breaking into a house &c.	64
" released from prison to his master "	65
WOODWARD	
George, costs to John Palmer for not prosecuting	67
to pay witness fees to Richard Chadwell.	68
granted damages against William Dinely for not prosecuting.	72
James, servant of S^r. Richard Saltonstall, wigwams burned by, (order as to recompensing Indians)	11
to be set in the bilboes for being drunk	26
to be whipped for running away from his master &c.	27
John, &c., case of, (drinking too much)	180
WOOLASTONE or WOLLASTON	
———, Mr., case of, (being privy to, and concealing an escape).	109
Edward, &c., will of Thomas Morrice testified to by,	124
WOOLCOT, WOOLCOTE (See WOLCOTT.)	
WOOLDRIGE. (See WOOLRIDGE.)	
WOOLESTON RIVER or Orkhussunt River, land near Salem bounded on the east by, granted to Capt. Jo: Endicott	24
WOOLRICH, WOOLRIDGE or WOLRIDGE, WOOLDRIGE. WOOLRIGE	
———, Mr., &c., to take an inventory of goods &c. of Alex: Wignall	33
to require the Indians to set out the bounds of lands sold by Chickataubut	55
John, Mr., fined for drunkenness.	84
(or Wollcott), John, of Roxbury ment^d. (order as to Richard Brown).	71
John, admonished &c. for drunkenness	73
Mr., &c., respited until the next Court	83
case of, (drunkenness)	88
bound to his good behavior and his servant Hester Ketcham freed	92
discharged from his bond	97
Mr., case of, (drunkenness &c.)	126
WORKMEN	
to work all day allowing time for food and rest	37
reduction in wages of, ment^d. (order as to price of commodities)	39
WORMEWOOD, ———, &c., to be sent to England " as unmeet to inhabit here "	10
WRIGHT or RIGHT	
———, Mr., shallop of, ment^d. (inquisition on body of William Bateman)	7
&c., to be sent prisoners to England	10
Goodman, &c., to go with Ensign Jennison &c. as to bounds of land sold to Mr. Pinchon	55

WRIGHT or RIGHT, *continued*.
 George, bond for appearance and bound to his good behavior . . 136
  discharged 139
 Richard, John Legge to be whipped for striking, ... 14
  Thomas Dexter &c. differences between, referred to Mr. Endicott &c. 35
  &c., gift towards the Sea Fort 42
  heifers kept by, difference as to, referred to Mr. Winthrop . 56
  to stave the canoe from which three persons were drowned . 78
 Robert, case of, (distemper in drink) 134
WULCOTT. (*See* WOLCOTT.)
WYAR }
WYER }
 Robert, &c., case of, (ravishing two young girls) 121
  put to Leonard Bowtle with his masters consent . . . 122
  fined for drinking with Samuel Bacon 132
WYTHES, SARAH, &c., to be whipped, (case of Robert Wyar &c.) . . 121

YONGE, PAUL, Henry Webbe &c. granted power as to estate of, . . . 107

www.ingramcontent.com/pod-product-compliance
Lightning Source LLC
Chambersburg PA
CBHW030545080526
44585CB00012B/261